THE HISTORY OF
BRITISH
MOTORING

A CHRONICLE OF CLASSIC CARS AND BIKES

Abbeydale Press

ISBN-10 digit: 1-86147-197-1
ISBN-13 digit: 978-1-86147-197-0

1 3 5 7 9 10 8 6 4 2

Published by Abbeydale Press, an imprint of
Bookmart Limited, Registered Number 2372865
Trading as Bookmart Limited, Blaby Road,
Wigston, Leicester LE18 4SE, England

Material for this publication has been taken from *Classic British Cars*
and *Classic British Bikes*, published by Bookmart Limited.

PHOTOGRAPHIC CREDITS
A number of images have been supplied by the photographic library
of the National Motor Museum at Beaulieu. We are indebted to the
librarian, Jonathan Day, for his help in compiling this book. The
photographs appearing on pages 254-5, 356, 362-3, 364-5, 376-7
were kindly supplied by Graham Robson.

Printed in Thailand

Contents

THE HISTORY OF BRITISH BIKES

THE HISTORY OF BRITISH CARS

THE HISTORY OF
BRITISH
BIKES

Introduction

The motorcycle is little over one hundred years old. At the start of the 20th century it resembled a spindly motorised bicycle whose large but often unreliable engine offered a performance little better than a modern moped. By the end of the century, it had developed into a sophisticated and comfortable superbike, in some cases capable of sustaining speeds in excess of 150mph for hours on end.

For well over 50 years, British bikes helped to force the pace of technological change, and for several decades could honestly claim to be the best in the world. British-built machines set speed records, won races and endurance trials, carried out seemingly impossible stunts – and carried their owners to work, day in, day out.

They were the favoured mounts of princes, film stars, industrialists, soldiers – and the ordinary working man and woman. They provided their owners with entertainment and freedom, kept the wheels of commerce turning, and played a major part in both world wars as well as many lesser conflicts. British motorcycle factories exported to half the globe – and the cousins of the machines that won races in Europe could be found earning their keep in rural communities across a British Empire that spanned almost every continent.

And then it all went wrong. In part the victim of increasing affluence, in part of mismanagement and shortsightedness, the British motorbike industry collapsed. In little more than 20 years it went from being the pride of the world to a half-forgotten footnote that owed its very existence to the dedication of a small band of enthusiasts.

Even so, the names of the great marques lived on: names such as BSA, Matchless, Norton, Sunbeam, and, above all, Triumph – a name which has been proudly reborn to take on the best in the world, winning sales and performance records alike, and well able to look forward to the next century.

Classic British Bikes tells the story of the machines for which the label 'Made in England' was a badge of pride. Featuring detailed historical analyses of almost one hundred machines, it chronicles the technical innovation, engineering expertise and ingenuity that for decades made the industry a world leader, as well as the numerous efforts to restore it to its former glory.

A century of progress has taken the motorcycle from its bicycle origins (left) to become a sophisticated high-performance machine (below). The history of the machines produced by the British motor cycle industry illustrates every step of that process.

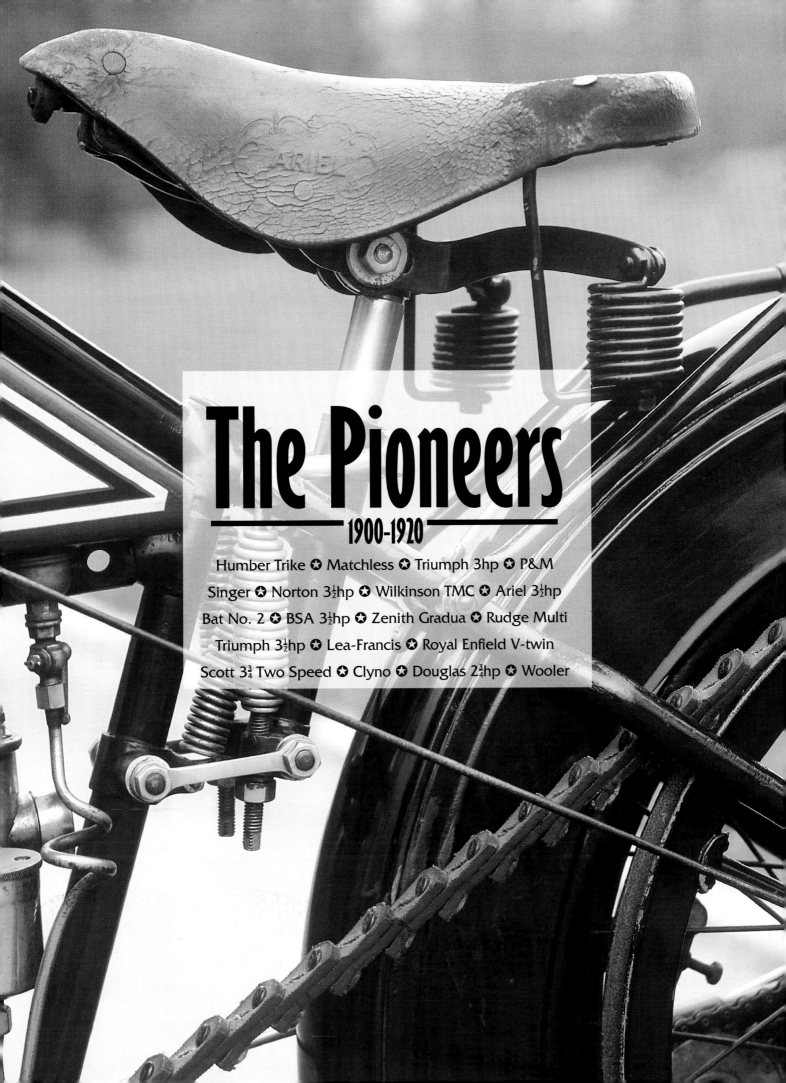

The Pioneers
1900-1920

Humber Trike ✪ Matchless ✪ Triumph 3hp ✪ P&M

Singer ✪ Norton 3½hp ✪ Wilkinson TMC ✪ Ariel 3½hp

Bat No. 2 ✪ BSA 3½hp ✪ Zenith Gradua ✪ Rudge Multi

Triumph 3½hp ✪ Lea-Francis ✪ Royal Enfield V-twin

Scott 3¾ Two Speed ✪ Clyno ✪ Douglas 2¾hp ✪ Wooler

The Pioneers

No one can really say where the motorcycle began, for it was the result of many simultaneous experiments in different countries.

Most historians date the motor industry from 1885, when two Germans, Daimler and Maybach, put the first really practical four-stroke engine into a wooden test-vehicle that they called the Einspur. As it had two wheels, albeit with a small pair of supporting wheels on each side, this can be said to be the first motorcycle, although Daimler and Maybach themselves saw it simply as a stepping stone to building the first car. But the British industry also got off to a flying start for, at around the same time, British inventor Edward Butler put forward his design for a twin-cylinder tricycle, which, in featuring electric ignition and a proper carburettor, was in many ways more advanced than Daimler's. Sadly, as with so many bright ideas before and since, ambitious plans to go into production failed to materialise, and Butler went no further than a prototype.

What is beyond dispute is that the first commercially successful motorcycle appeared in 1894, and it was the German Hildebrand and Wolfmüller. In France, De Dion was building tricycles in 1895, closely followed by the Werner motocyclette of 1897.

Unlike developments on the Continent, developments in Britain had been hampered by the Locomotive Acts of the 1860s, which restricted speeds to less than a fast walking pace and were responsible for the notorious red flag that had to be carried in advance of any motorised vehicle. When this law was repealed in November 1896 it was the cause of celebrations that are commemorated to this day in the form of the London to Brighton Run.

The repeal helped a fledgling industry to get started, at first mainly through the efforts of established bicycle manufacturers eager to get to grips with the new technology. Most of them bought proprietary engines from the French manufacturers, such as De Dion and Minerva, while others obtained a licence to build the De Dion or Werner machines.

There were many snags in getting the industry off the ground. Even if the basic design was sound – and many were not – public acceptance of the motorcycle was a long time coming. To start with, they were invariably expensive to buy and running costs were high. There were no wayside fuel stations, and the road more often than not consisted of an unmetalled, rutted track covered with mud and horse manure. Speed traps were common, and there

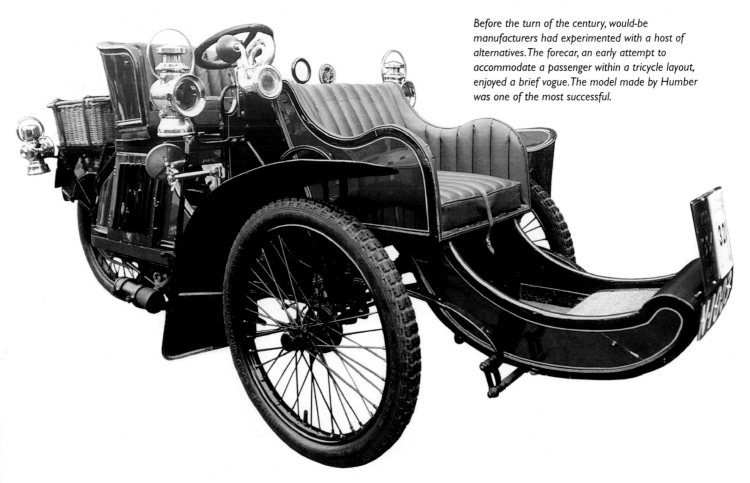

Before the turn of the century, would-be manufacturers had experimented with a host of alternatives. The forecar, an early attempt to accommodate a passenger within a tricycle layout, enjoyed a brief vogue. The model made by Humber was one of the most successful.

were many other legal restrictions on the pioneer motorist.

Unreliable, low-powered engines were the norm, and this helped to delay the development of a proper motorcycle, since what was euphemistically termed 'light pedal assistance' was looked on as essential not only for starting but also for going uphill or even into a headwind. As a result, it was a long time before motorcycles dispensed with pedalling gear completely and became something other than motorised bicycles.

The need to retain the pedalling gear, as well as a natural desire to experiment, led to considerable debate about such matters as the location of the engine. There were many weird and wonderful alternatives, while the problem always on the designer's mind was the dreaded 'side-slip', or skidding, a natural result of poor road surfaces, skinny tyres and what was often a very high centre of gravity.

It is perhaps surprising that the motorcycle evolved at all, but all the trials and tribulations must have been worth it for the occasional opportunity to fly effortlessly and unhindered down an open road.

The pioneer motor trade developed from the bicycle dealers and blacksmiths who served an earlier generation. In 1913 Douglas dealer Frederick Turpin (above) also offered Scott, Clyno, Premier and Bradbury machines from as little as 25 guineas. Almost 100,000 motorcycles were registered that year.

A pioneering spirit helped the early enthusiasts over the inevitable tribulations, while early magazines and books (right) were soon on the market to advise on everything from the choice of a machine to tackling roadside repairs.

The ingenuity and the enthusiasm of the designers knew no bounds, while the astonishing flexibility of the pioneering engines allowed them to triumph, despite the fact that most bikes lacked such items as a clutch or gearbox. Machines were generally started by a run and bump, and stalled when stopping, which initially limited their appeal to fit (and tall) young men.

Even so, the fledgling British industry produced some astonishing designs, including the world's first four-cylinder motorcycle. Development of the Holden began in 1896 and a water-cooled version was launched in 1899. With an engine that ran at just 400rpm and a power output of some 3bhp, it completed a run of over 100 miles in 1900.

Such experiments apart, it was clear for the most part that developments would centre mainly on single-cylinder side-valve engines with simple air cooling.

Clearly displaying its bicycle origins, the layout of the motorcycle settled down in the early years of the 20th century. It became the convention to have the engine in the position of the bottom bracket, with a simple belt drive to a large rear-wheel pulley, as on this 1903 Kerry. Pedals were still necessary to start off, as there was no clutch, and to assist the engine when the going got tough.

It was not until the beginning of the 20th century that machines that were recognisably related to the modern motorbike became generally available on the British market. The French Werner helped to pioneer the conventional position of the engine in place of the bicycle's bottom bracket, and many British manufacturers had their own variations on the theme. Although many of these early machines were too primitive and too demanding to appeal to anyone but committed and well-heeled enthusiasts, the majority went surprisingly well, and were capable of turning in some astonishing speed and endurance records.

The problem of accommodating a passenger, which had led to strange inventions such as the trailer and forecar, was now resolved mainly by the equally mechanically odd sidecar. This, however, had the significant advantage that the passenger was separated from all the fuss and dirt of the motorcycle itself.

While road racing had been a spur to development in mainland Europe, British roads could not legally be closed for motor sport. As a result, many of the early speed races and competitions were undertaken on the banked tracks built as a result of the cycle boom, or on the driveways of private estates. This contributed to the popularity of such events as reliability trials and hill-climbs. But the bar to pure

War and peace: the sidecar (left) developed as family transport, but soon found a new use on the battlefields of Europe (above), where the 'Trusty Triumph' single became the staple military machine.

road racing was removed with the construction of Brooklands in Surrey, a banked road track designed by Holden, where the first full-scale motorcycle race was held in 1908. A year before that, an even more significant event had taken place. With its own legislature, the Isle of Man was not subject to mainland restrictions, and as a result had been the site of the first Tourist Trophy – effectively a cross between a race and a reliability trial – in 1907. Won at little over 36mph, it was a small beginning for a race that would become a dominant force in the British industry, and then the world.

Before World War I, racing and commercial pressures had forced the pace of technological change, and most of the features of modern motorcycles had been tested in some form. Although the majority of machines still used a direct belt drive linking the engine and rear wheel, the advantages of a variable gear had been more than amply demonstrated, while numerous ingenious suspension systems had been tried. Chain drive, shaft drive, telescopic forks, four-valve engines, four-cylinder engines, water-cooled engines, overhead-camshafts and many other features recognisably similar to those of modern machines had all been seen – many of them British inventions. And with the outbreak of war, the light, manouevrable motorcycles produced by the leading British manufacturers found a host of applications, which earned them respect in the most taxing conditions in history.

The following pages tell the story of the many and varied experiments that ultimately led to the development of the modern form of the motorcycle. The story features such well-known names as BSA, Norton and Triumph, which went on to become legends of the industry in their own day – as well as the many that failed to survive those early pioneering days.

Humber Trike

Based on a pioneering French design, the tricycle format of the Humber offered greater stability than a two-wheeler on the rough roads of the day. It was one of the first truly successful motorcycle designs, produced in a variety of capacities both by the original makers and licensees such as Humber.

Humber Trike (1898)

Years in production: 1898

Engine type: single-cylinder side-valve four-stroke

Compression ratio: 4:5

Transmission: direct gear drive to rear axle

Top speed: approx 40mph

In the very early days of the motor industry there was a host of inventors prepared to make all manner of fanciful claims for their designs – and a host of entrepreneurs who were only too eager to prosper from them. Most of these schemes came to nothing, but where a few succeeded, the industry began. One such scheme was the brainchild of Humber.

Humber was established as early as 1868 by one Thomas Humber, whose aim as a bicycle pioneer was to build the best quality machines possible at his works in Beeston, Nottingham. In this aim he succeeded, and although he quit the business in 1892, before it had any connection with powered transport, his bicycles had already achieved a fine reputation. In 1884 they had pioneered the first diamond frame, a design that would become almost universal for bicycles, as well as forming the basis of most pioneer motorcycles.

During the cycle boom of the 1880s, Humber was built into a very large company indeed, with works in Beeston, Coventry and Wolverhampton – partly because of its association with an entrepreneur named Hooley, a man with a somewhat shady reputation for financial dealings. It was typical of the time that such men prospered, and a few years later two more appeared on the scene. These were Edward Joel Pennington, an American given to impossibly extravagant claims on behalf of the motorised gadgets and patents he peddled, and Harry Lawson, an English entrepreneur.

At Lawson's behest, in 1896 Humber started work on a number of prototypes of an experimental machine. Although Humber and Lawson spent a great deal of money, none of the prototypes ever came to anything. The most promising was a version of a Humber tricycle that had a single rear wheel and passenger seat between two steerable front wheels, and a De Dion engine mounted behind the rear wheel. In the years before 1900, the French De Dion company was the biggest name in proprietary engines, which were used by many fledgling manufacturers in Britain. The company was also behind the extremely successful French De Dion and Leon Bollée tricycles.

Harry Lawson's Motor Manufacturing Company (MMC) acquired the sole rights to the De Dion engine, which he built in Coventry. He also held the rights to the three-wheeler, which he passed on to Humber in 1896. This time the experiment was successful, and although the Humber works were destroyed in a fire soon after the first machines were completed, the company was by then firmly established as a motorcycle manufacturer.

In 1902 the firm (by now under new management) acquired the rights to the P&M design and started to make this as the Humber Beeston. They had also begun experiments with their first cars, which would prove even more successful. Humber continued to build motorcycles up until 1930, and in 1911 even won the first Junior TT held over the Mountain Circuit. Some years later, motorcycle production ended as a result of the depression, and the bicycle business was sold to Raleigh. But under the ownership of the Rootes group the Humber name would live on for a century after the company was founded.

The De Dion-based engine design (left) owed a great deal to pioneering Daimler, who made the first truly practical internal combustion engine. The aluminium alloy crankcase, radial finning and long holding-down bolts were De Dion innovations. Drive to the rear axle was by spur gear and pinion.

Matchless

Matchless was one of the true pioneers. Having become one of the first manufacturers in Britain, the firm really established themselves in 1907 by winning the single-cylinder class of the inaugural Isle of Man TT race. The company would go on to become one of the mainstays of the British industry.

Theirs was a familiar tale, moving from bicycle manufacture to motorcycle production, although, unlike most of their rivals, they were not based in the Coventry or Birmingham area, but in Plumstead, London. The firm was founded by H H Collier, whose young sons Harry and Charlie joined him before the end of the 19th century. Their first motorcycle had its French-made engine bolted under the front downtube of a bicycle-type frame. This appeared in 1899.

In 1902-3, their first production machines appeared. The early machines had the engine slung under the front downtube, below the steering head. There was much experimentation with the engine position, including between the seat tube and rear wheel. Stability was improved by a later model, in which the engine moved to the inside of the downtube. This machine used a version of the popular $2\frac{3}{4}$ hp De Dion engine, manufactured under

licence by the Motor Manufacturing Company (MMC). Ignition and carburation were primitive, using a total-loss battery and coil arrangement, and spray carburettor, but the models sold well enough to see further development, with an engine that finally settled in the centre of the frame, ahead of the pedals.

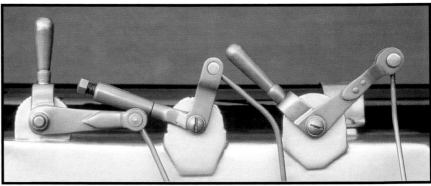

Juggling act (above): early engines had few automatic functions, so a host of tank-top levers was necessary to keep the ignition and carburation on song.

The 1902-3 model (below) has its engine placed under the front downtube, but the Collier family experimented with a number of different layouts in the pioneering years. The bicycle origins of the frame are clearly visible.

The inventive Colliers continued to experiment, and in 1904 launched a tri-car, with a pair of front wheels and single rear wheel. It was designed to provide transport for a passenger who sat ahead of the driver, between the wheels. The tri-car failed to sell well, and was dropped in 1905. But Matchless had already launched a new motorcycle that year, using the new V-twin engine built by fellow Londoner J A Prestwich (JAP) of Tottenham.

Transmission was by the conventional direct belt, but where the model really showed the forward thinking of its makers was in its pioneering front and rear suspension. That at the front was by leading-link forks, while at the rear it consisted of a swinging fork with spring box under the saddle.

On such a model Harry Collier – no mean sporting rider – represented Britain in an international race in France. The following year, both he and his brother Charlie were entered, with Charlie coming third.

Charlie Collier won a famous TT victory on a model powered by a single-cylinder overhead-valve JAP engine, which was exhibited in 1907 together with a new spring-frame V-twin and a racing model. Harry Collier had recorded the fastest lap in the 1907 TT, and together the

The Collier name is cast into the crankcase of the side-valve V-twin. A three-speed hub gear is fitted, although there was a six-speed variant that combined a variable pulley and movable rear wheel, similar to both the Rudge Multi and the Zenith Gradua.

brothers continued their winning ways, taking first place in the 1909 and 1910 TTs, while in 1908 a V-twin topped 70mph at the newly opened Brooklands racetrack.

As World War I approached, Matchless continued to develop their product. In 1912 they introduced a three-speed hub gear, and also began making their own engines. Surprisingly, they produced almost no motorcycles during the war, although the factory made an enormous contribution by manufacturing parts for munitions and aircraft. They would go on to become one of the significant marques of the British industry.

By the time that the 1912 V-twin (below) was built, motorcycle design had settled into a conformity – although on the way, Matchless had pioneered advanced suspension and many other features, including the dropped frame tube to lower the seating position. While the V-twin was a tourer, the company's racing machines had dominated many important events prior to 1910.

Matchless 5hp V-twin (1912)

Years in production: 1912

Engine type: V-twin side-valve four-stroke

Bore and stroke: 85 x 85mm

Compression ratio: 4:1

Capacity: 770cc

Transmission: direct belt drive with three-speed hub gear

Top speed: approx 60mph

Triumph 3hp

With its rebirth in the modern era, Triumph has become the longest-lived of the British marques. This dates from the 1905 3hp, the first machine entirely of Triumph's own manufacture, a true landmark in the history of the British industry.

Like so many other pioneers, Triumph was originally a bicycle company, founded in 1885 by a German expatriate, Siegfried Bettman. Together with a fellow German, engineer Mauritz Schulte, he set up in business in Coventry, choosing a company name that he believed would appeal to French and German buyers as well as the English. In fact, in the year that Triumph built its first motorcycle, a subsidiary German company was set up in Nuremberg, only separating in 1929.

That first Triumph motorcycle was designed in 1902 and used a proprietary Minerva engine in what was essentially a bicycle frame. The next, in 1903, had a JAP engine in a similar frame, but sales were slow and Triumph decided that they needed to build their own power unit. Designed by Schulte in 1905, and backed by considerable commitment on Triumph's part, it was a simple side-valve single, but used a much more advanced design than the engines they had been fitting.

Practical features abounded. At a time when many rivals relied on hit-and-miss 'automatic' inlet valves opened by suction, Triumph's was operated by a cam, a mirror of that used for the exhaust. The strong bottom end included proper main bearings, rather than bushes, and a heavy flywheel to keep the engine running smoothly through the power pulses.

One of the key developments was a proper magneto. While earlier pioneers had relied on the unreliable and potentially dangerous hot-tube ignition, electric ignition was starting to find favour. However, the early systems often relied on a coil and trembler powered by an 'accumulator' or battery to provide a spark. As there was no charging system, the battery had to be recharged after a run. Some of the early Triumphs used this system, but the 3hp offered the option of a magneto for the first time. Starting was improved and the rider was freed from reliance on a well-charged battery.

The 3hp model still used a bicycle-type frame with direct drive to the rear wheel, but soon demonstrated its advantages to would-be customers. With rigid, braced forks, it was light and manouevrable. The next year it gained a stronger frame and a primitive form of front suspension in the form of Triumph's own design of fork. This pivoted fore and aft, controlled by a large horizontal spring.

The engine was also improved, and in the first Isle of Man TT, held in 1907, J Marshall and F Hulbert took second and third place in the single-cylinder class. Sales took off and reached a level of some 20 a week. From such simple beginnings, Triumph was on the way to becoming one of the major forces of the British industry.

The simple side-valve engine (right) would cruise at around 35mph and return a top speed of around 50mph for a miserly 90mpg. This model is equipped with battery ignition.

Triumph 3hp (1905)

Years in production: 1905-07

Engine type: single-cylinder side-valve four-stroke

Bore and stroke: 78 x 76mm

Compression ratio: 4:1

Capacity: 363cc

Transmission: direct belt drive

Tyres (front/rear): 2 x 22in/2 x 22in

Wheelbase: 49in

Weight: 125lb

Top speed: approx 50mph

Little more than a heavyweight bicycle (around 125lb) with a 363cc engine fitted ahead of the pedalling gear, the 3hp model was the first true Triumph motorcycle. For its period, it was remarkably advanced and reliable, helping to set the company on the road to fortune.

P&M

P&M was one of those firms that, having had a great idea, stayed with it and refined it so that it effectively became the company's trademark. In the case of P&M this was so much the case that the idea lasted for 66 years.

The great idea dated back to 1900, when Joah Carver Phelon went into business with one Harry Rayner to develop a motorcycle. In those days, there was considerable debate and experiment into how to accommodate a motorcycle engine within the confines of a bicycle-type frame, and many were the weird and wonderful alternatives. Phelon's solution was to remove the front downtube from the frame and fit the engine in its place. It was an attractive solution. Not only was the engine – potentially at least – as strong as the tube it replaced, but it was well out in the cooling air, the centre of gravity was low and the drive was conveniently positioned. More of Phelon's forward-thinking was evident in the choice of chain drive to the rear wheel, when almost all manufacturers opted for belts.

The tank-mounted lever controls the two-speed gear.
Pulling it back engages the clutch connected to the low-ratio
sprocket; pushing it forward engages the high-gear chain.

Despite the machine's promise, the Yorkshire-based company was tiny and had limited resources. Their first engines were fitted to frames made by Humber, but from 1902 the design was licensed to Humber themselves. In this form the motorcycles proved very successful, achieving distinction in the 1902 RAC trials, using a 344cc engine with automatic inlet valve.

Phelon's original partner died in 1903, and in 1904 he went into a new partnership called Phelon and Moore, with the trademark P&M of Cleckheaton, Yorkshire. At Moore's instigation, P&M renegotiated the Humber licence, with a view to using the engine/frame design in conjunction with a new two-speed gear.

Again, the new model was well ahead of most of its rivals. The two-speed ratios were achieved by using a pair of primary chains and engine sprockets, together with expanding clutches that enabled the drive to be disengaged. This was a major advance in the days when

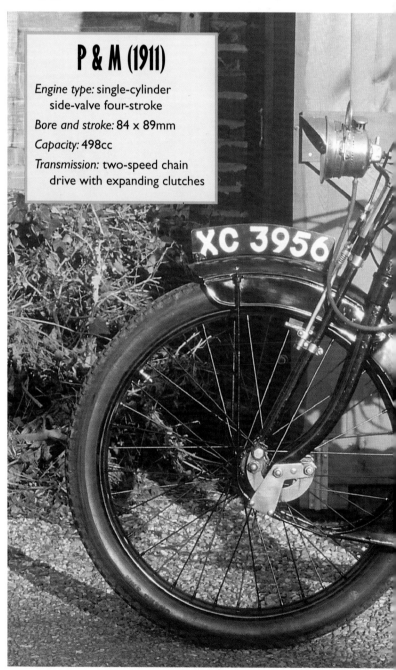

P & M (1911)

Engine type: single-cylinder side-valve four-stroke

Bore and stroke: 84 x 89mm

Capacity: 498cc

Transmission: two-speed chain drive with expanding clutches

XC 3956

most machines had to be bump-started after every halt. A patented half-compression device was also fitted to make starting easier – a feature that the model's descendants would retain over half a century later.

Mechanical inlet valves were introduced in 1910, with other refinements, but the two-speed gear remained. P&Ms were very reliable and performed well in trials and endurance tests. This was to stand the firm well in the future.

P&Ms were the Royal Flying Corp's service model of choice in World War I. Both solo and sidecar models were auctioned off in 1919.

Civilian production of a similar machine returned in the 1920s, and there would be some creditable trials and racing performances. From 1926, the trademark 'Panther' was adopted, and although the years wrought many changes, when the last Panther left the Cleckheaton works in the 1960s, it still used its engine in place of the front downtube.

The steeply inclined engine (left) runs from headstock to bottom bracket of the frame, in place of the normal downtube. As well as having strong castings, high tensile steel rods run the length of the engine to provide additional stiffness.

P&M's original design dated to a time when manufacturers were still undecided about where to put the engine. Such was their foresight that it helped to establish both their own firm and Humber, while the addition of a workable two-speed gear in 1904 again put them well ahead of the competition.

Singer

Among the early pioneers, Singer was an innovative company whose products were soundly designed and beautifully engineered. But like several of its contemporaries, Singer was a manufacturer of cars as well as motorcycles, and although its two-wheelers were deservedly popular, they lost out when the company decided to concentrate on the more profitable end of the motor business.

Based in Coventry, like so many of the early manufacturers, Singer first made a name for themselves with a product called the Singer Motor Wheel. This was a novel idea, first developed before the end of the 19th century, at a time when manufacturers were experimenting with all kinds of solutions to the problem of where to put the engine in a conventional pedal cycle frame. The motor wheel was the brainchild of a company called Perks and Birch, who patented it in 1899. It included a complete engine, together with tank and transmission, built inside a wheel that would fit into the rear forks of an ordinary bicycle.

Singer, already makers of bicycles and tricycles, took over the patent and refined the design. Fitted to the rear wheel of a bicycle or the front wheel of a tricycle it became popular at once and sold well. Simple to operate, the 208cc

Pioneer ergonomics dictated placing the controls where it suited ease of manufacture (left.). Levers fitted to the tank were not necessarily easy for the rider to operate, but with little traffic, it was possible to take time to make running adjustments.

Light but sturdy, Singer's pioneer machines were beautifully engineered by a company that made all the components in-house.

engine had a single speed control lever that was fitted to the handlebars, while the ignition used what was probably the first effective motorcycle magneto. The pedalling gear of the bicycle was left in place so that the rider could use it for starting, and for the 'light pedal assistance' that most pioneer motorcyclists were expected to provide on hills.

Singer had always made all the components themselves, and after 1904 it was a short step to making a motorcycle of more conventional appearance. This was similar to well-established contemporary designs, such as the Triumph, and placed a single-cylinder engine centrally in front of the pedalling gear of the bicycle, using direct belt drive to the rear wheel. The magneto moved to the front of the engine, and carried a distinctive external horseshoe magnet. With its flat tank, its pepperpot silencer and strutted, braced girder forks, this was almost the archetypal pioneer layout.

Several variations on the theme appeared, including 350cc two-strokes and, later, water-cooled four-strokes. The most popular were the conventional air-cooled side-valves of 299, 499 and 535cc.

Singers were entered in competition, but with limited success. One of the $2\frac{1}{2}$ hp models came fifth in the Isle of Man TT in 1913, but racing was never their forte. All were popular, usable machines, and the larger models were often fitted with sidecars of the open, wicker construction then popular. Meanwhile the Singer car had developed from early experiments with threewheelers, and by World War I had become the company's mainstay. After several mergers, the Singer name lived on in the British car industry until the 1960s, long after the motorcycles were forgotten. As for the Singer Wheel, an almost identical concept made a brief resurgence in the years after World War II, as part of the cyclemotor boom – with the BSA Winged Wheel as perhaps the best known. A similar engine in the wheel even appeared as a Honda moped of the 1960s.

Singer (1911)

Years in production: 1904-15

Engine type: single-cylinder side-valve four-stroke

Capacity: 299cc

Compression ratio: 5.5:1

Gearbox: direct belt drive

Wheels and tyres: 26 x $2\frac{1}{2}$in

Top speed: approx 45mph

Norton 3½hp

Few individual machines become so famous as to acquire their own nickname. But the Norton 3½hp, called 'Old Miracle', amply justified its name, with over 100 records and a performance that, with a top speed in excess of 80mph, was hardly to be credited from an unsophisticated, belt-drive single.

The first Nortons were made in 1902, the product of James Lansdowne Norton, bicycle fittings manufacturer of Birmingham. The first machine to bear his name used an imported clip-on engine, and although it was effectively a power-assisted bicycle, Norton was a man of high standards, and the model was neatly constructed. It was not long before improvements and experiments with a variety of other proprietary engines were on the way.

One such machine was powered by a V-twin Peugeot engine; it was aboard a privately entered example of one of these models that H Rem Fowler won the prestigious twin-cylinder class of the first-ever Isle of Man Tourist Trophy in 1907, as well as setting the fastest lap.

It was partly in response to this famous victory that Norton began to build his own engines, starting at the 1907 Stanley Show with his Model No.1, the Big Four. A 633cc side-valve single, it would continue in production (albeit heavily updated) until 1954.

In 1909 Norton introduced a smaller version. Rated at 3½hp, it was actually of 475cc, with 82 x 90mm bore and stroke. A new model appeared two years later for the 1911 Senior TT races. This had a 490cc engine derived from the relatively long-stroke 79 x 100mm dimensions that would grace Nortons for a further 50 years. Again called the 3½, it would grow into the Model 16 and then the immortal 16H.

In 1911, that first year of the new model's appearance, Norton himself rode one of the new machines in the TT, but as he was in poor health this was far from wise. As in previous years, he failed to place, but others had already begun setting records with the machine. Dan Bradbury was the first rider of a machine under 500cc to top 70 mph, while in 1912 Jack Emerson won the 150 mile Brooklands TT by some 13 minutes, setting a string of records in the process.

Simplicity was part of the keynote of Norton's success. The circular crankcase contained full-circle flywheels and a substantial big-end. The head and barrel were cast in one, but had substantial finning and a good clear passage for cooling air, with a simple sweep of the exhaust pipe providing the most efficient path for the emerging gases. The rest of the machine followed the normal Norton pattern of long, low frame, girder forks and flat tank, which the factory claimed

Simplicity characterises the engine (left), with smooth surfaces and easy curves. Rugged construction, plus the easiest possible passage for the gas and a cooling airflow are the secrets of its performance and reliability.

The tyre inflator atop the flat tank is a reminder of the hazards of pioneer motorcycling, while having to operate the tank-mounted hand-pump for engine oil was an accepted part of the rider's art (right).

Simplicity as an art form. The length of the frame emphasises the spareness of the layout, consisting of little more than engine, drive belt and the lightest possible cycle parts.

'set the fashion in the motorcycle world'. Whatever the truth of this, the handling was legendary. Norton had already started to use the slogan 'The Unapproachable', which would stay with the company down decades of racing success. In 1913 Norton advertised themselves as holding seven world records, including the mile at over 73mph. Such phenomenal performance was little short of a miracle.

When war intervened, production went into temporary abeyance. Although the Norton 3½hp was resurrected in 1919 little changed from before, it was as the Model 16 that the next part of its story would be written.

Norton 3½hp (1911-14)

Engine type: single-cylinder side-valve four-stroke

Bore and stroke: 79 x 100mm

Capacity: 490cc

Tyres (front/rear): 2½in clinchers

Brakes: rim

Top speed: 80+mph

Wilkinson TMC

Wilkinson's luxurious four-cylinder touring motorcycle must surely have been the most sophisticated machine of its age – and certainly the most comfortable, with a specification that included front and rear suspension and a car-type upholstered seat. The product of the old-established and prestigious Wilkinson Sword Company, it demonstrated engineering of the highest quality and a design that was years ahead of its time.

Wilkinson had dabbled with motorcycle manufacture as early as 1903, chiefly as a way of occupying its workforce when military contracts were at a low ebb, but that had been a relatively simple machine using a proprietary single-cylinder engine.

The model that next took their fancy, in 1908, was quite different. Young designer P G Tacchi had patented a design for what he intended as a military scouting machine, equipped with a Maxim machine gun on the handlebars. As military suppliers, Wilkinson were attracted by the scheme, and despite their failure to win an army contract they decided to persevere.

The original Tacchi design had used a proprietary V-twin engine and forks, but in many other respects, including the rear suspension, it resembled the Wilkinson that followed. Called the Touring Auto Cycle (TAC), it was shown in public during 1909 and was aimed at the civilian touring market. Powered by a 676cc four-cylinder air-cooled engine, it featured a car-type clutch and three-speed gearbox, plus shaft drive. There was a new fork designed by Tacchi, which used quarter-elliptic leaf springs, as at the rear. Steering was either by long, swept-back handlebars, or a car-type steering wheel. The machine was greeted enthusiastically, and production began at Wilkinson's works in West London.

A couple of years later there was a major change to the design, with the launch of the Touring Motor Cycle (TMC).

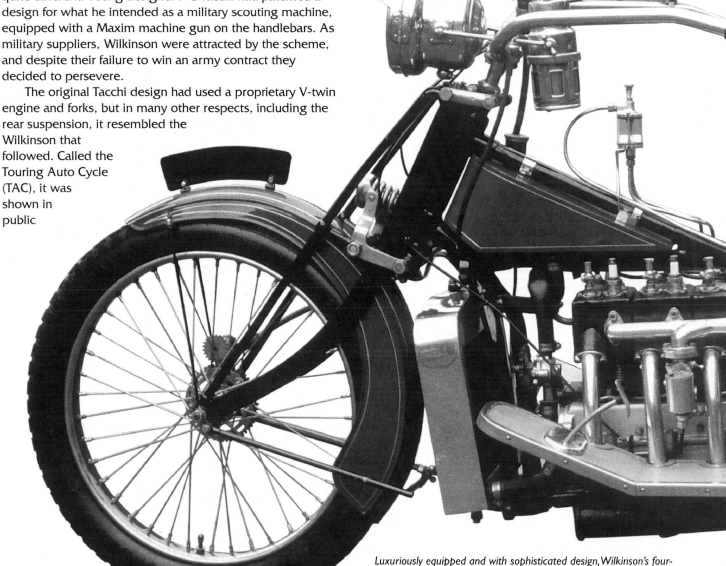

Luxuriously equipped and with sophisticated design, Wilkinson's four-cylinder machines were dubbed the 'two-wheeled Mercedes' but were only ever built in small quantities. This example has minor modifications to the lubrication and cooling systems, a legacy of its use to pull a sidecar.

The massive Jones speedometer is positioned for maximum visibility.

Wilkinson TMC (1909-16)

Engine type: four-cylinder water-cooled side-valve four-stroke (TMC)

Bore and stroke: 60 x 75mm

Capacity: 848cc

Transmission: car-type three-speed gearbox and shaft drive

Carburettor: Stewart Precision

Suspension: Saxon front forks, quarter-elliptic rear springing

Top speed: approx 50mph

The most obvious alteration was the use of a water-cooled side-valve engine, now of 848cc. There was also a return to a more conventional type of proprietary front fork, and there were numerous detail changes to the transmission and frame.

In fact, there were many changes throughout the development of the Wilkinson, which was hand built in small numbers. A larger, 996cc engine was offered in 1913, mainly for the benefit of the potential sidecar user. There were also internal changes to the engine and different bodywork.

World War I, and the ensuing rise in demand for armaments, meant that Wilkinson suspended production. But rights to the TMC, and a light car that Wilkinson had also been working on, were taken over by Ogston, another West London firm. When peace returned, Ogston concentrated their efforts on the car, while Wilkinson turned the factory over to making garden tools – a practical example of swords into ploughshares. Only a couple of hundred Wilkinson fours had ever been made, but their demise spelt the end to one of the most interesting pioneers of the British industry.

Ariel 3½hp

A chain-driven magneto (right), positioned in front of the engine, and a float carburettor were two features that Ariel offered from the first; they helped to set Ariel ahead of the competition.

In 1870 James Starley and William Hillman patented the first wheel to use tensioned wire spokes. Much lighter than previous built-up wheels, it was used to build a patented penny-farthing bicycle that they called Ariel, after the mythical sprite of the air. Justly popular, the bicycle company grew until, in 1896, Starley merged his company with another engineering concern, Westwood Manufacturing, in order to make bicycle components. The resulting company was also closely associated with Swift, another pioneering motorcycle manufacturer which was based in Coventry.

The first motorised Ariel came two years later, in the form of a quadricycle, or quad, effectively a four-wheeled bicycle using a French De Dion engine driving the rear axle. This was soon modified into a motor tricycle, based on the De Dion design but with a number of improvements – principally that of carrying the engine nearer the centre of the frame to improve roadholding. Carefully designed and well constructed, the tricycles sold in large numbers.

The first Ariel motorcycles appeared in 1902, and were somewhat in advance of most of the competition. Using an engine manufactured by Kerry, they featured proper carburettors and magneto ignition, at a time when unreliable surface carburettors and hit-or-miss hot fuse ignition was the norm.

The company itself was called Components Ltd, and was now run by Charles Sangster, a man with a pioneering spirit. Under his guidance, Ariel was chosen by the Auto Cycle Club (ACC) to represent Britain in the 1905 International Cup Races. Rider J S Campbell won the event at an average speed of over 40 mph. Other early Ariel proving stunts included the 'end-to-end' run from John O'Groats to Lands End, and in 1904 the first Ariel car was launched with a successful ascent of Mount Snowdon.

Even so, sales were slow, despite financial inducements in the form of generous part-exchange offers. This was more a reflection of the high price of a motorcycle in general – then around a year's wages for the average worker – than any failings of the product. Models with 2 and 3½ hp engines were on offer at £25 and £50 respectively.

Ariel 3½hp (1913)

Years in production: 1913

Engine type: single-cylinder side-valve four-stroke

Bore and stroke: 85 x 88mm

Capacity: 499cc

Transmission: direct belt drive

Top speed: approx 55mph

In 1910, Ariel launched a new model with a powerful 4hp side-valve engine built by White and Poppe. This was such a sound design that it would still be in service until 1925. In 1911, Components Ltd bought the design and then undertook to manufacture the machine themselves.

By the beginning of World War I, the range included a 500cc side-valve engine, and a 6hp V-twin. It also embraced the Arielette, a lightweight 350cc two-stroke designed and patented by Sangster himself. Despite advanced ideas such as a kick-start, three-speed gearbox and clutch, the war put paid to this promising design. For a time, more attention was given to cars, under the guidance of Sangster's son Jack. But a number of Ariel motorcycles saw armed service, and by the end of the conflict, the company was well positioned to take advantage of the postwar boom.

Solidly conventional, the Ariel solo was well engineered and set enviable standards of reliability, helping the marque to become one of the industry's leading names.

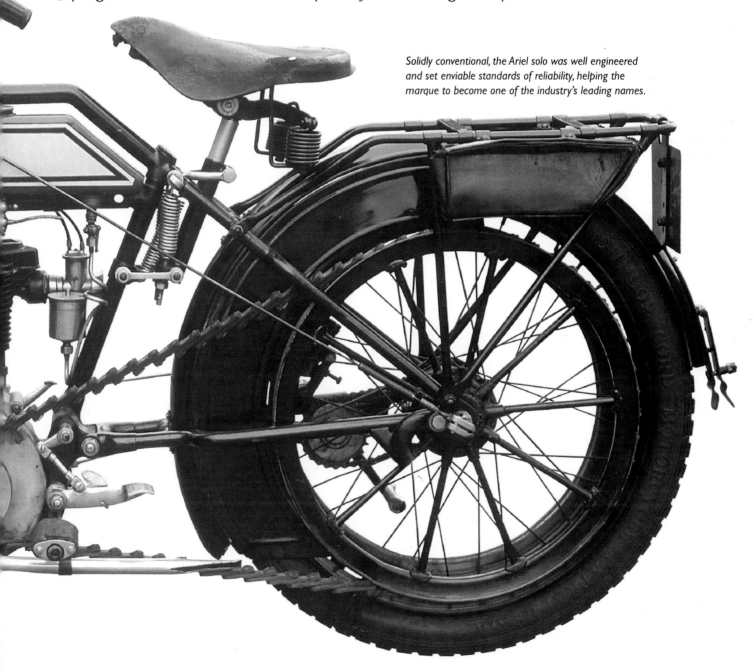

Bat No. 2

Among the early British pioneers, Bat was perhaps the first to make a serious effort to exploit the publicity available from racing and record-breaking. But their impact was much deeper than this, for the firm also produced some of the most technically sophisticated machines of the era, setting standards that others were soon to follow.

The company was based in Penge, South London. It was founded in 1902 by a Mr Batson, from whose name the bikes took theirs – although it was sometimes said that it was derived from an advertising slogan that claimed they were 'Best After Tests'(BAT). The company's Model No.1 was built using a $2\frac{3}{4}$ hp De Dion engine, and although it was basically a sound product, poor sales resulted in the founder selling the company within two years to one Theodore Tessier, a very able rider. From the first, Bat motorcycles demonstrated their maker's desire to advance the state of motorcycle engineering, for they dispensed with the pedalling gear that most rivals considered an essential backup for when the going got tough, such as riding up hills. They fitted a clutch, well in advance of most of the rest of the industry, and also patented one of the first recorded examples of a fully sprung suspension system. The front fork was a short leading-link design similar in principle to those that would be offered by a number of makers some 50 years later, while at the rear, the saddle and footrests were carried on a subframe. The subframe was suspended on springs from the main frame.

Sales boomed, partly because of the quality of the product, but also because Tessier was a skilled publicist. Launching a single cylinder $3\frac{1}{2}$ hp model in the first year after the take-over, he set about racking up a score of over two hundred wins and speed records. V-twin machines using engines supplied by the Tottenham firm JAP followed,

Bat No.2 (1913)

Engine type: V-twin side-valve
    four-stroke

Bore and stroke: 72 x 78mm

Capacity: 770cc

Compression ratio: 5.5:1

Top speed: approx 75mph

with 650, 770, 964 and 980cc power units fitted. Tessier rode a Bat in the very first Isle of Man TT in 1907, and although it failed to place, the next year's Bat entrant W H Bashall took a second in the twin-cylinder class, also scoring the lap record of 42.25mph. Two years later, in 1910, H H Bowen upped this to 53.15 – but although Bats were regularly entered prior to World War I, this would be the last time that they would figure in the TT record book. Reliability was probably their greatest weakness, for they were technically competent and of proven performance.

The year 1911 saw the introduction of the mountain section at the TT, in response to which many manufacturers

Short leading-link forks were a Bat hallmark from the early days. The principle was similar to that employed by makers such as Greeves half a century later.

fitted gearboxes, including Bat, which offered a two-speed unit as an alternative to the direct belt drive used previously. Both systems continued to be offered in parallel for two years.

By 1913, Bat machines had become more conventional. The spring frame was dispensed with and the new models had a combination of gearbox and belt drive to the rear wheel. World War I then intervened, contriving to dent Bat's fortunes over some machines supplied to Russia's armed services for which they were never paid. This left them in a poor position to exploit the postwar demand for cheap motorcycle transport.

Even so, Bat were in a better position than the fledgling Martinsyde company, which built its first machines in 1919, but foundered in 1923. Bat took over the company and sold Bat-Martinsydes for the next three years. Finally, underfunded and in the face of too much competition, Bat itself succumbed to the inevitable in 1926, after almost a quarter century in which they helped to establish the motorcycle in its modern form.

Bat's 1913 No. 2 Light Roadster was a sports touring machine with a 770cc JAP side-valve V-twin engine.

BSA 3½hp

The company that was to become Britain's largest motorcycle factory was rather late getting started in the new industry. But when they put their first machine on the market, its shrewd combination of the best features pioneered by others helped it to establish a reputation for quality and reliability that formed a solid foundation for BSA's later fortunes.

The company was an old one, for BSA, which stood for Birmingham Small Arms, was originally a gunmaker's trade association with its roots dating back some three hundred years. The BSA company proper was founded in 1861, and made guns for the next 20 years until they took up with the new bicycle industry in 1880. Then the outbreak of the Boer War meant an increased demand for guns, and bicycle manufacture was shelved until peace offered a new market.

During the early years of the century, many of BSA's fellow bicycle manufacturers enthusiastically launched their pioneer motorcycle designs – in fact, BSA made parts for a number of the early motorcycle makers. But although BSA experimented with a proprietary engine fitted into one of their bicycle frames in 1905, it was not until 1909 that they themselves began seriously to develop a product.

The fruits of their labour appeared in 1910, with the launch of their 3½hp belt-driven single. Part of the reason for waiting may have been to let the market develop. By this time, the early spate of experimentation had settled down somewhat and it must have been clear to BSA that this type of machine was by far the most popular, particularly in the form of the contemporary Triumph – which was already well-established as a practical all-rounder.

The new BSA bore a considerable resemblance to the Triumph, which had been in production for some three years. However, the BSA offered a number of advantages from the outset, and the firm proceeded to improve on them from year to year.

The simple side-valve engine was very close to the Triumph design; indeed, it has been said that several of the components are virtually identical. But in 1913 BSA modified the engine, using a désaxé design in which the cylinder is mounted ahead of the crank axis, the theory being that this results in smoother running and less wear. The carburettor was BSA's own design.

The racing form of the early BSA dispensed with such touring concessions as the pedalling gear – which was fitted behind the engine – for the ordinary road rider. Its dropped frame tube and lowered saddle anticipated such a move by many of its rivals.

The vintage side-valve displays typical concern for easy valve replacement. Removable caps over the valve heads made it simple to deal with a decoke or a broken valve stem, although the shape of the cast-iron cylinder made it a complex casting.

The frame was conventional and clearly based, like its contemporaries, on pedal cycle technology. But in 1912 the top tube was bent down behind the tank to permit a lower seating position – a fashionable and practical change in which BSA anticipated Triumph by a year or so. Where they scored a real mark over their rivals, however, was in the use of a parallelogram-type front fork, with a cantilevered spring – a vastly better suspension system than that offered by most other makers – notably the infamous Triumph fore-and-aft pivoted design.

Other features, such as the hand-pumped total-loss lubrication, were exactly like their contemporaries, although BSA included several practical little refinements designed to ensure fuss-free use. These included a two-speed rear hub gear and conical clutch (altered to a multiplate type in 1913)

at a time when such fitments were unusual, and machines commonly had to be started with a run and a bump, and stalled on stopping.

The model sold well until World War I, and was joined by a larger version aimed at the sidecar market. This became the basis of a military model, and together with a huge demand for munitions helped BSA to grow almost four-fold by 1918 when it was ideally positioned to exploit the postwar boom.

BSA 3½hp (1913)

Years in production: 1910-14

Engine type: single-cylinder side-valve four-stroke

Bore and stroke: 85 x 88mm

Capacity: 499cc

Carburettor: BSA

Tyres (front/rear): 2¼ x 26in/ 2¼ x 26in

Wheelbase: 55in

Top speed: 50mph

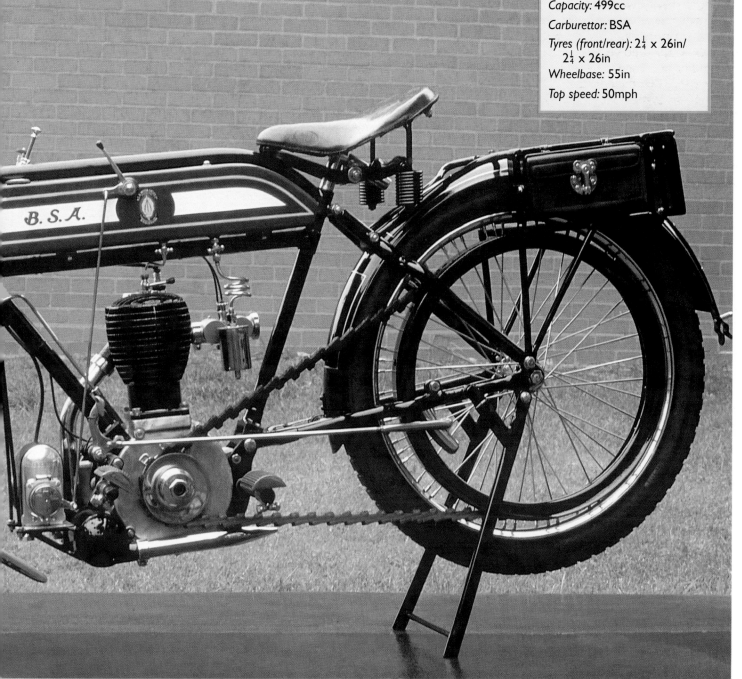

Zenith Gradua

Among the machines favoured by sporting riders in the years before World War I, Zenith machines fitted with the factory's Gradua gear were among the first to offer a really practical variable drive ratio. For a few years they were so successful in hill-climbs and other early events that they were barred from single-gear competitions. The company took this as a compliment and even added the word 'Barred' to their badge.

The earliest pioneer machines relied on direct belt drive to the rear wheel. Although their engines were designed for maximum flexibility, the fixed gear that resulted meant that a machine that could start off and pull up hills easily would have a severely limited top speed. The alternative, adopted by early sporting riders, was to use an adjustable pulley, which could be opened to give a smaller effective diameter,

and hence a higher gear. The only problem that this posed was that the belt tension was lost and it had to be shortened to suit. One early rider's manual devoted two pages to the simple process of climbing a hill, and a similar amount to descending at speed afterwards.

Zenith changed all that with a belt drive system, the ratio of which could be varied on the move. Although technically limited, it was good enough to ensure the marque's success in many important competitions, and having demonstrated the virtue of variable gearing, it paved the way for even more practical alternatives.

Zenith was established in 1904 in Stroud Green, North London. Like most pioneers, they used a variety of proprietary engines, fitted to a bicycle-type frame with direct belt drive. But in 1908, designer Freddie Barnes came up

Zenith manufactured a wide range of machines using the Gradua system. Some versions adopted a chain-cum-belt drive, with a short chain to a separate pulley in front of the engine, as seen on this 1914 V-twin.

The flanges of the front pulley (left) are opened and closed to give a smaller or larger effective diameter.

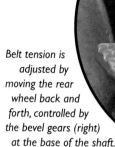

Belt tension is adjusted by moving the rear wheel back and forth, controlled by the bevel gears (right) at the base of the shaft.

with his development of the variable engine pulley. This had a pair of flanges that could be moved in or out by winding a handle while the machine was on the move. To maintain constant belt tension, the handle was also connected to a linkage that moved the rear wheel forward or backward in a pair of slots in the rear fork. There were a number of theoretical limitations to this device. Unlike the chain drive that would eventually take over, belts were prone to slip in the wet, while the limited gear ratios still demanded a large and flexible engine to make the best use of them. But with the JAP V-twins fitted to the majority of early Zeniths, the theoretical limitations faded into the background.

Zeniths were originally designed in the shadow of Muswell Hill, one of the steepest slopes in the area, and the Gradua was able to climb it easily and even achieve a hill-start. The system was the key to their success in the popular sport of hill-climbing, run on private slopes with a suitable incline. In 1911, Zenith achieved over 50 major wins, improving on their score the following year. Improvements to the Gradua system followed, including a variation in which a chain transmitted power to a 'gearbox' forward of the engine. Transmission from there on was by Gradua belt drive. More sophisticated alternatives had begun to appear, such as the Rudge Multi, while the chain-driven countershaft gearbox would soon eclipse all the pioneers' belt drives.

Zenith continued in production from a new site in South London, making machines powered by everything from a lightweight Villiers-powered two-stroke single to a 1100cc side-valve V-twin. Postwar, they restarted with a 750cc V-twin, but in 1950 ceased production, mainly because of the lack of suitable proprietary engine makers.

Zenith Gradua

Years in production: 1908-20

Engine type: single cylinder or V-twin side-valve four-strokes

The 1912 model (below) used a JAP engine single-cylinder side-valve engine made by J A Prestwich in Tottenham, North London.

Rudge Multi

Rudge Multi (1913)

Years in production: 1912-23

Engine type: single-cylinder inlet over exhaust four-stroke

Bore and stroke: 85 x 88mm (3.5hp) 85 x132mm (5/6hp)

Capacity: 499cc, 750cc

Carburettor: Senspray

Tyres (front/rear): $2\frac{1}{4}$ x 26in/ $2\frac{1}{4}$ x 26in

Top speed (racing model): 83mph

Produced by one of Britain's foremost makers, the Rudge Multi was not just a single motorcycle but a new concept, which represented an important stage in the development of motorcycle transmission systems, taking over from the equally influential Zenith Gradua. Launched in 1912, after the 1911 TT had shown the value of its multiplicity of drive ratios, it would remain in production for 10 years.

Rudge was already a long-established firm. Founded in the 1860s by Dan Rudge, a Wolverhampton publican and keen racing cyclist, Rudge bicycles had patented numerous technical advances and established a name for quality by the time Rudge died in 1880. The firm was kept going through various mergers, and by the end of the 19th century, after a merger with the Whitworth company in 1894, was producing nearly 400 bicycles a day, under the guidance of Charles Pugh, ex-director of the Whitworth company, and John Pugh, works director.

At about this time, Rudge Whitworth undertook a distribution deal with the Werner company of Paris, pioneer motorcycle manufacturers, but it was 1909 before they undertook development of their own first motorcycle. As perhaps Britain's best bicycle maker (a claim that became the company slogan), they were making some 1500 machines a week, and had the resources to undertake all the development in-house.

The Rudge Multi prototype embodied many sophisticated features, several of which were patented, including a new fork shackle and enclosed fork spring, plus an easily removable rear mudguard for dealing with punctures. The engine was a compromise between a side-valve and an overhead-valve, known as an F-head, but the machine was otherwise conventional, including a direct belt drive to the rear wheel. The first Rudge motorcycle was completed in 1910, in just under two weeks from drawing to metal. Following numerous road tests, including competition, the model went on sale at the end of the year.

In 1911, four Rudges started at the Senior TT, the first year in which the course included the climb over the Mountain. By this time, experiments with proprietary variable gear pulleys made by Mabon had proved the value of such a device on the demanding new course. However, Rudge's first efforts at the TT were not so promising, with two riders retiring, and only a 21st and 22nd place.

Nevertheless, convinced of the value of a variable gear, John Pugh continued development of what was to become the Multi system. Rudge had already patented a clutch that was attached to the engine shaft, outboard of the pulley. To this was added a device that allowed the pulley flanges to open and close. As it did so, the

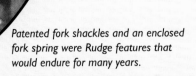

Patented fork shackles and an enclosed fork spring were Rudge features that would endure for many years.

belt would ride up the pulley, changing the effective diameter of the drive. To maintain belt tension, a linkage went to the rear wheel pulley, or belt rim, which closed and opened to balance the front. This gave ratios between 3.5 and 7.5:1, as well as, in theory, continuously variable selection.

Fitted to the 499cc TT model, the Multi was first entered for the 1912 TT.

The tall, exceptionally long stroke engine gains even greater height as a result of its use of an overhead inlet valve – the 'F-head' arrangement (right). Conventional overhead-valves, as used later, were not popular, as valve breakages were common.

Appearing on a 1913 model of 750cc, the Rudge Multi (below) soon become renowned for its advantage in speed trials and racing, as well as for the average rider.

Although Rudge failed to place, the Multi gear achieved successes at numerous trials and speed events, and was fitted to both the 3.5hp and 5/6hp models. In 1913 a Rudge Multi took second place at the TT, losing only by a narrow margin, and in 1914, Cyril Pullin (who had taken numerous long-standing speed records on his Rudge) won the event. During World War I, Rudge built a few machines for military use, but the main part of the factory was turned over to munitions work. When peace returned, so did motorcycle manufacture, starting with the 499cc Multi in Roadster or TT form. In 1920, the first Rudge to use a three-speed gearbox appeared, but the Multi continued in production until 1923, its cheapness, simplicity and lightness appealing long after the technical superiority of chain drive and a countershaft gearbox had been proved.

Triumph 3½hp

Triumph's pioneering 3½hp (500cc) models probably did more than any other machine to influence the mass acceptance of the motorcycle. Certainly, Triumph were one of the first to undertake mass production on a really major scale, and the reliability of their early models led to their later machines becoming known as 'Trusty' Triumphs.

By 1907, Triumph's solidly engineered 3hp singles had gained the company a good reputation as makers of reliable machines with a fair turn of speed. Part of that reliability came from the Triumphs' integrated design, and in keeping with their principle of controlling all elements of the design, Triumph developed their own twin-barrel carburettor and a magneto system which they fitted for the 1908 season.

It was around this time that the 'Trusty Triumph' nickname first appeared. Although belt drive was still used, Triumph also offered a new transmission system, using a Sturmey-Archer three-speed rear hub, similar to that used on pedal cycles. It was fitted with a clutch, incorporated into the hub.

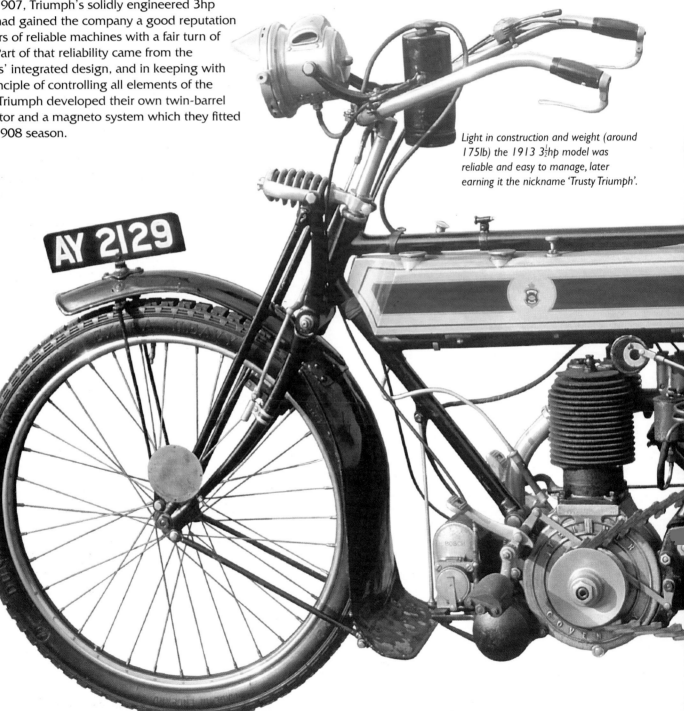

Light in construction and weight (around 175lb) the 1913 3½hp model was reliable and easy to manage, later earning it the nickname 'Trusty Triumph'.

A simple side-valve design (above), the engine uses direct belt drive to the rear wheel. A hub gear and clutch made for a much easier life than the alternative fixed gear, which meant a run and bump start after every stop.

More models joined the range, including the 225cc two-stroke 'Baby' and sporting variants aimed at the large number of riders who wanted to take part in motorcycle competitions. Triumph's own efforts had paid off with a win for Marshall in the second TT of 1908, and places in 1909 and 1910. Although Triumph machines failed to place in 1911, the marque's endurance had been proved by an epic Land's End to John o'Groats run undertaken by Ivan Hart-Davies, who rode 886 miles in just over 29 hours, the last time such a record run was permitted.

By 1911, the flagship of the range was the $3\frac{1}{2}$hp model. Developed from the earlier 3hp machine, it carried many detail improvements, while the capacity had been increased by some 163cc. More new models followed, until the range embraced a direct belt-drive Roadster, a de-luxe version with a pedal-operated clutch in the rear hub, a sporting TT Roadster and a full TT racing model.

Such machines were capable of high sustained speeds – a TT racing Triumph could top 75mph – while Alfred Catt proved the $3\frac{1}{2}$hp machines' reliability with a phenomenal ride of over 2500 miles in six days, on roads that in the main were little better than cart tracks. His own health was permanently affected, but the Triumph just kept on and on, earning it a place in motorcycle history.

Another development would soon earn the company an even bigger place in history, with a larger 4hp (550cc) version called the Model H appearing just before World War I. The motorcycle mainstay of the war effort, some 30,000 of Triumph's Model H were built, despite the evident weakness of the front fork, the spring of which was prone to snap on rough going, causing collapse of the front end. A favourite despatch rider modification was to strap a heavy leather belt around the fork in case of such a mishap. That failing apart, the side-valve Triumph single lived up to its 'Trusty' nickname, and stayed in use for many postwar years.

Triumph 3½hp (1913)

Years in production: 1906-14

Engine type: single-cylinder side-valve four-stroke

Bore and stroke: 85x 88mm

Capacity: 499cc

Carburettor: Triumph twin-barrel

Tyres (front/rear): $2\frac{1}{4}$ x 26in/ $2\frac{1}{4}$ x 26in

Wheelbase: 49in

Top speed: approx 55mph

Lea-Francis

At a time when all motorcycles were something of a luxury item, the products of Lea-Francis were aimed at the top of the market. Concentrating on quality rather than quantity, they built on a solid reputation that had already been established by Lea-Francis bicycles.

Bicycle manufacture had begun in 1895, when Graham Ingoldsby Francis and Richard Lea went into partnership in Coventry. The company's 'safety bicycles' were built to the highest standards, and they had a smart showroom in Piccadilly, London.

Unlike many others, Lea Francis dabbled in car manufacture before undertaking serious experiments with

Lea-Francis (1913-14)

Years in production: 1913-14

Engine type: JAP side-valve V-twin four-stroke

Bore and stroke: 85 x 88mm

Capacity: 430cc

Carburettor: Amac

Transmission: all-chain with two-speed gearbox and multiplate clutch

Top speed: 55mph

Rider conveniences abounded on the quality machines produced by Lea-Francis at their Coventry works. The kickstart, footboards, enclosed chain drive and excellent weather protection were all rarities when the model was introduced, while the patented brakes were supposed to be the best of their kind.

The JAP V-twin (left) was a popular choice of many motorcycle manufacturers, with few weaknesses except for a tendency to overheat. Lea-Francis teamed it with their own two-speed gearbox, which resulted in one of the most likeable packages of the time.

motorcycles, although they did try fitting a proprietary engine to one of the bicycles in 1902. The Lea-Francis car appeared the following year, but it was never a commercial success.

The first motorcycle proper came out in 1912, with a 430cc JAP V-twin side-valve engine. It had a two-speed gearbox and a hefty price that emphasised its quality and concentration on providing the rider with the best of everything. This included excellent weather shielding, with large mudguards, footboards and full enclosure for the all-chain transmission. An under-tray swung forward to act as a stand, and the front brake used a dummy belt rim and friction block. The brakes, like the firm's reflex rear lamp, were patented and said to be 'above suspicion'.

The chain drive and multiplate clutch were both advanced features for the time, when most makers relied on the simple belt. The method of tensioning the chain was also ingenious, for the gearbox was cylindrical, with an eccentric mounting. Simply rotating it in its housing provided a wide range of adjustment – a system that was seen almost 50 years later, when it was taken up for AJS and Matchless lightweights.

All this was the work of designers Norman Lea, the son of the founder, and Charles Ingle, and was very well received by the public despite the price. Norman Lea and Gordon Francis, son of the other partner, entered the new models in several reliability trials in 1913, and won awards in the Six Days' Trial and the Scottish Six Days' Trial, further enhancing the machine's reputation.

In 1914, Lea-Francis exhibited a range of new models with 430, 500 and 750cc JAP or MAG engines. A three-speed gearbox would have gone into production had it not been for the outbreak of war, which interrupted operations. A small number of machines were built for military use, but production virtually came to a halt.

After the armistice, the V-twins returned much as before and continued to win a fine reputation, especially for their performance in the major trials. The three-speed gearbox finally appeared in 1920, but by 1924 the company had decided to concentrate on car production, so motorcycle manufacture was discontinued, leaving a fine reputation behind them.

There was a postscript to the story, however, for young Gordon Francis had joined his father-in-law Arthur Barnett, a former Singer director, in 1919. The motorcycles they built were designed not so much for quality and exclusivity as reliability and economy. Yet the Francis-Barnett marque went on to build its own enviable reputation, including racing and off-road awards, and as part of the AMC Group, survived until as late as 1964.

A famous partnership: the Lea-Francis' tank badge (left) is flanked by the lever for the two-speed gear and the sight glass for the hand-pumped lubrication system.

Royal Enfield V-twin

Right from the beginning, Royal Enfield were proud to associate their motorcycles with their interests in small arms manufacture. 'Made like a gun' became a company slogan, and the pioneer machines gained an enviable reputation for reliability.

Longevity was another of the company's qualities, for having made their first machines in the early years of the century, they were one of the last to founder in the 1970s. The marque attained a kind of life after death, for Enfields are still made in Madras, India, to a design based on an original British pattern.

The first Royal Enfield was a quadricycle made in 1898, and together with tricycles that also used the ubiquitous De Dion engine, these comprised the bulk of the

company's output for some years. The Enfield Cycle Company had started as a bicycle manufacturer run by the Townsend family, but in the 1890s was absorbed into the Eadie concern.

Eadie itself was absorbed by BSA in the early 1900s, and Royal Enfield went its own way. Though based in Redditch, Worcestershire, the firm was closely associated with the Royal Small Arms factory in Enfield, Middlesex, for which it made components. It was through this connection that the bike's name and badge, which depicted a rifle with fixed bayonet, originated.

Royal Enfield V-twin (1914)

Years in production: 1913–1920

Engine type: inlet-over-exhaust V-twin four-stroke

Capacity: 450cc

Transmission: chain, with cush-drive hub

Top speed: 65mph

The V-twin Enfield became an enduring favourite, whether in solo or sidecar form. With the company's own design of transmission, most were powered by Swiss Motosaccoche engines, the London-built 6hp JAP being an exception.

The first two-wheelers, which appeared in 1901, had a 211cc Minerva engine clamped to a bicycle frame, with twisted-belt drive to the rear wheel. One design had the engine in front of the steering head, another mounted on the front downtube. Both these options soon proved to be inferior to the Werner solution with the engine in the centre of the frame and this was rapidly adopted. An early Enfield idea that persisted through the company's life was the notion of carrying the lubricating oil in a chamber that was cast into the crankcase.

For the next few years, the firm dabbled – rather unsuccessfully – in car manufacture, which meant that it was not until 1910 that real progress on the motorcycle front resulted. This time, the power unit was a 346cc V-twin designed by the Swiss company Motosaccoche. The new machines also included a two-speed gear using paired primary chains like the contemporary P&M or Scott. Another innovation was the use of a rear hub with rubber inserts to provide a cush-drive – again a persisting Enfield feature.

The firm expanded, and started to build its own engines, mostly V-twins of various sizes. Although Enfield regularly entered competitive events such as long-distance trials, it was not until 1914 that they had a really successful venture in the TT, when they fielded a strong team that was placed solidly up the field. Sadly, their best placed rider crashed on the last lap and despite finishing third, suffered a fatal collision at the conclusion of the event.

Soon after this, production was cut short by the war. Their V-twin sidecar outfits were used by the military to great effect as machine-gun platforms, but only in limited numbers. But in the postwar era, the firm's fortunes would rapidly revive, thanks in part to a new departure – a lightweight two-stroke single that had been launched, but not fully exploited before the conflict began.

The Enfield's V-twin engine (above) is an inlet-over-exhaust design, with the advanced feature of automatic lubrication via a double-acting pump. At a time when most makes relied on a hit-or-miss hand pump supplying oil on a total-loss basis, this was a significant advance.

Scott 3¾ Two Speed

One of the true pioneers, Alfred Angas Scott was an original thinker whose contributions to the fledgling motorcycle industry were many and various. Although Scott himself left the company he founded as early as 1919, the two-stroke machines built in the 1920s and 30s were some of the most charming motorcycles of the era, while Scott's ideas continued to influence successors as late as the 1970s Silk.

The list of Scott firsts and patents is extraordinary: including first rotary valves on a two-stroke, first telescopic forks, first kick-starter, one of the earliest parallel twins, and water-cooled motorcycle engines, and one of the first fully triangulated frames.

The man himself was born in 1874 in Bradford. Trained as an engineer, he worked for a time on marine steam engines, the layout of which had an influence on his designs. He began his own experiments early. In 1897, he patented a new type of bicycle brake, and around the end of the 19th century completed a twin-cylinder two-stroke engine, which he used to power the front wheel of his bicycle by friction drive to the tyre.

The experiments continued and the machine gained a transmission to the rear wheel. In 1904, Scott patented the engine design.

The first fully fledged Scott motorcycle was drawn up in 1908, and Scott contracted Jowett brothers, local engineers to manufacture the design for him.

Unconventional in almost every respect, but superbly logical, Scott's water-cooled two-speed twin-cylinder two-strokes won many competitions in the pioneer days and endeared themselves to owners.

Scott 3¾ Two Speed (1914)

Years in production: 1908-26

Engine type: parallel twin-cylinder
    water-cooled
    two-stroke

Bore and stroke: 73 x 63.5mm

Capacity: 532cc

Carburation: Scott carburettor

Gearbox: two-speed drive by chains
    with alternative ratios

Wheelbase: 55½ in

Weight: 250lb

Only a few were made before Jowett decided to concentrate on developing their own car design, but the 333cc air-cooled twin showed most of the features that would become Scott hallmarks. The frame was entirely made of straight tubes, and there was a revolutionary two-speed gear, effectively two entirely separate transmissions giving high or low ratios.

These early machines proved unreliable, but Scott took one to the local motorcycle club's hill-climb in July 1908, carrying off the top award. Three weeks later, at an important annual national hill-climb, he won three top awards, in the Open, Twin Cylinder and Variable Gear classes. The immediate result was that the governing ACU handicapped the Scott on the grounds that its extra firing intervals gave it more power.

In 1910 the machine was the first two-stroke to finish a TT, while the following year it set the record lap. In 1912 it led from start to finish. A further win followed in 1913.

Scott's civilian production continued until 1916, although the founder himself had been actively pursuing military contracts since 1912. His ideas found concrete expression with the design of a military three-wheeled gun carrier, and in 1919 he left the company to concentrate on the design of an unconventional three-wheeler called the Sociable, based on the gun-car. This never caught on and in 1923 Scott contracted pneumonia from which he died. He was only 48, and the company that he founded had many successful years to come.

Clyno

Solid and well-engineered, the Clyno V-twin had reached its peak of development on the eve of World War I. Its qualities were not lost on the military authorities, who adopted the machine as the main standard issue for the Motor Machine Gun Service. Equipped with a sidecar platform and a heavy machine gun, and operating in threes, the machines provided a highly mobile attack force.

Clyno itself had begun manufacturing motorcycles only a few years earlier, but had been formed in 1908 as an accessory maker, based in Thrapston, Northamptonshire. Founded by two cousins called Smith, the outfit's first product was a patented, adjustable inclined driving pulley, from which the firm took its name – a play on the word 'inclined'. The pulley was joined by a range of other useful accessories, and Clyno was soon profitable enough to go into motorcycle manufacture using proprietary V-twin and single-cylinder engines made by the Wolverhampton firm of Stevens, and fittings from Chater Lea in London.

The new machines first appeared at the end of 1909 and were very successful, but a year later there was a problem with the supply of engines. Stevens was another family firm, founded by four brothers, and had been

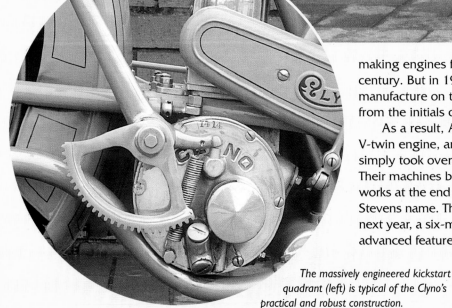

The massively engineered kickstart quadrant (left) is typical of the Clyno's practical and robust construction.

making engines for the trade since the end of the 19th century. But in 1910 they decided to go into motorcycle manufacture on their own account, as AJS, taking the name from the initials of the senior brother.

As a result, AJS decided to give up manufacturing their V-twin engine, and planned a move to new premises. Clyno simply took over the old Stevens works and machinery. Their machines began to appear from the Wolverhampton works at the end of 1910, the engines at first carrying the Stevens name. The single-cylinder bike was dropped. The next year, a six-model range was on offer, all with the advanced feature of all-chain drive, a kickstart and even a two- or four-speed gearbox offering a choice of alternative chain ratios.

By 1913 the Clyno had become a byword for convenience, with such

features as quickly detachable wheels and cast-alloy footboards. With a neat and workmanlike finish, it was robustly engineered, as befitted its favoured role as sidecar haulier. These qualities helped it to win favour at the military trials organised in 1914, and the substantial demand that followed led to the company engaging extra staff and working long shifts to build the armoured combinations. The Clynos were ridden to the south of England and then shipped to France, while from 1917, the Russian army was also supplied with a similar model.

Clyno might have been expected to profit from the postwar boom, but just as they were on the point of launching a new model, their chief designer left for rivals Raleigh. Meanwhile the founder had turned his attention to the light car market. Ultimately this policy spelt doom for the company, as it was unable to ride out the Depression.

Clyno (1914)

Engine type: Stevens/Clyno side-valve
   V-twin four-stroke

Capacity: 744cc

Carburettor: Amac

Transmission: all-chain with three-
   speed countershaft gearbox
   and clutch

Lubrication: semi-automatic, with
   hand-operated Best & Lloyd pump

Top speed: 55mph

Handsome and sturdy, the Clyno typified the final development of the pre-World War I motorcycle as a practical, comfortable solo or sidecar mount. It was these qualities that won it an important military contract, which saw it built in substantial numbers throughout the war years.

Douglas 2¾hp

Douglas flat-twin motorcycles won undying fame, and fortune, with their performance in World War I, when the company equipped army despatch riders with some 25,000 machines. Technically advanced, they demonstrated the smoothness of an engine type that was adopted by numerous other manufacturers, and used by Douglas themselves as late as 1957.

The Douglas Engineering Company was founded in Bristol in 1882, by Scottish brothers William and Edward Douglas, as a general engineering company and foundry. But the Douglas motorcycle really grew out of the efforts of one Joseph Barter, who founded a company called Light Motors Ltd in nearby Kingswood. Barter had developed a design called the Fairy – which used a horizontally opposed engine of advanced design – after being impressed by the smoothness of this type of engine. Despite its technical advantages, Barter failed to make enough money to enable the firm to

Gear selection is controlled by the handle on top of the tank (left), which selects low or high ratio. Also visible is the hand pump used to supply oil to the engine.

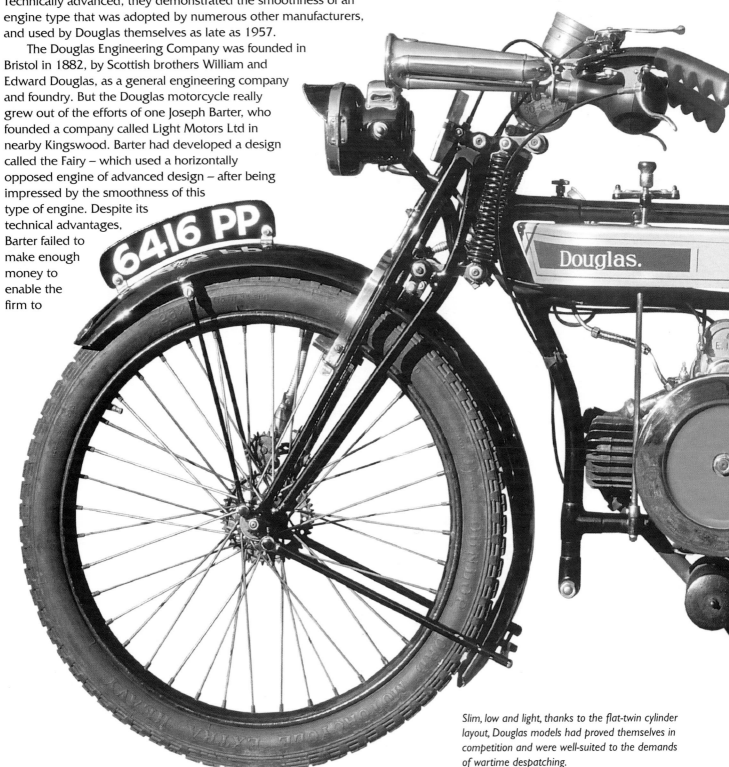

Slim, low and light, thanks to the flat-twin cylinder layout, Douglas models had proved themselves in competition and were well-suited to the demands of wartime despatching.

survive, and in 1907, Douglas took over manufacture of a model based on the Fairy, using direct belt drive. Barter became an employee of the company and helped to develop the machines. His original design had been of 200cc, but under Douglas ownership it was enlarged to 2¾ hp (340cc).

After a couple of years of very limited sales, a turning point came in 1910, with the introduction of a two-speed gearbox fitted under the gearbox and operated by a handle on top of the tank. Belt drive was used and no clutch was fitted – the machine was started simply by pushing off.

The new model soon won an important reliability trial, and before the end of the year scored an important success by setting a record for the Lands End to John O'Groats run. The various technical advances of the Douglas had paid off handsomely, and in 1911 there were more competition successes. In 1912, the engine gained new, mechanically operated valves that gave a power output of some 8bhp. At that year's Isle of Man TT, there were several Douglas entries, which gained an outstanding success, with 1st, 2nd and 4th places, despite the bad weather. Many other racing successes followed and Douglas' fortunes seemed assured.

By the end of 1914, Douglas had sold around 12,000 machines and were well-established, soon becoming one of the most important makers of military machines.

For a small side-valve, the Douglas twin was quick, and being light, it was easy to manhandle. The front plug could short out in the wet, but on the whole the machine was very reliable and smooth running. After the war, a civilian version of the Douglas twin went back into production in 1919, but many ex-WD examples were reconditioned and sold off to the public, giving long and honourable service in peace just as they had done in war-time.

Douglas 2¾ hp (1919)

Years in production: 1912-22

Engine type: horizontally opposed (fore and aft) side-valve four-stroke twin

Bore and stroke: 60.8 x 60mm

Capacity: 348cc

Power: 8bhp

Carburettor: Douglas two-lever

Tyres (front/rear): 2¼ x 26in/2¼ x 26in

Weight: 170lb

Top speed: 40mph

Wooler

Despite its date of manufacture, Wooler's unorthodox twin is a true pioneer in spirit. A tiny manufacturer, led by a visionary who seemed to delight in the unusual, the company survived until the 1950s, albeit with a gap of 17 years when no machines were produced. Unusual engine configurations and suspension designs were a Wooler hallmark, as was styling designed to turn heads.

John Wooler built his first motorcycle in 1911, and it set the pattern for the future. The engine was a horizontal single-cylinder two-stroke with a double-ended piston, eliminating the need for normal crankcase compression. The power was transmitted by a long pin that stuck through slots in the crankcase walls external connecting rods to the flywheel. There was a front and rear suspension, way ahead of its time, using a patented plunger system. The patent also covered a fuel tank that enclosed the steering head, supposedly as a means of achieving greater fuel capacity. Using belt drive, there was a pedal-operated device for adjusting the pulley to change gear.

That first machine had a 230cc engine, but by the time it went into production – at the nearby Wilkinson works, as

Wooler had no production facilities – the engine had been enlarged to 344cc. There were numerous minor improvements, including some thoughtful ideas such as knock-through wheel spindles and nuts of only two sizes. That led to a trademark of a double-ended spanner (the only tool needed!) and the word 'Accessibility'. The Wilkinson Wooler was in production until 1913, and manufacture ceased during World War I.

The Wooler that appeared in 1919 was similar in layout but very different in almost every detail of the engine. This was now a

Wooler (1920)

Years in production: 1919-23

Engine type: horizontally opposed (fore-and-aft) inlet-over-exhaust four-stroke

Engine type: single-cylinder side-valve four-stroke

Bore and stroke: 60 x 60mm

Capacity: 348cc

Transmission: initially by variable ratio belt, later by chain drive

Weight: 162lb

Top speed: approx 55mph

350cc four-stroke flat-twin, similar to the popular Douglas, but of inlet-over-exhaust layout rather than a side-valve. The forward-projecting tank was completely redesigned, but the suspension and variable belt-drive systems were there as before.

A real lightweight, the Wooler was also astoundingly economical. During a special test, it achieved an amazing 311 miles on a measured gallon. Entered in the 1921 Junior TT, its performance was unspectacular, coming only 34th, but at Brooklands it broke 29 world records for long-distance endurance. Its 'Flying Banana' nickname is supposed to have been gained after the TT.

After 1923, Wooler fitted new semi-overhead-cam 350 and 500cc versions of the engine; the fuel tank was of conventional shape. For 1926, John Wooler tried a much more conventional machine with rigid frame and fairly conventional girder forks. It had an intriguing overhead-cam 511cc single-cylinder engine, but it was set aside when he bought the ailing Packmann & Poppe company. Moving to Wembley, Wooler's small factory produced a small range of motorcycles until 1930, when it closed down.

As early as 1936, Wooler began work on another incredibly unconventional design, a 500cc transverse four with pistons interconnected by rocking beams to a single big end. News of this broke during the war, but it was not until 1948 that it was seen in the metal. Sadly, this incredibly lightweight design did not proceed beyond the experimental stage.

The horizontally-opposed engine (below) was extremely efficient, covering 311 miles on a gallon of fuel in a special test.

The Wooler gained the nickname 'Flying Banana' from the size, shape and colour of its tank. Despite its unconventional appearance it embodied original thinking that was good enough to gain 29 world records for speed and endurance.

Manufacturers' badges from 1900–1919

Vintage Days
1920-1940

ABC ✪ Levis Popular ✪ Norton 16H ✪ Velocette Two-stroke

Triumph Ricardo ✪ BSA Round Tank ✪ James V-twin

Brough Superior SS100 ✪ Ner-a-car ✪ Cotton TT

Sunbeam Model 90 ✪ Velocette KTT ✪ Norton CS1

Scott Squirrel ✪ Matchless Silver Hawk ✪ Excelsior Manxman

Norton International ✪ Vincent Rapide

Triumph Speed Twin 5T ✪ BSA Gold Star ✪ Rudge Ulster

Vintage Days

Although World War I ended in November 1918, rationing remained in force for some time and it was not until the following year that motorcycle factories were allowed to go back into production.

However, the end of the war coincided with an enormous demand for transport, fuelled by the returning servicemen and women, many of whom had their first experience of motorcycles or cars while at arms.

At first this demand was met by secondhand prewar models or reconditioned military machines, of which there were many thousands – mostly the ubiquitous despatch riders' Triumph single or Douglas twin. Prices were high, there were long waiting lists and fuel was in short supply, but demand was steady. The situation was tailor-made for ingenious dealers and accessory manufacturers, several of whom offered ways to make an old model appear like a new one, or economise with gadgets such as fuel-savers, 'hot' exhausts and plug protectors.

When restrictions on manufacture were lifted, there still remained the problem of limited raw materials, including most metals and rubber. Manufacturing capacity was no problem at all; there was a host of factories that had been forced to turn their attention from profitable and intensive war work to the civilian market. For firms such as Triumph, it was simply a matter of reopening the production lines, but there were many others with no prewar experience, for whom the sellers market was impossible to resist. Factories that had until recently been building aircraft, tanks or even components for the munitions industry began to turn their attention to motorcycles.

Typical of a host of small factories in the immediate postwar years, Sheffield-Henderson was a sidecar maker that assembled machines around proprietary engines from Blackburne – in this case a sporting overhead-valve model.

By the end of 1919 there were 50 new manufacturers and within a couple of years this had risen to over a hundred. More than two hundred models were exhibited at the first postwar Olympia show in 1919. Some of these were gimcrack designs, hastily rushed into production, others were simply 'assembly jobs' relying on bought-in engines, frame parts and running gear. But among the dross there were still gems to be found.

For the most part there was little immediate technical advancement, for the war had demonstrated in the clearest fashion what was worthwhile and what was not. The emphasis tended to be on reliability and convention. BSA, Matchless, Sunbeam and Clyno all showed machines that

Large factories such as railway and shipbuilding conglomerate Beardmore also got in on the act under the name Beardmore-Precision. This is a 1921 350cc model.

Working bikes (right): after the wartime despatch riding experience, motoring organisations were quick to catch on to the practicality of the motorcycle. In 1922, these four RAC patrolmen were equipped with Ivy 250cc two-strokes.

Motorcycles were a staple form of transport in the inter-war years. Lightweights, mostly two-strokes, were favoured by the taxation laws. This 225cc Royal Enfield (below) from the early 1920s was designed to be as cheap as possible but with modernisation lasted right through the Depression, virtually until World War II. It actually became cheaper and cheaper with the passing years.

would have seemed familiar six years earlier. Others were prepared to experiment, such as Royal Enfield with their prototype four-cylinder machine, which failed to go into production. But the star of the show was the revolutionary ABC, manufactured by the Sopwith Aviation company. Representing an enormous technological leap, this above all seemed to presage a new direction for the industry, although the detail flaws and financial muddle that attended its launch were indicative of the age in a less attractive way. Other industrial giants were not far behind, such as the Beardmore combine with the Precision design that again proved to promise more than it delivered.

Production got into full swing in 1920, but the euphoric promises of a year before all too often proved impossible to keep. Many prices were much higher than had been suggested and this would prove the downfall of many a hopeful. A distraction was offered by a brief craze for the scooter, inspired by an American device called the Autoped, which was more of a motorised skateboard than a true scooter. After a couple of years of ingenious but frequently hopeless variations on the theme, the bubble finally burst.

On a more serious note, competitions had also returned in 1919 and were enthusiastically greeted. Hillclimbs, sprints and trials regained all their prewar popularity and

more, while the Isle of Man TT and Brooklands were back in 1920. An ABC won at the first Brooklands event, while Sunbeam, AJS and Levis took the TTs.

The 1920s ushered in what many have called a 'Golden Age' of motorcycling. According to the strict definition, a 'Vintage' bike is deemed to be one constructed before 1930, although since the term was coined just after World War II, perceptions have changed.

As prosperity returned, customers increased in numbers and the successful factories boomed. A host of proprietary engine and component factories including JAP, in London, Villiers, Blackburne and Chater-Lea supported the smaller manufacturers, while the larger ones started a period of expansion and consolidation. Dealers grew larger and more affluent, while motorcycling was seen as socially acceptable for all classes.

On the one hand, a motorcycle could provide family transport or a workaday tool, especially if fitted with a sidecar. Sidecars were built with enough seats for a large family, or purpose-designed for butchers, bakers and even motorcycle dealers to transport their wares. On the other hand, a solo motorcycle was a fashionable accessory for a sporting young man or woman who could afford the very latest 'race replica'.

The basic motorcycle was still recognisably similar to its prewar counterpart – usually a 500cc single cylinder side-valve – turned out in hundreds of thousands by firms such as Triumph and Norton. There were technical improvements in items such as valves, which could now be relied on not to break frequently, and the emphasis was on practicality. There was also a boom in lightweights, partly as a result of taxation, which, after 1921, included a classification on weight – under 200lb and the tax was halved. Simple, lightly built and usually two-stroke powered, such models as the Levis and Royal Enfield offerings were cheap and simple enough to appeal to a new breed of riders.

At the other end of the scale, speeds began to rise and sports machines grew in popularity. In 1924 a Blackburne-engined Chater-Lea became the first 350 to exceed 100mph

Family transport (above): throughout the 1920s motorcycles and sidecar outfits were an eminently respectable means of travelling, and sales boomed.

The Isle of Man TT exercised an enormous influence over manufacturers and public in the interwar years. In a famous incident in 1924 (above) the great Stanley Woods corners his Cotton ahead of Norton's Joe Craig, fallen at Governor's Bridge. Both men would go on to great things, Woods as the most successful rider of his generation, Craig as head of Norton's race shop during their glory days.

Pressed-steel and a Villiers engine were Francis-Barnett's solution to providing low-budget transport. The 1937 Cruiser model offered comfort and cleanliness and was a popular 30s alternative.

at Brooklands, and machines of this size were seen as a real sporting alternative to the 500s. There also grew up a small but significant demand for luxury, high-performance machines, which was satisfied by specialist manufacturers such as Brough Superior and HRD.

Much of the interest in motorcycling was fuelled by the glamour of racing, and in particular the TT, which attracted huge audiences throughout the period. Stars such as Stanley Woods, Jimmy Simpson and Wal Handley were household names, while riders such as Bert Le Vack and Freddie Dixon became famous for their record-breaking exploits, hoisting the world record to almost 130 mph by the end of the decade. Norton and Velocette, among other manufacturers, built their reputations with a string of wins that proved Britain really did build the best bikes in the world. Such new sports as dirt-track (speedway) sprang up, and proved hugely popular with the crowds.

It was only at the end of the 1920s that light cars such as the Morris Minor and Austin Seven began to offer a serious challenge to the motorcycle. There were around three-quarters of a million bikes – a third of the world's total – on Britain's roads in 1929, the year of the collapse of the New York stock exchange.

The shock waves of the Depression that followed soon reached Britain. That year's show had seen the buoyant

launch of new luxury models, but economy would soon become the byword. Weaker manufacturers went to the wall, while others turned to more profitable enterprises. Even so, many prospered, partly as a result of cost-cutting and new commercial ideas such as hire purchase. Prices went down and down, reaching rock bottom in 1932, when the annual show at Olympia was cancelled, and a year later the taxation classes were revised to favour small capacity machines. By 1936 the situation had resulted in machines such as the 250cc pushrod-engined Red Panther, offering well over 110 mpg and costing less than £30 cash, payable in weekly instalments of some 33p. Even so, the big Brough Superiors continued to find small numbers of customers at prices of some £180.

Motorcycle sport continued to prosper, perhaps as an antidote to the drab austerity of the times. But commercially things failed to improve. Many famous factories were forced to close or merge – Ariel, the second largest concern in the land, AJS, Douglas and Sunbeam among them. From the mergers that arose at this time, the final shape of the British industry began to emerge.

One of the most significant factors in the shape of the postwar industry was also taking place in the Midlands, where Edward Turner, late of Ariel, now of Triumph, was laying down the form of the Speed Twin, a model that for better or worse would dictate the form of the motorcycle for three decades and more.

But another cloud was gathering, and its influence could be seen in an increasingly significant continental challenge to British sporting supremacy. The great Stanley Woods had switched his allegiance to Moto Guzzi and in 1935 won two

BSA, for a time the biggest manufacturer in the world, got big by making good honest workhorses like the 1934 'Sloper'. The sloping engine and twin fishtail exhausts were fashionable items, but the bike itself was stolid rather than speedy.

TTs for the Italian factory. An even greater challenge was being mounted closer to home. With massive state encouragement, BMW, NSU and DKW were fielding technically advanced racers and record-breakers with the objective of demonstrating Germany's engineering supremacy. With BMWs first and second in the 1939 Senior TT and DKWs placed in both the Junior and the Lightweight, they did just that.

The British answers, including the ambitious supercharged offerings from AJS and Velocette were virtually stillborn, for by the closing years of the 1930s, most of British industry was already gearing up for a conflict that seemed inevitable. Within months Europe was at war, drawing another chapter in motorcycle history to an end.

Norton and Velocette were a British racing double-act throughout the 1920s and 30s. Norton star P (Tim) Hunt pushes off in the 1932 Junior.

ABC

In 1919, many manufacturers who had been involved in war work found themselves facing the prospect of cutting back their activities unless they could diversify into other types of production. One such was Sopwith of Kingston-on-Thames, Surrey, an aircraft company that faced a sudden downturn in demand. Proprietor Tommy Sopwith believed that motorcycle production could be the answer, and turned to the prolific designer Granville Bradshaw for help.

The solution that Bradshaw offered was the astonishingly bold ABC flat-twin – even more extraordinary because the design was completed in a mere 11 days. He had bet the incredulous Sopwith that a prototype could be produced in three weeks – and backed this claim with a deal whereby he staked £100 per day over that time, while Sopwith would pay a similar sum for every day less. As a result, Bradshaw netted £1000 on the deal, an enormous sum at a time when a basic motorcycle could be bought for as little as £50.

An Achilles heel was the valve gear (left), which in its original form proved too weak. Accessory manufacturers offered solutions, but the firm's financial difficulties meant that they were never able to develop the ABC as needed.

A machine built in such a short time might have been expected to be crude, or at the least a copy of an existing design, but the ABC was neither. Its horizontally-opposed twin-cylinder engine employed overhead-valves when most makers, including the slightly later BMW that used a similar layout, stuck with the conservative side-valve layout. It had an integral four-speed gearbox, when many machines still used direct belt drive or, at best, two speeds. Only the chain drive from the gearbox to the rear wheel was perhaps not as advanced as the shaft adopted by BMW.

Part of the reason for this may have been that Bradshaw had decided on a fully sprung frame, which made it harder to accommodate a shaft. The main frame was a double-cradle, ingeniously splayed wide enough to support legshields and footboards, while providing protection for the engine in the event of the bike being dropped. The front fork was a girder design, with quarter-elliptic springing.

At the rear, Bradshaw had designed an early swinging-arm suspension, again leaf-sprung. There were many other features aimed at providing

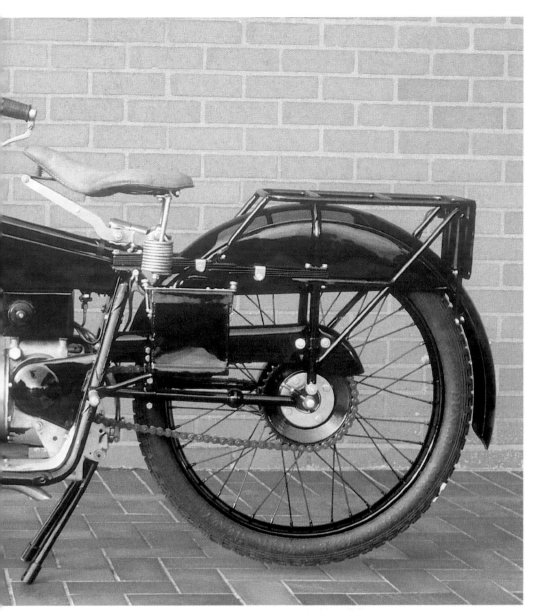

Rider comfort was a key part of the ABC concept. Front and rear springing, wide footboards and legshields offered a relaxed ride, while sophisticated controls made the ABC easier to ride than most of its contemporaries. Unfortunately, this promising newcomer was beset by teething problems and financial setbacks.

ABC (1919)

Years in production: 1919-25

Engine type: horizontally-opposed twin-cylinder overhead-valve four-stroke

Bore and stroke: 68.6 x 54mm

Capacity: 398cc

Carburettor: Claudel-Hobson

Gearbox: four-speed with H-gate

Top speed: 70mph

Rider convenience: the four-speed gearbox (below) was a real innovation, and the carburettor was simpler to control than that of most contemporaries. Less satisfactory was the lubrication, which had to be changed from wet-sump to a hand-pumped design.

rider convenience and luxury, and when it was launched, the ABC captured the imagination of the reviewers. Light in weight and quiet, the machine had a brisk performance, as well as being comfortable and stable. Orders began to flood in and the French company Gnôme et Rhône were signed up to produce the design under licence.

Then the troubles began. Initially priced at £70, the ABC proved too expensive to manufacture, and the design had to be modified to sort out some mechanical problems. Sales should have begun early in 1919, but when the first machines appeared in May 1920, the price had risen to an astronomical £160, and even at this price the makers were hardly covering their costs.

Only some 2000 were made. Although the ABCs proved capable of winning two speed records in the year they were launched, it soon transpired that the valve gear was weak and prone to breakage. While accessory makers offered cures for its mechanical problems, the factory itself quietly let the unprofitable ABC fade away. The last one made by Sopwith was built in 1923, although Gnôme et Rhône made a few up until 1925. After that it was left to others – especially the flat-twin BMWs – to demonstrate what the concept might have offered.

Levis Popular

As simple as it was possible to be, and cheap with it, Levis' lightweight was typical of the machines that provided everyday transport for the masses in the years just after World War I. But with its quality of engineering, it was also perhaps the best of its kind, and the name Levis went on to become a byword for two-stroke machines that were reliable, light and quick.

Levis motorcycles were made by Butterfields Ltd, an engineering firm started in Birmingham in 1906 by two brothers, William and Arthur Butterfield. Some years later, the firm began experimenting with motorcycle design, and in 1910 successfully tested their own two-stroke engine. The first machine they produced using this engine was only a little more substantial than a bicycle, and very light. With its 196cc two-stroke engine and direct belt drive to the rear wheel, it was capable of some 35mph. For their slogan, Butterfields adopted the Latin phrase 'levis et celer', meaning 'light and fast', and took the name Levis for the name of the motorcycles.

When the machine went into production as the Levis Model 1, the engine size had been increased to 269cc, while there was also a smaller version of 211cc, the Baby Levis. In the years before World War I, Butterfields went on to offer a number of versions of these models, together with a 349cc De-Luxe. In 1914, the 211cc Popular, which had a higher specification than the Baby, was introduced, along with a 175cc Levisette. Under the guidance of works manager Howard Newey, the firm also took its first steps in racing, although there were few events for lightweights.

The war, of course, put paid to much further development, although the firm experimented with engines for the aircraft industry. But in the years immediately after peace returned, there was an urgent need for cheap transport, which Levis stepped in to fill.

Levis had also begun racing again, and in 1920 entered 250cc machines in the Junior (350cc) TT, which included a newly introduced trophy for machines of 250cc or less. But for a crash, Levis was in contention to beat the best 350s; as it was, they still took first, second, and third in the 250cc class, as well as scoring a fastest lap that was 3mph better than the overall speed of the race-winning 350cc AJS.

Simple and light, the 211cc Levis (above) has few frills or unnecessary fittings. An unusual feature is the front downtube of the frame, which splits to allow the exhaust pipe to run centrally.

Unusually for a simple two-stroke of the time, the carburettor (left) supplies only a petrol/air mixture. Oil is provided from a separate reservoir, which feeds directly to the bottom end of the engine.

Levis Popular (1921)

Years in production: 1914-24

Engine type: single-cylinder two-stroke with drip feed lubrication

Bore and stroke: 62 x 70mm

Capacity: 211cc

Carburettor: Amac

Tyres (front/rear): 2¼ x 24in/2¼ x 24in

Weight: 118lb

Fuel consumption: 150mpg

Top speed: 35mph

Two years later, Levis won the first Lightweight TT run as a separate event. They also won continental Grands Prix in 1922 and '23.

Among the machines that provided Levis' bread and butter, the Popular was perhaps the most important. It was very simply constructed, with a light frame and forks and a transmission consisting simply of a belt looped around the engine pulley, driving the back wheel. With no kickstart or gears, starting was by pushing or scooting off, using a decompression lever to help the engine turn over easily. A large external flywheel kept the engine running evenly, although it might slow to a fast walking pace when pulling uphill. Brakes were simple, too, with a bicycle-type stirrup brake on the front rim and a heel-operated rear brake working on the belt rim.

But such simplicity did not mean crudeness. The Levis was well-engineered and simple to repair. It even included such sophistication as separate oiling, at a time when most two-strokes relied on a pre-mixed petroil. It was a formula that kept it in production until 1924 – a run of over a decade – when more apparently sophisticated models from both Levis and their rivals had come and gone.

Norton 16H

Tracing its lineage back to 1911, the Norton 16H was by turns a TT racer, wartime despatch machine and family sidecar slogger, in a remarkable career that spanned 33 years. In all that time, the engine's basic layout and dimensions remained unchanged – it was simply that the world moved on around it.

In 1911, the Isle of Man TT included a 500cc Senior class for the first time, and Norton had a new design ready to contest it. A side-valve of 490cc with dimensions of 79 x 100mm bore and stroke, it was listed as the '3½'. Founder James Norton rode one of the firm's entries himself, but failed to place. Yet, the very next year, a similar machine won the Brooklands TT, and three world records in the one event. In 1913, versions on sale included the Brooklands Special (BS) and Brooklands Road Special (BRS), which with their single-speed belt-driven transmission were guaranteed to have lapped Brooklands at more than 70mph (65 for the BRS), while many were in fact capable of exceeding 80mph.

Norton 16H (1922)

Years in production: 1921-54

Engine type: single-cylinder side-valve four-stroke

Bore and stroke: 79 x 100mm

Capacity: 490cc

Compression ratio: 4.9:1

Power: 12bhp

Tyres (front/rear): 3¼ x 26in

Top speed: 78mph

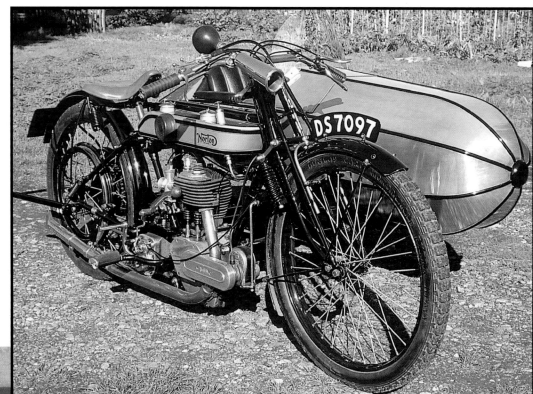

Sporting sidecar (right): the 16H was often linked to a sidecar throughout its long production life, although by the end it was providing family transport rather than race entries.

Lean and low-slung, the 1922 Norton 16H helped to establish a style for fast sporting 'flat-tankers'.

A chain-driven version was developed, but with World War I intervening it was 1919 before the 490cc Norton was back in civilian production. The catalogued Model 16 now featured chain-drive with a three-speed Sturmey-Archer gearbox, and was directly related to the competition machines that were holders of some 21 world records.

In 1920, the year of the first postwar TT, Norton moved to Bracebridge Street in Birmingham. At the TT, Norton's Douggie Brown was pipped to the post by Sunbeam's Tommy de la Hay, but could take satisfaction from knowing that more than half the finishers were riding Nortons.

The next year, Norton launched a new model, called the Colonial. Aimed at the expanding market in less developed areas of the Empire, it had a higher ground clearance than the standard machine, which gained an even lower riding position and a new designation – the 16H ('H' for Home) model. In the TT, although Norton failed to score better than sixth place, it was still the most popular marque represented.

In 1922 Norton's race development effort switched to the newly designed overhead-valve Model 18, but only one works machine was used in the TT, with another privately entered. A further dozen side-valvers were entered. By the next year the side-valver was no longer a works TT mount, but was still a popular private entry.

Out of the spotlight, the 16H found a new role as a popular sporting tourer, with styling and detail changes, such as a switch to a saddle tank, coming slowly over the next decade. The engine was reworked in 1931, but the next major development came in 1936, when after earlier successful trials the army began to place regular orders for 16Hs (modified for off-road work). These orders continued right through the war, with more than 80,000 delivered, spanning a decade in all, and some machines staying in service until the late 1950s.

Velocette Two-stroke

Slim, low and light with a sophisticated engine, the Velocette two-stroke won many admirers, and gave its name to 60 years of successors.

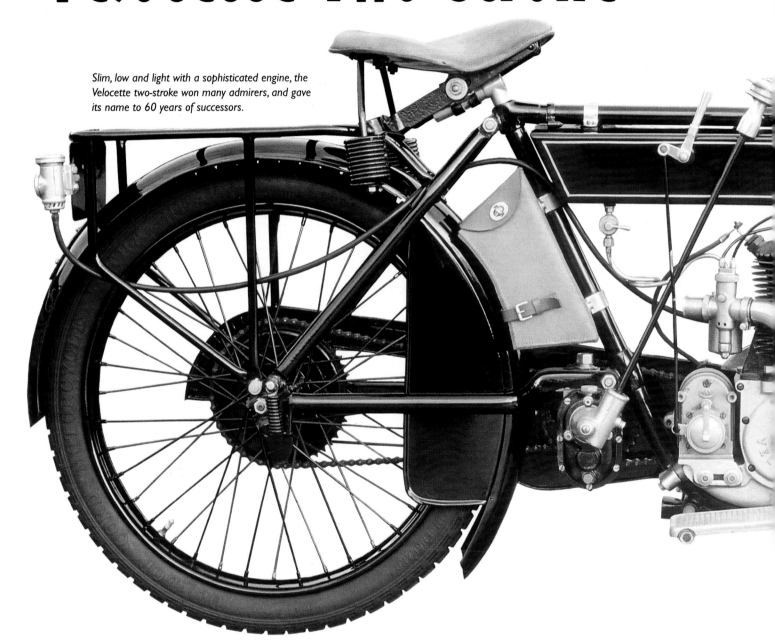

The British manufacturing company Veloce was founded in 1905 by John Gutgemann, a German whose name was anglicised to Goodman when he was naturalised a few years later. Veloce was a family concern in which Goodman's sons, daughter and grandsons would come to play an important part. The company made a wide range of products, including bicycles and conventional 500cc motorcycles. When they decided to add a speedy lightweight two-stroke to the line-up, the name Velocette was chosen to suggest that it was a baby version of the bigger machines. In time the new baby became so popular that the company was named after it rather than the other way around.

Although beautifully engineered and commendably light, the frame and forks were conventional for the time, and the real interest lay in the engine and transmission. These were both very sophisticated for their day, and offered many advanced features.

The transmission was by chain throughout – at a time when many competitors relied on the much less reliable belt. It had the luxury of a two-speed gearbox, although no clutch was fitted. The gearchange was by a large knob looking something like a bathroom tap, fitted on the right of the tank.

Part of the reason for the absence of a clutch (in itself not uncommon for the period) was the crankcase design, which helped lead to the adoption of a very unconventional

clutch on later models. The crankcase chosen was very compact and very narrow, contributing to a very stiff bottom end. On the early two-stroke, only one main bearing was used, and the crank was overhung. To balance it, the flywheel was fitted externally, and the drive chain ran inside this. A result of the narrow drive line is that the final drive chain is outside the primary sprocket, making the type of clutch adopted by most other designers an impossibility.

The benefit of the crankcase design was its strength, aided by a lubrication system that offered reliable oiling under all conditions. Most two-strokes then and for the next 50 years relied on hit-and-miss oiling by petroil lubrication. This was both messy and unreliable. Velocette offered a positive lubrication

system via a small container in the crankcase, which was automatically pressurised by the engine. This fed oil directly to the main bearing through an adjustable jet.

The top end was conventional for a two-stroke of the period, using a side-mounted induction tract and deflector-type piston to control the gas flow. Because of the absence of a clutch, a compression relief-valve was fitted to the front of the cylinder head to allow the engine to spin easily when starting off. In use the little Velocette was reliable and economical, while the absence of a clutch was no hardship at a time before heavy traffic existed. Light, simple and well-engineered, it paved the way for a company which would become one of the chief pioneers during the 1920s and 30s.

Triumph Ricardo

Having established an enviable reputation in the early days of motorcycle competition, Triumph chose to ignore events such as the Isle of Man TT for several years. So when they performed an abrupt about turn in 1922 it could be expected that they were pretty confident of the machine that they chose to enter – the super sports 'Ricardo'.

Sir Henry (Harry) Ricardo was a renowned combustion expert who had worked on behalf of many companies when he was asked by Triumph to advise on a replacement for their trusty side-valves. Ricardo produced a number of alternatives before Triumph announced that their new overhead-valve model would use a four-valve head design. In fact, from the cylinder barrel down, the rest of the machine was virtually identical to Triumph's tried-and-tested Model H side-valve – including cycle parts that were becoming dated by comparison with its rivals.

The theoretical advantages of a four-valve head were numerous. Gas flow could be more efficient, the spark plug could be positioned centrally for more efficient combustion, while the lighter components would respond quicker, allowing higher revs. In fact, Ricardo's design was quite conservative, using small ports and unusually recessed valves. Each pair of valves was parallel, set at 90 degrees to each other, with stems and springs exposed; the piston, which was of light alloy, had a concave crown and a slipper-type skirt. The cylinder barrel was made of solid steel and had very deep finning, while the head, which had two parallel exhaust ports, was iron. The valves were operated by rockers running in bearings carried in lugs cast into the top of the head. Two long, exposed pushrods ran up the outside of the engine.

Fully equipped for the road,
the Ricardo was marketed as a
super sports model, rather than a pure racer.

Triumph Model R (1923)

Years in production: 1921-28

Engine type: single-cylinder four-valve ohv
four-stroke

Bore and stroke: 80.5 x 98mm
(changed to 85 x 88mm)

Capacity: 499cc

Power: 20bhp @ 4600rpm

Carburettor: Triumph twin barrel

Tyres (front/rear): 3 x 26in/3 x 26in

Transmission: Triumph
three-speed gearbox

Weight: 250lb

Top speed:
approx 70mph

From there down, the engine was based on the Model H. The flywheels were slightly smaller, to allow free revving, while the lubrication, relying on constant-loss fed by hand pump, was later changed to dry sump fed by external oil pump. The resulting Model R Fast Roadster was marketed as a fully equipped sports model and attracted favourable reports. In this form it lapped Brooklands at 68mph, having survived the test of a flat-out lap in first gear. A racing version with modified ports also took the hour record at almost 77mph, and a flying mile at nearly 84mph.

Three were entered for the 1921 TT, alongside a back-up team of side-valve Triumphs. Handling deficiencies of the standard Triumph forks meant that proprietary alternatives were substituted, but in this first foray only one finished, well behind its side-valve team-mate.

A year later, the Ricardo was back with the new lubrication system, stronger valve gear, a modified cylinder with new dimensions and made of cast iron, a three-speed gearbox and new front fork. This time, it finished second in the TT, and the following year went on to take a number of continental wins and gold medals in the ISDT.

After 1924, Triumph switched their development efforts to a new model, although the 'Riccy' stayed in their range as a sports model until 1928, when the looming Depression forced Triumph to reduce their range. But the four-valve layout had proved its potential, and in the hands of Rudge and others, in the future would go on to demonstrate its winning worth.

BSA Round Tank

For a long period in the interwar years the giant BSA conglomerate dominated a booming motorcycle market in a way that no other British factory could claim to have done. 'One in four is a BSA' was a factory advertising slogan, and it was no idle boast. Part of the reason why BSA became so big was that they understood the needs of the market. While their machines were far from the most glamorous – and for many years were never even involved in racing – they satisfied the demand for reliable, basic transport that even today underpins the exotic machines from the Japanese giants.

At one end of the market this meant heavyweight sloggers such as the BSA V-twins and 500cc singles, often seen pulling sidecars as family transport or workaday hacks. At the other end of the market it meant affordable lightweights and, in particular, 250cc singles, a market niche that BSA made very much their own. Their attack on this market began in 1924 and was very much a new departure for BSA. It was known to be a difficult market, for the public had been treated to many poorly designed and underengineered budget specials from other makers.

The little BSA Round Tank was a well loved utility machine that established its makers in this important market. Reliable and rugged, it put thousands of people on wheels and found favour with institutions as a hard-working despatch bike.

Perhaps as a result, the little BSA was solidly conventional, with a side-valve four-stroke engine in place of the often unreliable two-strokes usually offered. It was small and light and simple enough for a novice, while strong enough to take all that the most uncaring rider could throw at it. And it was cheap – less than £40. There was belt-and-braces lubrication, with a new-fangled mechanical pump as well as the old-fashioned hand pump, plus a sight feed to reassure the anxious owner that all was well. The oil was contained in the front section of the tank that gave the model its name. Handsomely finished, but rugged and simple like the rest of the machine, the oil tank was a simple cylinder with no weak seams to split, and was suspended within the frame by two simple metal straps.

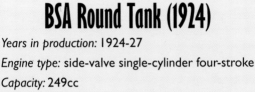

BSA Round Tank (1924)

Years in production: 1924-27

Engine type: side-valve single-cylinder four-stroke

Capacity: 249cc

Bore and stroke: 63 x 80mm

Tyres: 24 x 2¼in beaded-edge type

Brakes: friction block on dummy belt rim (rear only – two independent systems)

Gear box: two-speed

Top speed: 43 mph

Practical details abounded. The mudguards were surely some of the widest ever fitted to a motorcycle, genuinely capable of guarding against mud splashes in almost any conditions. Indeed, they were so wide that the front forks actually passed through them. All-chain drive was used, while the gearbox was operated directly by a long hand lever.

Ruggedness was such a concern of the factory that they boasted that the prototypes had been battered for hours on a special bumping machine to simulate years of heavy use. There were, of course, no breakages.

With such a concern for practicality it might seem odd that the factory chose not to fit a front brake. This was dictated by a feeling, dating back to pioneer days, that such a brake might be hazardous to the inexperienced rider, because of the risk of locking the wheel or skidding. It was felt that, with a modest top speed, a back brake should be perfectly adequate. In fact, BSA's design coincided with a new legal requirement that all machines should have two independent means of stopping. The factory solved that one simply by fitting two entirely separate systems to the back wheel. In addition to the footbrake, a friction block operated by the handlebar lever pressed on the dummy belt rim on the rear wheel.

The resulting machine was a pleasant utility bike that did a great deal to establish BSA's reputation for quality and reliability. One was even used in May 1924 as part of a BSA stunt, climbing Mount Snowdon in Wales in just over half an hour, alongside the mountain railway track. It sold in large numbers – some 35,000 – and was adopted by the Post Office for telegram delivery. This remained a familiar role for BSA lightweights for many years, right up to the era of the BSA Bantam and the twilight of a once-great British company.

Suspended between the frame rails on two nickel-plated suspension bands, the tank that gave the model its name comprised a separate oil compartment in front of the main petrol tank. Rather unkindly, the machine was also dubbed the 'Flying Marrow'.

James V-twin

In their later years, when they were simply part of the giant AMC group, the name of James would come to be associated almost exclusively with the kind of budget two-strokes that represented the final fling of the British industry. But in the early days of the industry, the picture was very different, and the marque adopted the slogan 'The Famous James' for its twin-cylinder flagship.

The company had been founded in the late 1870s as a bicycle manufacturer, taking the name of founder Harold James. The James Cycle Company, based in Greet, Birmingham, soon grew to a substantial operation. It produced its first motorcycle in 1902. Like most other pioneer motorcycle experiments, the first James product was virtually a conventional pedal cycle modified to take an engine, with belt drive to the rear wheel. As well as this model, the company produced another version in which the engine drove a friction roller in contact with the rear tyre, an idea that was used in some cyclemotors of the 1950s.

The earliest James machines used proprietary engines, but within a few years the company was manufacturing its own two-stroke and four-stroke power units, as well as experimenting with advanced ideas such as drum brakes and quick-change wheels. The 1908 'Safety' model was influential on rival makers, and in 1911, James introduced a model with such 'modern' features as multi-plate clutch, a kick-start, two-speed gearbox and all-chain drive.

During World War I, James machines were used by the Allied forces, but a fire at the factory prevented them from going back into peacetime production immediately. The earliest postwar models produced were 250 and 350cc side-valve singles, and these were soon followed by popular V-twins of 500cc. An overhead-valve model was made as well as the side-valve version pictured here. Both included advanced features for the time and were a popular choice of the family man (with sidecar attached) and sporting rider.

Unusually, James made most of the components themselves, unlike the majority of factories which relied on many bought-in components. This included making the castings for parts such as the distinctive silencer box carrying the 'James' name cast into the side.

Popular as they were, the bigger James models were expensive to make and to buy. By the end of the 1920s, the Depression was starting to bite the motorcycle industry and James were able to buy up the ailing Baker company, makers of lightweight motorcycles. From about 1930, smaller machines powered by proprietary Villiers two-strokes became the mainstay of James' business, until they themselves were taken over after World War II.

The gearchange quadrant on the side of the tank (left) is a special alloy casting made in James' own foundry.

The carburettor (right), a Mills, is a forerunner of the later Villiers design. It uses a concentric float bowl and mixing chamber, unusual at the time, but later to become a common design feature.

James V-twin (1924)

Years in production: 1914–1932

Engine type: side-valve V-twin four-stroke (overhead-valve engine also manufactured)

Capacity: 496cc

Bore and stroke: 63x80mm

Compression ratio: 5.5:1

Carburettor: Mills

Transmission: all-chain, via three-speed gearbox

Top speed: 65mph

Resplendent in its green James livery, the 500cc side-valve model features the handsome alloy castings that were a factory trademark. Electric lighting was a luxury item for its day.

Brough Superior SS100

The Brough Superior has been called the first superbike. The aim of its designer George Brough was to build a machine that was the best at everything – the fastest, best looking, most advanced and best finished – and in its day the Brough Superior earned itself the title of the 'Rolls Royce of Motor Cycles'. The SS100 could top 100mph when half that speed was considered good going, looked like it cost a fortune – and did – and was the natural choice of the rich and famous.

George Brough's father William was a well-established motorcycle manufacturer who had built a range of reliable machines at his Nottingham factory since the 1890s. But George, an excellent competition rider, wanted something with more performance than the Brough product could offer. So in 1919, after failing to convince his father of the rightness of his ideas, son George set up his own works, also in Nottingham. The name, a friend's idea, was meant to suggest the bike was superior to everything else on the

road, but George's father could have been forgiven for taking it personally.

In fact almost every part of the Brough Superior was the product of another factory; engines mostly from the JAP factory in Tottenham, London, gearboxes by Sturmey-Archer, brakes from Enfield and so on. The forks were Harley-Davidson, later copied by Brough under their own 'Castle' trademark. But George Brough had chosen the best components available and put them together with a keen stylist's eye, to create something with a visual appeal that no other machine could better – and a performance to match. The earliest Brough Superiors had side-valve V-twin engines but were no slouches – 80mph being well within reach. The finish, with acres of nickel plate and enamel, was superb, and the tank, a Brough's crowning glory, was like no other.

George Brough was an excellent publicist, helping to sell the machines with his own exploits. In 1922 he rode his personal Brough Superior SS80, nicknamed 'Spit and Polish'

Brough Superior SS100 (1925)

Years in production: 1924-39

Engine type: 45 degree V-twin ohv four-stroke

Bore and stroke: 85.5x86mm

Capacity: 998 cc

Carburettors: Binks

Tyres (front/rear): 3 x 28in/3 x 28in

Wheelbase: 59½in

Weight: 330lb

Top speed: 100mph

The distinctive, handsome Brough tank (right) carries filler caps for oil and petrol and a sight-gauge for the oil feed, as well as a handsome chronometric speedometer, then considered as an extra.

The featured bike is believed to be Lawrence of Arabia's fourth Brough. A 1925 SS100, it has exceeded 108mph. Supplied by Brough's London agent, it was fitted with several extras, including a specially modified tank, a toolbag and electric lights.

The Brough name on the magneto drive (above) only told part of the story, for the V-twin engine was the product of the JAP factory in Tottenham, as attested by the crankcase casting.

to win a Brooklands race at over 100mph, and took over 200 awards for his riding in trials and races. In 1922-3 he won 51 out of 52 sprints he entered – and the last was won by the bike without him, when he fell off forty yards from the finish!

In 1924 the first SS100 appeared. It had a 1000cc overhead-valve JAP V-twin engine and was based on the model on which rider Bert le Vack had taken the world speed record to 119mph. When launched, an SS100 cost between £150 and £170, according to specification – a huge sum when a modest house might cost £300 – but every model was guaranteed to have been tested at over 100mph and had handling to match, thanks to the excellent forks and frame. Sadly, the forks also led to the SS100's one weakness – the lack of a decent front brake. To add to the rider's comfort, the handlebars were made to suit the original owner, and many other options could be specified. Acetylene gas lights were the standard fitting on early

machines, as there was insufficient room for a dynamo, although later bikes came with electric lights.

Those who could afford it loved the SS100. One enthusiast was T E Lawrence, who as 'Lawrence of Arabia' had become a national hero. He owned seven Broughs in all – six of them SS100s – clocking up a total of over 300,000 miles and writing vividly about the excitement of his rides on 'Boanerges' (his nickname for his bikes).

The SS100 continued to be produced in small quantities, as befitted its high-quality status. In 1928 a long-stroke engine was introduced, which offered more power at the price of some flexibility. The JAP engine was redesigned in 1933 and in 1935 a Matchless engine was introduced. But in 1940, after two decades at the top, the Brough factory turned its production over to the war effort. When peace returned it ushered in a period of postwar austerity, and with no suitable engines being made, it was to be the end of Brough motorcycles.

Ner-a-car

The Ner-a-car was one of the most genuinely innovative 'motorcycles' ever made. A complete concept, it owed little to convention when it was designed, and embodied ideas that are still considered radical today. This makes it even more remarkable that in its day it was commercially successful enough to remain in production for some five years and sell in reasonable numbers.

Ner-a-car took its name from a double pun. Not only was it 'near a car' in its design principle, it was also the brainchild of an American called Carl Neracher. Working in a factory in Syracuse, New York State, Neracher built his first models in 1921, with the idea of making a machine that was more stable and comfortable than a conventional motorcycle could ever be.

The basis of the design was a low-slung platform of pressed steel, which housed the engine, transmission and rear wheel. Initially, there was no rear suspension, although this was later added. At the front, the frame splayed out to house the front wheel, which was suspended on coil springs and turned on a king-pin similar to a car's.

This form of hub-centre steering helped to make it possible for the machine to have an ultra-low centre of gravity and a more inherently precise control of steering and suspension. Its attraction is such that a similar principle has surfaced from time to time throughout motorcycle history, including on top of the range models from Yamaha and Bimota. Its chief drawback is the limited steering lock; in the case of the Ner-a-car leading to a turning circle of nearly 20 ft (over 6m).

This was a small price to pay for the machine's uncanny stability – such that it could easily be ridden hands-off – while with the huge front mudguard and wide footboards it offered excellent weather protection. The engine was under a cowling, which also helped to keep the rider clean. A later de-luxe model offered a windshield and instrument panel to give shielding as good as the best modern fairings.

At first, the power unit was a 211cc two-stroke single, and in this form the model was launched in Britain at the 1921 TT. The engine drove a large external flywheel, which also provided the unusual transmission. This consisted of a friction wheel in contact with the face of the flywheel, linked to the final drive sprocket, so that as the flywheel turned, it spun the friction wheel and hence the drive chain. A gear lever was used to track the friction wheel across the face of the flywheel, giving different gear ratios, while a twistgrip control could be used to disengage the friction wheel completely, acting as a clutch. The makers licensed the design to

the British company Sheffield Simplex, who at first uprated the engine to 285cc. Later, to provide more power, they fitted 350cc side-valve and pushrod engines from proprietary makers Blackburne, together with a more conventional three-speed gearbox. The price of what had been an expensive machine came down, while Ner-a-car riders won an impressive number of awards in road trials.

It won customers who were a long way from conventional motorcyclists – much as the later scooters were to do – and by 1926 Sheffield-Simplex was catering to their needs with the de-luxe model's car-type seat and dashboard. Sadly, the market for such sophistication remained a limited one, and towards the end of the year production ceased for good.

Ner-a-car (1925)

Years in production: 1921-26

Engine type: single-cylinder side-valve four-stroke

Capacity: 350cc

Gearbox: Sturmey Archer three-speed

Wheelbase: 59in

Turning circle: 19ft 6in

Weight: 168lb

The front wheel is carried on a subframe suspended on coil springs. It turns on a swivel arm mounted in the hub.

Carburettor, crankcase and transmission (left) are normally concealed by a steel casing.

Incredibly low, the Ner-a-car's pressed steel frame encloses the crankcase and front wheel completely. The handlebars have a linkage to connect them to the steering.

Cotton TT

Built to prove a design principle, the vintage Cottons went on to win two 1920s TTs and score a further seven places – as well as launching the career of one of the greatest road racers in history.

Many engineers deplored the traditional motorcycle frame's dependence on inherently weak bent tubes, but few put their ideas into practice. Willoughby Cotton was a law student rather than an engineer, but he succeeded where so many others compromised. Before World War I he set out a principle of design in which all tubes were to be straight and fully triangulated. All tubes should be in compression or tension, rather than subjected to bending forces. The design he sketched achieved all these objectives, with the secondary advantages that, as well as strength, it offered lightness and a low centre of gravity.

A prototype was constructed by Levis, but Cotton decided to go into manufacture in his own right. Abandoning his law career, he raised the capital to establish a factory in Gloucester shortly after the end of the war.

As a small factory, entering three machines in the 1922 Isle of Man TT was a bold stroke. Even bolder was offering a ride to an unknown Irishman aged just 17.

Cotton JAP TT (1927)

Years in production: 1927

Engine type: single cylinder
    overhead-valve JAP four-stroke

Bore and stroke: 85.5 x 85mm

Capacity: 490cc

Compression ratio: 6.5:1

Front forks: TT type

Gearbox: three-speed close-ratio

Weight: 285lb (approx)

The straight, triangulated tubes from headstock to rear wheel spindle were the principle on which Cotton was established, and are clearly visible on this 1927 500cc racer.

Stanley Woods was an aspiring racer without any real experience, who had written to every Senior TT manufacturer asserting that he already had a Junior (350cc) entry and now needed a machine for the Senior race. He had repeated this entirely fictitious claim in reverse for the Junior, backing up both claims with a largely fabricated testimonial. Cotton was the only marque that swallowed the fiction, although when Woods saw the tired old racer that they provided for the Junior, he reflected that maybe they had had the last laugh.

Despite enormous adversities, which included himself and the machine catching fire during refuelling, Woods rode a furious race to finish fifth, more than justifying Cotton's faith. The following year he stormed home to win ahead of a field that included the extremely competitive AJS and Douglas machines. Moving on to other marques, Woods would go on to win a total of 10 TTs, as well as a host of Grands Prix.

Cotton themselves continued to contest the TT throughout the 1920s, and in 1926 took all the first three places in the Lightweight (250cc) race. But such efforts always had to be supported by the manufacture of roadsters, powered by a wide variety of proprietary engines. After their popularity peaked towards the end of the 1920s, the Depression of the 1930s hit production badly and resulted in falling sales.

With the outbreak of World War II, motorcycle manufacture was curtailed and Cotton found themselves unable to diversify into other operations. They went into liquidation in 1940.

The firm was revived by new owners during the 1950s, as manufacturers of lightweight commuter machines. However these bore little relation to the original bike. In addition, their conventional frames were a far cry from the great design principle that had been laid down by the founder – one of the great innovators of chassis design.

The Cotton tank badge (right) reflected the triangulated principle of the frame, in which all the tubes were braced and subjected only to forces along their length.

Sunbeam Model 90

Such were the fine qualities of Sunbeam's roadster models that they were dubbed 'gentleman's motorcycles', but the Model 90, Sunbeam's most sporting machine of the 1920s, was more than capable of holding its own against all comers.

John Marston & Company, the firm that built Sunbeams, was founded in Wolverhampton, originally as makers of saucepans. In 1890 they began to make bicycles, which gained a reputation for fine finish and durability, as well as a practical chain enclosure – 'the little oilbath'. Marston's first motorcycle was built in 1912, and while conventional, was a sound design produced almost entirely in-house. The range expanded, and although Sunbeams were not cheap, they acquired a reputation for quality and reliability. After World War I, during which Sunbeams were used by the Russian and French forces, production of both singles and V-twin models continued.

The firm began entering reliability trials straight after the war, and re-entered racing soon afterwards. Riding side-valve 500cc machines, Tommy de la Hay won the 1920 TT with team-mate George Dance taking the lap record.

In 1922 Alec Bennett won again on a similar machine. Sunbeam had to wait until 1928 for another win, but this time it was their latest overhead-valve model ridden by the diminutive Charlie Dodson that secured them the honours.

Although the company had experimented with an overhead-cam design in 1925, the winning machine was effectively a works-prepared version of the catalogue Model 90 racer, itself similar to the Model 9 sporting roadster. To prove that his win was no fluke, Dodson repeated the performance in 1929, followed home by Alec Bennett on a similar machine. Many other wins were scored in continental Grands Prix, making the Model 90 effectively the last pushrod single-cylinder engine to be competitive in world class racing.

Early Model 90s followed the classic flat-tank styling and sported Sunbeam's renowned black and gold finish.

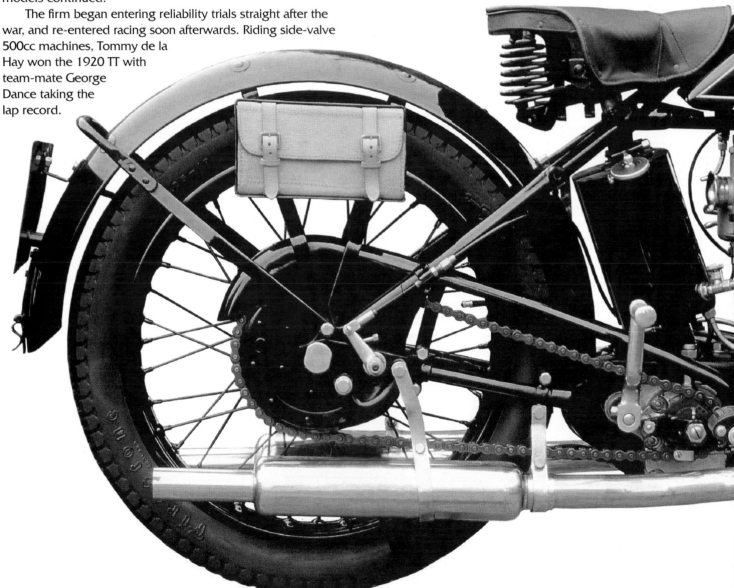

They were distinguished by their workmanship and immaculate finish, rather than the ingenuity of the design. The engineering was simple and solid, with long, hollow pushrods enclosed in separate tubes, exposed valves and twin exhaust ports for better cooling of the cast iron head. Large, well-balanced flywheels and a short, stiff con-rod characterised the bottom end, while the high compression piston and effective combustion chamber were the only secret of the top end. A close-ratio gearbox, racing cam profiles and hairpin valve springs were other distinctions between the Model 90 and its humbler brothers.

Dodson's own machines had to be specially adapted to suit his short stature, with lowered saddles and handlebars.

By 1929, when he won his second TT, a larger tank of the more fashionable saddle-tank design (and a modified frame) had been adopted, and a foot-change gearbox was used.

The Model 90 was made until 1933, and variants of the original design continued to be produced under differing model numbers until 1935, shortly before the company was taken over, and motorcycle production ceased with World War II.

Sunbeam Model 90 (1928)

Years in production: 1928-33

Engine type: single-cylinder ohv four-stroke

Bore and stroke: 80 x 90mm

Capacity: 499cc

Compression ratio: 7.5:1

Top speed: 90mph

The handsome chaincase (right), a Sunbeam speciality, is cast in light alloy. Twin exhaust ports were supposed to aid cooling.

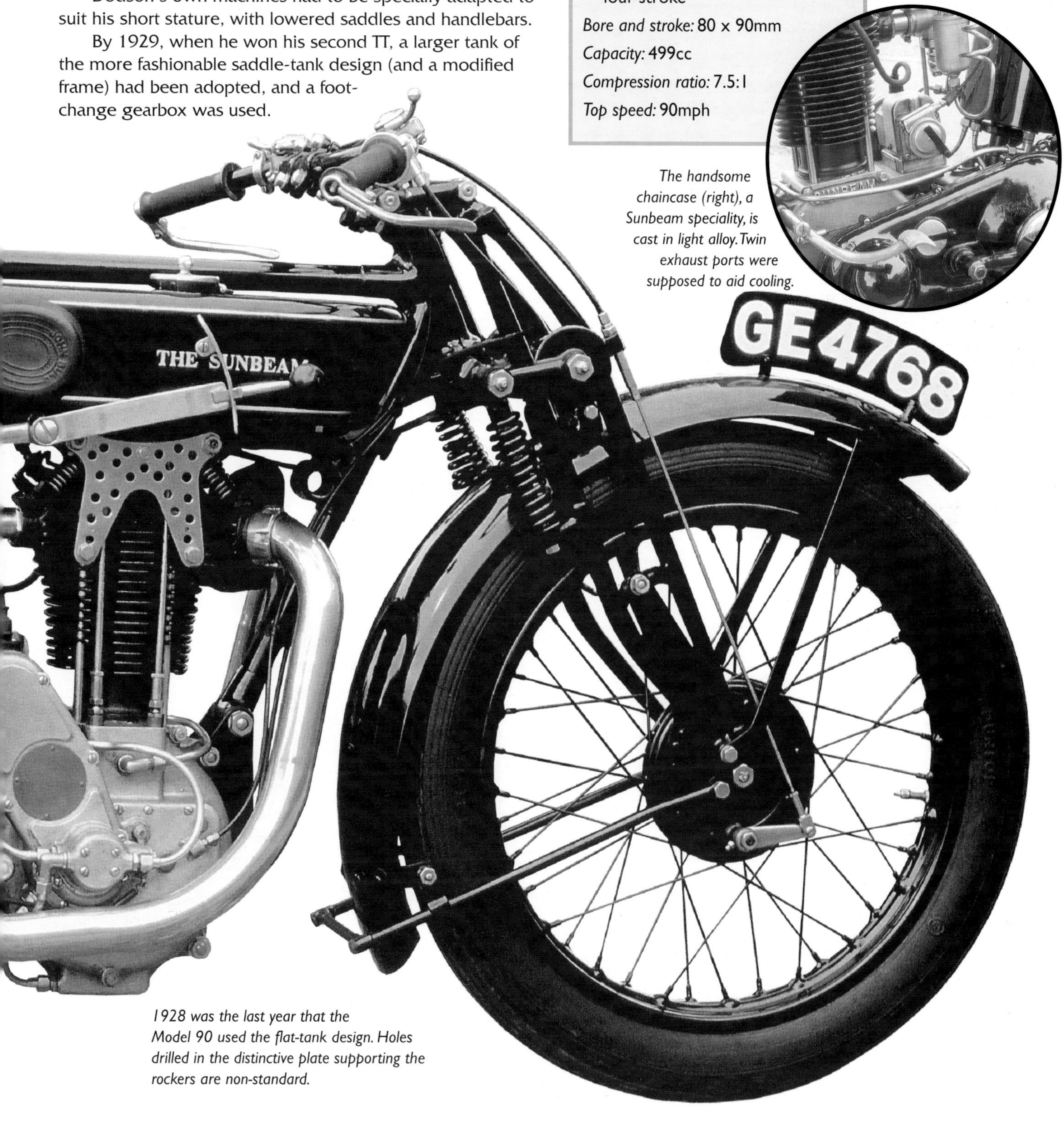

1928 was the last year that the Model 90 used the flat-tank design. Holes drilled in the distinctive plate supporting the rockers are non-standard.

Velocette KTT

Throughout the 1920s the Velocette factory achieved a host of racing successes, thanks to innovative design and superlative engineering. The overhead-camshaft 'cammy' KTT models swept the board towards the end of the decade, particularly at the Isle of Man TT, which was then the most influential road race in the world.

Percy Goodman, the son of the founder, started work on a overhead-camshaft design as early as 1924 – when such ideas were extremely advanced. However, while it attracted much attention, the prototype was far from a success and the model had to be heavily redesigned after its 1925 racing debut resulted in retirements.

This time, the design was an almost immediate winner, taking first place at the 1926 Junior (350cc) TT. In 1928 it became the first Junior machine to lap the Isle of Man at speeds of more than 70mph, and in total won eight TTs and Grands Prix.

From 1929 the KTT model was available to private owners as a 'race replica', which could be purchased for £80, and in private hands, cammy Velos went on to be the

The alloy casting (left) houses a pair of bevel gears driving the overhead-camshaft via the vertical shaft up the side of the cylinder barrel. Short rockers projecting from the cambox operate the exposed valves.

most successful amateur racing machines of the era, filling the first eight places at the Manx Grand Prix (the amateur version of the TT). By then a KTT had also put the world 350cc Hour Speed Record up to 100.39mph – the first time a 350 had topped 100mph. This feat was carried out at Brooklands by Velocette's own designer Harold Willis, one of the most innovative designers of his day and a brilliant development engineer.

In an era when cumbersome hand-change levers on the tank were the norm, the advantages of foot-change for racing had been recognised for some time. Several machines sported foot- or knee-change levers so that gears could be selected without letting go of the handlebars – but these were simply modified hand levers that had to be positioned exactly right for the chosen gear.

Willis devised the now virtually universal positive-stop gearbox, in which a single movement of the lever automatically selects the next gear up or down; the only limitation on the early KTT was that it retained a three-speed gearbox – changed to a four-speeder in 1932. The positive-stop gearchange was a brilliant innovation, which helped Velocette to become an even bigger success in competition and was immediately copied by most other manufacturers.

The 'K' series – a model letter that stood for camshaft – was developed throughout the 1930s, with variants such as the KSS (Super Sports) and KTS (Touring Sports). (TT of course meant TT replica.) Harold Willis even experimented with supercharging the works KTTs for two seasons.

Mass production of the KTT was discontinued in 1935, but the works racer continued to be developed. After reaching a peak just before World War II, the KTT series continued after the war with the MkVIII – itself to become a legend.

Velocette KTT (1929)

Years in production: 1925-50

Engine type: single-cylinder overhead-cam four stroke

Bore and stroke: 74 x 81mm

Capacity: 348cc

Compression ratio: 7.25:1

Power: 20bhp

Modified for racing, this KTT originally left the factory in July 1929 and was ridden to fourth place in the Manx Grand Prix that year. The rear subframe, a 1932 type, is a later modification.

Norton CS1

Norton CSI (1929)

Years in production: 1921-34

Engine type: single-cylinder side-valve four-stroke

Bore and stroke: 79 x 100mm

Capacity: 490cc

Compression ratio: 7:1

Power: 25bhp

Carburettor: Amal

Tyres (front/rear): $3\frac{1}{4}$ x 26in

Top speed: 85mph

Low-slung in the frame, the tall Norton CS1 engine set the tone for a generation of 'cammy' Nortons after it established its dominance in the 1927 TT.

By the late 1920s racing had long been a main driving force of Norton's development, although the pace of technological change had accelerated rapidly. Until the beginning of the decade the main sporting effort had been carried by the firm's simple side-valvers, but in 1924 it was the new pushrod Model 18 that carried the factory to victory in the first TT since 1907. All that was about to change, for a scant three seasons later, the first of a long line of overhead-camshaft Nortons was to appear.

The CS1, standing for Camshaft One, was the brainchild of Walter Moore, a brilliant designer who had joined Norton

The engine's clean lines and sturdy construction are typically Norton. But where on earlier models the crankcase itself linked the front and rear downtubes, engine and gearbox are carried above a forging that forms the bottom of a cradle frame. The three-speed gearbox has no positive stop, so gear selection requires very careful footwork.

long shaft housed in a tube running up the side of the barrel, splined to a second pair of bevel gears driving the overhead-camshaft. A pair of two-piece rocker arms projected from the camshaft housing to operate the exposed valves, which were returned by coil springs. The exhaust port was noticeably offset to the left to permit the smoothly curved exhaust pipe to clear the frame easily. The magneto was moved to the rear of the engine, with a diagonal chaincase fitted inside an extension to the chaincase on the left-hand side.

The new engine was fitted into the factory's full cradle frame, which now had a separate forging linking the front and rear tubes, housing the three-speed gearbox and the engine, where previously the crankcase had bolted directly to the front and rear tubes. Partly for this reason, the frame carried additional bracing stays to the rear wheel. Webb girder forks were fitted at the front, as was a large 8in diameter brake. A true saddle tank was fitted, concealing a frame that had to be tall, in order to accommodate the great height of the overhead-camshaft engine.

The new machines were ready for the 1927 TT, an event which they dominated in the hands of works riders Stanley Woods, Joe Craig and Alec Bennett. Woods led for much of the race and raised the lap record to over 70mph before retiring with a broken clutch. Bennett went on to win the race.

The next year a 348cc version appeared, and in 1929 was shown as the CJ, Junior model. Although there were few racing honours in either year, this was more a result of misfortune than the weakness of either the machines or the riders. The CS continued to demonstrate its superiority, and might have continued to do so for many years, were it not for the departure of its creator.

Walter Moore had accepted a lucrative offer from the German company NSU, for whom he would create a number of influential machines before he left with the outbreak of war. One of his first designs, however, was so closely based on the CS1, apart from using a four-speed gearbox, that the new 1930 NSU Rennmaschine was jokingly dubbed 'Norton Spares Used'. As Moore claimed the original design had been done in his own time, there was little that Norton could do to prevent him. They rapidly put together an alternative design, while Moore's NSUs were good enough to continue racing until 1935.

after stints at Douglas and ABC. Although he had been instrumental in developing the Model 18, Moore had long favoured the overhead-camshaft layout. After Velocette achieved a win in the 1926 Junior with their new 'cammy' model, and following rumours of other similar developments, Norton got the spur he needed. Taking up a design he had already sketched out, Moore laid down the machine that would carry Norton's works effort in 1927.

The bottom end closely followed the traditional Norton design, but cast into the side of the crankcase was a housing for the oil pump and a pair of bevel gears. These drove a

Scott Squirrel

Scott Squirrel (1928)

Years in production: 1926-40

Engine type: parallel twin-cylinder water-cooled two-stroke

Bore and stroke: 68.25 x 74.6mm

Capacity: 596cc

Carburettor: Binks

Gearbox: three-speed with hand change

Tyres front/rear: 3 x 20in/3 x 20in

Wheelbase: 55½in

Weight: 325lb

Top speed: 70mph

Scott built their reputation by flying in the face of convention. In the pioneer days, their delicate but never frail two-stroke twins were a delightful and effective alternative to the bicycle-framed, girder-forked, four-stroke single norm. But with the death of the founder in 1923 all that began to change. The late vintage Squirrel began a slow slide towards conformity that would eventually lose much of the charm of the originals. At the time, however, it seemed an attractive answer to satisfying the demands of an ever conservative mass market, and was a favourite machine for many competition riders.

The Squirrel name came into being in 1921, on the new 500cc sports model. It was an appropriate name for a cheeky, agile machine that was third in the Senior TT of 1922, made a fastest lap in the 1923 event and was second in 1924. At first, the Squirrel remained true to Alfred Scott's original open frame, two-speed concept. But from 1922, the company began to dabble with a three-speed design, using a conventional gearbox and clutch, and a three-speed

Handsome and more conventional in appearance than its predecessors, the three-speed Flying Squirrel suffered only from a thirst for fuel and a hefty price tag. Although the frame is still fully triangulated, the large fuel tank fills the centre of the frame.

Squirrel was shown in 1923. It was considerably more expensive than the two-speeder, and the company needed the income, for mounting debts forced an Official Receiver to take charge of the company.

Although the two-speed models remained in production until 1931, much of the development centred on the newer version. In 1926, the racing version's gearbox was much improved, but more importantly, the frame and forks were completely revamped. The frame was made of heavier tubing, and the fork was extensively braced. Although the frame was still triangulated, there was a top bracing tube, and the tank filled the open frame in a way that had already appeared on racing machines.

The desirable TT Replica of 1930 embodies racing features such as quick-action fillers and foot-change gearbox, but uses substantially the same mechanical design.

The resulting machine had a much more conventional appearance, but had gained around one-third in weight. Although the engine was also heavily revised, the extra power was scarcely in proportion to the change in power-to-weight ratio. Although the new Scotts made a poor showing in the 1926 TT, this model was the basis of the roadster Flying Squirrel models that followed. The 500cc machine that appeared at the 1926 Earls Court Show was effectively identical, along with a 600cc option. There was a considerable increase in price, making them around twice the price of a sporty four-stroke.

The year 1928 saw Scott's last place in a Senior TT, a third, and towards the end of the season the factory put a Replica on sale. It would become one of the best loved models. As part of a cost-cutting exercise for 1929, which saw the Squirrels drop in price, they also launched a more basic Tourer at under £70.

By 1931 Scott's financial straitjacket and the mounting recession had the firm in serious difficulties. There was no entry at the TT, nor the annual motorcycle show. There were detail modifications to the range each year, but the most significant efforts were reserved for a prototype three-cylinder two-stroke. Although this was proudly shown in 1934, Scott lacked the resources to exploit the design.

The original Scott went out of production during the war and never really recovered after it. In 1950 the firm was sold to Matt Holder's Aerco company, based in Birmingham. Holder continued to sell bikes from the assets acquired, and it was not until 1956 that a new machine was built. The 'Birmingham Scotts' had a conventional swinging arm frame and a 600cc version of the Scott engine. Prototypes for variants were floated occasionally, but these came to little.

The hand-change gate for the gearbox is carried behind the traditional and very effective Scott honeycomb radiator (left).

The front forks, which use a plunger-type suspension, are also heavily braced (right).

Matchless Silver Hawk

The London-based Matchless company was among Britain's leading companies in the 1930s. Despite the depression it was sufficiently buoyant in 1931 to buy up the ailing AJS concern and merge it into Associated Motor Cycles Ltd (AMC).

In the autumn of the previous year, Matchless had demonstrated its buoyancy to an astonished public by launching an outstanding new model at the Earls Court Show. With a technical specification that reads more like the 1980s than the 1930s, the new machine was a 600cc four-cylinder design with overhead-camshaft, rear-sprung frame and coupled brakes, plus a stylish appearance and sporting performance.

Although its single-cylinder block made it hard to see the engine configuration, it was in fact a narrow-angle V-four. This was not the first time that Matchless had tried such a design – the company's earlier Silver Arrow had a similar layout. But the Silver Arrow had been a 400cc side-valve V-twin with two bores at an angle of 26 degrees to each other inside the single block. The engine was superbly quiet, but the model had been expensive and was too heavy to have a good performance. It also suffered from overheating, a side-valve trait aggravated by the substantial cylinder casting. It only remained in production for three years.

Designer Bert Collier, one of the two brothers behind Matchless, had decided to retain the best features of the Silver Arrow but give the sporting public the performance it craved. As on the Silver Arrow, the cylinder casting was in one piece, but this time there were four bores, with two

The instrument panel (above) was a practical feature borrowed from the earlier Silver Arrow.

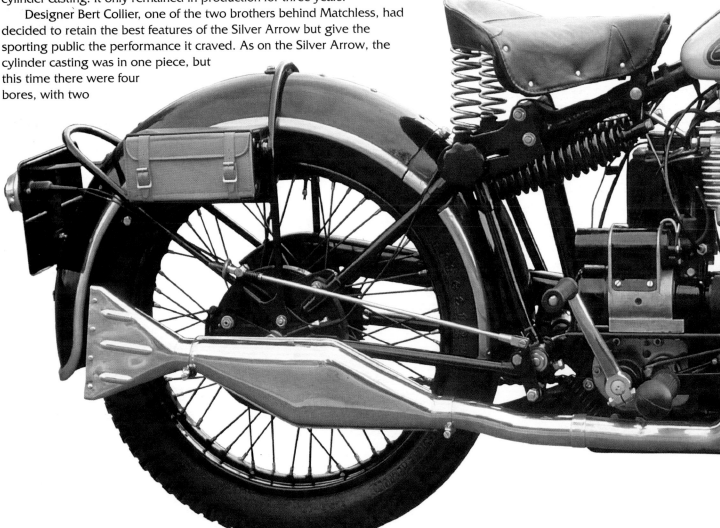

pairs at the same 26 degrees to one another. The crankshaft ran across the frame, and the conrods were offset in two pairs so that the front and rear cylinders could be in line. Now that the valves were above the combustion chambers, it was possible to cast-in cooling air spaces between the cylinders. The overhead-camshaft and valve gear was driven by a shaft taken from one end of the crankshaft.

A single carburettor was fitted, with a cross-shaped induction tract that fed all four inlet valves, although in practice, gas delivery was far from even. The exhaust

Matchless Silver Hawk Model B (1934)

Years in production: 1931-35

Engine type: narrow-angle V-four overhead-cam four-stroke

Bore and stroke: 50.8 x 73mm

Capacity: 592cc

Gearbox: four-speed Sturmey-Archer

Top speed: 76mph

ports were coupled and a pair of exhaust pipes fed a single silencer.

The sporting 600 was fitted to a frame that was virtually the same as the Silver Arrow's. It included a rear fork pivoting on bonded rubber bushes, with a pair of springs and a friction damper under the single saddle. Handsome and stylish, the whole machine was designed very much in the current fashion and looked to have a bright future. The engine was so easy to start, it was said that it could be done by hand. Top speed was more than 80mph – very impressive for the time. The engine was flexible enough to potter along in top gear, an important consideration of the day when the awkwardness of hand-changing meant that riders liked to stay in top for as long as possible.

Sadly, just as with the Silver Arrow, there were overheating problems. The engine was hard to maintain, although it could be decoked in the frame. Other models suffered similar teething problems and overcame them through development – the Ariel Square Four, launched at the same time as the Silver Hawk, had its share of problems. But the Hawk proved just too expensive to survive more than five years, with not enough benefits to offer the limited number of customers who could afford it.

A handsome example of 1930's styling, the Matchless Silver Hawk had a lively performance and exotic specification that made it a star of the show when it was launched in 1930.

Excelsior Manxman

The Excelsior Manxman was one of the most successful products of the first company to build a British motorcycle. Excelsior was also to become one of the industry's last survivors.

Excelsior was founded in Coventry in 1874 as a bicycle manufacturer, but well before the turn of the century it had built Britain's first commercial motorcycle. During the pioneer years before World War I, the company produced small numbers of interesting machines, including an 850cc single, and was the first marque to achieve a mile-a-minute in a speed trial.

The firm was taken over by one of its suppliers after World War I, and the new management proved to be the spur to the firm becoming heavily involved in racing, as well as offering a range of everyday lightweight machines powered by proprietary JAP, Villiers or Blackburne engines. Their racing effort led to several successes – and when Excelsior's Syd Crabtree won the Lightweight TT in 1929, the firm offered replicas for sale the very next season.

Rather than rely on proprietary engines like so many others, Excelsior then decided to develop their own design, and in 1933 came up with a world beater. A 250, designed by Excelsior's Eric Walker and Blackburne's Ike Hatch, it followed Rudge's pioneering work on four-valve technology. Technically advanced but complicated, it used fully

Excelsior Manxman (1935)

Years in production: 1934-39

Engine type: single-cylinder single overhead-cam four-stroke

Bore and stroke: 63 x 69mm (250) 75 x 79mm (350)

Capacity: 249cc

Compression ratio: 6.5:1

Cylinder head: two-valve aluminium-bronze

Gearbox: three-speed close-ratio

Weight: 280lb

radial valves operated by pushrods driven from twin camshafts, and both inlet ports had their own carburettor. As Excelsior lacked their own engine building facilities, a small batch was built for them by Blackburne. Dubbed the 'Mechanical Marvel' this experimental engine won the 1933 Lightweight TT at a record speed in its first outing, despite atrocious weather.

The feat was not to be repeated, however, and in 1935 Walker and Hatch came up with a completely new design, the much more conventional Manxman, a two-valve machine using a bevel-driven single overhead-cam. Easier to build than the Mechanical Marvel, it was also very reliable and handled well, although it was rather heavy – perhaps as a result of being somewhat over-engineered.

The following year, as success still eluded Excelsior, the Manxman gained a four-valve head and took second place in both the 1936 and '37 Lightweight TTs, while a 350cc version scored a third in the 1937 Junior. More importantly for the company's fortunes, replicas were on sale to privateers, who kept the Manxman's name to the fore in racing for many years to come, while the model was also popular with sporting road riders.

At the TT, Excelsior continued to place each year until war brought an end to racing. In 1938, when they took second and third places, Excelsior used a spring frame, which added to the already good road-holding qualities. The performance was good enough to achieve Lightweight thirds in the first and second postwar events, but the company itself was not to return to the field in which it had once been so strong a contender.

Bronze head, widely spaced fins and overhead-camshaft (above) are characteristic features of the Manxman.

A lightweight racer that was a little too heavy for ultimate success, the 250cc Excelsior Manxman was nevertheless a fitting tribute to Britain's oldest motorcycle manufacturer.

Norton International

Designed by development engineer Joe Craig in association with Arthur Carroll, the Model 30 appeared in 1930. The following year Norton achieved a host of wins around the world, so the name International was a natural choice for its premier racer. It had neatly trounced the opposition in the Senior TT, a feat repeated by the 350cc version in the Junior. In the autumn it took the one-hour record at Montlhéry at more than 110mph.

From 1932 the International that went on sale to the public was effectively a TT replica, equipped with road fittings – and many of the cycle parts were common to lesser models in the range with only minor modifications. The Roadholder forks were made by Norton in place of the Webbs fitted previously, and the frame was shorter and lower than the CS1 had used. Newly designed quickly-detachable wheels were a practical benefit of racing experience, while a large tank with sporting lines became an International hallmark and added greatly to the model's visual appeal.

Above all, it was the engine that defined the International. With a very strong bottom end and massive flywheels, the cylinder barrel and head were held down by long through bolts. The camshaft was housed in a completely separate casting that bolted to the top of the head. Long rockers protruded from slits in the cambox to operate the valves, the stems of which were completely exposed. The valve springs, originally coils, were changed to a hairpin type to allow rapid racing changes. A labyrinthine oil system fed lubricant to the big end, cylinder wall, cambox and valve guides via adjustable jets. Performance was in the 100mph region.

Minor improvements followed year-on-year. The forks and gearbox were redesigned in 1933 and from 1935 the gearbox was made by Norton

rather than Sturmey-Archer. From 1936 the racing specification included an alloy cylinder barrel and head with a bronze combustion chamber and aluminium fins.

The big change for 1938 was the adoption of plunger rear springing, as used on the 1937 works racers. By this time the Inter, sold with racing fittings, had begun to diverge widely from the standard sports models and had become very expensive. And from 1937, the true works

racers had gained a double overhead-camshaft – the first step on the road to the evolution of the Manx Norton. But the Inter itself remained one of the most desirable motorcycles on offer, even if more urgent matters had begun to intrude. Production ceased in 1940 with the advent of war – the end of the first chapter in the International's story.

Tower of power (left): Norton's long-stroke single carries its valve gear in a separate casting bolted to the top of the cylinder head, resulting in a tall engine dominated by the polished tube housing the drive-shaft to the overhead-cam. The head and barrel are in cast-iron, but alloy was an option. While immensely tough, oil leaks from the cambox are a common feature of the design.

Norton International Model 30 (1936)

Years in production: 1931-39 (rigid) 1938-39

Engine type: single overhead-cam single-cylinder four-stroke

Bore and stroke: 79 x100mm

Capacity: 490cc

Compression ratio: 7.23:1

Power: 29bhp

Carburettors: $1\frac{5}{32}$ in Amal TT

Tyres (front/rear): 3 x 27/ $3\frac{1}{4}$ x 27in

Wheelbase: $54\frac{3}{4}$ in

Top speed: 93mph

Girder forks and a rigid rear end are the hallmark of the early Inter. Two years after this model was made, Norton's newly developed plunger rear suspension was adopted, while postwar models gained telescopic forks.

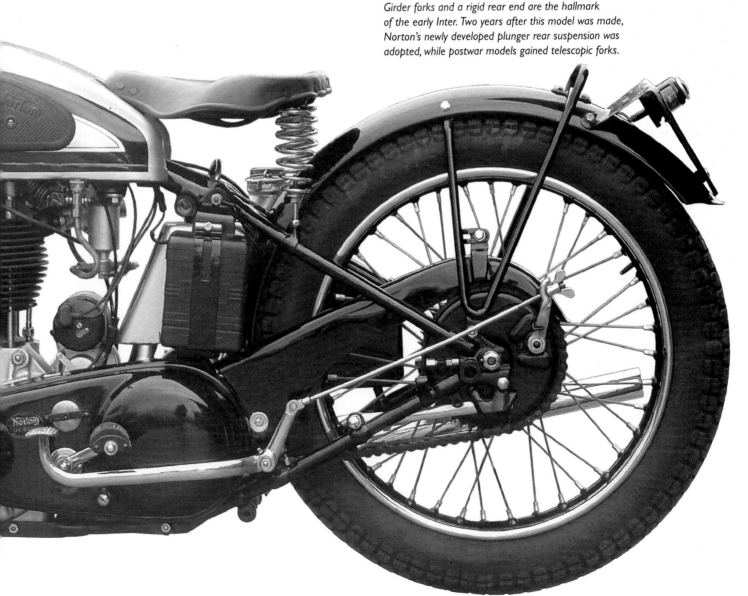

Vincent Rapide

The Vincent motorcycle began and ended with an uncompromising vision: to be faster, more powerful, better at handling, and better all round than anything on the market. In many ways it succeeded, albeit at the cost of complexity and a price tag that put it out of reach of most customers. The ultimate form of the machine was very much the personal vision of the company's founder, Philip C Vincent. But it goes back even further than that, to another man with a personal view of what a motorcycle should be. This man was Howard R Davies.

Davies was a racer of no small ability, and won the 1921 500cc Senior TT on a 350 AJS. But becoming increasingly disillusioned with the failings of standard products, he founded his own company, HRD, in 1924. The bike was largely an assembly of proprietary parts – JAP engine, Druid or Webb racing forks, Burman gearbox – but he chose the best of everything, including larger brakes than most of the competition, and put them together with an expert's knowhow (and the aid of some capable designers). A low seating position and one of the first saddle tanks gave them a sleek appearance and good handling. In 1925 Davies proved his point by winning the Senior TT with one.

Always exclusive, HRDs sold in small quantities and foundered financially after just two years. The company and assets were bought by competitors OK Supreme. Enter PC Vincent. Educated at Harrow, Vincent had owned a 1923 BSA the defects of which so incensed him that he decided he could do better. Schoolboy sketches included a triangulated rear end with suspension units under the seat. Going on to study engineering at Cambridge, he built his first prototype while only 19 years old. It embodied those first ideas and attracted the attention of the influential editor of *The Motor Cycle*, who suggested that Vincent should purchase a known name, rather than try to attract the public with his radical ideas.

A proprietary JAP single-cylinder engine was a feature of the original HRD motorcycle. After Philip Vincent bought the name he continued for a time to fit these popular units, although now using a spring frame of his own design (below). Sales were slow at first, as the motorcycle looked complex and unconventional.

Few could argue with the phenomenal performance that resulted from the happy accident of the V-twin's design (right). Scarcely larger or heavier than a single it developed almost twice the power, while the spring frame gave the handling to cope with it and the twin front brakes provided the necessary stopping ability.

Vincent Rapide (1937)

Years in production: 1936-39
Engine type: 47.5 degree V-twin ohv four-stroke
Bore and stroke: 84 x 90mm
Capacity: 998cc
Compression ratio: 6.8:1
Power: 45bhp @ 5500rpm
Carburettors: $1\frac{1}{16}$in Amals
Tyres (front/rear): 3 x 20in/$3\frac{1}{2}$ x 19in
Wheelbase: 56in
Weight: 430lb
Top speed: 105+mph

H·R·D

Complexity became an art form in the shape of the Series A Rapide, dating from 1937 (left). The bike had a web of external oil pipes, which led to the model being dubbed a 'Plumber's Nightmare'.

Backed by his father, Vincent took over HRD's assets from OK Supreme in 1928. The factory was set up in Stevenage, north of London. The first products carried the HRD tank badge, but little else of Davies' designs remained. In place of the neat, stylish singles, Vincent's offerings looked complex. At their heart was a familiar JAP engine, but Vincent's triangulated spring frames were a far cry from the neat diamond familiar to most motorcyclists.

They were slow to sell, although matters improved after Vincent fell in with a young Australian engineer who was touring the world. Phil Irving would become his partner in making Vincent into a world beater. Supremely practical, Irving possessed the skill and vision to turn Vincent's ideals into a machine that looked sufficiently conventional to appeal to conservative riders, while giving it the performance that would turn heads.

Sales picked up in the early 1930s. In 1935 Vincent offered their own engine for the first time. A pushrod 500cc single, its most unusual feature was valves that were operated from the middle of the stem, supposedly decreasing wear and keeping the engine short.

The single began to gain enthusiastic followers, but in 1936 Vincent took the final step to legendary status. The turning point came when Irving noticed a drawing and a tracing of the 500cc Comet engine lying together. He realised that with few modifications a V-twin could be simply created, and that it would fit into the single's frame.

For little extra weight, the difference was phenomenal. Awesome power was available from the $47\frac{1}{2}$ degree twin, its angle an accident deriving from the necessity to line up the single's timing gear. The Series A Rapide could top 110. Some 80 were built before the war. After it, they would spawn one of the greats of the British industry.

Triumph Speed Twin 5T

The Speed Twin changed the face of motorcycling. Before it, most motorcycles, sporting or otherwise, were singles. But the Speed Twin was so immediately successful that almost all other factories jumped on the bandwagon with their own versions. Its parallel twin engine configuration was to endure until the demise of Triumph – and the industry – some four decades later.

One man can take most of the responsibility for the Speed Twin – Edward Turner, who had been the man behind Ariel's Square Four. Moving to Triumph, Turner quickly revitalised the firm's 250, 350 and 500cc singles as the Tiger 70, 80 and 90. Good looks and the exciting performance suggested by their name ensured the new models' popularity. However in 1938 Edward Turner brought out the range leader that would really put the Triumph company firmly back on the map.

There was nothing new about vertical twins – they had been tried by Triumph (among others) in the pioneer

days, and again Turner's new Speed Twin was light and smaller than the Tiger 90, enabling it to slot into the same frame. Weighing 5lb less than the Tiger 90, it cost only £5 more at £75. At a glance, it even looked like a twin-port single, a distinct advantage in a notoriously conservative market. But it had better acceleration, pulled more smoothly and revved more freely, with valve gear many supposed to have been influenced by the sporting Riley cars.

The first Speed Twins had a one piece iron cylinder block with six studs holding the base. This proved a weakness and was soon changed to eight studs. The head was also cast iron. Camshafts in front and behind the crankcase opening drove pushrods between the cylinders, operating the valve gear in separate alloy boxes bolted to the head. Ignition and lighting were

by a Lucas Magdyno fitted behind the cylinders, and lubrication was by double-plunger pump. Transmission was by a separate four-speed gearbox.

The appealing finish was Amaranth red and chrome with gold lining. The model looked clean and fast, and it was; delivering some 26bhp, the engine was good for around 90mph. In 1939 the factory produced a sports model, the Tiger 100, costing £5 more with a tuned engine, or £10 for an aluminium-bronze head. Finished in black instead of red, this model would top 100mph. Fitted with a supercharger, it took the Brooklands 500cc lap record to over 118mph.

Had it not been for the war, which soon interrupted production, the trend-setting Speed Twin might have dominated the market even sooner. As it was, it ushered in a period during the 1950s when BSA, Norton and a host of marques such as Royal Enfield and Ariel all eagerly followed Triumph down a parallel twin route, which some detractors of the layout would call a blind alley.

Triumph Speed Twin 5T (1938)

Years in production: 1938-40

Engine type: 180 degree parallel twin ohv four-stroke

Bore and stroke: 63 x 80mm

Capacity: 498cc

Compression ratio: 7.2:1

Power: 27bhp @ 6300rpm

Carburettors: 1in Amal

Tyres (front/rear): 30 x 20/3¼ x 20in

Wheelbase: 55in

Top speed: 95mph

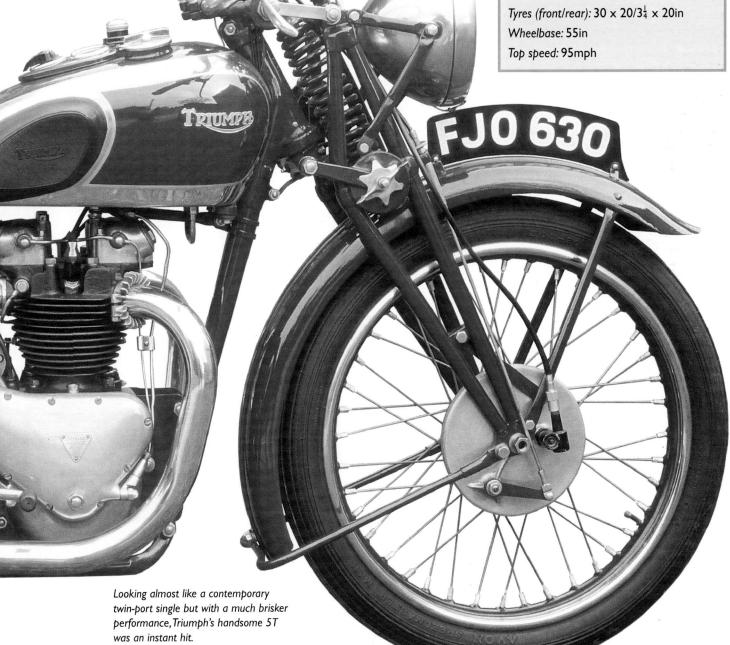

Looking almost like a contemporary twin-port single but with a much brisker performance, Triumph's handsome 5T was an instant hit.

BSA Gold Star

By 1937, BSA was Britain's largest motorcycle manufacturer, but it had built its reputation on providing good, solid workhorses, rather than racers. After a disastrous outing at the TT in 1921, BSA had turned its back on speed events, preferring to promote the product through reliability trials and other, off-road events.

So it was with some surprise that the Brooklands spectators noted the entry of a BSA 500cc Empire Star at a track meeting on 30 June 1937. Even more surprising was the rider, Walter 'Wal' Handley, one of the most accomplished racers of the day.

A sporting model introduced to mark the King's Silver Jubilee of 1935, the Empire Star had established a reputation for reliability and endurance, although with its iron-barrelled pushrod engine and heavy frame, it was not really considered a speed machine. But for 1937, designer Val Page had made major engine modifications, and the model had gained a new, much lighter frame.

In fact, Handley's mount was far from being a standard Empire Star. The riding position was adapted for racing, and the weight had been reduced. Inside the iron barrel it had a high compression piston suitable for alcohol fuel, and was fitted with a racing carburettor and magneto, plus special gearing. Races at Brooklands were run to a handicap, but even so, Handley stormed past the slower riders to lead from lap two. His fastest lap exceeded 107mph and he won the race at more than 102mph.

It was a long-standing Brooklands tradition that anyone who completed a lap at more than100mph during a race was awarded a special enamel badge bearing a six-pointed star and the number 100 – the 'Gold Star'. It was no easy task to win one, and it was only natural that when BSA decided to capitalise on

Based on the Brooklands trophy that gave the model its name, the BSA's Gold Star badge (above) dominates either side of the handsomely chromed fuel tank.

BSA Gold Star (1939)

Years in production: 1938-39

Engine type: single-cylinder ohv four-stroke

Bore and stroke: 82 x 94mm

Capacity: 496cc

Compression ratio: 7.8:1

Power: 28bhp @ 5250rpm

Carburettor: Amal TT

Tyres (front/rear): 3 x 20in/ $3\frac{1}{2}$ x 19in

Wheelbase: 54in

Top speed: 92mph

Listed as 'the fastest standard sports machine' of its day, the BSA Gold Star represented a pinnacle of 1930s design and of pushrod engine technology. The frame had a conventional front fork and rigid rear, but nevertheless made a comfortable 90mph mount.

their success with the launch of a new sporting 500 in 1938, the tuned Empire Star would be called the Gold Star.

Listed as the model M24, the Gold Star was in fact substantially different from the machine that inspired it. For one thing, it had an aluminium head and barrel with cast-in pushrod tunnel, while the gearbox was cast in magnesium alloy. A racing Amal TT carburettor was used and a plain-barrelled silencer took the place of the Brooklands-can type that Brooklands racing regulations required. Engines were bench tested to give a guaranteed power output. Most of the rest of the machine followed the Empire Star, although both a trials version and a racer were also catalogued.

In fact, sales were poorer than might have been hoped, perhaps because the trend setting Triumph Speed Twin was launched at the same time as the Gold Star, while the new sports model was not as civilised as most BSA customers expected. But some competition success kept it in production and the next year a modified version appeared.

For 1939, the last year of production before the war, the gearbox had reverted to aluminium, and there were detail changes to the engine. Much more handsome in appearance, the new Gold Star was catalogued at £77/10/- as 'the fastest standard sports machine you can buy'. It was the beginning of a model that would become a legend.

Rudge Ulster

Rudge Ulster (1939)

Years in production: 1929-39

Engine type: single-cylinder, four-valve semi-radial ohv four-stroke

Bore and stroke: 85 x 88mm

Capacity: 499cc

Compression ratio: 7.25:1

Brakes: 8in coupled, front and rear

Power: 45bhp @ 5300rpm

Carburettors: $1\frac{1}{16}$in Amals

Tyres (front/rear): $2\frac{3}{4}$ x 21in/ $2\frac{3}{4}$ x 20in

Top speed: 85mph

Rudge Whitworth's final sporting model was named after the race in which it won its greatest victory – the Ulster Grand Prix, billed as the world's fastest motorcycle road race. As it was first offered to the general public, the machine was virtually a race replica, although in later years roadster refinements were added.

Rider Graham Walker (later a journalist and father of motorsports commentator Murray) had been appointed Rudge sales manager in 1926. When he took first place in the 1928 Ulster Grand Prix, after an epic battle against rival Charlie Dodson on his Sunbeam Model 90, it was the first time a road race had been won at over 80mph. It was a win that had been eagerly expected – if Walker's Rudge had not suffered oiling problems on the last lap, he would almost certainly have won the Senior TT in the Isle of Man two months before, and the Ulster might have had another name.

Before the year was out, Ernie Nott took the world two-hour record at 100mph-plus, and there were further records in 1929. In Grand Prix racing, there were mixed

The clean lines of Rudge's top sporting roadster – as well as its four-valve engine – derive directly from the machines that won the Ulster Grand Prix and many other races of the 1930s.

fortunes until 1930, when the first two Senior TT and the first three Junior places all fell to Rudge.

The winning formula was a triumph of technology and engineering. For years, Rudge had championed the four-valve head as the means to improved combustion efficiency and power. The 500cc models used a pent-roof head design, with two pairs of valves operating on parallel slopes like a pitched roof. The 350cc Junior version used a more complex radial-valve layout with all four valves angled in to the hemispherical combustion chamber. An efficient four-speed gearbox and massive drum brakes which were a byword for power helped the rider to make the most of the engine performance.

All three 1930 Junior Rudges were home at more than 70 mph, the first machines to break this barrier. It was the last year in which a pushrod machine would win the race, although the Lightweight TT fell to the 250cc version in 1931. As late as 1934, a trio of 250s privately entered by Graham Walker scored a Lightweight hat trick.

The 1931 (below) Ulster, shown in racing trim, is small and lithe with a leaner look than the later machine.

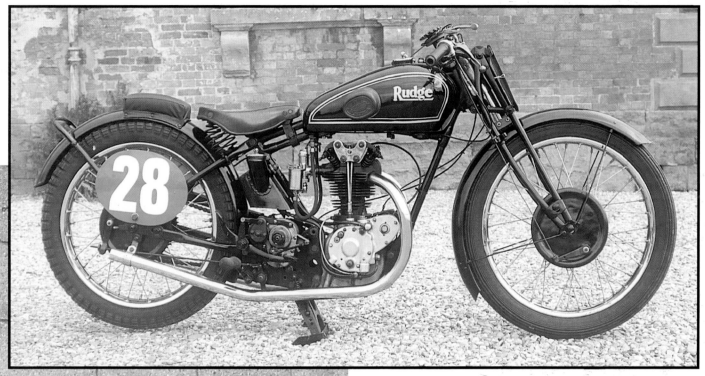

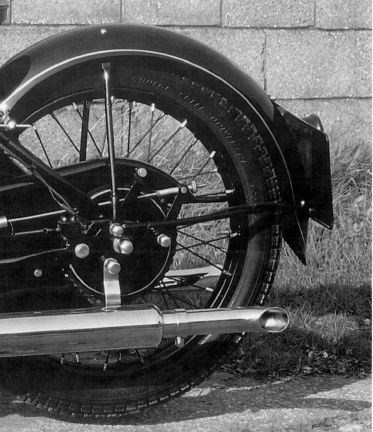

As a result of the factory's racing achievements, the range-leading Sports models were rechristened the Ulster in 1929. Refinements included dry-sump lubrication, a new crankcase and enclosed valves. Later models acquired contemporary styling, while the performance kept pace with the times – a claimed 100mph in 1930.

Financial troubles were a constant factor for Rudge. The years 1931 and 1932 saw very poor sales, and in 1933 the company had to halt many of its development projects, as well as giving up racing –although private entries continued throughout the 1930s.

Later that year, Rudge went into receivership, but this was not to be the end, and in 1936 the music and electrical company EMI, a major creditor, took over Rudge. One of the first developments to affect the Ulster and Special model was a new aluminium cylinder head with enclosed valves and revised oiling. During 1937 the factory was moved to EMI's base at Hayes, Middlesex. Sales gradually improved, but it was not enough to save Rudge. With the outbreak of war, EMI had to concentrate on its main business, chiefly the assembly of radio and rader equipment. Although they had intended to resume production when peace came, this was not to be, and in 1943 the Rudge name and tooling were sold off to Raleigh – a sad end to a great pioneering marque.

Manufacturers' badges from 1920–1939

The Classic Era

1940-1960

BSA M20 ✪ Excelsior Welbike ✪ AJS 7R

Triumph GP & Trophy ✪ Vincent Rapide ✪ Velocette KTT

LE Velocette ✪ BSA Bantam ✪ Norton Model 18 & ES2

BSA A10 Golden Flash ✪ Royal Enfield Bullet ✪ Sunbeam S8

Vincent Black Prince ✪ Ariel Square Four ✪ Douglas Dragonfly

Norton Dominator ✪ Velocette MSS ✪ Norton International

BSA Gold Star ✪ Triumph Tiger Cub ✪ Panther M120

The Classic Era

World War II meant the end of one era and the beginning of another. Economically, it would sap Britain's reserves and precipitate the break-up of an Empire that had once formed a captive market for British goods, and a cheap source of raw materials. It would also give wider horizons to a postwar generation. But first, there was the reality of a conflict in which every available resource had to be mobilised.

Of course this included the motorcycle industry, although not necessarily in the production of motorcycles. Some of Britain's most prestigious names ceased production and were turned over to making precision parts for other industries, or machines that were more suited to the war effort. For the big firms, motorcycle production did continue, for the most part, although on a severely restricted basis. Most manufacturers had been attempting to interest the War Office in the machines they thought most suitable, but in the event the military fell back on the tried-and-tested. BSA produced a stream of 500cc side-valves, the M20, while Norton turned out vast quantities of the similar 16H. Matchless produced the most forward looking of the machines built in quantity, the lightweight 350cc overhead-valve G3, which, when it gained 'Teledraulic' telescopic forks, became a forces favourite.

Of the major makers, only Triumph was not largely involved in wartime production. They would have been, had it not been for the Coventry blitz, which destroyed their factory early in the conflict. Other factories made machines in smaller numbers, including the specialised lightweight folding bikes from Royal Enfield and Excelsior, designed to be landed with paratroops. Norton made a Big Four-powered sidecar outfit designed as a gun platform, adopting an ingenious sidecar wheel

Norton in defence and defiance on all fronts

Wartime innovations tended to concentrate on the specialised. Norton's Big Four driven-wheel sidecar outfit (above) was capable of impressive off-road performance, but was deemed so hazardous to drive under ordinary conditions that the sidecar wheel drive had to be removed before any were sold off as Army surplus

On active service (left): the military motorcycle, typified by BSA's M20 and Norton's 16H side-valve performed essential service in many theatres of war. But although wartime proved the technical spur for advances in aviation and other fields, most service bikes were based on worthy but basic prewar designs.

In the immediate postwar period there was a massive demand for transport, yet motorcycles and the petrol to power them were both in short supply. Autocycles, precursors of the modern moped, provided one answer.

drive to enable it to negotiate rough terrain, and there were many other weird and wonderful offerings that failed to get into production.

Although Germany made great use of BMW sidecar outfits and lightweight solos in their 'lightning war' tactics, in the end the main use of the Allied military machines was, as in World War I, as despatch and convoy escorts. Over 400,000 British WD bikes were made, and thousands of riders were trained to use them.

When peace returned, as in World War I there was an immediate demand for transport. This time, there were many more experienced riders who were hungry for machines, and as before the demand was met with a mixture of reconditioned ex-service bikes, secondhand machines and finally a trickle of new models.

Again echoing a previous conflict, there were numerous shortages. Many materials were in short supply, but the chief disadvantage for the ordinary rider was the rationing of petrol. Supplies of a low octane, unbranded 'Pool' petrol began in mid 1945, but private owners were restricted to three gallons a week, or two for machines under 250cc.

New models were not long in coming. Triumph, courtesy of a new factory, was first in production with a postwar range of parallel twins. BSA and AMC rapidly followed suit, although it would be a long time before any of the returning servicemen and women could aspire to anything so exotic. For many, the route on to two wheels was via an autocycle, forerunner of the moped, or even a bicycle assisted by a clip-on motor.

The prewar depression had seen declining numbers of machines on the road from an all-time high in 1929, but within a year of peace there were half a million bikes in use – nearly double the 1939 total. All this despite an 'export or die' policy imposed to pay off crippling war debts, which meant most of the new machines produced went overseas. Machines had also become more expensive, thanks in part to the new purchase tax imposed during the war.

As a result the machines that most people were riding were extremely basic and in a low state of tune. Wartime experience had made most machines reliable, but many of the commonest conveniences were still considered extras – items such as pillion seats and footrests, air filters and speedometers. And despite the Brave New World promised by makers such as Triumph, most of the 'new' models on the market were warmed-over 1930s designs, dependent on worn tooling in factories that had seen only limited investment for years.

The mood, though, was one of optimism. There were bright ideas aplenty, including some, such as BSA's Bantam and Sunbeam's S7, that were copied from, or inspired by, successful enemy designs. Competition riding had returned

Despite postwar austerity, there was still room for the superlative, such as the Vincent Black Shadow, amply able to boast that it was the world's fastest, and prove it, time and again.

Motorcycle production boomed throughout the 1950s, buoyed up by an eager home market and healthy export business.

as early as June 1945. At the same time, a new movement was under way, with the formation in 1946 of the Vintage Motorcycle Club to ensure that older machines were valued and preserved. Major competitions began to return that year with the first postwar Manx Grand Prix.

The winner of the Senior race proved prophetic. Ernie Lyons was mounted on a new Triumph twin, with a specially developed alloy engine. Over the next few years the type would become the staple diet of the British industry, with BSA, Norton, AJS, Matchless, Ariel, Royal Enfield and others offering their alternative parallel twins.

TT racing returned the next year, although shortages or raw materials meant the cancellation of the planned industry show. Many of the technical improvements of the prewar racers had centred around supercharging. Such 'artificial aids' were now banned by the sport's organising bodies and, as a result, several of the British industry's most promising designs lost their advantage. Postwar racing tended to centre on the single-cylinder overhead-cam Manx Norton, with similar offerings from AMC and Velocette making up the field. Occasional exotic designs such as the AJS 'Porcupine' surfaced, but despite the undoubted success of the singles, there was little with a technology that could challenge the four-cylinder Italian racers soon being fielded by Gilera, or the technically advanced Moto Guzzi singles.

As the 1940s turned into the 1950s, things still looked good, however. The British industry was booming, with exports at record levels. British bikes were winning races and

setting records, with machines such as the exclusive Vincent twins setting the standard by which all others were judged.

There were still shortages, however. With petrol supplies settling down, the Korean War meant that chroming had to be restricted, resulting in a couple of years of painted rims and other items. And behind the scenes the British factories were suffering from a shortage of real investment.

The German factories, starting for the most part from scratch, were coming out of a period of restricted production with machines that formed the basis for their own postwar expansion, as well as the model for Japan to do the same. Italy was offering a host of new ideas, including the scooter. The Vespa, launched in 1946, would spawn a European boom in which any British offerings were too little, too late. Owing little or nothing to anything that had gone before, or motorcycle convention in general, the Italian scooter was poorly understood and all-too-easily dismissed in Britain.

Many famous names failed to reappear after the war and many succumbed soon after it, including Douglas, which soldiered on for a scant 10 years. Despite the attraction of models such as the much-prized 90 Plus, chronic under-investment would eventually prove the downfall of the company.

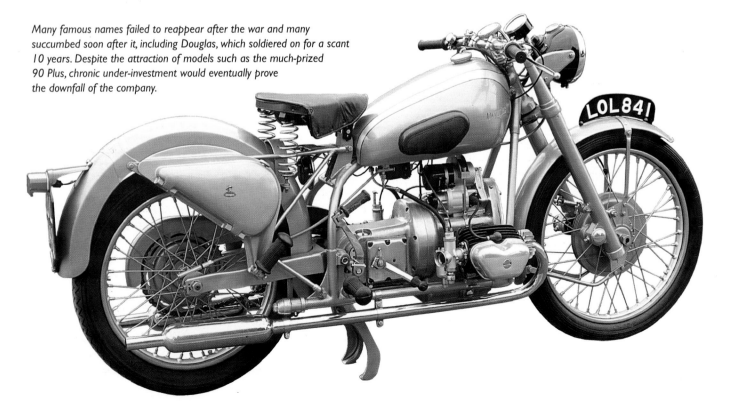

This was caused in part to sales that were booming without the need to adopt such foreign ideas. In 1953, motorcycles topped the million mark, and Prime Minister Harold Macmillan's vision of a Britain that had 'never had it so good' was entirely believable. Britain was the largest motorcycle producer outside the Iron Curtain countries, and in a position to dictate its own terms.

Several motorcycle manufacturers had their own ideas of a Utopian machine that would provide transport for the masses. Velocette offered the LE and Ariel the Leader, in both cases backing their hunches with massive investment, which would prove ill-judged despite the clear advantages of the machines themselves. More conventionally, Norton had a frame, the Featherbed – even if, strictly, it had been developed independently in Ireland – and suspension that would set the standard for years to come. However, this would in itself mask for a few years the advances in engineering design that had been made by the continental opposition, and not just in the field of racing.

This was not to say that British machines did not still lead the world. One only had to look at the competitive records achieved by machines such as the Triumph twins, BSA's Gold Star, the Manx Norton, the AJS 7R and the racing Velocettes to see that, while machines such as the Vincent were still offering a performance that no rivals could match. But there were also external factors that were affecting the market for the British industry's products. In the early 1950s motorcycles were still everyday transport, for prosperity had still not improved to the degree where cars were affordable by the mass market. Lightweights provided commuters with a ride to work, while larger models suited the sporting rider or sidecar user. Sidecars were still commonplace family vehicles. But all this was changing, and at a pace that was too fast for most of the British industry to perceive.

Light cars such as the Mini were under development, at a price that would soon challenge the family sidecar outfit, while offering their owners far greater convenience. The Italian racing bikes, which started to demonstrate their technical superiority in the mid 1950s, had now espoused streamlining, offering still greater speed potential. Sales of two-wheelers were going up, it was true, but many of them were scooters.

By the end of the decade motorcycle sales had reached a peak that had not been seen for 30 years. But in truth there were troubles behind the scenes throughout Europe. The Italian companies that dominated road racing – Moto Guzzi, Mondial and Gilera – had withdrawn, in part as a result of the high costs. German factories were closing as the economic pendulum swung back in favour of the light car. And in Britain the image of the motorcycle, as well as its economic position, was altering fast.

What had been accepted as family transport a decade before was now increasingly associated with the youth market, and at that, the undesirable 'coffee-bar cowboys' who had latched on to the image of the motorcycle outlaw portrayed in the banned 1953 film *The Wild One*. Softened and detuned, this provided a model for suburban rebellion across Britain. With the ready availability of relatively cheap, fast and raw machines from all the British factories, the scene was set for a major shift in public attitudes to motorcycling.

Technologically, things were also changing fast. It was prophetic that while the last TT of the 1950s was dominated by the Italian MVs and the British Nortons, that year's competition also saw the debut of a new name – Honda – and a new challenge to British industry.

BSA M20

When World War II began, BSA was Britain's major motorcycle factory, with the proud boast that 'one in four is a BSA'. The firm had supplied the armed forces in World War I, and as befitted a company that began as an armament manufacturer, had geared up to produce munitions as early as 1935. They would go on to become the biggest supplier of motorcycles to the forces, in the somewhat unlikely form of their model M20.

Originally launched in 1937, mainly as a sidecar model, the M20 used a 500cc side-valve engine in a heavy frame. BSA had been supplying the War Office with a variety of models for evaluation, and in some cases purchase, since the late 1920s. But following the failure of their 1935 submission, the 35-6, the company submitted the M20 in 1936, only to see this fail, too, owing to heavy engine wear. Resubmitted the next year, it passed, but only marginally, and a small batch was purchased in 1938.

The War Office then issued specifications for a lightweight model, specially designed for service use, and BSA, along with the other major manufacturers, developed their own prototype. Although this was well received and a few were built, the official policy then changed to favour the machines that were already in service, whose reliability was well known, principally the Norton 16H and M20. Large quantities of the BSA model were purchased, until it eventually became the leading service model, although far from the most popular with its riders.

Heavy, bulky, slow and with limited ground clearance, the M20 had far from an ideal specification, but it was rugged, generally reliable and easily repaired. Special fittings included a long, spiked prop stand for field use and a large headlamp, fitted with a blackout mask in many areas of operation. There were other detail changes up to 1942, when shortage of rubber led to the replacement of rubber items such as hand grips with canvas fittings and footrests with simple metal ribs. A large air filter mounted on the tank and coupled to the carburettor by a hose was fitted for use in dusty climates such as the African desert. As a result part of the rear of the tank had to be cut away.

Comprising details from various years between 1940-42, this BSA M20 is typical of WD models that were rebuilt many times, losing their original identity in the process. The rear frames for canvas panniers are a standard military fitting.

The M20 used BSA's heavyweight girder forks (left), here liberally finished in khaki paint like the rest of the machine.

BSA M20 (1940)

Years in production: 1937-55

Engine type: single-cylinder side-valve four-stroke

Bore and stroke: 82 x 94mm

Capacity: 469cc

Compression ratio: 4:9:1

Power: 13bhp @ 4200rpm

Top speed: 60mph

Simplicity itself, the M20's rugged side-valve engine had massive flywheels, a low compression ratio and soft valve-timing which made it both forgiving and flexible, with plenty of low-down torque, coupled to a standard BSA gearbox. The primary drive chaincase was a sheet steel pressing secured by a host of small screws, but the exposed rear chain had to take its chances in the desert sand or northern mud.

Purchased for despatch and escort duty, the M20 served in many theatres of war. Over 125,000 were purchased by the armed forces. Finish consisted largely of applying khaki paint liberally, often including the engine,

tyres and even the saddle, with different camouflage schemes in various countries.

Vast numbers of M20s were discharged at the end of hostilities, and after gaining a new coat of paint were snapped up by a transport-hungry public. However the model stayed in service in smaller numbers for many years – in some cases as late as 1971. The vast quantities built mean that ex-WD M20s are still in use in many parts of the world, and it is even possible to find that new spares are still available. The civilian model was manufactured until 1955, with its 600cc cousin the M21 soldiering on until 1963, the last side-valve built in Britain.

Excelsior Welbike

The Excelsior Welbike was an ingenious oddity that grew out of the special needs of wartime. Intended to be dropped by parachute or landed by glider as front line transport for the Airborne Forces, the machine had to be cheap, lightweight, small and expendable.

The motorcycle to fit the bill was not designed by the Excelsior factory themselves. A long established engineering concern, Excelsior could lay claim to being the first British maker of motorcycles for sale to the general public, but was never a major manufacturer. In fact, at the beginning of the war the factory undertook contract engineering rather than motorcycle production.

Instead, the prototype was produced at the government's military research centre in Welwyn in Hertfordshire – the reason for it being named the *Wel*-bike. Its designer, a Mr. Dolphin, began with a standard airborne equipment container and sketched a miniature motorcycle with handlebars and saddle that folded to fit inside. Powered by a 98cc two-stroke Villiers autocycle engine, the result was crude, but tough and effective. There was no suspension, no lights and only one brake, the bare minimum necessary. The tiny fuel tank had to be pressurised by pump as it was too low to supply petrol by gravity feed – but this could be done before it went into action. To ready the Welbike for use, the handlebars simply had to be swung up and outwards until they locked on spring-loaded pins. The saddle was then pulled up and the footrests pushed down until they locked.

1943: a paratrooper unpacks the lightweight Welbike, which has been dropped in the special container shown.

Excelsior was contracted to build the machine, and after some refinements it went into production with Excelsior's own 98cc autocycle engine. As planned, the Welbike could be made very cheaply and quickly – so quickly that frame, engine and all were painted in one go while still on the production line.

Almost 4000 were built and saw action in parachute drops as well as beach assaults from 1942 until the end of the war. The bike's use, however, was limited by its low performance, especially over rough terrain. In the heat of battle, even the few seconds needed to remove it from its container and unfold it were seen as a drawback. As a result many saw more use as airfield transport than on the front line.

After the war some were sold off – although, without fitting a front brake, they could not legally be used on British roads. Meanwhile the original designer had been developing a civilian version, which he showed to the general engineering concern Brockhouse Engineering just after the war. Brockhouse built the model in small numbers and sold it as the Corgi, using the single-speed Excelsior engine. It soon proved to be too slow and too unrefined even for a transport-hungry postwar economy, and was soon discontinued – although the concept returned in a much more sophisticated form with the folding Honda 'monkey bikes' of the 1960s and 70s.

Meanwhile Excelsior continued production of their own autocycle and later built a popular two-stroke 250cc twin, the Talisman. The firm survives today as the makers of Britax accessories.

An early Welbike with 98cc Villiers autocycle engine. Rubber shortages led to the use of brass and canvas handlebar grips seen here. Also clearly visible is the pump for pressurising the fuel tank.

Excelsior Welbike (1942)

Frame: twin loop tubular with folding handlebar and telescopic seat tube

Suspension: none

Gearbox: none – single speed

Engine type: two-stroke, petroil lubricated

Capacity: 98 cc

Ignition: flywheel magneto

Lighting (on Corgi): 6 volt dynamo in flywheel magneto

Wheels: 10in, 20 psi front, 35 psi rear

AJS 7R

Known as the 'Boy Racer', the 350cc AJS 7R was one of the most successful club racing machines of its time – dominating the amateur Manx Grand Prix for many years. It is directly related to the 500cc Matchless G50 that came to be a major force in classic racing decades later.

   Well before World War II AJS had successfully developed the R7 model, which used a tensioned chain drive to its overhead-camshaft. Although the firm had been absorbed by Matchless and become part of Associated Motorcycles Ltd (AMC), when the 7R appeared in 1948 it bore significant similarities to the earlier design. Although it was accused of being a copy of Velocette's KTT model, sharing the Velo's dimensions, the valve drive was again by chain, rather than shaft as on the KTT, and the 7R had a much more modern frame with welded construction and telescopic fork – AMC had pioneered the use of such technology with the much-copied wartime Teledraulic fork. Many castings were in light alloy, including magnesium, which was used extensively. As a result the 7R was much lighter than the KTT, and looked altogether like a postwar design rather than an update of a prewar machine.

   The year 1948 was not perhaps the best time to launch a performance machine, for the low-octane petrol restriction of the time stifled performance. It was four years before the

7R demonstrated the force that it would become, with a win in the 1952 Junior (350cc) Manx Grand Prix by rider Bob McIntyre, who trumped this with a seond place in the 500cc race the same year.

AJS development engineer Jack Williams then took a hand, using early gas flow experiments to help develop a more efficient head design, together with an improved cam and valve setup. These ultimately took the power up by nearly 15 per cent, while the weight also went down by some 8 per cent by late 1954, turning the machine into a potent racing force.

The distinctive gold-finished chaincase (right) for the drive to the overhead-camshaft, was fitted with a Weller blade tensioner.

In traditional black and gold finish, the AJS 7R was the epitome of the British postwar club racing single. The factory development went on to win a TT, while countless amateurs achieved personal triumphs.

While these improvements were under way, the works was also developing an experimental model using three valves (a single inlet and twin exhausts) designed in 1952 by Ike Hatch. The idea was to improve cooling and allow the sparking plug to be placed in the theoretically better central position. The earliest version used a modified version of the normal AJS chain-driven overhead-cam. A later version improved the power output – however, the complexity of the redesigned valve gear meant that the drive had to be by shaft rather than the normal chain.

In a record breaking attempt later that year at the banked Monthléry track near Paris, the three-valve AJS machine took a total of five world records. Two years later, in 1954, the development team's efforts paid off when rider Rod Coleman won the Junior TT, followed home by D Farrant, thus ending a period of four straight Norton wins. Unfortunately the works abandoned the development of this machine soon after, leaving the successful two-valve to soldier on as the mainstay of a racing effort that sustained hundreds of privateers long after the factory itself had ceased production.

AJS 7R (1948)

Years in production: 1948-54

Engine type: single-cylinder single overhead-cam four-stroke

Bore and stroke: 74 x 81mm

Capacity: 348cc

Compression ratio: 10.8-12.2:1

Power: 37bhp @ 7500rpm – 42bhp @ 7800rpm

Weight: 285lb

Top speed: 102mph

Triumph GP and Trophy

Before World War II, Triumph had laid the foundation of the sporting parallel twin with its ground-breaking Speed Twin. A decade later, the company's racing machines showed the high-speed potential of the format and helped to confirm the postwar popularity of the format.

Triumph might have been expected to play a major part in the war, but the bombing raids on Coventry so damaged the factory that it was only able to resume limited production during 1942 at temporary premises in Warwickshire. Triumph intended to concentrate its military production on a 350cc machine based on the Speed Twin, but in fact the only model built in quantity was a 350cc single. Something that was to have more postwar relevance was not a motorcycle at all, but an auxiliary generator unit built for the Air Ministry. This used a lightweight, all-alloy version of the twin engine with ducted cooling, coupled to a direct current generator.

Production of the Speed Twin and Tiger 100 resumed in 1945, and these models were soon modernised with telescopic forks. It was shortly afterwards that Triumph staff realised that the leftover stock of cylinder barrels from the

generator unit offered the potential to create a lightweight, high-performance version of the Tiger 100. In particular, they provided a means of curing the overheating, to which highly tuned Triumph twins were prone.

Prototypes were prepared by Freddie Clarke, a prewar record-breaker, and one was entered in the 1946 Manx Grand Prix, ridden by Ernie Lyons. The model achieved a famous win ahead of the second-place Manx Norton, but it was said that managing director Edward Turner, who was opposed to racing, was not pleased that the model had been developed in his absence and without his approval.

Nevertheless, the race-prepared machine produced between 25 and 30 per cent more power than the sports roadster, and went into limited production. The generator-based engine was housed in a basically rigid frame fitted

Triumph's first postwar racing twin won the Manx Grand Prix in 1946. This is a 1948 model, with the all-alloy engine based on the wartime generator, racing megaphone silencers and sprung-hub rear suspension.

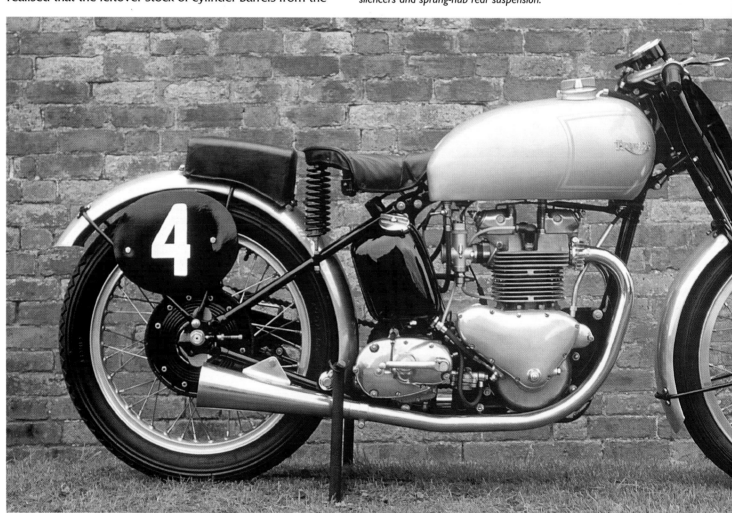

with Triumph's telescopic fork. A form of rear springing was offered by the Turner-designed sprung-hub. This comprised a large drum, inside which was a plunger springing unit. Although it could be fitted to a rigid frame without modification, the sprung-hub provided a limited degree of movement and was also prone to rapid wear, which could result in severe handling problems.

Despite this, in 1948 the GP model, as it was called, won the Manx Grand Prix again, and over the next few years made its mark in road racing. It was phased out in 1950, making way for race-kitted versions of the T100, but it had already become part of the Triumph legend.

There was another side to the story. In 1948 Triumph had entered an official team in the International Six Days' Trial in Italy, and had created three special machines. Again they had used the light alloy cylinder barrels, again they were based on the roadster twins. Sweeping all before them, the ultra-lightweight twins scooped the manufacturer's award.

In honour of the event Triumph launched a very special model – the TR5 Trophy. A versatile, dual-purpose machine, this used a single carburettor in place of the roadster's twin-carb setup, and the engine was much more softly tuned. But in its heyday club riders could use it as everyday transport, and at the weekend remove the headlamp in minutes and be competitive in any form of off-road competition.

No larger than a contemporary off-road single but with a much brisker performance, Triumph's handsome Trophy model was an instant hit.

Triumph GP/TR5 (1948-51)

Years in production: 1948-50 (GP), 1948-58 (TR5)

Engine type: 180 degree parallel twin ohv four-stroke

Bore and stroke: 63 x 80mm

Capacity: 498cc

Compression ratio: 6:1 (TR5)

Power: 40 bhp (GP), 25bhp (TR5) @ 6000rpm

Carburettors: Amal Mk 6

Tyres (front/rear): 3 x 20in/4 x 19in

Wheelbase: 53in

Weight: 295lb (TR5)

Top speed: 85mph (TR5)

Vincent Rapide

Power and speed: it's a formula that sells superbikes today, although in the grim period of postwar austerity few could afford such luxuries. But who could resist the pull of a one litre machine that advertised itself as 'The World's Fastest Standard Motorcycle'? Phil Vincent and his designer Phil Irving had begun to plan the successor to their Series A Rapide as early as 1943, working on their ideas after hours, or when the Stevenage factory's war work schedule permitted. The machine was to be a 1000cc high-speed, ultra-reliable touring bike.

The layout of the engine was similar to that of the 'Plumber's Nightmare' Series A, but cleaned up with unit construction and smooth alloy castings. Even so, the power unit was still slightly longer than before. To make the bike itself more compact, Irving and Vincent came up with a radical solution. The engine and gearbox unit was so massive and rugged that they could do away with the frame. This had the double advantage that there was no need for the conventional frame tubing that was then in short supply. Instead of a frame, the rear swinging arm pivoted directly behind the gearbox, while on top

Vincent Rapide (1948)

Years in production: 1946-50

Frame: 50 degree V-twin ohv four-stroke

Capacity: 998cc

Bore and stroke: 84 x 90mm

Compression ratio: 6.45:1

Power: 45bhp @ 5300rpm

Carburettors: $1\frac{1}{16}$in Amals

Tyres (front/rear): 3 x 20in/ $3\frac{1}{2}$ x 19in

Wheelbase: $56\frac{1}{2}$in

Top speed: 110mph

of the engine a sheet steel box was bolted, which formed an attachment for the rear suspension and the steering head for the front forks. Cleverly, it also doubled as the oil tank.

The forks were conventional Brampton girders, which would later be replaced with Vincent's own design. The twin drum brakes of the Series A remained – at first with steel drums, later with alloy. Convenience was also a feature of the design, which abounded with practical features for the rider. Footrests and pedals were adjustable to suit the length of riders' legs and even the size of their feet. Among other firsts was a dual seat with a linkage that allowed it to move independently of the suspension. The kickstart could be fitted to either side of the bike, which allowed it to be used with a sidecar on the right or the left. Click-stop adjusters made light work of common chores such as chain

tensioning, and tommy bars were fitted to the wheels so they could be removed with a minimum of tools.

When the new Rapide was launched in 1946 it caused a sensation – but by law, at least 75 per cent had to go for export, making the machine a rare beast in the early years. In any case, its price made it a luxury item, and since the factory recommended a thorough warm-up for the engine, with a trip of at least 12 miles, it would have been a poor choice for riding to work - but who would want to?

Vincent claimed 45bhp for the engine – low by modern standards, but astounding for its day and the poor quality 'pool' petrol of the time. And it was good enough for 110mph, a staggering speed for those days.

Two years later, Vincent topped even this, launching the legendary Black Shadow. With a massive 5in, 150mph speedometer, it was obvious that this was meant for speed. And it delivered it, with 10hp more than the Rapide and 125mph performance, straight from the crate. Excellent brakes, roadholding and steering made it one of the world's most desirable motorcycles, particularly after Rollie Free took one to a world record of over 150mph at Bonneville Salt Flats in 1948.

A legend was born.

As befitted the 'world's fastest' standard motorcycle, the Rapide is an imposing machine, dominated by the castings of its engine. In contrast, the Brampton forks fitted to the series B give a rather spindly look to the front end; they were soon replaced by Vincent's own Girdraulics.

Velocette KTT

Velocette's enormously successful KTT series had been steadily developed for 14 years when the MkVIII appeared at the Earls Court Show in 1938. Priced at £120, the model was another 'race replica' in the great Velocette tradition, and included a host of innovations seen on the works machines that had won that year's Junior TT.

With a host of lightweight alloy parts, sophisticated oiling and a pioneering rear suspension design, it showed all the benefits of a consistent programme of race development. The most noticeable feature of the engine was its massive cylinder head casting, with its squared-off light alloy fins virtually filling the frame. This had been introduced on the works racers in 1937 and

sold to the public as a limited run of Mk VII KTTs early in 1938. Similar finning extended to the rocker box, which contained a labyrinth of oilways to lubricate the bevel gears and cams.

The Mk VII had a fairly modest state of tune (with an 8.75:1 compression ratio) and a rigid frame with few special fittings. The Mk VIII was an altogether different proposition. It featured 'swinging arm' rear suspension and Dowty oleo pneumatic rear shock absorbers, in which the springing was by air under pressure, with oil damping. It had lightweight magnesium alloy brake hubs and a telescopic housing for

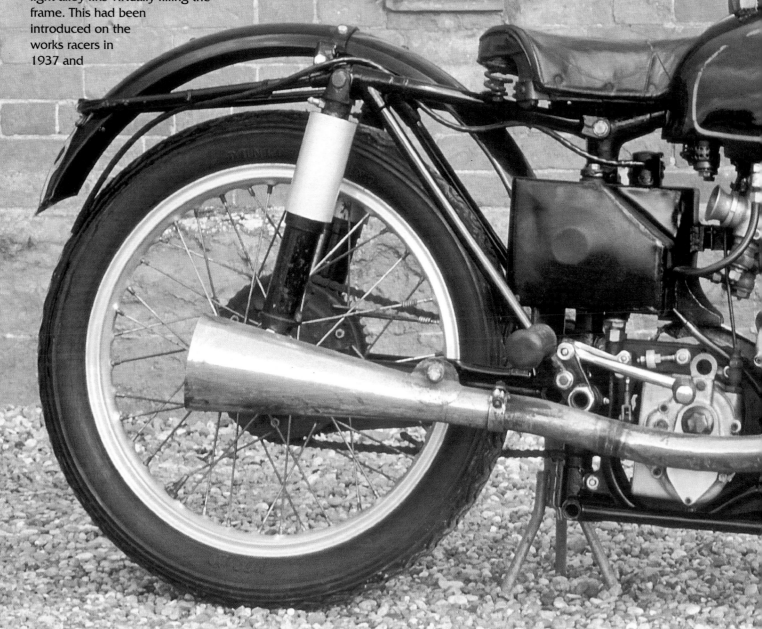

Velocette Mk VIII KTT (1949)

Years in production: 1938-50

Engine type: single-cylinder overhead-cam four stroke

Bore and stroke: 74 x 81 mm

Capacity: 348cc

Compression ratio: 10.9:1

Top speed: 110mph

the front fork spring, while the engine had been beefed up to an 11:1 compression ratio. The valves on the works bikes were filled with sodium for better cooling.

Ridden by Stanley Woods, the Mk VIII won the 1939 Junior TT for the second year running, just after Velocette's great designer Harold Willis had died of meningitis. The model did well in private hands too – one privately owned KTT became the only 350 to lap the Brooklands circuit at more than 100mph on petrol rather than alcohol racing fuel.

War then brought a close to racing as to so many other things, and Velocette built around 2200 versions of its pushrod models for military use. When production resumed after the war the Mk VIII was good enough to take two 350cc world championships and to win the Junior TT three years running.

The postwar engines used the lower compression ratio head, owing to the restriction of fuel to low-octane 'pool' petrol. Production continued until 1950, by which time the double overhead-cam Manx Nortons were taking the honours in world class 350cc racing. But with a top speed of 105mph, the production models enjoyed a long competitive career in the hands of enthusiastic amateurs, who continued to celebrate the brilliance of a design that enjoyed almost a quarter of a century at the top.

Velocette's pivoted fork rear suspension design was innovative at a time when most manufacturers were toying with plungers, if they had embraced rear springing at all. On this example, the early air-sprung rear dampers have been replaced by a later type.

LE Velocette

One of a number of postwar designs aimed at producing everyday transport for everyman, the LE Velocette owed little to convention and featured many interesting concepts. But although it enjoyed a production run of some 16 years, like all its peers that dared to be different, the little Velocette was ultimately unsuccessful, never meeting its maker's optimistic sales target.

In the early postwar years, the bulk of Velocette's production consisted of updated versions of their prewar pushrod models, the MSS and MOV. But in 1948 the firm unveiled the new design that would take their place. Literally, indeed, for the model that Velocette were introducing was designed for mass production, and building it needed all the space the factory could provide.

Its design owed little to anything that had been seen before. The 'frame' was a pressed-steel box, which offered the same advantages that had been seen in the car industry, of quick, cheap and strong

construction – albeit with the disadvantages that it was costly to tool up and difficult to change the design.

The telescopic forks were bang up-to-the-minute, while the rear swinging-arm suspension was state-of-the art, with shock absorber units that could be moved in curved upper mounting slots to change the spring rate and damping – a Velocette patent.

Cleanliness, quietness and convenience were important features of the design, which was intended to appeal to people who would not consider a conventional motorcycle. Voluminous mudguards, built-in legshields and footboards looked after the cleanliness, while convenience included built-in luggage capacity, a hand starter lever (matched by a hand gearchange on the early

models), and shaft drive housed in one leg of the swinging arm.

It was the quiet aspect that dictated the choice of the engine design. A horizontally-opposed twin, the design offered smoothness and a low centre of gravity, in addition to an easy transmission run to the shaft drive. The side-valve design allowed the engine to be relatively narrow, while watercooling helped to keep the noise levels low, at the same time allowing the engine to be tucked away while keeping the temperature under control.

The model name LE was chosen for 'little engine', and little it was. Just 149cc when it first appeared, the Velocette fitted most of its designers' objectives, but although the engine was easy to start, its performance was decidedly limited.

Other weaknesses and teething troubles came to light, mainly to do with the lubrication system and transmission – and in 1950 the LE was redesigned. It now had a 192cc engine, with internal modifications, developing some 8bhp.

Sales were slow, for although the potential for a utility bike is enormous (as the later scooters and even more successful Honda step-thrus were to

LE Velocette (1950)

Years in production: 1948-68 (variants including Valiant and Vogue)

Engine type: horizontally-opposed side-valve four-stroke twin

Bore and stroke: 50 x 49mm

Capacity: 192cc

Power: 8 bhp @ 5000 rpm

Top speed: 52mph

prove), this is probably the hardest market of all to crack. What kept the LE in production for so long was its appeal to the police, who found it a perfect choice for urban patrol work. This led to the nickname 'Noddy' bike, supposedly as the result of a directive that police patrolmen meeting a superior officer should nod rather than salute, which would have meant taking a hand off the handlebars.

A luxury version with twin headlamps and scooter-like bodywork, called the Vogue, failed to catch on – a fate that also befell the Valiant, introduced in 1956. This featured an air-cooled engine and a four-speed foot-change gearbox with kickstart, as well as a 'motorcycle' tube frame and styling.

The gearbox found its way on to the LE in 1958, the last major change to the design. The LE continued to be sold in small numbers into the 1960s, but long before this, the disappointing level of sales had forced Velocette to return to building conventional motorcycles, a range that would outlast the LE by over a decade, although the last police 'Noddy' bikes remained in service until 1971.

A motorcycle for Everyman, the Velocette LE offered comprehensive weather protection and luggage space, allied to easy starting and a whisper-quiet engine.

BSA Bantam

BSA Bantam (1951)

Years in production: 1948-63

Engine type: piston-ported two-stroke single

Bore and stroke: 52 x 28mm

Capacity: 123cc

Compressor ratio: 6.5:1

Power: 4.5bhp @ 5000rpm

Top speed: 50mph

One of the most successful lightweights ever produced in Britain, the Bantam was actually 'borrowed' from a prewar German design.

Before World War II the German manufacturer DKW was one of the great innovators of two-stroke technology. Until then most two-strokes had used a cumbersome 'deflector piston' which had a massive hump in the middle to control the flow of gases. DKW's version used a symmetrical, flat-top piston – together with clever transfer porting – to direct the gas flow for better power and reliability.

As part of the reparations of war, German designs were offered to the Allies. One such was the DKW RT125, a popular little prewar lightweight. The design was turned down by Villiers, Britain's major maker of lightweight two-stroke engines, but was rapidly adopted by BSA. The same design was also taken up by the other Allies. Harley-Davidson, Voskhod and WSK all made their own variants – in the latter cases, for decades later. Even Yamaha borrowed the design.

Although the BSA was a direct copy, the original design had the gearchange on the left in European, rather than

The neat egg-shaped 123cc power unit (right) contained a three-speed gearbox and a flywheel magneto. The battery lighting used on this model was optional – the first D1s all used direct lighting.

British fashion. So BSA simply reversed the drawings to make a mirror image of the DKW with a 'conventional' gearchange. Inside the egg-shaped engine castings was a three-speed gearbox in unit with the engine, which had a pressed-up full-circle flywheel. The cylinder barrel of cast iron contained opposed transfer ports, and the cylinder head was of aluminium alloy; capacity was 123cc. Lubrication was by petroil mix, fed by a tiny $\frac{5}{8}$ in carburettor with integral air filter. Ignition and lighting were by a Wipac flywheel magneto fitted to the left of the crankshaft. Lighting was direct, with no battery fitted.

The new BSA was announced early in 1948, and initially it was suggested that it would be supplied as a proprietary engine unit only. But in June that year the first complete machine was launched. As was common at the time, it was first listed 'for export only' and called the D1. However, by October it had gained the Bantam name, and gradually became available on the home market.

The first model had a rigid frame made of welded steel tubes, a somewhat crude, undamped front fork and front mudguard with a distinct deep valance that was even bigger than the rear. The silencer was teardrop-shaped and very flat in section. Producing $4\frac{1}{2}$ bhp, it was good for about 50mph on a miserly 120mpg, and despite a few niggles, with its £60 price tag, the model sold as fast as BSA could produce it. The finish was mist green, except for pale cream-yellow panels on the sides of the tank.

In 1950 the Bantam was improved and updated with an optional plunger rear suspension, deeper rear mudguard valance and smaller front one, as well as many minor refinements. A new electrical system based on a Lucas alternator was also offered. A competition version designed for trials or scrambles was also catalogued, while some owners modified machines for lightweight racing.

In 1954 a larger 150cc version called the D3 was introduced. It had heavier forks, plunger springing as standard, and a larger front brake, among minor variations. It gained a new swinging-arm frame in 1956, but this was dropped in 1957. The D1 continued in production until August 1963 with little change. There were minor improvements to the electrics, engine and frame, and in 1956 the rigid version was dropped. It had sold some 20,000 a year and was much-loved by owners all around the world. A workhorse whose duties had included telegram deliveries, commuting and farming in the Australian bush, examples soldiered on for a decade or more as a mainstay of some rider training schemes. Meanwhile, derivatives of the original design would continue to be produced as late as 1971.

Plunger rear springing added comfort to the original D1's rigid rear end, but both front and rear suspension remained undamped except by friction.

Norton Model 18 & ES2

Norton Model 18 & ES2 (1947/52)

Years in production: 1921-54 (Model 18),
   1928-63 (ES2)

Engine type: single-cylinder side-valve
   four-stroke

Bore and stroke: 79 x 100mm

Capacity: 490cc

Compression ratio: 6.45:1

Power: 21bhp

Carburettor: Amal Monobloc 276
   (1947 Mod 18)

Ignition: Magneto (prior to 1958)

Weight: 374 lb (1947 Mod 18)

Top speed: 78mph

Pushrod Norton singles date back to 1922, but their heyday really began in 1924 when they carried the factory to a string of race victories. That role was to last a scant three years, supplanted by the more efficient overhead-cam racers. But as roadsters they would continue until 1963, gradually outclassed in the performance stakes, but offering occasional reminders of their sporting heritage.

The Model 18 was the first pushrod Norton, but it adopted a bottom end and 79 x 100mm that went back almost to the dawn of the marque. It was soon followed by a host of variants, including the 600cc Model 19 and sports ES2. The origin of the latter model number is uncertain; one theory is that it stands for 'Enclosed Springs' for on the first Model 18, pushrod and return springs were both exposed.

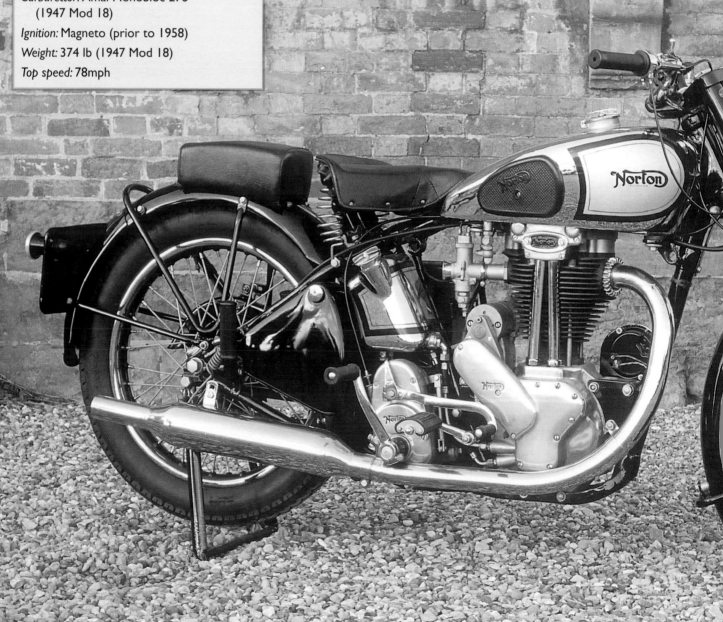

The ES2 (above) shared its heritage and most of its fittings with the Model 18. On the immediate postwar models, the most obvious difference between the two was the ES2's plunger rear suspension – a mixed blessing.

Postwar the Model 18 was the first pushrod Norton to go back into production, appearing in 1946 in something similar to its prewar form. In 1947 it gained Norton's famous 'Roadholder' front forks, yet retained a rigid rear end. The ES2, relaunched that year, had Norton's plunger rear suspension – something of a mixed blessing, for although it offered a degree of comfort it also added weight and was a constant maintenance chore.

While Norton advertised on the basis of the company's racing heritage, in truth they were simply good, solid sporting singles, robust and torquey; the handling, roadholding and brakes were predictable and sure. Many were used as sidecar tugs, still more, simply as basic transport. The Model 18 was also sold for trials use, but from 1949 to 1954 Norton offered a proper trials variant, the rigid 500T with a frame based on the wartime 16H. The trials models relied on the upright Norton gearbox originally fitted to the Model 18, but from 1950 on the roadsters gained the so-called laid-down gearbox, which offered a neater enclosure for the change mechanism.

A slow process of development followed and in 1953 the ES2 gained the swinging-arm frame used on the first Dominator twins. In 1954 the rigid Model 18 was phased out and the 600cc Model 19 was reintroduced in rigid (mainly for sidecar use) or swinging-arm frame. A 350cc the Model 50, joined the range in 1956, and a new gearbox with a triangular selection mechanism was fitted to all the singles.

In 1959 the Model 19 disappeared and the smaller variants found a new home – the revered Featherbed frame. After 1961 the singles gained the new Slimline frame, and this was the final chapter in their story. From then on, Norton would concentrate of their twins range, while the 1965/66 ES2 Mk2 was nothing more than a cynically rebadged Matchless.

Norton's 'long Roadholder' forks were fitted to the Model 18 from 1947. They offered good handling at the expense of a slightly heavy appearance at the front end.

BSA A10 Golden Flash

BSA's postwar parallel twins owed an obvious debt to Triumph's trend-setting Speed Twin of the 1930s, but in every detail the design was a true original. And in its own way, BSA was as influential as Triumph in making the layout such a staple of the British industry in the 1950s and into the 1960s.

There was a further link with Triumph, since some of the earliest design work on what would become BSA's twin was carried out by Val Page, the engineer responsible for the first

Solid, dependable and economical, the 650cc A10 twin shared a common heritage with Triumph's Speed Twin but had a character that was all its own.

Triumph parallel twin, the 650cc 6/1. Yet more design studies were carried out by Edward Turner, designer of the Speed Twin, during some time spent at BSA in the war years. Most of the detail work, however, was the responsibility of BSA chief designer Herbert Perkins, who had been with the company for many years. He was nearing retirement age when he laid down the basis of the 500cc BSA A7, which was launched in 1946.

Among notable differences from the Triumph design were the use of a single camshaft with four lobes, carried behind the engine, instead of separate ones for exhaust and inlet. The gearbox was also bolted to the back of the engine in semi-unit construction, instead of being completely

Plunger rear springing (above), a contemporary fad, offered only limited movement in comparison with rigid frames. Uneven chain tension could result in rapid chain wear, while wear in the under-lubricated suspension system itself would result in vague handling.

offered with the then-new plunger suspension system, which supposedly added to rider comfort, although as time would tell, at the expense of handling as the plungers wore. A rigid version was available until 1952, mainly for the benefit of sidecar users, for whom there was also alternative gearing. Perhaps the only serious weakness – especially for sidecar use – was the poor braking from the narrow steel drums originally fitted.

As the years wore on, there was a steady stream of improvements and options for both the A7 and A10. These included sports versions with high-performance carburettors and tuned engines. The first major change came in 1954, with the adoption of a new frame and swinging-arm rear suspension. This necessitated a change to the transmission. Alloy brake drums followed in 1956, with a corresponding improvement in stopping power. This was needed even more by the sports-tuned Road Rocket, introduced that year and good for 110mph.

The Golden Flash itself went on year by year, earning a reputation for dependability that endeared it to a generation of riders. As fashions changed, so BSA developed the unit-engined A65 model, and the A10 was phased out in 1961, although the more sporting Super Rocket continued until 1963. That last year saw the introduction of the definitive sporting derivative, the Rocket Gold Star. This used a tuned 650cc sports engine in a Gold Star frame – a hybrid that worked so well that it overshadowed BSA's own replacement for the pre-unit 650cc twins. It was a fitting swan song for a much loved model.

A handsome engine (below), proudly bearing BSA's 'piled arms' badge on the timing cover, the iron-barrelled A10 power unit had many detail differences compared to the rival Triumph and Norton offerings.

BSA A10 Golden Flash (1952)

Years in production: 1950-61

Engine type: twin-cylinder overhead-valve four-stroke

Bore and stroke: 70 x 84mm

Capacity: 646cc

Compression ratio: 6.5:1

Power: 35bhp at 4500rpm

Gearbox: four-speed

Weight: 395lb (plunger)

separate. The power from the earliest engines was 26bhp and the power unit was mounted in a duplex cradle frame with rigid rear end and telescopic forks that gave competent handling. A sports version was offered two years later. Some problems with the transmission and other features such as the lubrication were tackled in the ensuing years to make the A7 into a competent and reliable mount, though not one with a particularly high performance.

Much of the work involved in refining the original design was carried out by Bert Hopwood, a very experienced designer who had worked at most of the major factories. He soon had a further brief, for when news of Triumph's plans to introduce a larger version of their twin leaked out, BSA decided to follow suit, with a deadline of October 1949, the Earls Court Show. Starting in May 1949, the design work was carried out in around four weeks, and the model was in prototype form inside five months. Short-cuts had to be taken – such as ordering the tooling and assuming that there would be no major design changes – and many of the parts were shared with the 500cc A7. Even so, it was an incredible effort, with prototypes being continuously tested by teams of riders from the month of August onwards.

The rush job proved to be worth it, as the A10 Golden Flash was a success from the start, with few problems to mar its path to public acceptance. The Golden Flash name referred to the paint scheme, applied overall, although black and chrome was offered as an option. The new iron-barrelled engine gave a useful 35bhp and the machine was

Royal Enfield Bullet

Royal Enfield's much loved range of Bullet singles typify much of the best of British tradition. Unglamorous, but sturdy and reliable workhorses, they also possess the virtually unique distinction of having remained in volume production for a period approaching half a century.

The Bullet name, which harked back to Royal Enfield's association with gun manufacture, first appeared in the early 1930s. It was applied to a full range of 250, 350 and 500cc overhead-valve singles – lighter, tuned sports versions of the firm's existing models. But it was with the 350cc model that the name was most associated from the outset, and the Bullet range was particularly aimed at the sport of trials, which in those days was contested by modified road machines with little more special equipment than a high-level silencer.

With the start of the war Royal Enfield became a major supplier of motorcycles to the armed forces, some 30,000 of them being the overhead-valve 350cc WD/CO, based heavily on the prewar trials machines. These formed the backbone of the first few years of the

company's peacetime production, but in February 1948 the first postwar Bullet appeared.

Appropriately enough, the prototypes were entered in an important trial, where two first-class awards were gained. The Bullet was a pioneer of swinging-arm suspension, using two oil-damped shock absorber units carried at a steep angle on a pair of lugs that extended up from the frame. Although rear suspension was starting to gain favour for road use, it was much derided for trials, where the emphasis had always been on keeping the rear wheel in contact with the ground and relying on a slogging motor to carry the machine through.

It was later on in 1948 that the Bullet really started to prove itself by winning the trophy at the International Six Days' Trial, the ISDT, where two riders also took gold medals, the only ones awarded to 350s.

Royal Enfield Bullet (1952)

Years in production: 1948-1996

Engine type: single-cylinder ohv four-stroke

Bore and stroke: 70 x 90mm

Capacity: 346cc

Compression ratio: 6.2:1

Power: 18bhp

Gearbox: Albion

Carburettors: 1 in Amal

Tyres: $3\frac{1}{4}$ x 19in

The unmistakable shape of the Bullet engine (left) is visible in machines made four decades later in India, although more modern electrics have replaced the Magdyno behind the cylinder.

The production models came onto the market the next year, and were broadly similar to the prototypes. Following a Royal Enfield convention, the engine appeared to be a wet-sump design, but actually used an oil tank cast as part of the crankcase. The gearbox, a four-speed Albion design, was bolted to the back of this, resulting in a compact and rigid unit as befitted its competition status. The new frame had a single front downtube and swinging-arm rear suspension, as well as Enfield's own telescopic forks at the front. Both wheels had 6in brakes, and the rear wheel incorporated Enfield's cush-drive hub.

The new design was such a success that the competition version was soon joined by road bikes, while the trials and scrambles machines continued winning. In 1952, Johnny Brittain won the Scottish Six Days' Trial, and the following year he and fellow Enfield rider Jack Stocker were part of the team that won the ISDT without losing a single point.

The Bullets were developed over the ensuing years. A 500cc version appeared in 1953 – alloy brakes were introduced, and a new styling feature, the cast-alloy Casquette, formed a combined steering head, instrument panel and light housing. A revised frame was introduced in 1956, while Enfield's own full-enclosure fairing, the Airflow, was optional. A works replica trials version was catalogued in 1958, and there were a number of other variants before the Bullet range was dropped in 1962. But not quite. While Royal Enfield themselves used the name on a number of later models, the rights to manufacture the original had been sold to a company in Madras, India. Slowly developed over the decades, it remains in production in a variety of versions – eloquent testament to the soundness of the basic design.

With its upswept silencer and swinging-arm frame, the compact Bullet hints at its original trials derivation.

Sunbeam S8

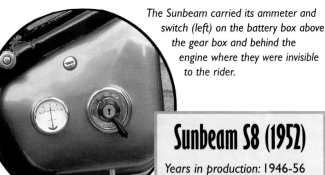

Designed as Britain's answer to the BMW, the Sunbeam S7 and later the S8 were an odd mixture of the inspired and the impractical, which ultimately condemned them to being an interesting backwater, rather than part of the mainstream of postwar motorcycling.

Several influences were at work, but the new machines were BSAs in all but name. Sunbeam had ceased to be a truly separate entity during the 1930s, and the trademarks now belonged to the giant BSA organisation, which reasoned that they could capitalise on Sunbeam's 'gentleman's motorcycle' image for their new tourer.

The design was the work of independent designer Erling Poppe, but was heavily based on the BMW R75, manufacturing rights to which had been offered to BSA as part of the war reparations. But while the double-cradle frame and telescopic fork echoed the BMW, the engine unit was a completely new design.

Displacing 487cc, the engine was basically a parallel twin not unlike that offered by BSA themselves in the form of the A7. But it was housed in alloy castings and turned around so that the crankshaft ran in line with the frame. And it seemed like a more sophisticated design than most contemporary motorcycles, thanks to the use of an overhead-cam, driven by a cam-chain at the front of the crankcase.

Sunbeam S8 (1952)

Years in production: 1946-56

Engine type: parallel twin (in-line) overhead-cam four-stroke

Bore and stroke: 70 x 63.5mm

Capacity: 487cc

Power: 24 bhp @ 6000rpm

Carburettor: Amal

Tyres (front/rear): $4\frac{3}{4}$ x 16in/ $4\frac{3}{4}$ x 16in

Wheelbase: 57in

Weight: 430lb (S7) 413lb (S8)

The first of the Sunbeam's problems arose from the choice of transmission. The intention was to use a shaft drive like the BMW, but for some reason the design adopted had a worm gear in place of the German machine's bevels. While much easier to manufacture, it was inherently weak, and on prototypes the worm was shown to strip its thread if the engine was used to its full potential. Rather than redesign the drive, BSA chose to cut the power – emasculating the engine to a paltry 24 bhp unit that the worm could handle. The second problem was vibration. This had been evident on the prototypes, but the warning signs were

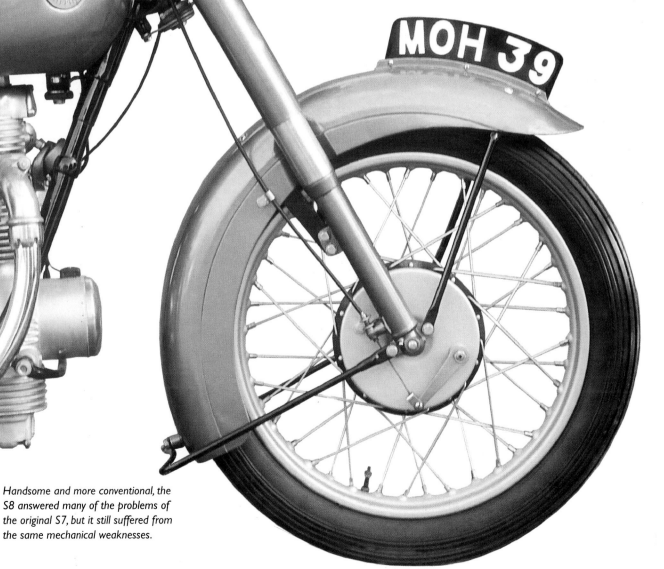

ignored until the bike went into production in 1946. When an initial batch was despatched to a police team intended to escort George VI on an official visit, it was reported that they were unridable. This time, the 'solution' was to replace the rigid engine mountings with flexible rubber buffers, allowing the engine to shake without communicating this to the rider. A consequence of this action was that a rust-prone section of flexible pipe had to be added in front of the silencer, which did not move with the engine.

The machine weighed more than 400lb – but looked heavier. Fitted with 16in 'balloon' tyres, its handling was prone to vagueness, which became aggravated as the plunger rear suspension units wore. Nor was it much success as a sidecar puller – the result of its limited power ouput. The finish, in BSA's rather drab 'Mist Green', can hardly have helped its showroom appeal, any more than the stories of its mechanical defects, and it was a poor seller.

In 1949 BSA decided to tackle both the performance and the styling by launching the new S8 as a sports alternative to the touring S7. Much lighter than its predecessor, this used cycle parts such as forks and wheels from other BSA models. It was a more popular machine than the S7, but was still far from a runaway success. BSA finally discontinued the Sunbeams in 1956.

Handsome and more conventional, the S8 answered many of the problems of the original S7, but it still suffered from the same mechanical weaknesses.

Vincent Black Prince

Phil Vincent was nothing if not a great innovator. Having pioneered his own suspension design and created the fastest road vehicle of its time, in 1954 riders expected Vincent's latest Series D to be something special. Indeed it was, for here was Vincent describing the lack of weather protection as a Stone Age idea and offering a pioneering, fully enclosed aerodynamic motorcycle.

As events would prove, this was a serious miscalculation on his part, for the customers who had loved the brutal exposed engines of his earlier machines were left cold by the Series D styling. Technically it was superb, and offered a glimpse of the fully faired sports machines of the future. Press tests extolled its weather protection, economy and speed, but all-important sales were slow to follow. Meanwhile, the competition was becoming faster, better suspended and, above all, cheap.

Yet Vincent's logic was impeccable. All motorcycles were facing competition from lower-priced cars, at a time when both still represented alternative modes of transport rather than leisure accessories. The Vincent was already faster and handled better than almost any motorcycle – so convenience must have seemed a logical route for improvement. And Phil Vincent had even consulted the owner's club about suggested innovations.

The Series D modifications were applied to the whole range: the Rapide, Black Shadow, Black Knight and range-leading Black Prince. Under the skin, technical changes included coil ignition and several engineering alterations. The chassis underwent major modification, for the fabricated steel backbone that formed an oil tank was replaced by a simple tube, which proved much weaker, and separate tank. There was a new rear subframe/seat support and an old Rudge idea was recycled, for there was a hand lever to remove the chore of putting the bike on its stand.

Problems with supply of the glass-fibre components meant that some Series D machines were supplied in naked form. Even so, being designed to be hidden, many thought the appearance ugly.

Motorcycle sales were slow – too slow to provide the much needed cash. Meanwhile another Vincent venture would help to deal a death blow to the company. Just as the Series D anticipated the fully faired sports tourer, the Amanda water scooter predated the jet ski by a quarter of a century. But technical and safety problems, plus the discovery that Vincent was actually losing money on bike sales, pushed the company into closure. The last Vincent was built barely a week before Christmas 1955. It is a strange twist of fate that the enclosed models, through rarity, are now among the most sought-after of the survivors.

Under the skin, Vincent's mighty 1000cc 50 degree V-twin (left) was much as before. But in the mid 1950s, it seemed that most customers preferred their power units on view.

Vincent Black Prince (1955)

Years in production: 1954-55

Engine type: 50 degree V-twin ohv four-stroke

Bore and stroke: 84 x 90mm

Capacity: 998cc

Compression ratio: 7.3:1

Power: 55bhp @ 5700rpm

Carburettors: $1\frac{1}{16}$ in Amals

Tyres (front/rear): $3\frac{1}{2}$ x 19in/ 4 x 18in

Wheelbase: $56\frac{1}{2}$ in

Weight: 460lb

Top speed: 120mph (est)

While the styling caused plenty of raised eyebrows, there was no denying the efficiency of the weatherproofing, or of the aerodynamics. The range-leading Black Prince had the practicality of a scooter with the performance of the mighty Black Shadow, but it was not what the market demanded and would shortly become history.

Ariel Square Four

Ariel's Square Four always had a special place in motorcycling mythology, almost regardless of how well it performed. A four-cylinder machine when such a thing was almost impossibly exotic, it was also a 1000cc machine at a time when a 650 or even a 500 was considered a big bike.

And from 1955, when Vincent ceased manufacture, the Square Four was by far the largest capacity machine on offer from the British industry.

The Square Four was an idea long before it was a workable bike. The idea started back in 1928, when Edward

A handsome machine, the late 1000cc version of Ariel's long-lived range leader was positioned as luxury tourer rather than sports bike. Tank-top flutes were a traditional Ariel styling feature, although by 1956 the company was but a part of the giant BSA group.

Turner – later to become famous as the designer of the Triumph twin and the head of the Triumph company – was a young hopeful hawking sketches of a revolutionary machine around the motorcycle industry.

The idea found a home at Ariel, then one of Britain's most important manufacturers, who took it up enthusiastically. What Turner had sketched was effectively a pair of across-the-frame parallel twins linked by a pair of gears. While there were theoretical problems

Four pipes typify the MkII postwar machine (right), while the large oil tank wrapping around the engine was first introduced in 1956.

with the linking gears, the beauty of the scheme was its incredible compactness and the fact that all the opposing forces could be balanced to result in a super-smooth engine.

The original prototype was a 500, so small and light that it could be fitted into the frame of the contemporary Ariel 250. Easy to start and smooth, it used an overhead-camshaft that probably contributed to its major weakness – overheating around the cylinder head. But after considerable development a revised version that was unveiled in autumn 1930 created a sensation. The machine had an obvious appeal for sidecar riders and in 1932 was offered in a 600cc form better suited to this use, while the 500 was dropped.

That the Square Four had speed potential was obvious, and so it was proved in 1933 when Ben Bickell took a much-modified 500 (a small-bore 600 fitted with a supercharger) to Brooklands. The machine narrowly failed to become the first British 500 to achieve 100 miles in an hour, despite lapping at well over 110. Every attempt failed as a result of the overheating bugbear.

In 1937 the engine was completely redesigned, partly to get around such problems. The overhead-cam was abandoned in favour of pushrods, and the crankcase and crank were completely altered. For the first time, a 1000cc version joined the 600, and as an option, rear springing using the link system devised by Frank Anstey was offered. This gave constant chain tension but little movement, and required frequent attention to its numerous plain bushes to prevent slop setting in.

After the war only the larger version went back into production, now with a modern telescopic fork. It was heavier than it should have been, however, and in 1949 the engine became all-alloy, gaining coil ignition with a car-type distributor a year later. Acceleration and handling both improved, while the cooling also got better.

The final development came in 1953 when the MkII version appeared. Sporting four separate exhaust pipes and numerous internal improvements, this was a flexible machine that proved an excellent high-speed tourer.

Ariel Square Four (1956)

Years in production: 1953-58 (4G Mk II)

Engine type: four-cylinder (square four) ohv four-stroke

Bore and stroke: 65 x 75mm

Capacity: 997cc

Compression ratio: 6.45:1

Power: 42bhp @ 5800rpm

Carburettor: SU

Weight: 460lb

Top speed: 107mph

That was to be virtually the end, however. The 'Squariel' was growing ever more expensive against the competition and the minor refinements introduced each year could not mask the fact that in some areas, such as cooling and rear suspension, it was not as refined as it could be. The year 1958 was the last year of full production, although the concept was developed as late as the 1970s by the Healey brothers, who put a modified Square Four engine in a frame built by the Swiss specialist Egli to complete around 20 specials – while Turner's linked crankshaft idea was employed to great effect by Kawasaki and others in racing.

Douglas Dragonfly

Against a background of financial uncertainty, the Douglas factory was always willing to rise to the challenge, pioneering innovative designs and modern styling. And so it was in 1954, when they launched a sophisticated and original looking design at the Earls Court show.

Developed during 1953, the model was intended to supersede the rather dated range then in production and take the company into a new era. Many of its design features foreshadowed those of the slightly later BMW, which went on to achieve considerable success.

Douglas' new engine design was a 350 based on their previous engine – which had enjoyed only slow sales despite a good performance – although it also borrowed heavily from an interesting 500cc prototype shown in 1951. The engine had been strengthened internally and cleaned up externally, with a streamlined appearance and a

crankcase that housed the electrics and other ancillaries, while the gearbox was attached to the rear. A single Amal Monobloc carburettor fed both cylinders. Coil ignition and alternator electrics were among the model's advanced features.

Most of the cycle parts were bought in – a departure from Douglas' normal practice. The frame was completely new, being an open duplex construction of welded tubes, manufactured on their behalf by the Reynolds Tube Company. A swinging arm with twin dampers (a modern feature for the time) looked after the rear suspension, while the front suspension used a design patented by

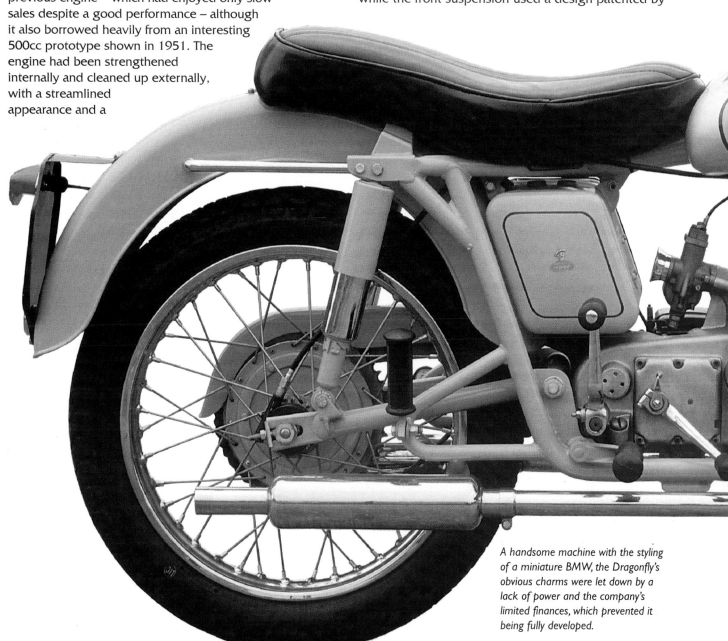

A handsome machine with the styling of a miniature BMW, the Dragonfly's obvious charms were let down by a lack of power and the company's limited finances, which prevented it being fully developed.

Douglas Dragonfly (1956)

Years in production: 1953-56

Engine type: horizontally-opposed twin-cylinder four-stroke

Bore and stroke: 60.8 x 60mm

Capacity: 348cc

Ignition: Coil, with Miller alternator

Carburettor: Amal Monobloc

Weight: 365lb

Top speed: 75mph

Midlands engineer Ernie Earles and built by Reynolds. This used a long swinging arm, controlled by twin dampers. A similar design was used by BMW on their production bikes, while MV Agusta, among others, tried it for racing.

The other main styling feature was the petrol tank and light unit. Containing a massive $5\frac{1}{2}$ gallons, the tank pressing continued forward of the steering head to house the headlamp and instrument panel, which did not turn with the steering.

Originally called the 'Dart', by the time of the show the model was called the 'Dragonfly'. Finished in a cream shade called 'light stone' with toning green panels or black-and-gold, it was an attractive if unconventional machine.

Unfortunately, after its much-vaunted show launch – when it appeared clamped between the jaws of a giant micrometer – Douglas was unable to offer quantity production for another nine months. Despite a favourable road test in April 1955, the price had gone up by almost 10 per cent by August, and a less favourable road test appeared in September.

Its handling could not be faulted, although the brakes were rather poor. But ultimately the problem for the Dragonfly came down to a mismatch of its capacity and its presentation. With the styling and fittings of a long-distance tourer, it had an engine that was pushed to top 75mph and cruised at considerably less.

It found few customers – only around 1500 were made – and Douglas' shaky finances did not help. Towards the end of 1956 the company was taken over by the Westinghouse electrical group, and production of motorcycles ended the following March.

Norton Dominator

Inspired by the popular success of Triumph's prewar Speed Twin, and aware that other factories were working on their own versions, Norton realised that if they were to have any future after World War II, they too needed a twin engine.

The job was undertaken by Bert Hopwood, who had worked on the development of Edward Turner's original Speed Twin design and had a vast experience in the industry. In 1947 Hopwood laid out his design, which aimed to improve on the Triumph's weaknesses, such as poor cooling, and incorporated some new ideas of his own. Chief among these was the use of only a single camshaft for inlet and exhaust valves, in place of the two used by Triumph and all the other factories.

The design had to work within the constraints of Norton's antiquated manufacturing machinery, as well as running on the poor quality postwar 'Pool' petrol. And for reasons of economy, it had to fit into the existing single-cylinder model's frame. Such thoughts as these were behind the choice of a single carburettor, with close inlet ports and splayed exhausts.

Fitted into plunger cycle parts from the range-leading ES2 single, with some cosmetic changes including a special tank and mudguards, this became the Norton Model 7 Dominator, launched in 1949. However it was the middle of the year before any Dominators found their way on to the home market.

With a soft tuning, it offered little real challenge to Triumph's twin – being more expensive to the tune of some £20 – and was little promoted by Norton against their traditional singles for the first few years. But it would still reach 90mph and offered excellent reliability and handling in the Norton tradition.

There was little change during the next few years. In 1953 it gained a swinging-arm rear suspension, and a year later an alloy cylinder head. It was phased out in 1956, having long been overshadowed by its replacement, the De-Luxe, or Dominator 88, which found its way on to the home market in 1953. The engine was much as before, but what made the 88 special was its frame, a close copy of the phenomenally successful 'Featherbed' used on the works Manx Norton racers. With the Featherbed's legendary handling, and weighing some 40lb less than the Model 7,

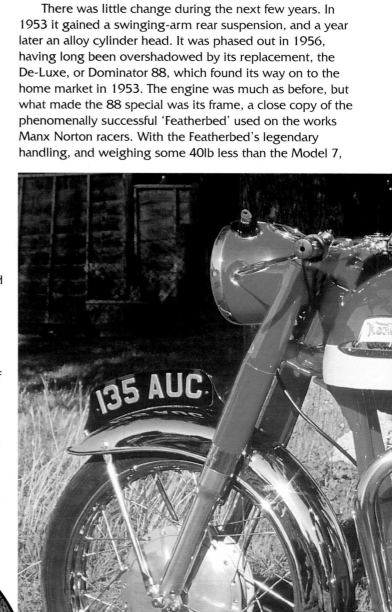

Flat Norton handlebars contributed to a comfortable riding position (right) and the famous 'Roadholder' forks assisted in the secure handling.

it handled and went rather better than its predecessor. In 1956 the 88 Dominator's engine received the benefit of some serious performance development. The engine was resized by enlarging both bore and stroke to give a new capacity of 600cc. Its power output went up from 29 to 31 bhp and the new model was called the Dominator 99. With a hotter camshaft and higher compression ratio, plus new carburettor, the model's number roughly equated to its top speed. There were refinements to the frame to match the performance, as well as other refinements.

The new engine also went into the Model 7's frame, the resulting machine being aimed at sidecar users.

The next important change was in 1961-62, when a new 49 bhp 650cc model was announced and both the 88 and 99 came out in SS (Super Sports) versions. The 600s were soon discontinued and in 1964 the first of a series of 750 models, the Atlas, appeared.

Norton Dominator (1956)

Years in production: 1956-62 (Dominator 99)

Frame: parallel twin ohv four-stroke

Capacity: 596cc

Bore and stroke: 68 x 82mm

Compression ratio: 7.4:1

Power: 31bhp @ 6500rpm

Carburettors: $1\frac{1}{16}$in Amal 376

Ignition: coil

Wheelbase: $56\frac{1}{2}$in

Weight: 395lb

Top speed: 101mph

With a 'slimline' version of Norton's famous Featherbed frame adding comfort, Norton's Dominator twin offered the best handling package standard package available.

Velocette MSS

The MSS first appeared in 1935 – a 500cc sports model designed to fit into the 'M' series that comprised the 250 MOV and 350 MAC. Like the rest of the series it was an overhead-valve single with Velocette's own development of a high camshaft driven by intermediate gears, and short pushrods. These were designed to give the low reciprocating masses of an overhead-cam model and similar revvability, and succeeded – giving the MSS a speed not too far short of the company's race-derived 'K' models.

Velocette MACs were among a number of machines produced for military use, but only one MSS was tested by the army, and production ended for the duration. The 'M' series reappeared soon after the war, but as the factory soon put all their efforts into the 'revolutionary' pressed steel LE, all but the MAC (including the old 81 x 96 mm long-stroke 500) were discontinued.

The MAC underwent a steady programme of development throughout the early 1950s. There were many detail changes to the engine, but the most important changes were to the chassis, with Velocette's own telescopic forks appearing in 1951 and a swinging-arm frame using Velocette's patented adjustable shock absorbers in 1953.

The year 1954 saw the relaunch of a model called the MSS, but in truth this was a very different proposition from

Velocette MSS (1956)

Years in production: 1954-68

Engine type: ohv four-stroke single

Bore and stroke: 86 x 86 mm

Capacity: 499 cc

Compression ratio: 6.75:1

Power: 23 bhp @ 5000 rpm

Weight: 375 lb

Top speed: 80 mph

prewar days. The engine was of much shorter stroke, giving 'square' dimensions in its alloy barrel. The bottom end was similarly updated, and although the engine was softly tuned it was a modern design with considerable in-built strength.

The frame was the same as used on the contemporary MAC, and it was even claimed that the engine dimensions had been dictated by the need to fit it in this chassis. That the model was planned as a tourer was evident from the fitted panniers, which could be supplied as an option, while sidecar lugs were built into the frame. The gearbox was beefed up compared to the earlier MAC's, and sidecar ratios were optional.

Despite the soft tune, the MSS was no slouch, being good for 80 mph or more, while the spring frame offered excellent handling. It was no surprise, therefore, that it started to be tuned for higher performance. In 1955 a very rare scrambles version was offered, while the following year launched the sports Venom model. This began a series in which higher and higher performance was achieved at the expense of the very flexibility and usability that had been the reason for introducing the pushrod models.

The underlying machine changed little, keeping outdated features such as the separate magneto long into the 1960s. It was such factors as the difficulty of obtaining supplies of components, coupled with the factory's increasing financial problems, that contributed to the end of the model in 1968. But its appeal lives on, with the qualities of the long-legged, economical single cylinder engine at the heart of the experience.

Classic single: a prewar finish and prewar virtues were evident in a machine that was relaunched, albeit heavily redesigned, almost 20 years after it first appeared in the 1930s. The major changes centred on the chassis, with modern telescopic forks and swinging-arm suspension, while the engine had been redesigned to give a much shorter stroke.

Norton International

In prewar days, the Norton Model 30 had been the racing flagship of the range, but by World War II the pure racers had already begun to diverge from the International that was on sale to the public. When postwar production resumed in 1947, the 'Inter' had found a niche as a fast sporting roadster, and its single overhead-cam engine had become a vastly different proposition from the double overhead-cam racing Manx models.

The Inters achieved steady, though limited, sales for the next few years, and while some diehard enthusiasts continued to race them in amateur competition, they were becoming dated against competition that included Triumph twins and the BSA Gold Star. Even so, several Clubman's TT winners of the late 1940s were mounted on Internationals fitted with special racing equipment, including an alloy cylinder barrel in place of the roadster's cast iron.

The final stage of development of the Inter came in 1953, when the alloy engine was installed in Norton's latest racing frame, the Featherbed, together with a new gearbox of the current design. In this form the International won its final Clubman's TT, although the Featherbed model was really intended as a sports special for fast road work.

The International's Featherbed frame was not quite a replica of the one used on the pure racers, but it was built to a higher standard than its humbler roadster brothers. In any form, the Featherbed became the standard by which all handling would be judged for two decades, and with some of the best telescopic forks in the business, and braking to match, it could be pushed to the limits of the considerable performance that the Inter's engine could deliver.

As a racing engine the 490cc overhead-cam unit made few concessions to practicality, although it was supremely rugged and reliable. It could be tricky to set up, with running clearances adjusted by a multiplicity of shims, and an oiling system that relied on several hard-to-reach adjustable jets. The valves remained exposed until the end of production, with the result that incurable oil leaks from the valve gear were a constant fact of life for Inter owners. Roadster silencing tended to stifle the engine's performance, and by the late 1950s it was possible to get the same level of power with much less fuss from later designs such as Norton's own Dominator twin.

But such complaints were to miss the point

completely, for the International oozed class, with an image second to none and a performance that was more usable than many of its rivals. Full of sound and fury, it handled and braked superbly, and allowed its lucky owner to believe that he was riding a real racer on the road.

Norton Model 30 (1956)

Engine type: single overhead cam single-cylinder four-stroke

Bore and stroke: 79 x100mm

Capacity: 490cc

Compression ratio: 7.23:1

Power: 29.5bhp @ 5500rpm

Carburettors: $1\frac{5}{32}$ in Amal TT

Tyres (front/rear): 3 x 19in/ $3\frac{1}{4}$ x 19in

Wheelbase: 55.5in

Top speed: 97mph

The International was always expensive and sold at a very low level. By 1956 it was being made to special order only, and there were detail changes as parts were used up or new fittings were employed. The last of the line left the works in 1958, when fewer than 20 were made. But to the end, the Inter had a pedigree borrowed from some of the most famous British racers ever made, and a performance that kept riders enthralled for decades.

Sharing something of the lines of the Manx racers, the International used a similar Featherbed frame, but an engine based on the prewar single overhead-cam racing power unit.

Rider's eye view (right): Norton's straight handlebars and fork-top instrument panel were standard for the road-going Featherbed framed models. It was only under the tank that the last Norton 'cammy' single displayed its prewar heritage.

799 BPC

BSA Gold Star

The heart of it all: the all-alloy pushrod engine was developed from BSA's prewar Empire Star, mated to a massive Amal GP carburettor and sports gearbox.

Before the war, the BSA Gold Star had already established itself as a legend. Postwar it would go on to become the definitive sports single – unequalled in production racing and a force to be reckoned with in almost every form of motorcycle competition from trials to scrambling (motocross).

The first postwar Goldie appeared at the 1948 Earls Court Show, but had already been seen in competition in amateur racing, including the 1947 Manx Grand Prix and 1948 Clubmans TT. Initially only on sale as a 350cc machine, its design included an alloy head and barrel that enclosed the pushrod tube, and many tuning parts were available from the outset. Most of the cycle parts were based on the contemporary touring B31, though new telescopic forks and a plunger rear suspension were added. A rigid version was on offer for the trials rider.

The top speed of the standard machine was much better than the B31, but on the low-octane fuel available was limited to less than 80mph. Fitted with the factory tuning parts, however, it could top 90mph, with a lively performance throughout the range. In 1949 a Clubmans model so equipped won the amateur 350cc race in the Isle of Man.

A 500cc version went on sale the next year, 1950. Both models gained a larger, 8in front drum brake and were in most respects identical. Detail improvements followed and by 1952 the 350 model could comfortably exceed 95mph. A more obvious change than the engine work, however, was the frame. Of all-welded construction, this had a single top tube and duplex cradle under the engine, kinked on the right-hand side to accommodate the prominent oil pump. Rear suspension was now by an effective swinging-arm design, with the engine and gearbox carried in substantial plates that added to the overall stiffness. By 1954, after steady development, the 350 could top the 'ton' in Clubmans trim. What was to become almost the definitive version of the 500 appeared after 1955 and was given the DB type designation. Fitted with racing accessories, this could top 110mph with ease.

In 1956 the ultimate Goldie appeared. The DBD34 was fitted with a host of race-proven tuning parts. These included what was to become the legendary Gold Star silencer, part racing megaphone, part roadster silencer. On the over-run it produced a characteristic 'twitter' that was to become a well-loved feature. The cylinder head was revised to suit the largest sports carburettor available, the $1\frac{1}{2}$in Amal GP. The gearbox was given ultra-close ratios and needle rollers in the sleeve gear, and its designation RRT2 became part of Gold Star mythology. The front brake was changed to an equally legendary and desirable Goldie component, the 190mm full-width alloy front drum. In Clubmans trim, the Goldie was fitted with the steeply angled clip-on handlebars, rearset footrests, swept-back exhaust,

Clubmans cockpit (left): steeply angled handlebars, twin clocks, jutting headlamp on tubular brackets – the Goldie look helped to breed a generation of café racers.

BSA Gold Star (1957)

Years in production: 1956-63 (DBD34)

Engine type: single-cylinder ohv four-stroke

Bore and stroke: 85 x 88mm

Capacity: 496cc

Compression ratio: 7.8:1

Power: 40bhp @ 7000rpm (42bhp with megaphone silencer)

Carburettors: 1½in Amal GP

Tyres (front/rear): 2¾ x 20in/ 3½ x 19in

Wheelbase: 56in

Weight: 305lb

Top speed: 110mph

The classic 1950s sports single – a BSA Gold Star DBD34 in the Clubmans trim, which included clip-on racing handlebars, rearset footrests, swept-back exhaust and 'twittering' Goldie silencer. Race-tuning extended to the close-ratio gearbox, which enabled a Gold Star to hit 50mph in first gear at the expense of a slow start-off.

light alloy fuel tank and paired speedometer/rev counter that set the style for a generation of 1960s café racers. On the Goldie it was no mere window dressing, for the model so dominated the Isle of Man Clubmans TT that the series became redundant. After its first win in 1949 it won every year until 1956, when the series was discontinued. In that last victorious year, only two of the 350cc field rode anything else. In the 500 race, Gold Stars took all the first six places.

Perhaps the most versatile sports machine of all time, Goldies also won many top-class trials and scrambles, although even during the 1950s it was becoming obvious that the days of heavy off-road singles were numbered. By the end of the decade the works team had switched to works-prepared versions of the current BSA lightweights.

With minor revisions, the customer Goldie continued until 1963 and was still being raced decades later.

Triumph Tiger Cub

Triumph's Tiger Cub was designed unashamedly to appeal to those who admired the company's sporting twins. With the hand of master stylist Edward Turner much in evidence, they offered an attractive alternative to a string of lightweights mostly powered by proprietary Villiers two-strokes. The 'Baby Bonnies' provided a desirable apprenticeship on two wheels for a generation of youths, and a ride-to-work bike with style. After 1960, when learners were restricted to bikes of less than 250cc, the Cub's appeal was enormously enhanced.

Although by the 1950s Triumph was very much associated with twins, thanks to its trend-setting Speed Twin and later derivatives, prewar much of its production had centred on sports singles. The first postwar single was the much more mundane Terrier – a 150cc machine very much aimed at the commuter market, which Triumph had tended to foresake in recent years. Looking much like the Cub that followed, the Terrier was designed as a baby version of the twins, taking all their styling cues, and was distinguished from many of its cheaply made competitors by an air of completeness and quality. Its weakest points were rear suspension by plungers, and a big end assembly that proved rather too short-lived. The engine was built in unit with a four-speed gearbox and enclosed in a streamlined casing.

The first Cub, the T20, was simply a larger version of the Terrier, using the same plunger frame and cycle parts. A weak area of the frame that persisted for years was the swan-necked and unsupported headstock. This was braced by the tank, which was constructed in such a way that a stiffening tunnel ran from headstock to just forward of the seat. If this was replaced with another type of tank, the frame could prove extremely flimsy.

Apart from an increase in bore and stroke to give a capacity of 199cc, the engine unit changed little from the near-square unit of the original Terrier, including some irritating foibles. In particular, it was difficult to change the chain, and a new sprocket meant major dismantling, while the alternator inside the primary chaincase would prove the seat of many an electrical problem. The clutch and big end had led to many dissatisfied Terrier buyers, and had had to be redesigned.

The Cub's bottom end was changed in 1956 to a plain bearing, but this also proved troublesome, especially in the hands of novice riders who would rev the engine before it had warmed up properly, or economical owners who neglected to change the oil frequently enough. Big end life in such circumstances was depressingly short, and Triumph suffered many warranty claims before this fundamental flaw was sorted out.

Triumph's diminutive 200 provided an attractive alternative to a host of two-stroke lightweights. With styling borrowed from its bigger brothers, and a four-stroke single engine, it was the passport to two wheels for many a learner motorcyclist in the late 1950s and into the 1960s and beyond.

The frame was modified in 1957 gaining a swinging-arm rear suspension with twin shock absorber units. A competition (off-road) version called the T20C appeared that year, sporting a high-level exhaust and modified wheels and suspension. The basic styling remained that of the larger Triumphs, with four-bar tank badge, nacelle enclosing the headlamp, instruments and upper fork legs.

There were numerous styling and mechanical changes over the years. Variations on a theme included sports and off-road versions, while in 1966 the Bantam Cub appeared – a hybrid with the baby Triumph engine in a BSA Bantam frame. The last Tiger Cub was the Super Cub, launched in 1967 and dropped a year later. But the Cubs had laid the seeds for its replacement by becoming the inspiration for the 250cc BSA C15, which appeared a decade later.

Triumph's nacelle was a familiar styling feature. As well as rotary switchgear and the speedometer, it incorporated a gear position indicator needle linked to the gearbox via a rack-and-pinion mechanism and cable.

Triumph Tiger Cub (1959)

Years in production: 1956-68 (all model variations)

Engine type: single-cylinder ohv four-stroke

Capacity: 199cc

Power: 14bhp @ 6500rpm

Carburettor: Amal

Tyres (front/rear): $3\frac{1}{4} \times 17$in

Weight: 230lb

Top speed: 60mph

Panther M120

For many years the biggest single-cylinder motorcycle in the world, Panther's 650 sloper announced that fact with a deep, lazy engine beat, which was said to 'fire every other lamppost'. With enormous torque and incredible economy, it was ideally suited to pulling the enormous sidecars that formed budget family transport.

The Model 120 was the final product of P&M of Cleckheaton, Yorkshire – the factory that had built its first motorcycle at the beginning of the 20th century with the revolutionary idea of using a sloping engine, instead of the front portion of a conventional frame. From first to last, it was this concept that defined Panthers, with gradual concessions to the engine and suspension designs of the changing years.

By the 1930s the form of the big single Panther had pretty much settled, and the firm also survived through the lean early years of the decade, thanks to the excellent volume sales of the ultra-cheap Red Panther 250cc lightweight which sold for under £30.

After the war the machines that appeared bore a close resemblance to the prewar models. The Model 100 Panther for 1946 was a 600cc single with rigid frame and girder forks. It was ideally

set up for economical sidecar use, with a fuel consumption in excess of 60 mpg.

The next year Dowty Oleomatic air-sprung telescopic forks were fitted – a form of front suspension that was very efficient when new, but gave problems when older as the seals wore. There were minor improvements to various parts of the bike until 1954 when a new, conventionally sprung fork was fitted, and a swinging-arm frame was adopted. Styling changes followed, and the rigid model was discontinued in 1957.

Handsome, solid and dependable, the 650cc Panther Model 120 was rarely seen in solo form; most performed sterling service as power for the family sidecar outfit.

The main news for 1958 was the development of the larger Model 120, which was closely based on the 600cc model, both bored and stroked. But that year's prototypes displayed a number of engine problems, largely a result of the increased stress and problems with Panther's unusual lubrication system. Based on a large sump cast into the front of the engine, this pumped oil up to the top of the engine, but return was hit-and-miss. With the more powerful, more stressed engine of the Model 120, the oil scavenging became less efficient and consumption became heavy.

The production bikes were substantially improved, and offered even lower fuel consumption – 70 mpg with a sidecar – than their predecessor. The Model 120 was ideally suited to sidecar use. In 1959 Panther's own sidecar chassis was an option – and this even included a towbar for a trailer.

The mode of progress of such an outfit was stately, but relaxing – once the machine had been started. The enormously heavy flywheels took considerable effort to get

Panther Model 120 (1959)

Years in production: 1959-66

Engine Type: single-cylinder ohv
    four-stroke

Capacity: 649cc

Bore and stroke: 88 x 106mm

Compression ratio: 6.5:1

Power: 27bhp @ 4500rpm

Gearbox: Burman four-speed

Tyres (front & rear): 3½ x 19in

Wheelbase: 59in

Turning Circle: 19ft 6in

Weight: 426lb

spinning, especially with the engine's long stroke. To ease this, Panther fitted its own patented aid to the normal exhaust valve lifter. A small lever on the timing chest raised a ramp on the exhaust cam, lifting the valve partly off its seat, thus reducing the compression enough to allow the engine to spin more easily.

The simple, generally understressed big Panthers offered vintage values in a changing world. But sales of all Panther's range had been falling since the end of the 1950s, and by 1962 the firm was in receivership. An enlightened receiver kept them in production for a few years, mainly using up existing spares. But when difficulties arose obtaining major components – the separate Lucas Magdyno and Burman gearbox, which were by then virtually outmoded – there was no realistic way forward.

The last Panthers were built in 1966, although they remained on sale for at least a year after that. They were extremely cheap, but times had moved on and there was no longer any demand for the big sidecar outfit, as cheap cars took over that role and big bikes began the move towards becoming leisure vehicles.

Slogging power (below): the long stroke sloper engine possesses a legendary torque, despite its antiquated layout. The forward projecting casting is an oil reservoir, part of a near-vintage lubrication system. Despite such dated features, it was more the use of a separate gearbox and magneto that became unavailable that spelt the end of the big Panther, rather than any design shortcomings.

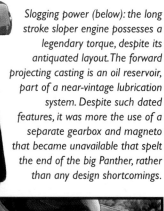

Manufacturers' badges from 1940–1959

Endings and Beginnings

1960-1997

BSA C15T ✪ Ariel Leader ✪ Greeves Sports Twin

Royal Enfield Constellation ✪ Norton 500 Manx

BSA A65 ✪ Velocette Thruxton ✪ BSA Rocket 3

Triumph T120 Bonneville ✪ Norton Commando (Fastback)

Norton P11 ✪ Norton Commando (Roadster)

Triumph Trident ✪ Rickman Enfield Interceptor ✪ Silk 700

Triumph T140 Bonneville ✪ Hesketh Vampire

Norton Wankel Rotary ✪ Triumph Trident

Triumph T595 Daytona ✪ Triumph Thunderbird

Endings and Beginnings

As the 1960s dawned, they ushered in a new era in motorcycling – and a combination of powerful forces that would soon see the British industry reduced from a world leader to an also-ran, and finally to near-oblivion. And yet, during a decade that would see the creation of some of the best-loved British machines of all time, it was hard to spot where the downfall began. A third of million new machines were registered in 1959 and everything seemed to be booming. While the scooter and other continental imports had made significant inroads into British bike sales, it seemed as though there was still plenty of room in the market place for everyone.

On the face of it, Britain still had a thriving industry. Great names such as AJS, BSA, Matchless, Norton, Triumph and Velocette were still offering a wide range of singles and twins with their traditional qualities of, on the one hand, dependable economy, and on the other, sporting performance. There were exciting new models either recently launched, or soon to be announced, such as the radical Ariel Leader/Arrow, and new twins from Norton, BSA and Triumph. Such smaller independent concerns as Cotton, Greeves and DMW offered a wide range of budget models with two-stroke engines, mostly from the long-established Villiers factory, while similar models from Francis Barnett or James came with the backing of the major industry groups to which these names belonged.

The shadows on the horizon are easier to spot with hindsight. One was the introduction of the Mini car. Costing around the same as a top-of-the-range motorcycle or sidecar combination – chic and fun to drive, with it – it was the beginning of the end for bikes as basic transport. Another factor was the launch of the Honda Dream in 1959. Its quirky styling masked, for a time, the fact that here was a 250cc machine that could run rings around many machines twice its size and had an electric-starter, to boot. Against this beautifully engineered overhead-camshaft twin, the British industry was fielding machines powered by the basically sound, but low-powered Villiers two-strokes and the recently launched and badly flawed Norton Jubilee pushrod twin. In 1961 Honda would be followed by Yamaha and Suzuki, both concerns which rapidly began to establish themselves as major forces in racing as well as roadsters.

Motorcycling itself was attracting a bad press, with scare stories in the papers about the antics of rockers and rising accident rate that proved it was more than just media hype. The year 1960 saw the introduction of a limit on learner riders to machines of under 250cc, while insurance rates started to creep up, sure-fire factors in discouraging young riders from making a start.

By this time, the British industry consisted mainly of two large combines, the giant BSA-Triumph group (which also included Ariel and other famous names), based in the

The 1963 film The Leather Boys (above) illustrated many of the problems which would come to bedevil the British bike industry over the next decade. Bikes were increasingly coming to be seen as a fringe pursuit with a questionable image, while the staple pushrod parallel twins were already looking dated when compared to developments abroad.

Traditional factories such as the Ariel plant (below) photographed in the 1950s, relied on labour-intensive hand building. But the BSA Triumph group, which owned Ariel, were alive to the need for change, installing new lines and computer controls at the BSA factory in Small Heath, which made the factory one of the most modern in the world.

Midlands, and the lesser Associated Motorcycles (AMC), which included AJS, Francis Barnett, James, Matchless, and Norton, largely based in Plumstead, South London. There were plenty of small independents, too, such as Royal Enfield or Velocette, although many of the great names, for example Vincent, had already disappeared.

Whatever the cause of the British industry's troubles, it was certainly not just a lack of foresight. Both the major conglomerates had invested considerable sums in development throughout the 1950s and on into the 1960s. AMC retooled extensively in the 1950s and BSA spent a small fortune a decade later equipping its Small Heath plant with the latest assembly line technology, including state-of-the-art computer controlled production and spares.

Some of this investment was misguided, since it required heavy cash injections that the BSA Group could ill afford, while the very size of the group meant that management was unwieldy and tended to the bureaucratic. One symptom of this was the installation in 1967 of a central research and development facility for the whole group at Umberslade Hall, an attractive country estate near Solihull, equidistant from each of the main factories. The trouble with such an arrangement (besides being very costly in itself) was that it tended to create a situation in which R&D staff were remote from the problems of production, while traditional rivalries between the factories still existed.

AMC had no such capital to invest in new measures and witnessed their traditional customer base being eroded by degrees. The group's once proud heritage in road racing was largely behind it by the 1960s, with the rightly famed Manx Norton winning its last TT in 1961, while the privateer racers, the 350cc AJS 7R and 500cc Matchless G50, were phased out in the mid-60s. As far as the roadsters went, the days of the traditional big single were virtually over, and, despite an enviable reputation for assembly and finish, the crunch came in 1966 against a background of falling sales. The Norton factory had previously had to be closed in 1962 and moved to London. Such rationalisation was too little, too late, and with funds having dried up, the company was acquired by the industrial group Manganese Bronze Holdings. At a stroke, Francis Barnett and James were no more. From that time until the late 1960s – when the original factory in Plumstead was closed and Norton was joined with Villiers in yet another industry amalgamation – only the bigger Nortons and Matchless models were made .

Many smaller factories were forced to close as a result of the Norton-Villiers merger, for Villiers was the last volume supplier of proprietary engines, and these were now cut off in a move to consolidate the engine supply for Norton-Villiers own project, the AJS Stormer scramblers. Of the important small independents, only Greeves had developed sufficiently to manufacture their own engines, and such names as Cotton and Dot were forced to look overseas, or fold, which eventually happened.

Another great name had disappeared in 1963, coincidentally the first year in which MOT tests were applied, initially for machines of over five years old. Ariel, as part of the BSA group had been moved from their Selly Oak factory to BSA's Small Heath plant, and ceased to be.

Final fling: the Norton Commando and Triumph Bonneville represented the ultimate development of an engine concept that could be traced back to before the war, although the innovative frame concept of the Commando in particular proved that there was still plenty of life in the old ideas.

The refusal of the workers at Triumph's old Meriden plant to accept redundancy culminated in a sit-in at the factory (left) and many months of unrest, after which new owners NVT were forced to accept defeat. Government funding helped the Meriden workers' co-operative to continue in production for several years in the late 1970s.

Great white hope (below): the Norton rotary was developed from one of the last projects of the old BSA research facility. Many years of steady development proved that the idea worked, and well enough to win races. But while the new Norton sold in small numbers to institutional users and enthusiasts, it was never able to achieve proper volume production and economies of scale.

The revamped Norton Villiers group started confidently with the appointment of a new chief designer and the development of a new model that would become a great name of the industry – the Commando.

Such new models were very necessary. The British industry's one-time confidence that the Japanese would confine themselves to small machines had been shattered by the arrival of the Honda 450 'Black Bomber' in 1965, and while this was never a best-seller, it paved the way for other larger machines from Japan. And by this time, it was also well known that Honda was working on the epoch-making 750 Four.

BSA-Triumph were in serious trouble. Almost all their new developments had failed to bring them the hoped for benefits, and many ageing models had been discontinued. But there were promising signs, too. In 1967 and 1968 the companies' sales efforts earned them Queen's Awards for Industry, while in 1968 the group announced its own new models, again to become legends. These were the Triumph Trident and BSA Rocket III – both derived, not so much from the group's new R&D headquarters, as an expedient reworking of the forty-year-old Triumph Speed Twin. Still, they were great bikes, that was the important thing, and were sorely needed.

Many of the major manufacturers' promising ideas had failed to make it into production. Of the smaller independents, Royal Enfield and Panther were already part of history, while Velocette was on its last set of wheels.

The launch of the first Japanese superbikes in 1969 hit the British bikes hard. Disastrous losses culminated in a rescue plan in 1972, which would merge BSA/Triumph with Norton Villiers to form Norton Villiers Triumph (NVT), as duly happened in 1973. There were some interesting footnotes, however. On the racing side, in 1972 Norton entered into a famous association with John Player cigarettes, which would go on to win fame and glory for the resulting JPN team. The same year, the little AJS Stormer, and the rights to the name, were sold off to former development engineer Fluff Brown, who continued to make small numbers of the FB-AJS off-roaders.

Great survivor (above): the Villiers-engined AJS Stormer was one of the last machines from the old AMC combine in the 1960s. Now updated and still made by former development engineer Fluff Brown, it represents the kind of enthusiastic small-volume production that survived the demise of the major manufacturers.

A reborn Triumph has embraced the best of new technology (left), including robots, as well as traditional skills to enable it to compete for world markets at the highest level.

But the biggest side effect of the merger came with the proposed reorganisation of the factories. This would have resulted in closure of the old Triumph plant at Meriden, Coventry, but the 1750 workers took exception to this and undertook a sit-in. After a year-and-a-half, during which NVT was unable to get access to the Trident parts held in the factory, the model had to be effectively discontinued. With falling sales of the Commando, NVT's Norton plant virtually gave up production after 1976, concentrating on the assembly of small numbers of mopeds using Italian engines, and small trail bikes based on Yamaha components. They moved to a new, smaller factory in Shenstone, Staffs, after 1978.

The great survivor, somewhat perversely, was Meriden, where after a long-drawn-out struggle, the government finally stepped in with funding to start the Meriden Co-operative in 1975. The Co-op would continue building what they knew best, Triumph twins, as well as continuing their own efforts to assemble machines from overseas parts.

Many smaller independents continued, including notables such as Rickman, Weslake, Seeley, Spondon and Silk. Such companies made an interesting range of specials, often including frames for Japanese machines, for this was an area where British expertise was still acknowledged. But such efforts were virtually doomed to remain small, for by this time most of the major component suppliers that had supported the British industry with parts such as electrics, carburettors, wheels, tanks and mudguards were themselves disappearing or diversifying.

This did not mean that there were not people prepared to try. In the late 1970s and early 1980s Lord Alexander Hesketh captured the public imagination with news of the latest British 'world-beater', a machine built to the highest standards and designed to take on the best foreign competition. It was the sort of good news which the industry needed – for in 1982, after a long struggle, the Meriden co-op folded, and the last remaining Bonnevilles were now being assembled in small numbers in Devon.

Hesketh's efforts failed, and from this time on, the British bike was virtually a cottage industry. It was condemned to depend on imports of foreign components for such rebirths as a new 'Matchless G50', which used the Austrian Rotax engine, although the burgeoning interest in older 'classics' helped to keep specialist frame-builders and skilled engineers in business.

The one obvious ray of hope during the 1980s was Norton, the inheritor of one of BSA's own 'world-beaters' using the new rotary engine technology. It was a story that could have been designed to appeal to the British psyche, as the little underdogs laboured against all the odds to produce a model that was not only successful in its own terms but actually managed a string of famous racing wins to demonstrate what might have been, if only. Sadly, it was a case of too little, too late, and Norton all but disappeared in a welter of accusation and counter-accusation of financial mismanagement.

And so it all might have ended, except for Triumph. Virtually unnoticed for several years, and deliberately avoiding the kind of publicity that Norton and Hesketh had courted, the new owner of the remnants of the old Meriden assets had set out to make a range of machines which would genuinely merit the 'world-beater' tag. Accepting the new era of design and the new commercial realities of the late 1980s and 1990s, the reborn Triumph had almost nothing to do with the old, except the name and the loyalty which that could command. Starting with a clean sheet and an open chequebook, it was the creation of a single entrepreneur – the kind of figure that had helped to create the industry a century before. But above all, Triumph is proof that the skills that helped to make the British bike the envy of the world still exist. As all those behind the mergers and start-ups of the last 20 years of the industry had hoped, it is simply a matter of providing the proper environment in which those skills can be expressed.

Volume production of a modern machine depends on components that are either made in-house, sourced overseas or from a handful of specialist suppliers, as many of the biggest names in British motorcycle components are no longer in business.

BSA C15T

BSA's lightweight singles of the 1960s came to symptomise much of what was wrong with the British industry at the time. Yet they provided transport for thousands of young riders, and the trials versions can also be said to have helped to usher in the modern era of off-road sport, while being very successful in their own right.

BSA had acquired the Triumph marque at the start of the 1950s, and while the company had been rightly famous for its lightweights in the past, those that appeared towards the end of the decade owed far more to Triumph than to BSA.

Chief among them was the 1958 C15 Star. A 250cc four-stroke, long a popular BSA configuration, its pushrod single-cylinder engine was almost totally derived from the 200cc Triumph Tiger Cub, albeit with an upright cylinder in place of the Cub's inclined unit. The Cub itself was derived from the earlier 150cc Terrier, and both had proved unreliable, with a weak bottom end, among other failings.

Even so, in its BSA incarnation the new model seemed both up-to-date and sophisticated, with its light weight and sophisticated electrics setting it apart from the competition. And with learners restricted to 250s from 1960, it was one of the most attractive alternatives – if one discounted the Honda twins that appeared in 1961.

As with its Triumph predecessors, the C15 and its derivatives suffered from minor electrical problems, oil leaks and somewhat complicated maintenance routines. But it went well enough and was mainly reliable. The SS80 sports version, which appeared in 1961, was faster, while the 350 version, the B40, offered more power and appealed to army buyers as well as the general public. In the mid 1960s a similar engine layout was seen in the shape of the 75cc Beagle and 50cc Ariel Pixie, two fatally flawed attempts by the BSA Group to launch an ultra-lightweight.

Over the years there were countless variations on the same theme, including sports and off-road versions, while the basic engine was stretched to 441 and finally 499cc. The engine even found its way back to Triumph, to power the street-scrambler-styled singles of the late 1960s and early 1970s. The last of BSA's C15 derivatives was the B50, built until 1973. Even after this, the specialist company CCM of Bolton built their own derivative of the B50 for off-road competition throughout the 1970s and on into 1981.

Off-road sport was long a speciality of BSA. In the postwar era, the 350 and

Despite its serious competition aspirations, the 250 still carried full road equipment (left) including electrics by the unreliable and unloved energy-transfer system.

Superficially the same unit as the roadster, the trials bike's all-alloy engine (left) concealed a host of minor modifications, as well as a set of gearbox ratios more suited to off-road use. The iron-barrelled engine was derived from Triumph's Terrier and Tiger Cub, and itself spawned a whole generation of derivatives.

Relatively lightweight, with taut handling and good suspension, BSA's C15T capitalised on the virtues of the roadster to produce a trials bike that helped to usher in the modern era.

500cc Gold Stars had been enormously successful trials and scrambles mounts, but the company correctly anticipated the modern era and its shift towards lighter, more manageable machines. The lightweight, unit-construction C15 offered a great deal of potential, and the competition shop soon developed works specials that were ridden with a great deal of success, notably by expert rider and BSA employee Brian Martin.

Production versions followed the C15S scrambler and C15T trials machine. Superficially similar to the roadsters, there were in fact numerous differences, which included frames, wheels and suspension, as well as a host of engine modifications. The gear ratios were of course specially chosen for off-road, while the electrics used the so-called energy-transfer system. This did away with a battery, saving weight, but was notoriously problematic.

Even so, the true competition bikes succeeded famously. On the 441cc derivative, Jeff Smith won the world motocross championship in 1964 and 1965. It was the design's finest hour.

BSA C15T (1960)

Years in production: 1958-73 (all variations), 1959-65 (C15T)

Engine type: single-cylinder ohv four-stroke

Bore and stroke: 67 x 70 mm

Capacity: 247cc

Compression ratio: 7:1

Power: 15bhp @ 5000rpm

Carburettor: Amal Monobloc

Exhaust: high level

Weight: 275lb

Top speed: 75mph

Ariel Leader

One of the most technically innovative offerings of the postwar years of the British industry, Ariel's futuristic two-stroke was designed from scratch for mass transport. As part of the giant BSA group, Ariel had been manufacturing its traditional four-stroke singles, the Square Four, and a version of the BSA 650 twin when, in 1955, BSA decided to turn the entire resource of the factory over to a revolutionary new design offering low maintenance and full weather protection.

In doing so they may have been influenced by the enormous boom in sales of (mainly imported) scooters, although the machine that was eventually produced was far from a traditional scooter. Instead, it was a full-size 250cc motorcycle, albeit with small (16in) wheels. It was built entirely of pressed steel, which ideally lent itself to mass production, and offered tremendous strength. Unfortunately, the high initial cost of the tooling meant that it cost a great deal to get into production, while it was expensive to modify the design.

Not that there was anything inherently wrong with the final design of veteran Val Page, the man behind some of the most successful products of the British industry. Assisted by Bernard Knight, every aspect embodied sound logical thinking. It was based on a strong box beam that contributed to the excellent handling, and which, by acting as a low-slung fuel reservoir, helped to keep the centre of gravity down. The trailing-link forks with dampers concealed inside the legs worked extremely efficiently despite their odd appearance.

The engine hung below the main beam, and was designed as an integrated unit. A 250cc parallel twin with 180 degree firing interval, the cylinders were angled at 45 degrees to help keep the weight low slung. There were a number of similarities between the engine design and that of the German Adler, which went out of production just before Ariel launched their Leader. But while the engine shared several important dimensions, there were so many differences and developments that it could hardly be called a simple copy.

When the Leader appeared in 1958 it offered a complete package, with integral fairing and windscreen, and a dummy 'petrol tank' that was actually a luggage compartment, plus a host of practical and

Ariel Leader (1961)

Years in production: 1958-65

Engine type: parallel twin two-stroke

Bore and stroke: 54 x 54mm (48.5 x 54mm)

Capacity: 249cc (199.5cc)

Power: 17.5bhp @ 6750rpm

Carburettor: Amal Monobloc

Tyres (front/rear): $3\frac{1}{4}$ x 16in/ $3\frac{1}{4}$ x 16in

Top speed: 73mph

On the Leader the 6-inch headlamp was housed in the fairing. On the Arrow (above), it is supported by extensions forwards from the tank.

844 VVX

decorative extras. But despite its practical appeal and initially good response, many traditional motorcycle customers were turned off by its styling, while others were wooed by the appeal of the cheaper scooter and the revolutionary Mini.

Its cost may also have been too high, and in an attempt to appeal to the more sporting motorcyclist, as well as offer a cheaper alternative, the Leader was redesigned as the unfaired Arrow, launched in 1960. Again, the styling was odd – the engine was never intended to be on view and the front fork and mudguard appeared rather clumsy. But the machine was lighter, with a decent performance, and it was much cheaper – as it needed to be in a competitive market.

Ariel's entire production was devoted to the new range, and in a good month well over 1000 were produced. Tuning experiments upped the power of a works-developed model enough for it to come seventh in the lightweight TT, and the position looked promising.

For 1961 a new cylinder head improved the power of the standard machines, and a super sports version, the Golden Arrow, was also launched. But the reliability and practicality which Ariel had hoped for were not what they should have been. Starting could be poor, the gear change was rough, and some maintenance jobs were tricky. Two-stroke technology of the time also meant that while the engine was quick, it was often smoky.

The construction of the beam frame, complete with dummy tank, is clear to see in the unfaired Arrow (above), introduced as a more sporting model. The trailing-link forks gave good handling, but the unconventional appearance and clumsy mudguard did not endear them to sporting riders.

In 1963 the Ariel factory was absorbed into the main BSA plant. With cleaner, more practical machines appearing from Japan, even the launch in 1964 of a 200cc version, could not mask the fact that a total production run of some 17,000 was much too few. Production ended in 1965, and with it the Ariel name, although it was resurrected for two spectacularly unsuccessful BSA-designed lightweights, the Pixie and the Ariel 3, over the next few years.

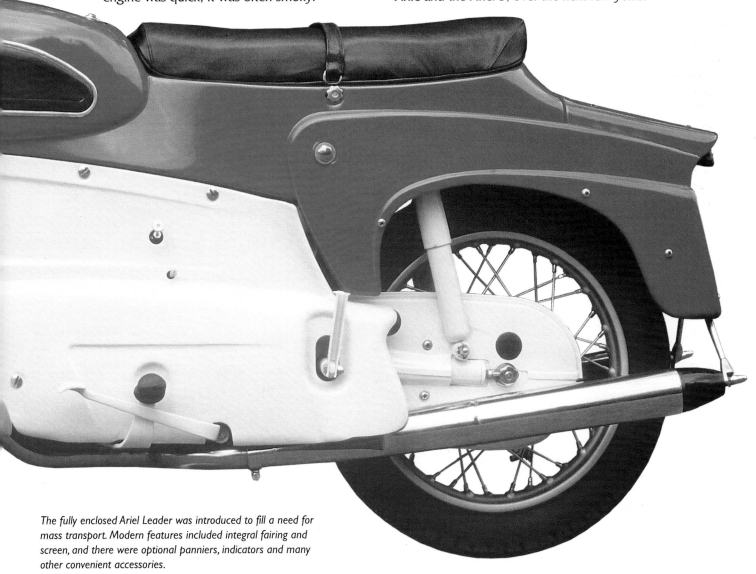

The fully enclosed Ariel Leader was introduced to fill a need for mass transport. Modern features included integral fairing and screen, and there were optional panniers, indicators and many other convenient accessories.

Greeves Sports Twin

Built by one of Britain's smallest manufacturers, Greeves lightweights were true individuals with an all-round quality that often put to shame the offerings from the major motorcycle factories.

The company took its name from one man, Bert Greeves, but it was really the product of two partners. The other half was Greeves' cousin Preston Derry Cobb, paralysed from birth but very much an active partner when they went into business shortly after World War II. In those early days the product was a motorised invalid carriage, and the company was called Invacar.

The invalid carriages sold well and established a firm foundation for the factory, which was based in Thundersley, near Benfleet in Essex. Although small, and reliant on proprietary engines that were produced by Villiers, the factory possessed its own foundry and very soon became expert in the new technology of fibreglass moulding. The invalid cars also featured some innovative design, notably suspension by rubber bushes that acted as self-damping springs when they twisted.

By the early 1950s Bert Greeves, an enthusiastic motorcylist and no mean off-road rider, was able to indulge his interests by constructing a prototype scrambler (motocross) machine. After this had been thoroughly proved in competition, production versions of both an off-road machine and a roadster appeared in 1954. Using Villiers or British Anzani engines, and front and rear suspension based on the invalid cars' rubber units, the frames illustrated another Greeves innovation. In place of the normal tubular fabricated front section and steering head was a

single aluminium alloy casting. This was an enormously strong H-section beam into which was cast a steel top tube and lugs for the engine mountings. Other fittings included the proprietary electrics and British Hub brakes used by a host of other small manufacturers.

It was the frame and front forks, which used short leading links, that really set Greeves aside from the rest. Despite their unconventional appearance, they offered superb handling on or off the road. For a time public resistance to the design meant that Greeves made some conventionally framed machines, too, but when experienced competition rider Brian Stonebridge joined the company in the mid 1950s, Greeves started to make a name for itself with an incredible series of giant-killing demonstrations, which vindicated their unconventional ideas.

Roadster production had centred on a range of modest lightweight twins, mainly powered by Villiers 250 and

Greeves 32DC (1961)

Years in production: 1956-63
  (with engine variations)

Engine type: 180 degree parallel
  twin two-stroke (Villiers 3T)

Bore and stroke: 57 x 63.5 mm

Capacity: 324cc

Compression ratio: 8.7:1

Power: 17bhp @ 5250rpm

Carburettor: Villiers 25mm

Tyres (front/rear): 20in/18in

Weight: 270lb

Top speed: 74mph

325cc units, after some early Anzani-engined models. By the 1960s the Sports Twins had become probably the best of their kind, thanks to Greeves handling and quality build. An indication of the regard in which they were held was their adoption as police bikes.

Numbers were inevitably small, however, with only around 300 racers and a few thousand roadsters appearing throughout the 1960s. As the decade wore on, Greeves fell victim to a number of pressures. First its engine supplier Villiers was taken over, and then the British market saw the first influx of sophisticated Japanese lightweights. Invacar, too, fell victim to the changing times. It was taken over in 1973, but in any case government support for specialist invalid cars ceased shortly afterwards. The last Greeves roadsters had left the factory in 1968, but they had designed a new motocrosser around their own single-cylinder 360cc engine. Its derivatives stayed in production until 1978, although a disastrous factory fire in 1976 was really the end of Greeves as a volume manufacturer.

Competition machines (above) ran in parallel with the roadsters. Typical of the breed was this 246cc Model 24MDS scrambler, modified to take part in the 1963 ISDT.

With the company's distinctive alloy front-beam frame and forks, and a finish in Moorland Blue, the Sports Twin in either 250 or 325cc form was one of Greeves' best loved roadsters. Despite its reliance on proprietary engine, electrics and brakes, it offered better handling and comfort than other Villiers-powered lightweights, plus a pedigree that was proven in competition.

Royal Enfield Constellation

Big parallel
twins may
have been the
staple fare of the
British industry in the
late 1950s and 60s, but there
were plenty of variations on the theme. With a character all
its own, Royal Enfield's twin offered one of several
alternatives to BSA/Triumph conformity, and was for several
years the largest of its kind.

Royal Enfield's first postwar twin appeared in 1948 and
owed more to the company's singles than to the
competition. A 500cc engine in the 350 single's swinging-
arm frame, it featured separate heads and barrels that
improved cooling and serviceability at some cost to
strength, while the crankcase incorporated a cast-in oil
container at the rear. Ignition was by battery, coil and
distributor, and although the Albion gearbox was a separate
unit, it was rigidly bolted to the rear of the engine. It was

rather unimaginatively called the 500 Twin.

A few years later the 1953 700cc Meteor went one
better than the rival 650s by offering what was
effectively a doubled-up 350 single. Technically it offered
some advanced features, such as a diecast cylinder head,
and a double-sided alloy front brake. This included
sophisticated adjustment and balancing arrangements, and
although only 6in in diameter was initially a good stopper.

Design changes for both models followed, including
such seemingly retrograde steps as a switch to magneto
and dynamo electrics. Major changes to the engine,
lubrication system and cycle parts resulted in the 1956
Super Meteor – an excellent all-rounder – while the 500
Twin was similarly improved. A year later, with the Vincent
V-twin already gone (and the Ariel Square Four being
phased out), the big Enfield achieved the distinction of
being the largest capacity twin on the market.

The 700cc Constellation was launched in the United
States in 1957, but first appeared in Britain in 1958, along

Royal Enfield Constellation (1961)

Years in production: 1958-63

Engine type: 360 degree parallel twin ohv four-stroke

Bore and stroke: 70 x 90 mm

Capacity: 692cc

Compression ratio: 8:1

Power: 51bhp @ 6250rpm

Carburettors: twin Amal Monoblocs

Tyres (front/rear): $3\frac{1}{4}$ x 18in/$3\frac{1}{2}$ x 17in

Weight: 403lb

Top speed: 116mph

Another classic Royal Enfield feature, the cast-alloy casquette (below) combined instrument housing, top yoke and light shell in one unit.

Beefy, purposeful and powerful, in its day the 'Connie' was the biggest British twin.

with a new and much lighter 500, the Meteor Minor. With new engine castings, the 'Connie' was a sportier design with a very robust bottom end, hot cams and, initially, a single racing Amal TT carburettor. With a suitably tuned cylinder head, the resulting bike was a real road-burner capable of well over 110mph. On test, it bettered 115mph.

The racing carb disappeared in favour of twin Monoblocs in 1959, but the bike was still fast – although it soon gained a reputation for fragility, while the front brake was inadequate for the power and speed. In fact, there were a number of niggles, which meant that the model never achieved the popularity of machines such as the Triumph twins, despite its theoretical advantages and better acceleration.

To counter complaints of heavy vibration, the crankshaft was redesigned. The rather weak clutch was altered in 1961, and there were a number of styling changes. This became the ultimate example of the 'Connie', because in 1963 Enfield launched the even larger 750 Interceptor (actually a 736cc design) while the Constellation was mainly relegated to sidecar duty before production ceased that year. The 750 twins only lasted a few years more. With the company suffering from the financial malaise of much of the industry, production suffered a short gap before the model bowed out at the start of the 1970s.

Norton 500 Manx

As a company, Norton came to be dominated by the demands of racing, and for many years a wide gulf separated their bread-and-butter products from the exotics developed in the race shop. While the policy might not have been ideal for commercial success, it nevertheless produced one of the most phenomenally effective racers of all time – the Manx Norton single.

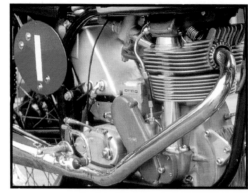

Finning that completely enclosed the bevel drive shaft (left) is a characteristic of the later, short-stroke models. The stiff crankcase in Elektron magnesium alloy extends right up to the bottom fins.

The Manx Norton was also one of the supreme examples of the value of constant development, in the hands of race engineer Joe Craig whose meticulous experiments kept squeezing more and more power out of the design as each season passed.

The Manx was itself a development from the single overhead-cam International racers. A dohc layout had been tried as early as 1937, with a larger cambox in which a gear train operated twin camshafts bearing directly on a pair of valve 'pushers' in contact with the valve stems. Inspired partly by experiments at rivals Velocette, this design was not immediately successful, although it reappeared in 1938 with revised engine dimensions and supposedly phenomenal power output.

The Manx name was first used late in 1939, but in 1940 all racing efforts ceased. The name appeared once again in 1946 before September's amateur Manx Grand Prix, where several entrants rode that season's new racer. With an engine based on the prewar International, the dohc cambox was used, while the machines sported the new telescopic front forks tried on the works bikes in 1938. Performance, however, was disappointing, partly as a result of the low-octane 'Pool' petrol then in use.

Gradually, a steady process of development began to pay dividends. In 1948 a twin leading-shoe brake appeared, and with 112mph potential, it was needed. By 1950, with 120mph performance, it was essential.

The year 1950 saw the most significant leap in Manx technology, with the adoption of the new 'Featherbed' frame designed in Ireland by the McCandless brothers and Artie Bell. The new frame and suspension were a quantum leap for motorcycling in general, and gave Norton a massive edge over the competition. Its name was coined by rider Harold Daniell, enthusing about its comfort.

After a triumphant debut in the hands of Geoff Duke in April, the Featherbed Nortons went on to win a

double hat trick at the TT, the first of many major wins. In 1951 both the 500 and 350 were listed as production racers – virtually identical to the works machines, the only significant differences between the two models being the engine size.

In 1953 the engines were redesigned with a much shorter stroke for improved revs, and many more wins ensued, despite the sophistication of the mainly Italian multi-cylinder competition. In 1954 streamlining was tested, resulting in yet more wins, but it was becoming clear that time was running out for the antiquated technology. Norton 'officially' withdrew from Grand Prix racing at the end of the season, although they continued to support works entries, and rivals Moto Guzzi continued to race single cylinders with considerable success until 1957.

The factory continued to develop the Manx, and gained many more wins, while the production models soldiered on as the mainstay of privateer competition for many years. Then, in 1961, Norton scored an amazing double hat trick at the TT – although most of the Italian makers were not competing that year. But the works efforts were switching to a new model, the Domiracer, which made its debut at that same event. It was effectively the model's swan song, although private enthusiasts developed and raced them for many more years. The last batch appeared in 1962, the year in which Norton works in Birmingham's Bracebridge Street closed, and the factory moved in with AMC in Plumstead, London.

Norton 500 Manx (1962)

Years in production: 1946-53 (long-stroke) 1953-62 (short-stroke)

Engine type: double overhead-cam single-cylinder four-stroke

Bore and stroke: 79.6 x100mm (1946-53), 86 x 85.6 (1953-62)

Capacity: 499cc

Compression ratio: 9.75:1

Power: 50bhp @ 7200rpm

Carburettors: 1½in Amal GP

Tyres (front/rear): 3 x 19in /3½ x 19in

Wheelbase: 56in

Top speed: 150mph (depending on gearing)

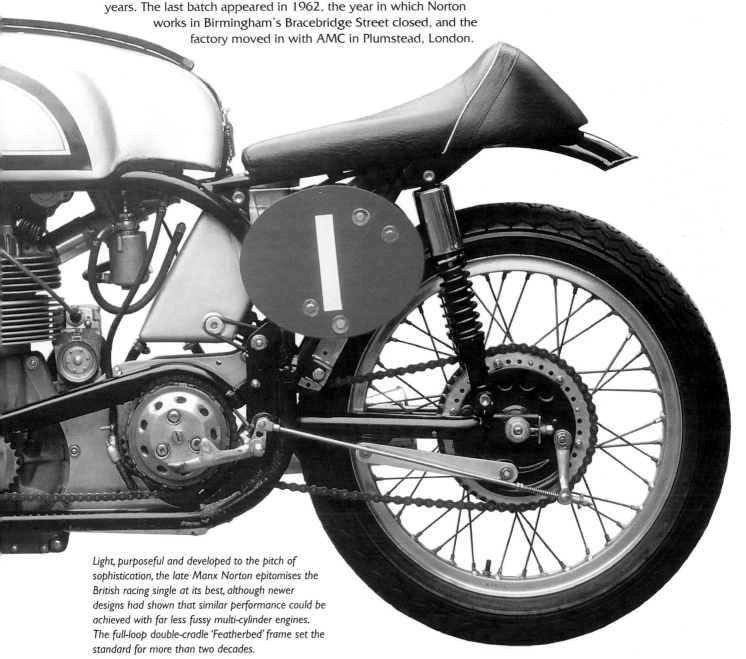

Light, purposeful and developed to the pitch of sophistication, the late Manx Norton epitomises the British racing single at its best, although newer designs had shown that similar performance could be achieved with far less fussy multi-cylinder engines. The full-loop double-cradle 'Featherbed' frame set the standard for more than two decades.

BSA A65

Along with its 500cc cousin, the A50, the problems that beset the A65 typify much of what went wrong with BSA towards the end of the company. The machines attracted a poor reputation for reliability and spares back up in particular, which helped to put the final nails in the coffin of a large part of the British industry. And yet the design had its good points, for with modification the engine unit proved itself in that most demanding of competition fields – sidecar racing – while surviving, hard-working bikes have clocked up tens of thousands of trouble-free miles.

By the 1960s BSA had become part of a large conglomerate with diverse interests. There had been a concerted effort to introduce new management systems, and there was an on-going drive to attract sales in the all-important American market. Despite the popularity of the existing 650cc twins, these were perceived as being of an increasingly antiquated design, which was losing out against the competition from Triumph in particular.

The new models were developed quickly, and many of their problems were the kind that a longer testing period would have ironed out. On the face of it, though, the new 650 offered promise, being more sophisticated and lighter than its A10-based predecessors. In place of their nuts-and-bolts separate engine, gearbox, magneto and dynamo, the engine

was a unit-construction design with fashionable 'power egg' streamlined styling and an alternator. Only a single carburettor was fitted, but with almost square dimensions, the engine promised to be free-revving, with room for an efficient combustion chamber design.

It was perhaps surprising, therefore, that it initially offered less power than the top-of-the-range A10-based machine, the Rocket Gold Star, although as the model was developed it became clear that there was much more available. The frame and forks were similar to the duplex cradle unit of the late A10s, but the geometry was changed to suit smaller wheels, and the bike was much more compact overall. The handling was generally quite good, although the rather crude damping of the front forks sometimes found the going tough.

When the A65 and smaller A50 were launched in 1962, they appeared to have plenty going for them. The styling fell into line with the clean, but rather lumpen BSA look of the period, with a weak point being the awkwardly large side panels, which extended forward, supposedly to tidy up the space behind the engine. The performance was not bad, with strong acceleration and a reasonable 100mph or so top speed – and the fuel economy was good.

The problems soon appeared, however. The engines were prone to vibration, but much more seriously, the main bearings self-destructed at depressingly low mileages, often blocking the oil pump and wrecking the engine. Oil leaks were common and the primary drive chain was also prone to rapid wear.

This did not prevent an A50 from taking Gold in the 1962 ISDT, while for the public, the A65 was soon offered in higher performance versions with sportier styling, higher and higher compression ratios, and latterly, twin carburettors. One such machine, the 650 Lightning, even managed to win a production race in 1965. For the American market initially, there were many variants, including scramblers.

'Power-egg' styling was a popular fashion in the 1960s, and the 650 BSA unit was perhaps the definitive version. All functions in the unit engine were smoothly faired in behind streamlined alloy casings.

BSA A65 (1966)

Years in production: 1962-72 (all A65 variants) 1966-68 (Spitfire models)

Engine type: twin-cylinder ohv four-stroke

Bore and stroke: 75 x 74mm

Capacity: 654cc

Compression ratio: 10 5:1 (Spitfire MkII)

Power: 54bhp @ 4500rpm (Spitfire MkII)

Gearbox: four-speed

Weight: 383lb (Spitfire MkII)

By 1966 the top of the range was the Spitfire MkII, which sported many racing fittings, such as close-ratio gears, a larger front brake and fibreglass tank. It was light and fast, with 120 mph within reach, and thanks to a new front fork, handled well. The introduction of 12 volt electrics was an improvement that benefited the whole range. But the problems were still there, as the awesome levels of vibration which were produced by sustained high speed running testified.

Much production was still aimed at the US market, and in 1967 BSA won an export award. The American market dictated many styling changes, which were less popular for the home market, such as high-rise bars and smaller tanks for several models.

There were several attempts at curing the engines' basic problems, but none that really succeeded, and from 1970 on, this flawed power unit gained a frame with problems of its own. This was the oil-in-frame unit, in which a large diameter backbone doubled as the oil tank. A similar design was adopted by Triumph, and although both handled well,

Handsome in a beefy way, the A65 eschewed the nuts-and-bolts looks of its predecessors in favour of a rounded, all-enclosed styling. With a highly-tuned, but fragile, engine, it offered true sports bike performance and the handling to exploit it.

they were so designed that the seat height precluded them being ridden comfortably by anyone who was much under six feet tall.

The model soldiered on until 1972, despite BSA's growing financial difficulties. By this time the seat height had been reduced to a much more workable level, handling was excellent and even the vibration seemed to have decreased. Sadly it was too late, and the A65 became a victim of BSA's need to make cuts.

There is a postscript, for a solution to the main-bearing problem had been proposed while developing the factory racers in 1966-7, but never adopted. After the model had been discontinued, ex-BSA workers offered this as an after-market conversion, consisting of a new set of main bearings an optional new oil pump and clutch modification.

Velocette Thruxton

The Thruxton Velo was the final development of Velocette's pushrod single – a machine that in essence dated back to the mid 1930s. Despite its simple and in many ways antiquated layout, this was a genuine 100mph machine, which could top 110 and still sip fuel at an astonishingly low rate through its massive racing carburettor.

Thruxton is the name of a race track in Hampshire – one of the many wartime airfields that found a new use during the 1950s. Racing at Thruxton centred on the endurance marathon for production machines, the 500-miler. The bikes had to be substantially catalogue models and the entries were shared between two riders who took turn and turn about. Over the years many British stars shone in the event, including Dave Croxford, Percy Tait, Ray Pickrell and Paul Smart. Machines that achieved great things there included the racing bersion of the Triumph Bonneville, to which the event also gave its name, the BSA-Triumph threes, the John Player Norton Commandos – and the Velocette.

Velocette singles evolved slowly over the years. Their basic formula was laid down by the 1934 250cc MOV, with the camshaft mounted high up and the pushrods kept as short as possible, while their narrow crankcase, slimline

clutch and outboard chain run dated back to the early vintage days. Larger capacities and shorter strokes followed over the years, and by the late 1950s the machine had evolved into the 350cc Viper and 500cc Venom.

These Velocettes had a sporting image and performance, and on 18–19 March a Clubman's Venom

The ultimate sports pushrod engine (right): tuning the Thruxton included a special head with extra large valves and a down-draught inlet port. This was matched to an enormous Amal GP carburettor that required special cut-aways in the tanks. Yet the engine was enormously flexible – there were only four ratios in the gearbox – and capable of astonishing fuel economy.

equipped with Velocette's own sports options and a full fairing set out to challenge the 24-hour speed record. After circulating the Monthléry speed bowl near Paris in the hands of a team of eight riders for a day and a night, it achieved an outstanding success. First the twelve-hour record fell at more than 104 mph, then the twenty four-hour record went at an average speed of 100 mph-plus – an enduring record.

In 1964 the high-cam Velo reached its ultimate development. The performance of the Clubman's Venom at Thruxton led to the makers offering a performance kit that included a special head with 2in inlet valve and an enormous Amal Grand Prix carburettor, plus oil and petrol tanks cut away to suit. For the following year, Velocette offered the Thruxton model with this kit, racing seat and footrests, swept-back exhaust and a twin-leading shoe alloy front brake.

Although the 1965 500-miler was held on an alternative circuit, the Velocettes dominated the race, with Dave Dixon and Joe Dunphy ahead at the last. The model soon found favour with sporting riders, for it was a genuine tuned roadster and was well able to cope with everyday use, despite being a fussy starter.

Its finest moment came in 1967, the year of the first Isle of Man Production TT. In the 500 class, Neil Kelly took the race at just under 90mph, as well as the fastest lap at over 91 mph. Fellow rider Keith Heckles was second.

Only a little more than 1200 Thruxtons were built, although the relative ease of converting a Venom meant that there were several more replicas constructed by private owners. In 1969 the ignition system had to be modified to coil ignition, as the traditional magneto had been phased out by Lucas. This was effectively the factory's swan song, for it bowed to commercial pressure in 1971, still a genuine family firm after 66 years.

Production racer: in 1967 the Thruxton dominated the inaugural Production TT, taking first, second and fastest lap. It was capable of more than 110mph and had proven endurance, having broken the 24-hour record.

Velocette Venom Thruxton (1967)

Years in production: 1965-71

Engine type: high-camshaft ohv four-stroke single

Bore and stroke: 86 x 86mm

Capacity: 499cc

Compression ratio: 9.2:1

Power: 41-47bhp @ 6200rpm

Carburettor: Amal GP

Tyres (front/rear): 3 x 19in/3¼ x 19in

Wheelbase: 54¾in

Top speed: 110mph

BSA Rocket 3

The late 1960s ushered in the age of the superbikes – machines with technical specifications and performances much superior to anything that had gone before. And although the bikes that really gave form to the name were Japanese, both BSA's and Triumph's triples were among the most important of the pioneers.

As part of the same manufacturing group, the BSA Rocket 3 and the slightly later Triumph Trident were based on the same original concept, although the differences between them went well beyond the name on the tank.

The original concept dated back to the early 1960s, when designers Bert Hopwood and Doug Hele realised that it would be quite simple to graft an extra cylinder on to the 500cc Triumph twin, producing a 750cc three-cylinder engine. The advantage of such a layout, apart from the increased capacity, would be that the inherent balance of a triple would result in a much smoother power delivery.

However, nothing was done with the idea for several years, until the company's board members were told of Honda's plans to produce a 750cc four-cylinder machine. A prototype was hastily put into production, and within a year it was developing a healthy 58bhp for a weight not much greater than the contemporary Triumph Bonneville twin.

To save time, the cylinder blocks had been made from cast iron, while the specially sand-cast crankcase components also added weight, so there was obviously plenty of potential. One clever feature of the design, even if it looked like production expediency, was the way in which

The crankcase (below) consists of separate castings bolted together, requiring care in assembly. Three exhausts lead into two pipes, terminating in the extraordinary 'ray gun' silencers with three short exit pipes.

Science-fiction styling and superbike performance were the two main attributes of the 1968 BSA Rocket 3, designed to appeal to a largely American market.

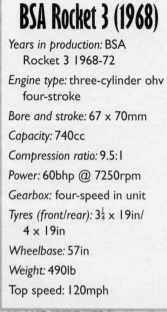

BSA Rocket 3 (1968)

Years in production: BSA Rocket 3 1968-72

Engine type: three-cylinder ohv four-stroke

Bore and stroke: 67 x 70mm

Capacity: 740cc

Compression ratio: 9.5:1

Power: 60bhp @ 7250rpm

Gearbox: four-speed in unit

Tyres (front/rear): $3\frac{1}{4}$ x 19in/ 4 x 19in

Wheelbase: 57in

Weight: 490lb

Top speed: 120mph

the crankshaft was made. To give even firing, this had to have three throws at 120 degrees to each other – a complicated forging. So instead, the shaft was forged•in one plane, then heated and twisted to the correct angles. Inevitably, part of the heritage of the engine design was that it was both costly and complicated to manufacture. Two versions – a BSA and a Triumph – were actually developed, using a different engine and frame layout, with the BSA's engine angled forward in a duplex cradle frame. The crankcase was a bolt-up assembly of five major castings in place of the two used by most of the competition, and indeed, the original Triumph twins. Care in component selection and engine building were essential.

Production of the first Rocket 3, as BSA were to call their version of the triple, began in 1968, and the machine was launched in Britain early in 1969 – slightly ahead of

Honda's revolutionary 750 four – to mixed reactions. Road tests showed that it was the fastest multi-cylinder production machine of the era, and although it was slightly slower to accelerate than either the Norton Commando or the Honda, it had the legs of both at the top end. In 1971 a Rocket 3 won the Daytona 200 in the United States, with a new race record speed, while a Trident placed second and another BSA placed third.

The styling was far less well-received. Designed by committee, and in response to the demands of the huge American market, the Rocket 3's slab-sided petrol tank, huge badges and 'ray gun' silencers were not what the traditional BSA buyer expected. Only about 7000 were built before financial difficulties meant production shut down in 1972, leaving the Triumph Trident to inherit the mantle of the triples.

Triumph T120 Bonneville

Triumph's Speed Twin had been one of the bikes that helped to set the pace before the war. After the conflict, the 500cc Speed Twin spawned many descendants, from 350 to 750cc capacity. Above all others, the 650cc Bonneville became the bike that set the standard throughout the late 1950s and 1960s – the era of the Rockers and Café Racers.

The first 650cc Triumph appeared in 1949, when the softly tuned 6T Thunderbird showed its pace at the Monthléry speed bowl before going on sale the next year. The model was an excellent tourer, marred only by two failings – the increased level of vibration that had caused one of the Monthléry entries to record a slower time than it should have, and the crude rear suspension offered by Triumph's sprung hub.

Even so, a Thunderbird racer, equipped with twin carburettors, hot cams and high-compression pistons, managed to better 132mph at Utah's Bonneville Salt Flats in 1951. A few years later, in 1956, Johnny Allen made a world speed record bid in a streamlined shell fitted with two 6T engines. Although he achieved 214.4mph, a record accepted by the US authorities, the world governing body refused to acknowledge it. Undaunted, American enthusiasts continued their efforts, and two years later a specially prepared Tiger 110 (a 650 with rear swing arm and hotter engine than the Thunderbird) managed to achieve over 147mph, ridden by Bill Johnson. The speed was good enough for a class record. That was in 1958, and the venue once again was Bonneville.

The first Triumph machine to bear the Bonneville name appeared in 1959. Based heavily on the Tiger 110, the T120 was fitted with the twin carburettors that were optional on the T110, together with the hot E3134 inlet cam. With a power rated at 46 bhp, the model was already good for a comfortable 115mph – perhaps more – but the engine had the potential to be tuned a lot hotter.

The first Bonnevilles could easily outperform the handling of their cycle parts, but from 1963 onwards they

Light and sporty, Triumph's 650 twin had an edge over its more staid competitors, which made it the machine that a generation aspired to. Although its general layout harked back some 30 years, it had been revised year-on-year, giving an unrivalled blend of power and handling.

Front braking (left) is by a twin-leading-shoe 8in diameter drum that stopped the light (370lb) package reasonably effectively.

gained a new frame, with extra bracing for the swinging arm and steering head. At the same time, the separate engine and gearbox became part of a new unitary design. As a result the power unit became more compact, and now contributed to the stiffness of the package. A couple of years later, the steering angle was changed and improved forks adopted.

All these improvements helped Triumph's Bonneville to match the all-round performance available from its rivals. In the styling stakes, however, it had no equal. Where the contemporary BSA was worthy but perhaps a little stolid, and Norton's offering lacked the absolute glamour of its racing forebears, the 650 Bonneville oozed get-up-and-go.

On the race track, it got up and went. In 1967 and 1969 it won Production TTs and British 500 mile races. The works T100R gave 55 bhp and was timed at over 140mph in the

TT. In 1969 it achieved a 1/2/3 in the Thruxton 500-miler, covering three more of the top seven places.

Bonnevilles attract strong supporters, and several different years have their proponents. In the opinion of many, however, the 1968 is the best of the breed. With good handling and more reliable electrics than its predecessors (including a new ignition system), all the good features were there in a package that was hard to beat. But it was almost the end of the line, for the 650 twin would survive a scant three years before it was replaced by a new 750 and Triumph began its slow slide into oblivion.

Triumph T120 Bonneville (1968)

Years in production: 1959-71

Engine type: twin-cylinder ohv four-stroke

Bore and stroke: 71 x 82mm

Capacity: 649cc

Compression ratio: 8.5:1

Power: 46bhp @ 6700rpm

Carburation: two $1\frac{3}{16}$in Amal Monoblocs

Gearbox: four-speed

Wheelbase: 55in

Weight: 370lb

Norton Commando (Fastback)

Launched to rapturous acclaim at the Earls Court Show in 1967, and four times voted Machine of the Year, the Norton Commando was perhaps the best loved product of the final years of the British industry. And yet it grew from a classic compromise. By the mid-60s, Associated Motorcycles (AMC), the parent company of the AJS, Matchless and Norton concerns – among many other great names of the British industry – was in trouble. In late 1966 the firm was taken over by Manganese Bronze Holdings, an engineering conglomerate which already owned Villiers. Under the chairmanship of Dennis Poore, the head of MBH and a one-time racing driver, the motorcycle interests were merged into Norton Villiers.

Prior to this production had consisted of a range of variations of AJS's, Matchless' and Norton's old twins and singles, many of which had been dropped as poor sellers after 1962. Virtually all the current product consisted of 650 and 750cc Norton twins, using either the ageing Featherbed or Matchless frame. It was clear that the new company needed a flagship – and quickly, preferably by the next year's show. Efforts initially centred on an existing design that had been underway some years before. Called the P10, this was a double overhead-camshaft parallel twin, but after several months development it was apparent that the machine would prove too heavy, too rough and potentially too unreliable.

With only some three months to go before the show, development engineers Bernard Hooper and Bob Trigg, together with engineering director Dr Stefan Bauer, suggested an alternative. Bauer had joined Norton Villiers in January 1967 from Rolls Royce. Not a motorcyclist, he argued that conventional frame design was contrary to good engineering principles, and suggested that the P10 should have a frame based on a single top tube. Bauer also insisted that engine vibration could not be tolerated – and it was vibration that was one of the chief complaints with the existing Norton twins.

Developed from the 497cc Dominator of the early 1950s, the twins had grown through 596 and 646cc, and finally to the 745cc unit used in the Featherbed-framed Atlas, gaining power at the expense of a little more roughness each time. The idea that was now put forward was completely radical – why not fit a modified version of the tried-and-tested

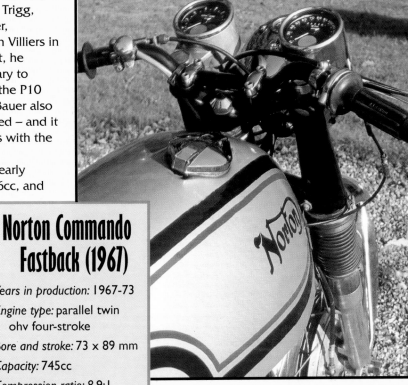

This model, one of the first ten made, is finished in conventional Norton silver with red and black striping, a far cry from the colourful show machine.

Norton Commando Fastback (1967)

Years in production: 1967-73

Engine type: parallel twin ohv four-stroke

Bore and stroke: 73 x 89 mm

Capacity: 745cc

Compression ratio: 8.9:1

Power: 58bhp @ 6500rpm

Carburettors: Amal concentric

Tyres (front/rear): 3 x 19in/ $3\frac{1}{2}$ x 19in

Wheelbase: $56\frac{3}{4}$ in

Top speed: 120mph

Atlas engine to a new frame based on Bauer's ideas? And to eliminate the problem of vibration, simply isolate the engine from the rider, together with the entire transmission train, including the rear wheel.

This was done by bolting the separate engine, gearbox and swinging-arm assembly together as one unit. The unit was then suspended from a spine frame based on a $2\frac{1}{4}$ in diameter top tube, using adjustable rubber bushes at three carefully calculated points. The idea worked superbly, allowing the engine to shake to its heart's content without disturbing the rider, and in 1969 the idea won an award for the most significant contribution to motorcycling. Inclined slightly forward, the modified Atlas engine had an aggressive stance and possessed enormous grunt.

Styling on the prototype was carried out by design consultants Wolf Ohlins, another company with no motorcycling experience. It included a silver frame and tank, and an orange seat with curious 'ears' projecting forward to hug the tank. Ar the rear it featured a racy hump, which led to the model being dubbed the 'Fastback'. Much lighter than its predecessors, the machine went as well as it looked. Acceleration was phenomenal for its day, under five seconds to reach 60mph, leading to a top speed of nearly 120mph.

Fastback styling took the motorcycle world by storm in 1967. A forward angled engine, fibreglass seat tail, and 'ears' coming forward from the seat to embrace the tank all hinted at the 120mph performance of which the machine was capable.

Norton P11

Norton's P11 'desert sled' was one of the British industry's inspired compromises. Something of a 'parts-bin special' it was a mix-and-match combination of parts from Norton and parent company AMC, designed to suit the American market and originally for export only. The result was so good that although few found their way on to British roads, those that did, along with many more recent re-imports, rapidly achieved cult status. With the enormous popularity of powerful, off-road twins that began in the 1980s, it can now also be seen as a machine that was way ahead of its time.

The P11 predated Norton's more famous Commando, but in many ways it shared similar reasons for its existence. The firm's Dominator twins had been developed to the limit while – despite the pedigree of its Featherbed frame – their 750cc derivative the Atlas was starting to look its age. With cutbacks becoming a necessity in the mid 1960s, AMC was keen to reduce the model variations and dispose of stock.

America still formed a big part of the market, where leisure motorcycling was far more significant than in Britain. Off-road sport in particular had long been an important sales area, and it was this that led to the launch of the P11. AMC's US distributor suggested that it might be possible to construct a machine especially for the popular West Coast desert races. AMC's Matchless G85CS had satisfied just such a market. Essentially a racing 500cc engine in a

Conceived as a racer first and foremost, in the late 1960s Norton's 'desert sled' took first place in California's Mojave desert for two years running. The powerful, lightweight package that resulted became a cult roadster.

lightweight scrambler frame, it had been very successful, but was now outclassed on power. In 1965 Norton had tried a version of the Atlas – the Scrambler – but it was far too heavy to be competitive.

And so the P11 was born. It used the Atlas engine as modified for the scrambler. But in place of the heavy roadster-based cycle parts, the frame was the lightweight unit of the Matchless. Lightness was the key, for together with the powerful Atlas engine it provided a brutal power-to-weight ratio. The tank was as small as practicable and made of alloy. Mudguards, silencer, side panels and other

fittings followed suit. Everything was built for one purpose only – winning. Win it did. In its intended home of the Mojave desert, the lightweight, powerful P11 reigned supreme through the closing years of the 1960s. That same power could get out of hand on the road, where with off-road tyres and a short wheelbase its handling was not always as sure as expected from a Norton.

Any criticism of its road performance missed the point, for no scrambler was equipped to deal with a performance of well over 100 mph on the tarmac. Lightweight, lean and purposeful, these machines were costly to build, because the Norton engine was a tight fit in the Matchless frame and needed special spacers to match up. Their schizophrenic existence was obvious from the fact that a near-identical model was marketed as the Matchless N15CS. But whatever their identity, the package worked superbly well, while their cut-down styling helped to define the street scrambler concept that would influence a whole generation of future roadsters. When both models were discontinued in 1969, they had already become a legend.

Norton P11 (1969)

Years in production: 1967-69

Engine type: 360 degree parallel twin ohv four-stroke

Bore and stroke: 73 x 89 mm

Capacity: 745cc

Compression ratio: 7.5:1

Power: 50bhp @ 6rpm

Carburettors: twin Amal Concentrics

Weight: 380lb

Top speed: 110mph

Norton Commando (Roadster)

The Norton Commando was well placed to exploit the dawning of the superbike era and it enjoyed a healthy level of sales right from the start. In 1969 a MkII version was introduced, along with the Commando S model, which had high-level exhausts, both running down the left of the machine, and the more conventionally styled Roadster.

The Commando was launched into competition right from the start, and it was not long before the 750 gained its first track success. It would go on to win a host of events and records, while the entry in the Production TT of 1970 narrowly missed a 100mph lap.

The 750 models continued until late 1973, with various styling and mechanical changes. These variants included the bizarre Hi-Rider, which had extreme Chopper styling featuring ultra high-rise bars and a seat with an extended backrest. But there was also a change that spelled near disaster. This was the introduction of the Combat engine in 1972, a year that also saw the use of a front disc brake for the first time.

The Combat engine was developed with the idea of improving the power and performance. It had a strengthened bottom end, hot cams, high compression and gas-flowed head. Although this seemed like a good idea, it was almost fatal for the model. The over-stressed main bearings frequently gave way after as few as 5000 miles, while oil leaks and damage from over-revving were depressingly common. Retrospectively, the problems were cured by fitting a new type of main bearing and lowering the compression ratio, but the Combat engine had been an expensive folly.

It was a pity that the record of the 750 had been tarnished in this way, for the potential of the design was well demonstrated by some spectacular success on the race track. Following his success in production racing with the early 750, Norton's brilliant rider-developer Peter Williams set out to see just what could be done to make the bike competitive in Formula 750. Sponsored by the John Player tobacco company, his development led to a

model with a monocoque version of an isolastic frame, which doubled as the fuel tank, and a tailored fairing that directed air to the engine and carburettors. Highly efficient, the fairing made up for a massive power deficiency against the opposition. After a run of frustration and disappointment, Williams came home in the 1973 Formula 750 TT to a famous win, with the fastest lap of 107.57mph. His team-mate Mick Grant was second.

The 750cc models were phased out in October 1973, by which time they were designated MkV models, and with the problems cured, were as attractive in their way as the original Fastback 750s had been.

The MkI 850cc replacements had appeared earlier that year, and would remain in production through three mark changes until 1975. By that time they had gained (rather ineffective) electric starting and numerous modifications,

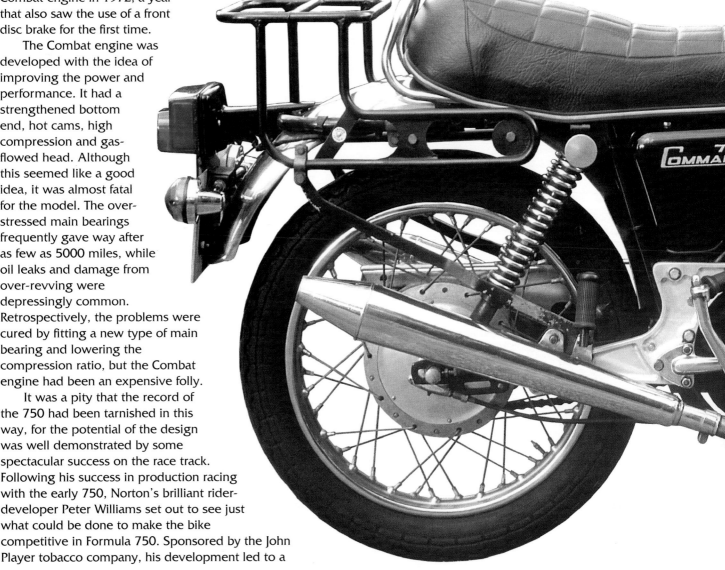

all aimed at helping the Commando to compete with the reliability and performance of its competition – chiefly the new generation of Japanese superbikes.

Sadly, by this time the parent company's financial difficulties and the problems of manufacture on worn, old machinery made it increasingly difficult to compete. While the machines were rightly loved by a generation of owners, it had to be acknowledged that running a Commando required a level of dedication and sympathy far higher than that demanded by a Honda or Kawasaki. And for Norton it would prove impossible to compete in selling what was effectively one design to a tiny proportion of the market. Despite its proud heritage and enviable record, the Commando succumbed to old age and market pressures, with a final trickle of machines in 1978. Although the Norton name would live on in the form of the rotary-engined machines built at Shenstone in Staffordshire, the Commando marked the end of a line that had begun a long way back in the pioneer era.

Norton Commando Roadster (1973)

Years in production: 1967-73 (750) 1973-78 (850)

Engine type: parallel twin ohv four-stroke

Bore and stroke: 73 x 89mm (750) 77 x 89mm (850)

Capacity: 745cc (750) 829cc (850)

Compression ratio: 9:1 (750) 10:1 (Combat) 8.5:1 (850)

Power: 60bhp (750) 68bhp (Combat) 60bhp @ 6000rpm (850) (claimed)

Carburettors: 30mm Amal Concentrics 32mm (Combat and 850)

Tyres (front/rear): 4.10x19

Top speed: 125mph (claimed)

Like the other later variants of the Commando, the Roadster was conventionally styled compared to its predecessors. Refinements included flashing indicators and a front disc brake. The disastrous 'improvement' of the over-tuned Combat engine used on other models was abandoned in 1973, the year of this 750cc MkV model.

Triumph Trident

The story of the Triumph Trident began as part of the same development process that had spawned the BSA Rocket 3. But where the BSA soon went out of production, it was the Triumph that really proved the concept.

The first version of the Trident had an upright engine in a frame based on the single downtube Bonneville, quite unlike the BSA's angled engine and duplex frame, which meant that most of the major castings were completely different. By contrast to the BSA's radical styling, which had helped to contribute to its poor sales, Triumph's version, the T150 Trident, had a family likeness to the contemporary twin, especially after a redesign in 1972.

Whatever the reason, the Trident sold much better than the Rocket 3, and about 45,000 were made. This was despite weaknesses in quality control, as a result of which oil leaks and electrical faults were distressingly common. The drum brakes initially used were weak for a machine with such high performance, and had to be modified, although

The T150 version of the Trident (above) has an upright engine, like the upright Triumph twin on which it was based. The frame has a single downtube similar to the twin's, and unlike the BSA version of the triples.

discs were fitted to later models. The engine, too, needed heavy maintenance over a lengthy running-in period. Fortunately the unconventional crank, produced by twisting a straight forging, eventually proved strong enough to last throughout the model's production life and to cope with uprated power outputs of around 100bhp.

There was a much happier story in competition, as the triples proved competitive right from the start; although they were not without a few problems. One Trident racer acquired legendary status after a massive oil leak at the 1970 Bol d'Or, which led to it acquiring lurid handling and

Triumph Trident T160 (1974)

Years in production: 1969-1974 (T150)
1974 (T160)

Engine type: three-cylinder ohv four-stroke

Bore and stroke: 67 x 70mm

Capacity: 740cc

Compression ratio: 9.5:1

Power: 58bhp @ 7250rpm

Gearbox: four-speed in unit

Tyres (front/rear): 4.10 x 19in/4.10 x 19in

Wheelbase: 58in

Weight: 525lb

Top speed: 115mph

the nickname 'Slippery Sam'. Even so, triples won most of the important short-circuit competitions, as well as taking the first three places in the 1971 Production TT.

In Rocket 3 form, the triples' styling had already veered to the flamboyant, but in 1972 it was taken to excess with a model styled by the young American designer Craig Vetter. Planned as a limited-edition model to appeal to American tastes, it was called the X75 Hurricane, and blended elements of a stripped flat-track racer with the chopper styling brought into vogue by the recent film *Easy Rider*.

Considered outrageous at the time, in hindsight it can be seen to have had an enormous effect on motorcycle styling.

From 1974 Triumph offered a new and much more conventional triple, the T160, using a version of the BSA's inclined engine, with, for the first time, an electric start to augment the kick-starter.

A number of variants of this model found their way on to the British market as the Cardinal. They were in fact part of a batch that had been destined for police use in the Middle East, but redirected when the deal fell through. This was effectively the end of the design. There had been plans to launch a 900cc version, as well as a 1000cc four, but this was not to be, and with the imminent financial collapse of the parent company, Triumph was forced to concentrate on the much simpler twins.

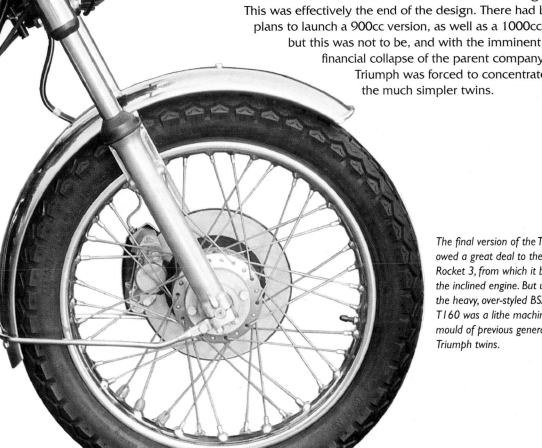

The final version of the Trident owed a great deal to the BSA Rocket 3, from which it borrowed the inclined engine. But unlike the heavy, over-styled BSA, the T160 was a lithe machine in the mould of previous generations of Triumph twins.

Rickman Enfield Interceptor

The Rickman Interceptor mated one of the biggest engines produced by the British industry to one of the best frames. Much lighter than its forebears, it had better handling and one of the first really effective disc brakes. It should have been a splendid success, but in reality it represented a glorious swan song for one of the industry's great pioneers.

By the late 1960s the Rickman brothers Don and Derek were firmly established as makers of high-quality frames for sports machines, off-roaders and even police bikes. Over the years they would produce packages for the popular Japanese engines, then diversify into accessories and kit car manufacture.

As Rickman began their rise, so Royal Enfield began to sink. Their flagship, the 750 Interceptor, had been launched in 1963, but while it was a promising new model the company was already in the same kind of financial trouble that had gripped much of the industry.

The company's new owners had launched an ambitious programme of new models and had thrown themselves enthusiastically into racing, but further cutbacks proved necessary, and the old Redditch works was closed in 1966. Engines and other parts were now built in a new factory, while the once-popular 250 singles ceased manufacture, and production of Interceptor frames was farmed out to Velocette. The company changed hands again in 1967, becoming part of the Norton Villiers group. Velocette now took over the spares operation, which they ran until they themselves closed in 1971.

Interceptors continued to be made throughout this period, although there was a gap between 1965 and 1967, when the model reappeared as the Series 1A. In 1968 the Series II

model was launched. Substantially different from the earlier machines, these had a Norton front end, redesigned engine, clutch and ignition. Powerful and generally reliable, they were offered in an American styling with high bars that made hard work of the high top speeds possible, while the outmoded gearbox was awkward to use.

Around 1000 engines had been made when Royal Enfield abruptly ceased trading, leaving these power units surplus to requirements. Several hundred were bought by the American Floyd Clymer, a publisher who had recently aquired the Indian name, intending to relaunch the marque. The Indian Enfield 750 was sold in America from 1969.

The remaining batch went to Rickman, who built a short run using their nickel-plated duplex frame with their own design of front fork, 10in disc brakes and fibreglass body parts. Styling was an odd mix of café racer and tourer with high-rise bars clamped to the fork stanchions. Despite their quality and an excellent performance, the bikes were hampered by a high price as well as reservations about the engine and, particularly, the gearbox. Sales were slow, and under 140 were built in two years. Despite that, their charm and rarity ensured that they rate as one of the true classics from the declining British industry, while the survival of the Enfield name was a timely reminder of a firm that had helped to bring about its birth.

Rickman Enfield Interceptor (1974)

Years in production: 1970-2 (some registered later)

Engine type: 360 degree parallel twin ohv four-stroke

Bore and stroke: 71 x 93mm

Capacity: 636cc

Compression ratio: 8.5:1

Power: 56bhp @ 6750rpm

Carburettors: twin Amal Concentrics

Tyres (front/rear): $4\frac{1}{8}$ x 18in/$4\frac{1}{8}$ x 18in

Weight: 365lb

Top speed: 120mph

Stylish and purposeful, the Rickman frame package included their own frame, forks and pioneering disc brakes, as well as fibreglass tank and bodywork. Refinished in red, the result is far more effective than the original models, which were finished in blue apart from side panels in white – seemingly an incomplete afterthought. One of the last batch made, this model was not registered until 1974.

Silk 700

In the mid 1970s the Silk gained a reputation for being one of the best-handling machines of the day – although its reliability and outright speed never attracted quite the same eulogies. It might have been unfair to expect any more, for the Silk, built by a small specialist engineering company based in Derbyshire, was a direct descendant of the venerable Scott two-stroke.

Company founder George Silk was a precision engineer who had trained with an ex-Scott employee and restorer, while his own father was active in the owners' club. He himself rode and tuned vintage Scotts in the 1960s, and when, at the end of the decade, he set up in business as a specialist engineer, Silk Engineering offered a repair and parts service for Scotts as a sideline. The services included a number of modifications aimed at providing increased reliability and power, improving both the bottom end, the lubrication and the gas flow.

The chief improvement, however, lay in a frame that offered modern technology in a concept much closer to Alfred Scott's original ideas than anything produced in the previous 30 years. The frame was a product of nearby Spondon Engineering, a relative newcomer to the world of specialist frame-building for racers. Spondon's frames for Japanese racing two-strokes were light, stiff and well triangulated, with modern suspension at both ends. They made their own forks and

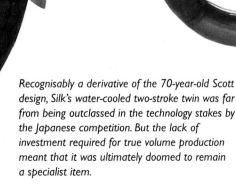

Recognisably a derivative of the 70-year-old Scott design, Silk's water-cooled two-stroke twin was far from being outclassed in the technology stakes by the Japanese competition. But the lack of investment required for true volume production meant that it was ultimately doomed to remain a specialist item.

brakes, too – and the whole package could easily be adapted to the engines that Silk was building.

The radiator was either a Scott-type or borrowed from an LE Velocette, and the final piece in this most British of jigsaws was the gearbox – based on the late Velocette four-speed design, modified to allow it to be a built in unit with the engine. The 20 Scott-based Silk Specials constructed by 1975 were just that – specials built as a blend of disparate components.

With assistance from some of Britain's foremost engineering specialists the Scott-based engine was substantially redesigned, with a patented scavenging system backed up by specially developed silencers, resulting in a smooth, powerful engine with good fuel economy. Other modern features, such as state-of-the-art electronic ignition, were designed in from the start.

Silk 700 (1978)

Years in production: 1975-79

Engine type: twin-cylinder water-cooled two-stroke

Bore and stroke: 76 x 72mm

Capacity: 653cc

Compression ratio: 8 5:1 (MkII)

Power: 54bhp @ 6000rpm (MkII)

Gearbox: four-speed

Weight: 309lb

The result of all this work was the Silk 700S – clearly derived from the previous Specials, but a proper production machine with parts manufactured by Silk or its suppliers. Although clearly a limited volume, hand built machine, it bristled with clever ideas and practical features such as rear chain enclosure. In a time when superbikes were becoming heavier and heavier, the most attractive feature of the 700S was its very absence of weight – less than many Japanese lightweights for the power output of a middleweight. Together with the excellent Spondon frame, this contributed to the superb handling and good acceleration.

Producing such a machine in small numbers was fraught with difficulties – not least financial – and Silk found the going hard at a time when most of the British industry was collapsing. There was no way in which the Silk could have attracted a mass market or financed volume production. Fewer than 150 were built.

Triumph T140 Bonneville

The Triumph Bonneville was nothing if not a survivor. Clearly based on Edward Turner's prewar concept, it continued to uphold the traditional values of the company while trying to adopt the modern conveniences that a new generation of riders demanded. And despite a number of obvious shortcomings, it continued to win friends and admirers throughout the superbike era.

The last of the long line of Triumph twins had an inauspicious beginning, when its launch was delayed by a whole series of design problems. It began in 650cc form when the current Bonneville engine gained a new frame in 1971. It was heavily based on the frame used for the BSA A65, sharing its oil-in-frame design, and had similar shortcomings as a result of an excessively high seat. There were also numerous teething troubles, but the bike was reasonably well received.

A year later the frame was lowered and there were a number of detail changes, including the introduction of a five-speed gearbox option. By now, 'mod-cons' such as indicators were the norm, but with its drum brakes and kick-start, the T120 Bonneville was years behind such competitors as the Honda 750 Four launched three years earlier. Vibration and oil consumption were also a problem, but the handling continued to set a standard that the Japanese competition could not match.

The first 750cc versions appeared the following year as the T140V. Essentially, this was a bored-out 650 and, apart from minor variations, it shared the smaller bike's cycle parts, which now included a new front disc brake. The first few models were 724cc, but this soon settled at 744cc with a slightly larger bore. More softly tuned than the 650, the engine was also strengthened, with more positive location for the head and an extra holding-down stud; the transmission was beefed up, and there were other detail changes.

The parallel twin's vibration was worse on the new model, and it was slow to gain acceptance, especially while the 650cc ran alongside it. Worse still, the Meriden factory's problems reached a head late in 1973, ultimately resulting in the workers' occupation. No new machines appeared until mid 1974, and those that did emerge showed evidence of hasty finishing. The following year matters improved as the workers' cooperative got underway and settled down to doing what they knew best. Existing machines were sold off to make way for a new model, with an engine that had been modified to suit the American market's insistence on a left-foot gearchange – a regulation that was introduced in 1974.

Triumph T140 Bonneville (1978)

Years in production: 1973-88

Engine type: twin-cylinder ohv four-stroke

Bore and stroke: 76 x 82mm

Capacity: 744cc

Compression ratio: 7.9:1

Power: 49bhp @ 6500rpm

Carburation: Two 30mm Amal Concentrics

Gearbox: five-speed

Tyres front/rear: $4\frac{1}{8}$ x 19in/$4\frac{1}{8}$ x 18in

Wheelbase: 55in

Weight: 395lb

Top speed: 111mph

Quality control proved a problem with antiquated machinery and limited funds, but by 1977 the factory was able to offer a limited-edition Jubilee model, to mark the Queen's Silver Jubilee. With a number of minor refinements introduced in 1978, the T140, as the model was now styled, had become a reasonably sound, if anachronistic, option.

The year 1979 brought the launch of the T140E – which had a new cylinder head and carburettors aimed at meeting new American emission laws – and the T140D, a custom special. Around 20,000 machines based on the new design were built before Triumph finally went to the wall. These included an 'executive' tourer, latterly including the first electric start model, an economy 650 version, a trail variant and finally the eight-valve TSS and custom TSX.

The Meriden cooperative went into liquidation in 1982. The assets were bought by John Bloor, although he assigned limited rights to build the Bonneville to Les Harris's Devon-based company. Harris built a limited number of Bonnies between 1985 and 1988, but although this spelt the end for the old twin, by then Bloor's own plans to write a new chapter in the Triumph story were well-advanced.

Old world charm for the new world: American specification features include high bars and traditional streamlined Triumph tank. The simple controls and instruments show little concession to the ergonomics which were starting to dominate design thinking in the 1970s – although they are efficient enough to operate for all that.

The traditional virtues of Triumph's 750cc twin included light weight, simplicity and good handling. But there were few concessions to the contemporary world of superbikes, with the exception of a front disc brake and flashing indicators. The engine was clearly heavily in debt to the 40-year-old Speed Twin, with 'modernisations' such as the left-foot, five-speed gearchange very much an afterthought.

Hesketh Vampire

By the late 1970s it was obvious to all that the British industry had been in terminal decline for a long time. So when it leaked out that someone was preparing to invest substantially in a completely new model, it was greeted with enthusiasm from many sides. If, for all its good points, the motorcycle that they got failed to live up to its promise, it came to be seen as just another symptom of the British malaise.

The man behind the machine was colourful character Lord Hesketh, a fully fledged baron with a substantial inheritance, which included an impressive estate in Northamptonshire. In 1973 Hesketh, then aged just 22, had run a Formula One car-racing team with impressive results, and in 1975 came fourth in the World Championship.

Financially, however, things were not going so well and in 1974 Hesketh decided to supplement his company's racing car engineering work by developing a motorcycle

Hesketh Vampire (1984)

Years in production: 1982-83

Engine type: four-valve 90 degree
   V-twin four-stroke

Bore and stroke: 95 x 70 mm

Capacity: 992cc

Compression ratio: 10.5:1

Carburettors: 36mm Amal MkII
   Concentric/Dell'Orto PHFs

Wheelbase: 59½in

Weight: 506lb (V1000) 544lb
   (Vampire)

Top speed: 120mph

Impressive instrumentation (right) included a clock and a gauge to show the ambient temperature. Hydraulic operation for the clutch was a Hesketh innovation.

that could capitalise on both their racing record and the kind of British handmade exclusivity that went with his lordship's name.

Several ideas were floated, including buying the near-defunct Norton factory or making frame kits for Japanese bikes. But motorcycle sales were enjoying a boom and outside the Japanese four-cylinder conformity, European twins were growing in popularity. In 1977 Hesketh began talks with engine specialists Weslake that would result in the development of the company's own 1000cc V-twin – a classically British type of engine that was proving to be a great success for Ducati.

Unfortunately the project soon ran into trouble, while behind the scenes finance was proving difficult. Many of the troubles centred on the conflicting demands of Hesketh's largely car-based team of designers with Weslake's own engineers. The engine was heavily based on Weslake's successful four-valve singles, widely used in speedway.

Heavy and tall, the Vampire was a last-ditch attempt to make a success out of the failed Hesketh V1000 by turning it into a tourer. But the fairing offered inadequate protection, and the bike still suffered from the basic engineering deficiencies caused by a lack of development. Few sold, and the company foundered for a second time in the early 1980s.

But restrictions on the design meant there had to be many compromises, particularly in the layout of the gearbox.

Although problems began surfacing fairly early on, an enthusiastic press launch went ahead in the spring of 1980. The bike that went on show was traditionally styled, with a small cockpit fairing and handsomely plated frame. Its layout was similar to the contemporary Ducati 90 degree 'L-twin', although its chunky looks were a world away from the lithe Italian. At over 500 lb, the chunky looks were backed up by the facts.

As no existing factory was able to take on quantity manufacture, Hesketh set up his own at Daventry. Experienced staff were hired, and the process of putting the V1000 into production began.

In 1981 the first went on press test, with the result that criticism of the clunky gearchange, engine noise, handling and price became public. Urgent revisions were put in hand, but it became clear that Hesketh was short of money. When the bikes went on sale in February 1982 it was a matter of too little, too late. Only 100 or so were sold before the company was wound up in August 1982.

The postscript was not long in following. Hesketh and partners had formed a new firm, whose small team would sell a package of modifications for the existing machines, at the same time developing a new fully-faired tourer, the Vampire. But the gearbox faults, which included a host of false neutrals, persisted, while the engine was noisy and the fairing restricted the turning circle without giving adequate protection. After a couple of years only a handful had been sold, and there were further lay-offs. While members of the enthusiastic team continued their own development work, it was the end for Hesketh himself and yet another last hope for the British industry.

The unfaired V1000 (left): the massive Hesketh engine – the cause of most of the troubles – was slung from a simple, plated tube frame. Problems included oil leaks from the chaincases to the overhead-camshafts, heavy vibration and a lumpy gearchange, despite a low state of tune.

Norton Wankel Rotary

Although it ended up wearing a Norton badge, the British rotary spent years being batted about between the various company groups that formed as the industry went into terminal decline. When it finally appeared, years after the concept first saw metal, some viewed it as little short of a miracle, while others were sceptical about the long-term potential of an engine type that was already being seen as something of a lost cause.

When Norton rotaries started to win races, some were overjoyed, while others enjoyed wrangling about the technicalities of the engine classification and whether it was competing fairly. Whatever else, the Norton rotary was a brave effort by a small and dedicated team that added an important chapter to the story of the British motorcycle.

The Wankel engine was invented by Germany's Dr Felix Wankel, who took a first patent on the principle in the late 1920s. It was not until the late 1950s that a workable prototype was developed by Wankel, then working at NSU. The engine was used in some NSU cars, notably the Ro80, and showed so much promise that manufacturers worldwide rushed to buy licences to build them.

The Wankel's apparent advantages were numerous: doing away with the dozens of moving parts of a conventional piston engine, and replacing them with a simple rotor around which the normal cycle of induction, compression, ignition and exhaust were continually taking place, offering incredible smoothness. Unfortunately it was not that simple, with early problems arising as a result of the complexity of sealing and lubricating the rotor.

Rotary-engined machines appeared throughout the 1970s, including motorcycles from Suzuki, Hercules/DKW, Van Veen Kriedler and a prototype Yamaha. Only the Suzuki RE5 was built in any quantity, and it proved too heavy and thirsty to become anything more than a curiosity. The only company to make much of a success of the concept was Mazda, notably with the RX7 sports car.

Among the experimenters was the BSA group, at that time a massive conglomerate with extensive R&D facilities.

The unconventional shape of Norton's air-cooled twin-rotor engine (above) harks back to a prototype developed by BSA as early as 1971. The concept originally developed by Dr Felix Wankel, working for NSU in Germany, offered smooth power with few moving parts. The practice was not so simple.

Using a proprietary German engine with a single rotor and fan cooling, an experimental machine was built in 1969. Having identified several problem areas, BSA built its own prototype in 1970, using an air-cooled twin-rotor layout, and a year later came up with an idea that greatly improved cooling efficiency.

As the decade wore on, BSA's increasing financial difficulties led to cutbacks that threatened the programme, but it was still alive as BSA was taken over by the Norton-Villiers-Triumph group. Prototypes were press tested in 1974, but a year later NVT collapsed.

The rotary project was salvaged from the collapse and given to a small but expert team based at Shenstone in Staffordshire. There they continued development on a tiny budget. Their work bore fruit in the early 1980s when several police forces and the armed forces took delivery of the Interpol II, with an engine clearly derived directly from the BSA prototype in a pressed-steel frame. The engine also found a new home as a power unit for ultralight aircraft.

There were several problems with the police bikes, although they showed obvious promise. It was not until 1987 that the company launched the limited edition unfaired Classic, designed to test the market. At the end of

Behind its fairing, the Commander concealed a liquid-cooled version of the twin-rotor engine developing 85 bhp, good enough to propel the tourer to around 125mph. The panniers were initially integral with the bodywork. The brakes, like the front wheel, were culled from the XJ900 Yamaha, and helped to slow a heavy machine that possessed minimal engine braking, like a two-stroke.

Norton Wankel Rotary (1987)

Years in production: 1987 (Classic)

Engine type: twin-rotor air-cooled rotary

Capacity: 588cc

Compression ratio: 7.5:1

Power: 79bhp @ 9000rpm

Carburettor: 1½in constant vacuum

Tyres (front/rear): 100/90 V18/ 120/80 V18

Wheelbase: 58½in

Weight: 498lb

Top speed: 120mph

Classic Norton: the unfaired silver machine with red and black coachlining was deliberately designed to recall traditional values. Based on the company's police bikes, the Classic was produced as a limited edition, complete with authentication certificate, as a means of testing the civilian market.

the year, the fully-equipped Commander, with a liquid-cooled version of the engine, was launched to many plaudits, despite its premium price and rather high fuel consumption.

A prototype racer was also under development, and when this finally took to the track it showed enormous potential, although there was a dispute as to whether its unconventional engine should be classified as a 588cc, as Norton claimed, or much more. Eventually the governing bodies settled on a formula that enabled it to compete as a 1000cc machine. By the end of the decade, with new sponsors JPS, the Nortons had won the British Formula One and Shell Supercup, and the Norton name was seen on a TT leaderboard for the first time since 1973.

From then on the Norton story became a bitter tale of dedicated engineers continuing to produce a trickle of motorcycles, against a bewildering backdrop of corporate manoeuvring through a dire financial morass. But it may be premature to draw a line under the Norton story; after one hundred years in production, it is perhaps to be hoped that the firm may see its rebirth as a major force in the same way as Triumph.

Triumph Trident

Triumph Trident (1995)

Engine type: liquid-cooled double overhead-cam in-line three-cylinder four-stroke

Bore and stroke: 76 x 65mm

Capacity: 885cc

Compression ratio: 10.6:1

Power: 98bhp @ 9000rpm

Carburettors: 3x36mm flat slide constant vacuum

Tyres (front/rear): 120/70 ZR17/ 180/55 ZR17

Wheelbase: 58½in

The reborn, modern Triumph is a machine that can hold its head up with the best in the world. The marque that proved Britain could still produce a world-class motorcycle manufacturer after so many 'new British world-beaters' had foundered, Triumph has prospered by adopting the design traditions of the very Japanese machines that had helped to kill off the British bike. As far as most of the world was concerned, Triumph had come to an end with the collapse of the Meriden cooperative in 1981, although there had been an attempt to keep the Bonneville going beyond the death of the parent factory. But there were those who believed that the Triumph name still had something going for it – not least its thousands of devoted owners and enthusiasts. It was these people that the new owner of the Triumph name was counting on, when, out of the rubble of the old factory,

In its basic, unfaired touring form the Trident demonstrates the essence of the Hinckley Triumph concept. Recognisably modern and owing much to the Japanese tradition, the three-cylinder engine is in a class of its own, while the simple spine frame and suspension are adequate to the task without being over sophisticated.

The rider's eye view (left) revels how Triumph adopted the modern idiom with instruments and controls to rival those of its competitors.

a new company suddenly emerged at the end of the 1980s.

The owner was John Bloor. A large-scale property developer, he had amassed a considerable personal wealth by the time the old Triumph site was offered for sale. Together with the land, it turned out that the Triumph name and rights were also part of the package, a package that made Bloor the owner of the Triumph heritage.

What followed was a long period of secrecy, speculation and rumour. Finally, in 1988, the rumours were laid to rest when Bloor's company began building a new factory on a site at Hinckley, Leicestershire, where it was revealed a new range of Triumphs was to be built.

Secrecy still prevailed, however, perhaps because so much damage had been done to past revivals such as Hesketh and Norton by premature launches and too much speculation. The facts that did emerge made it clear that there was no connection other than name between Bloor's Triumph and the old Meriden company. Staff, machinery, designs and components were completely new.

The factory was completed in 1990 and the first machines were seen later that year at the German motorcycle show in Cologne – significantly the homeland of BMW rather than the old British industry, and an important international showcase. The first machine was the unfaired, touring Trident – its name and choice of three-cylinder engine being an important link with the old Triumph heritage. Production built up slowly but steadily from the first full year in 1992, with more models added on a gradual basis.

Triumph T595 Daytona

As the millenium approached, it was becoming clear what class of bike would rule the roost in the late 1990s. Sports bikes, as epitomised by Ducati's stylish 916 and Honda's hi-tech Fireblade, were the the machines that grabbed the headlines. For a new manufacturer like Triumph to compete at this level, a machine was needed that was both distinctively different and able to deliver the goods – no small undertaking for such a new company.

The solution was the T595 Daytona, which rapidly established itself as a bike with the capability to beat the best on the track as well as being a supremely usable street machine. Based on Triumph's trademark triple engine, it was in fact an all-new 955cc design with a double-overhead cam, and liquid-cooled power unit developed in association with the Lotus car race engineers. The object of the exercise was to optimise porting, valve and combustion chamber shapes,

improving breathing. Stronger components ensured reliability at higher engine speeds and outputs, while new materials for non-stress-bearing components saved weight.

The engine management system, claimed to be the most complex and smartest ever fitted to a motorcycle, controlled the fuel injection and air induction, and could easily be adjusted to suit legislation in various markets, simply by replacing a tuning card. The full-power version gave 128bhp at 10,200rpm, with a massive 74 ft lb of torque peaking at 8,500rpm.

Matching the new engine was a new twin-spar perimeter frame that offered a radical departure from Triumph's successful spine concept, as well as an improvement on the competitors' offerings. Fabricated from aluminium extrusions and built-up sections, the frame used the engine as a stressed member to keep the weight down.

With a single-sided swinging arm and Japanese Showa suspension front and rear, handling was impeccable, while wheels, tyres and brakes were to the highest specification.

Versatility was one of the objectives of the design, which was aimed at providing the ultimate street bike as well as offering race-winning potential. The tucked-in silencer could easily be replaced with a full race component, while the sophisticated frame and forks were well up to the 160mph-plus potential of the stock machine.

Trumph also offered a stripped version of the same machine, the T509 Speed Triple, which allied a slightly lower performance to the fashionable 'street-fighter' look. Together, both machines demonstrated the technical capabilities of the new Triumph factory and showed that the British industry had fully shaken off its past problems to face a new era of motorcycling.

The slimline fairing with twin headlamps (above) offers the height of contemporary styling but conceals the hi-tech aluminium frame, the twin spars of which snake over the top of the three-cylinder power unit.

The distinctive three-spoke alloy wheels were designed by Triumph and produced in Italy aspecially for this model. The brakes, sourced in Japan, use four piston calipers with floating discs. The tucked-in silencer, designed to take advantage of the single-sided rear suspension, can be replaced with a racing unit.

Triumph T595 Daytona (1997)

Years in production: 1996–

Engine type: double overhead-cam four-stroke four-valve in-line triple

Capacity: 955cc

Bore and stroke: 79x65mm

Compression ratio: 11.2:1

Fuel system: Sagem fuel injection

Power: 128bhp @ 10,200rpm

Transmission: six-speed gearbox

Top speed: 161mph

Triumph Thunderbird

Although factory founder John Bloor had ridden a motorcycle in his youth, he was far from the mould of some of the many passionate enthusiasts who had tried to revive the British industry in the 1970s. As a hard-headed and successful businessman, he knew the value of brand loyalty and recognised the potential asset represented by such a well-respected name as Triumph.

Although the Triumph logo itself had been subtly redesigned, it was recognisably the same as the one that had graced the best-loved models in the company's history. Similarly, there were echoes of the old Triumph in the choice of a basic three-cylinder engine, and in the choice of the model names. With the average Hinckley Triumph buyer approaching 40 years of age, such historic resonances might be expected to strike a chord.

Triumph Thunderbird (1995)

Engine type: liquid-cooled double overhead-cam in-line three-cylinder four-stroke

Bore and stroke: 76 x 65mm

Capacity: 885cc

Compression ratio: 10.6:1

Power: 70bhp @ 8000rpm

Carburettors: 3 x 36mm flat slide constant vacuum

Tyres (front/rear): 110/80 18/160/80 16

Wheelbase: 58½in

With a tank, seat and mudguards which deliberately echo the styling of twins from Triumph's heyday, the Thunderbird proved an instant hit. The new model appealed to lovers of the British tradition while offering the sophistication that many new riders considered essential.

Nowhere was the sense of heritage stronger than with the new Thunderbird. Again, the model name was borrowed from the past, but this time, so was the styling. Happily for Triumph, a significant niche had opened in the market for machines that echoed the look and simplicity of older models, while offering the sophistication and reliability of new ones – an area that was already proving profitable for Japanese factories.

Triumph had a significant advantage in their choice of frame design. Although older in concept and inherently taller than the aluminum beam frames of contemporary fashion, the tubular spine frame was much simpler to construct or modify, while proving more than adequate to the task. Thus the Thunderbird acquired a tank and seat that were recognisably derived from the twins of the 1950s and 60s, old style mudguards and an engine that retained the modern features of the other models, including liquid-cooling – but was cleverly redesigned to look like its air-cooled forebears.

With power delivery to match the best of the competition, build quality intended to match BMW's and considerable development potential, Triumph's rebirth has almost single-handedly confounded the critics and proved that the British motorcycle has a future as well as a past. And with the 'retro' styling of its revived Thunderbird, Triumph has brought the British tradition full circle – even if, for some, it is a pastiche that flies in the face of everything the original stood for.

Manufacturers' badges from 1960 to present day

THE HISTORY OF
BRITISH
CARS

Foreword

It was Herbert Austin who said 'I make motor cars for the man in the street'. He was referring, of course, at the time to the Austin Seven. Motoring and the motor car have changed so much in the last 115 years, as initially, only the wealthy could afford a car. A little unfairly, the automobile has often been referred to as the plaything of the rich.

The 1920s and 1930s, brought motoring within the reach of more people and in the process, changed the landscape. It produced bigger and better roads, roadside garages and cafes, and above all a change in the architecture of the urban landscape. There was ribbon development and the arrival of the integral garage which was to change the shape of all houses. Now, a high proportion of the population either own a car or have access to one.

One of the most difficult jobs for a curator or director of a motor museum, is the choice of vehicles to put on display to the visitor. Certainly at Beaulieu we are continually refining the collection, rather than adding to it, as space is always at a premium. I had a similar dilemma when selecting cars to feature in this book. In choosing cars from the earliest to the latest, I ultimately opted for the more popular models; I was determined, however, to be a little unpredictable so you will find examples of the obscure and some of the less well-designed.

Probably the most difficult selection was vehicles to appear in the modern classic section. When choosing vehicles for the National Motor Museum's collection, we like at least twenty years of hindsight!

Michael E. Ware
Director, National Motor Museum, Beaulieu, England

1903 Wolseley Horizontal Twin

1993 McLaren F1

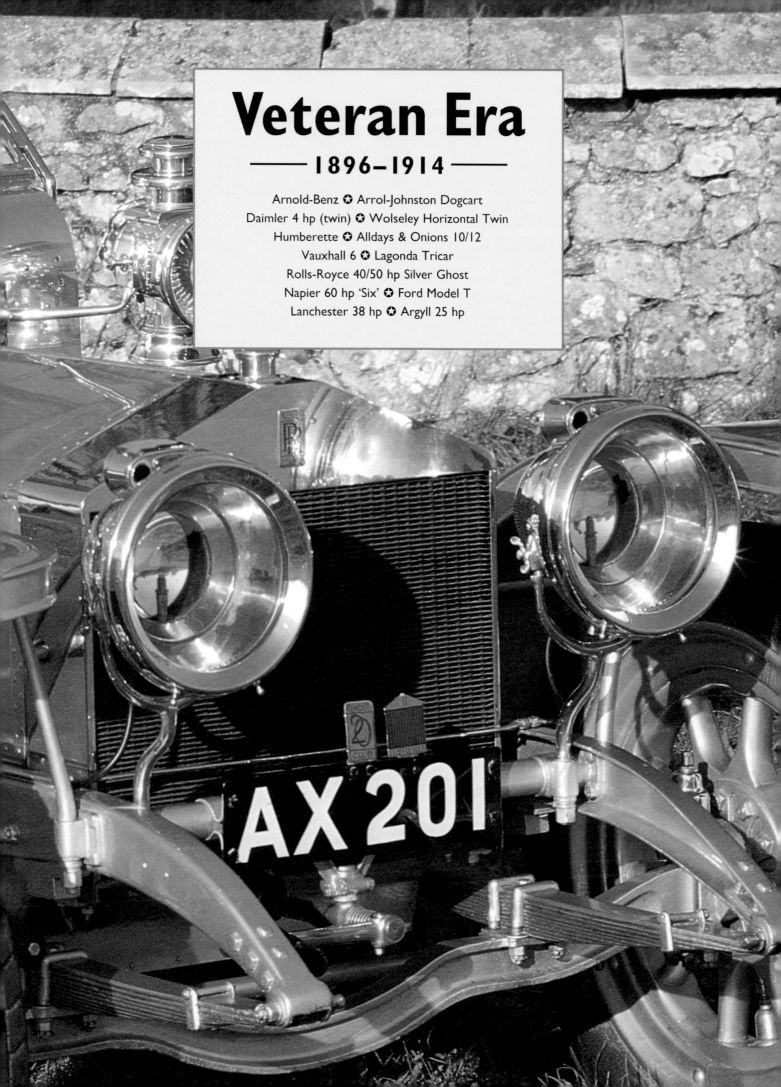

Veteran Era

—1896–1914—

Arnold-Benz ✪ Arrol-Johnston Dogcart
Daimler 4 hp (twin) ✪ Wolseley Horizontal Twin
Humberette ✪ Alldays & Onions 10/12
Vauxhall 6 ✪ Lagonda Tricar
Rolls-Royce 40/50 hp Silver Ghost
Napier 60 hp 'Six' ✪ Ford Model T
Lanchester 38 hp ✪ Argyll 25 hp

Veteran Era

Although a number of British motor cars can be counted among the 'greats' of the 20th century, Great Britain was not actually a motoring pioneer. The world's first cars were built in Germany, where Nicolaus Otto designed the first practical petrol-driven engine, and where Benz and Daimler made the first practical 'horse-less carriages'. It was in France, however, that a fledgling motor industry was first founded. Panhard & Levassor and Peugeot were soon joined by De Dion Bouton, after which expansion was swift. Both France and Germany were well ahead of Britain, and although the Americans started late, they soon overwhelmed everyone with their low-cost/mass-production expertise.

Although steam-driven monstrosities had been tried on British roads in the early part of the nineteenth century, horse-drawn machinery (particularly the personal carriage, and the stagecoach) was not easy to dislodge. Petrol-driven cars were not really established until the late 1890s. This was not through lack of interest from forward-looking individuals, but because of official legal obstruction to such machinery, which were classified as 'light locomotives'

according to legislation passed in 1865 and 1878. At that point, all such vehicles were limited to speeds of two mph in towns, and to four mph in the countryside, and had to be attended by three persons. Originally, an attendant walking ahead of the 'locomotive' was obliged to carry a red flag as a warning to nervous horse owners, but this requirement was dropped in 1878.

Society was slow to embrace the technological advances heralded by the motor car, partly because the vested interest of much of the Establishment rested either in railway travel or in the huge industry surrounding horse-drawn transport – farriers, ostlers, breeders, traders and carriage makers. It was only after spirited lobbying and ridicule from the first few motorists who had imported cars from Germany or France, that the 'Locomotives on Highways', or 'Emancipation Act' came into force in 1896, which freed vehicles under 1.5 tons (1,524 kg) of all restrictions, and permitted them to travel at speeds up to a sensational 12 mph. The original London-Brighton run of November 1896 was held to celebrate this great achievement.

Right: At the turn of the century, cars were expensive and invariably driven by the rich – as the size of the houses in the background of this 1899 photograph of the Holloway brothers (front) and passenger Warwick Wright (back) in their Daimler 4 hp Twin confirms.

Opposite page: The Emancipation Run. Walter Arnold driving one of his Arnold cars from London to Brighton, in November 1896, was celebrating the increase of highway speed limits to 12 mph.

That speed limit, incidentally, would rise to 20 mph in 1903 (a speed which few cars could then achieve, never mind exceed). The speed limit was not changed, however, until 1930, by which time it was being widely ignored, in spite of ruthless policing (by speed trap) from local police forces.

BRITISH PIONEERS

While European cars dominated the market of the 1890s, one or two British inventors had worked to produce prototypes. Bremer's four-wheeler of 1894 was an unconvincing pram-like affair which never achieved reliability (or even went on sale), while the Knight (originally a three-wheeler) and the Petter of 1895 were more practical.

By 1896 in Birmingham the Lanchester brothers and Herbert Austin (for Wolseley) had both built commendably advanced prototypes, while Walter Arnold had built a dozen or so Benz machines, but Britain's first series-production motor car was the Daimler, which went on sale later in that year. Assembled at a converted cotton mill in Coventry, in a business run by company promoter Harry Lawson (who later went to jail for a variety of financial frauds), this was a surprisingly good car to emerge from a very shadily-financed concern. At first no more than an accurate license-built copy of the latest German Daimler models, this car gradually evolved, and from the early 1900s would not only be independent, but would have an altogether more respectable background.

Over the next few years there was a rush to mechanise Great Britain, first with motor cycles, then tricycles, and eventually with four-wheeler cars. Attend any old-machine event today, and you will see Rover and Singer cycles, Triumph motor cycles and Lagonda tricars, all of which confirm these trends.

By the mid-1900s British cars were not yet available in abundance, but they had become surprisingly reliable. Daimler and Lanchester had been joined by Rolls-Royce, Napier, Riley, Rover, Humber, Sunbeam and other more ephemeral makes, though at this stage all cars were essentially hand-built, hand-crafted, and expensive. In the early years of the century, cars in Britain were invariably owned by rich men with large houses or country estates; they garaged their new automobiles in motor houses once used to stable the horses and their carriages, and employed driver/mechanics (chauffeurs) to drive them around. Price was considered less important than style, presence and dependability – and since almost every car was faster than a trotting horse, a lack of performance was not critical at first. This not only explains why it took years for cheap and simple cars to be developed, but also why there was a sudden plethora of magnificent marques from which to choose. In the early years of the century Napier led, Daimler struggled valiantly to follow, and Rolls-Royce almost immediately joined in.

The first Napiers, from a long-established London company, were big, fast, impressive, and soon had an enviable motor racing reputation. Through their principal engineer/manager, S.F. Edge, they were always placed at the cutting edge of publicity, especially when they became the first to use a six-cylinder engine.

Daimler, unwilling to join such a competitive battle for motor racing supremacy, went for high style and elegant furnishings, along with high-tech engineering instead, and introduced a sophisticated series of double sleeve-valved engines from 1909. By this time they had also secured royal patronage, and therefore became the make of car which typified the gentry who bought them. Who needed advertising, when the list of owners included royal highnesses, dukes, earls and their descendants?

This, therefore, is the right moment to introduce Rolls-Royce, a company which started quietly in a back street of Manchester, but blossomed in 1906 after the introduction of the immortal 40/50 hp Silver Ghost, and shortly moved to a new factory in Derby. With this single model (there would be no other until the early 1920s), Henry Royce established a legend, and although it took decades for British royalty to take Rolls-Royce to their hearts, by 1914 they were recognised as the 'Best Cars in the World' – a phrase which the company itself was always happy to use in its promotional material.

By 1910, in fact, the British motor industry was well established, for not only had Lanchester and Rover started building sturdy, middle class machinery, but they had been joined by marques like Sunbeam of Wolverhampton (the noted engineer Louis Coatalen joined them from Hillman in 1909), and Talbot, which was already building cars in London's North Kensington. Cars were also being built north of the Border, in Scotland: by Argyll (whose new factory at Alexandria, near Loch Lomond, was a positive palace by previous standards) and Arrol-Johnston, which built cars in Paisley from 1906, but then moved, with great enterprise, to Dumfries in 1913.

Production of British cars built up steadily at this time, but it was clear to every tycoon that prices would have to be driven down considerably before Britain's burgeoning middle classes could join in the fun. One type of car which was still virtually unknown, not only here but in Europe, was the sports car. Cynics might say that because of their mechanical fragility and their character, every early car was a sports car, but this ignores the fact that sports cars should have two seats, open-top styling, and sparkling performance. Vauxhall's very rare 'Prince Henry', and one or two highly-priced Napiers qualified, but there would be none in numbers until the 1920s.

BIG HITTERS

None of Britain's 'big six' – the car makers whose cars flooded our roads from the 1930s to the 1960s – were among the pioneers, though once established, all of them soon took up dominant positions. Standard of Coventry was set up first in 1903 with a modest single-cylinder-engined machine, but would not become major producers until the 1920s.

Vauxhall, originally at Lambeth, in London, was founded in the same year, and made 76 cars in 1904, but made no real progress until the business relocated to Luton in 1905. Only a few years later, under a charismatic new chief engineer, L.H. Pomeroy (Senior), their sports cars and racing cars were among the best: true fame and serious production would come in the 1920s, not only because of the excellence of the 30/98 sports car, but because of Vauxhall's take-over by General Motors of the USA.

Opposite page: The chauffeur, clad in driving uniform complete with goggles, allows the proud owner to pose behind the wheel of his new Austin in this 1907 photograph taken outside Belvoir House in Fareham, Hampshire, while family and friends admire the car.

Left: This 1902 10 hp Wolseley was designed by Herbert Austin who later went on to start his own company in 1906. The Austin name was to play a significant part in British car manufacturing throughout the 20th century.

Austin, too, started modestly in 1906, though their founder, Herbert Austin, was already noted for his design work at Wolseley. Solidly established by 1914, huge expansion followed in the 1920s.

Hillman was set up in Coventry by William Hillman in 1907, but although this company built solid, middle class cars until the 1920s, it was not until they were forced into a merger with their next-door neighbour Humber in 1928 (both later being subsumed into the Rootes Group) that the size of the company began to matter.

The two biggest hitters of all – Ford and Morris – did not even get started in England until just before the First World War. Ford, of course, was an American firm, which had been in business since the end of the previous century, but true quantity production did not begin until the now-legendary Model T was announced in 1908. Henry Ford was finally persuaded to set up an assembly operation, for Model Ts, at a factory in Trafford Park, Manchester. As expected, he did nothing by halves, and this facility soon out-shone anything so far achieved by British nationals.

Although the Model T was incredibly cheap, and sold fast in the UK, its potential was always hampered by the annual car licence fee exacted on British cars, which favoured small-engined cars with tiny piston area: the 2.9-litre Model T had neither, and suffered. Even so, until the Bullnose Morris hit the market in numbers, the T was Britain's best-selling car.

Morris, which started production in 1913, was the last of the 'big six' to start work, and made little impact in this period. William Morris began in tiny premises with what is called an 'assembled car' (where the parent factory built almost nothing of its own, but merely screwed together components supplied by outside specialists), and very few facilities. Although Morris became Britain's best-selling car-maker in the mid 1920s, only 1,300 Morrises were produced in 1913, all of them Bullnose Oxfords, and the company's original market share was a mere 3.8 per cent.

By 1914, when the motor car had still only been legally approved for use on British roads for 18 years, annual production had risen to at least 34,000 cars. Until the late 1900s, horses and their carriages still outnumbered cars on British roads (particularly outside major towns and cities), but after that the motor car took precedence. The last pre-war British Motor Show was held at London's Olympia in 1913, when no fewer than 211 makes (from ten countries) were listed in *The Autocar's Buyers' Guide*. By the time the outbreak of war put paid to private car production in 1914, more than 130,000 cars (almost all British) were already on the roads, which themselves had changed immeasurably in just two decades.

But if such figures sounded impressive, what followed in the 1920s and 1930s would dwarf them all. At the turn of the century, motoring had been strictly for the rich, and by 1914 it was for the merely 'well-to-do'. By 1930 'motoring for the masses' would have arrived.

1896 Arnold-Benz

Britain's motor industry did not exist in 1894, not only because the motor car itself was new and rare, but because British legislation still discouraged its use. It was not until pioneers like Walter Arnold & Sons (of Kent) took the plunge that any sort of domestic manufacture took place.

In 1894 Walter Arnold imported a 1.5-litre Benz from Germany, believing that the climate for motoring must soon change, and that there was a market for the new-fangled 'horse-less carriages' in the UK. He agreed with Benz to produce a British version of the car. The first customer car was sold before the 1896 Act 'liberated' the British car, almost certainly making the Arnold-Benz the first 'British' car to go on sale.

Over in Germany, Benz was in direct competition with Daimler, whose UK branch in Coventry produced the first British-built Daimler cars from 1896. Unlike in Germany, however, the Benz-based cars did not prosper, and only a dozen machines were built and sold before Arnold abandoned its enterprise. This was not the end of the Arnold company, however, as a descendant of the concern exists in the UK today.

The very first Arnold car (an amalgam of British and German components and engineering), known as 'Adam', actually took part in the London-Brighton 'Emancipation Run' in November 1896, and is today on show in the National Motor Museum at Beaulieu. Like the Benz cars of the day, the Arnold was built around a wooden chassis frame, which was strengthened with iron flitch plates. The engine itself was an oversquare single-cylinder unit, with an atmospheric inlet valve (which opened when the cast iron piston sucked in the mixture on its induction stroke), and a gravity-fed surface carburettor.

The engine was located under the high mounted seats, driving the rear wheels through a two-speed 'fast and loose' pulley clutch, with final drive from the transmission cross-shaft by exposed chain (which had to be lubricated at least once every day). To start the engine, the flywheel was rotated by the chauffeur's gloved hand.

Like the running gear, the rest of the design was crude, with spindly wire-spoke wheels (those at the rear being much larger than the front), external-contracting brake bands at the rear, and a spoon brake on the solid rear tyre. A driver could count himself lucky if he completed a 30-mile journey (at 30 mpg fuel economy) without a breakdown of some sort. This, though, was pioneer British motoring, without which the motor car could never have progressed.

Arnold-Benz

Years in production: 1896–98
Structure: Mid/rear engine/rear-drive. Separate wooden chassis
Engine type: 1-cylinder, automatic inlet, side exhaust valve
Bore and stroke: 123.8 x 111.1 mm
Capacity: 1,190 cc
Power: 1.5 bhp @ 65 rpm
Fuel supply: Gravity fed surface carburettor
Suspension: Beam-axle front, beam-axle rear
Top speed: 16 mph

Below: Steering in the Arnold-Benz pistoned engine was by a vertical steering column and a twin open rack. Ten mph felt perilously fast in this machine, where the occupants sat up high, and totally exposed to the elements.

1898 Arrol-Johnston Dogcart

Arrol-Johnston was one of the most famous early makes of car in Scotland, and was introduced at a time when the fledgling industry looked like being an important part of Scotland's industrial fabric. This early promise soon faded, for no cars were made north of the Border after the 1920s until Rootes set up a new plant in the 1960s to manufacture Hillman Imps.

The Arrol-Johnston marque was founded very early in the life of the British motor industry, in 1897, when Sir William Arrol (the noted civil engineer) and George Johnston got together to develop the original 'Dogcart' model, which went into production in a factory at Camlachie, an industrial area of Glasgow. The city was not short of industrial skills, of course, but in the

Victorian era they had been applied mainly to heavy industries, such as shipbuilding.

A 'dogcart' was a particularly compact style of horse-drawn carriage, where two rows of seats were placed back-to-back. The carriage was so small and light that, on a private estate at least, it could be drawn by a pony or a large dog! Like many 'horseless carriages', the pioneering Arrol-Johnston's style was lifted from the earlier era, though in this case the solid-tyred wheels were altogether larger, and the flat-twin opposed-piston engine was positioned under the floor, driving the rear wheels by chain.

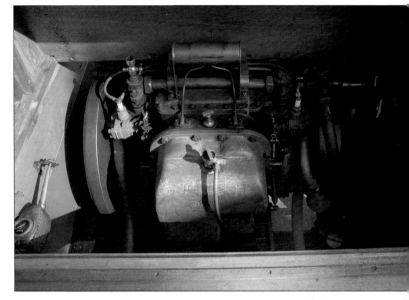

Above: The flat-twin pistoned engine was positioned under the floor, driving the rear wheels by chain, but its performance was limited.

Although the performance was distinctly limited (and, even then, it was beginning to look old-fashioned), this was such a strong, reliable, popular and practical layout that it was produced, with only minor changes, until 1907, by which time a more modern front-engined 12/15 model had appeared.

The brakes were arranged in the form of shoes which could be pressed on the back of the solid rear tyres – not very effective in dry weather, and virtually useless when it was raining. The suspension, on the other hand, was relatively comfortable, for there were full elliptic leaf springs at the front, and half-elliptics at the rear. Transmission and brake control levers were mounted close to the driver's right hand, and some cars were fitted with magnificent bulb horns.

Arrol-Johnston Dogcart

Years in production: 1898–1907
Structure: Mid engine/rear-drive
   Separate chassis
Engine type: Flat-2 cylinder,
   side-valve
Bore and stroke: 100 x 86.4 mm
Capacity: 3,230 cc
Power: 10 bhp @ unstated rpm
Fuel supply: One carburettor
Suspension: Beam-axle front,
   beam-axle rear
Weight: 2,350 lb
Top speed: 25 mph

Left and right: The Dogcart's layout owed as much to the past, as to the future – the large wheels were constructed from wood, there was no weather protection for the passengers, and the brakes were virtually non-existent.

This was a good foundation for the marque, which prospered into the 1910s and 1920s but, like many other companies, suffered badly from the arrival of cheaper, series-production machinery made in the Midlands. In spite of a move to Dumfries in 1913, and a merger with Aster (of Wembley, Middlesex) in 1927, the pedigree fell away, the last of all being produced in 1931.

1899 Daimler 12 hp

Although Daimler, of Coventry, was one of the very first British manufacturers to make and sell motor cars in any numbers, for the first few years it had to rely on license-built designs from the Daimler company of Germany. Even so, starting from premises in a converted textile mill, it soon built up its business, and began producing all-British models in the early 1900s.

The original Daimler, started life as the invention of Gottlieb Daimler, of Cannstatt, whose pioneering 'horseless carriage' had gone on the road in 1886. After producing internal combustion engines for sale to other concerns, Daimler began building cars in 1896. A licence to build these twin-cylinder engined cars in Britain was taken out by one Harry Lawson, a vigorous promoter of car businesses, whose intention seems to have been to corner the market. Using fair means and foul, he failed in this, and spent time in jail as a result, but the Daimler marque prospered.

Looking back with a century's hindsight, one could say that the first Daimlers were almost impossibly crude and spidery in the extreme, but we must also remember that they were among the first reliable machines which did not require horses, oxen or human power to move them down the roads. Without previous experience on which to draw, these 'horseless carriages' were just that – developments of carriages which might once have been pulled by horses, but now had a petrol engine mounted underneath the frame instead.

With a top speed of no more than 15-20 mph, and a cruising speed (if anything so chancy or restless can be described in this way) of no more than 10 mph, features such as suspension

and braking could be virtually ignored, handling meant nothing, and it was the fight for reliability which was paramount. The 12 hp model which followed in 1899 was altogether more sophisticated, for it had a more powerful four-cylinder engine in the nose. Described by *The Motor Car Journal* as 'the most up-to-date carriage built in this country', in

Daimler 12 hp

Years in production: 1899–1903
Structure: Front-engine/rear-drive. Separate chassis
Engine type: 4-cylinder, automatic inlet valve
Bore and stroke: 90 x 120 mm
Capacity: 3,054 cc
Power: 12 bhp @ unspecified rpm
Fuel supply: Spray-type carburettor
Suspension: Beam-axle front, beam-axle rear
Weight: Not quoted
Top speed: 25 mph (approx.)

July 1899 the Hon. John Scott-Montagu's car (which is illustrated) was the first-ever petrol-engined vehicle to enter the precincts of the Houses of Parliament.

Like many cars of its day, this machine has a front-mounted engine, a gearbox under the seats, and final drive to the rear wheels was by chain. Although pneumatic tyres were fitted to the front wheels, early examples had solid rear tyres.

Although the styling of late-Victorian cars differs completely from those of today, their mechanical layout was already edging towards what became an industry standard for many decades to come.

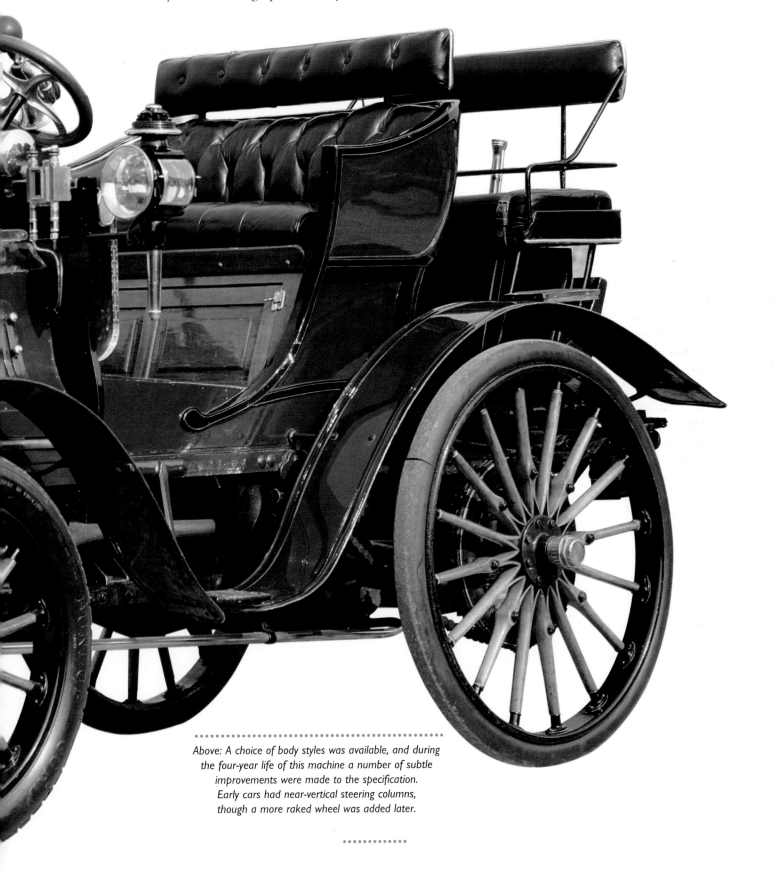

Above: A choice of body styles was available, and during the four-year life of this machine a number of subtle improvements were made to the specification. Early cars had near-vertical steering columns, though a more raked wheel was added later.

1903 Wolseley Horizontal Twin

The Wolseleys of 1900–1905, which were actually designed by Herbert Austin (who would later found his own car-making concern), were the first wholly British cars to be mass-produced. (Earlier cars like the Victorian Daimlers were inspired by Daimler-Benz cars from Germany). Prototype Wolseleys were the pioneering tricars of 1896 and 1898, and the first four-wheeler voiturette followed in 1899. Examples of the four-wheeler competed successfully in the Automobile Club's 1000 Miles trial of 1900, after which series production began in Birmingham.

The first Wolseley actually to go on sale was a single-cylinder model, which was speedily followed by others: twins and horizontally-aligned flat-four cylinder types, all with similar cylinder dimensions and valve gear details, and the same simple type of chassis and transmission.

Although the engines were physically large, they were not, of course, very powerful. They were located under the front of the chassis, ahead and under the toe-board, with cooling radiators and accessories above them, and a chain-driven final drive to the rear axle, which, with the exception of the French Système Panhard was the accepted layout of the period.

Cylinder heads pointed forwards, towards the nose of the car, which helped to keep them cool. The first twin-cylinder Wolseley arrived in 1901, and was effectively a doubling up of the original single-cylinder power unit, eventually pushing out a creditable 12 bhp. The early cars used an 'automatic' or 'atmospheric' inlet valve in their engines, which was opened by suction when the cylinder drew in fuel/air mixture, and which was forced back on to its seat by compression and combustion. This was inefficient, and was supplanted by a mechanically-operated inlet valve on later types. The transmission was complex – a Renolds chain drove from the clutch to a separate mid-mounted transmission, then through a four-speed gearbox, with twin chain drives to the rear wheels from the mid-mounted gearbox counter shaft, all the chains requiring regular (daily, ideally) attention and oiling.

The development of these cars came to an abrupt end in 1905, when Wolseley's directors wanted to see new vertical engine models introduced. Herbert Austin refused to carry out their wishes and therefore walked out, but this might just have been a good excuse, as the original Austin-badged cars, which followed within a year, had vertical engines.

The last horizontal-engined Wolseley was built in 1906, and a series of more conventional, Siddeley-inspired cars succeeded them.

Wolseley Horizontal Twin

Years in production: 1901–05
Structure: Front engine/rear-drive
  Separate chassis
Engine type: Flat 2-cylinder,
  over-head inlet-valve/side-
  exhaust valve
Bore and stroke: 114.3 x 127 mm
Capacity: 2,606 cc
Power: 10 bhp @ 700 rpm
Fuel supply: One Wolseley
  carburettor
Suspension: Beam-axle front,
  beam-axle rear
Weight: 2,130 lb
Top speed: 20 mph

Left: No fewer than 327 of all types were sold in 1901, rising to 800 in 1903. At the time this made Wolseley the most prolific of all British makes, a lead which it retained until the outbreak of the First World War a decade later.

1903 Humberette

If you are a lover of Classic (rather than Veteran) cars, you probably remember a Humber as a large, ponderous but well equipped member of the Rootes Group. If you are a vintage enthusiast, you will no doubt remember the famous 8/18s, 12/25s and 14/40s of the 1920s. But this is to forget the origins of Humber, which are in the 1890s, in Beeston, Nottingham.

Humber (like many other marques) evolved from a company which had originally made pedal cycles (for Nottingham had a thriving bicycle industry for much of the century). Although Beeston originally dabbled with the abortive Pennington car project, the first engine-driven, Humber-badged, machines from Beeston were motor tricycles and quadricycles, followed by tricars. The first cars had two- or four-cylinder engines, but they were succeeded by the tiny single-cylinder-engined Humberette (literally, 'small Humber'), a sturdy and well made machine with only a little power, yet the miracle was that it could carry a useful payload.

By comparison with previous Humbers, this was an ambitious project, for it featured a De Dion style of front-mounted water-cooled engine, with a leather-covered cone clutch, a two-speed gearbox controlled by levers under the steering wheel, as well as drive shaft to the rear wheels – the last being a real novelty in the early 1900s. The steering wheel, by the way, had only a single spoke, a characteristic of early Humbers, and quite 50 years ahead of the time when Citroen 're-invented' it. Braking, always a chancy business on cars of this period, was by externally contracting elements which were exposed to the weather. Even so, it was well made and (like other Beeston-Humbers) it was more substantially built and more expensive than equivalent cars from Humber's Coventry factory.

The original Humberette, while respected, was soon seen to be under-powered, so within a year the engine had been enlarged to 762 cc from 611 cc, though few cars were sold, and Humber rather dropped the idea of a 'small car' when the business was concentrated in Coventry in 1908. 'Humberette', though, was a intriguing name to use, so the company tried again in 1914, with an entirely different, larger, V-twin-engined car. In the 1920s Humber turned to building larger, more conventional cars, eventually merging with Hillman in 1928, and becoming a founder member of the Rootes Group.

Right: The original Humberette was probably the British car industry's first successful attempt to produce a popular light car, though as new-fangled motor cars still appealed mainly to the rich, it was difficult to get buyers interested.

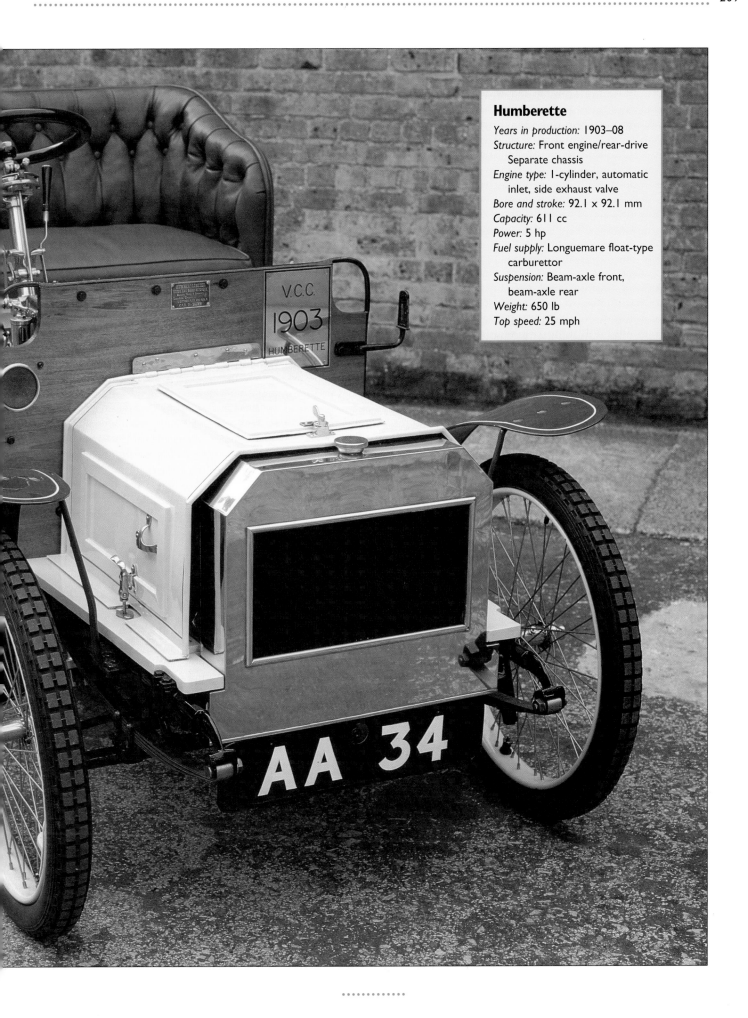

Humberette

Years in production: 1903–08
Structure: Front engine/rear-drive
Separate chassis
Engine type: 1-cylinder, automatic
inlet, side exhaust valve
Bore and stroke: 92.1 x 92.1 mm
Capacity: 611 cc
Power: 5 hp
Fuel supply: Longuemare float-type
carburettor
Suspension: Beam-axle front,
beam-axle rear
Weight: 650 lb
Top speed: 25 mph

V.C.C.
1903
HUMBERETTE

AA 34

1904 Alldays & Onions 7 hp

Alldays & Onions 7 hp

Years in production: 1904–08
Structure: Front engine/rear-drive.
    Separate chassis
Engine type: 1-cylinder, side-valve
Bore and stroke: 101.6 x 114.2 mm
Capacity: 926 cc
Power: 7 bhp at unspecified rpm
Fuel supply: Single carburettor
Suspension: Beam axle front, beam
    axle rear

Although this car's name was quaint, there was nothing strange about its engineering, or its behaviour. Established in Birmingham in 1899, the company started with a single-cylinder machine. As with most such British machines, inspiration came from overseas, for this 'Traveller' was merely a quadricycle with a French de Dion engine.

The company did not really make its name until 1905, when the original own-design twin-cylinder 10/12 went on sale. Although this was a major new undertaking, Alldays was confident of success. The general feeling in the company, and throughout Birmingham, where Britain's nascent motor industry was based, was that motor car sales were continually increasing, and that anything was possible.

The first twentieth-century Alldays & Onions model was the 7 hp of 1904, which had a modern-looking layout and style, but was powered only by a side-valve, single-cylinder, front-mounted engine. This was merely the start for the company's development, but it showed that the company already knew what would appeal to the public.

Like other early-1900s British cars, the 7 hp looked chunky and purposeful, with a sturdy frame, lofty seating positions, and a conventional chassis which included leaf-spring suspension and artillery-style wooden wheels. The original 10/12s had simple chassis frames, with artillery-style wooden wheels and pneumatic tyres (though these, alas, were by no means as puncture resistant as the makers would have liked). The engine was a water-cooled vertical twin with side-valves, and was soon renowned as a smooth, no-nonsense slogger.

Alldays were so ambitious (and self-confident) that in 1908 they absorbed the car-maker Enfield of Redditch (the same company with connections to the famous rifle and bicycle business), and developed new and more expensive cars. The 10/12 was therefore allowed to languish, and the last Alldays-badged cars were sold in 1918, for by this time the business had developed its alternative (and expensive) Enfield-Alldays range, which sold in limited numbers until 1925.

Right: Once seen as sturdy and long-lasting, its reputation spread rapidly by word of mouth and it became one of Britain's most successful 'small' cars. It was not until the market's stability was upset by the arrival of the Morris Bullnose model, and the cheap Ford Model T, that its popularity died away.

1904 Vauxhall 7 hp

When the first motor cars arrived on British roads, the Vauxhall Iron Works on the south bank of the Thames was only interested in marine engineering. Its first cars were inspired by the German Benz machines though there was some evidence of American influence too, and were designed as a co-operative effort between F.W. Hodges and the official receiver of the company. Even so, they had little chance to develop the cars, or the car-making business in London, for within a year the company had run out of space. Accordingly, it up-rooted itself, to a new greenfield site at Luton, in Bedfordshire, where it remains to this day.

Although the original Vauxhall was rated at, and named, a 5 hp machine, it was the 6 hp model of 1904 which was the first to go on sale. By the standards, and sales levels, of the day, it was an immediate success and 776 vehicles were sold in the year. At a time when most car designers looked back to the standard of horse-drawn carts, one advanced feature was the use of coil springs for front and rear suspension beams.

The low-revving single cylinder engine measured 1,029 cc (as large as a small four-cylinder family car of the late 1990s), but only produced 6 horsepower, and needed a two-speed gearbox to provide a top cruising speed of 15 mph. Contemporary pictures of those early cars show a compact four-seater layout – the wheelbase was only 6 ft 9 in, (2,057 mm) the overall length not more than about 9 ft (2,743 mm). Only one year later, the company introduced a radically different model, the 7/9 hp, which not only had a three-cylinder engine, but it was mounted at the front of the car.

This became the company's staple product for more than a year, and all types had distinctive, rakish, styling, complete with a vee-nose and a front-mounted radiator. Early types has a 1.3-litre engine and 7 hp, but were underpowered, so a larger, 9 bph, 1,436 cc engine soon became a standard fitting.

Except for its engine, this model was conventional by early Edwardian standards, for it had a three-speed sliding-type gearbox behind the engine, chain drive to the rear axle, and there was a transmission brake behind the gear-box. Pneumatic tyres were usually standard, this handsome machine being available in a variety of body styles. For Vauxhall, though, this was only the beginning, as L.H. Pomeroy went on to design a series of fine Edwardian and Vintage cars, before General Motors took over the business in 1925.

Below: The 7/9 hp was Vauxhall's first multi-cylinder model, a much more conventional machine than the original type. The three-cylinder engine was mounted up front under the shapely bonnet. There was a choice of body styles.

Vauxhall 7/9

Years in production: 1904–05
Structure: Front engine/rear-drive.
   Separate chassis
Engine type: 3-cylinder, side-valve
Bore and stroke: 76.2 x 105 mm
Capacity: 1,435 cc
Power: 9 bhp at unspecified rpm
Fuel supply: One carburettor
Suspension: Beam-axle front,
   beam-axle rear
Weight: 1,350 lb (approx)
Top speed: 30 mph

1905 Lagonda Tricar

Some of the most glamorous of marques have humble origins. Lagonda, so famous in the 1970s and 1980s for its supercars, started out by building motor cycles; its first 'motor car' was actually a motorbike-derived tricar.

American Wilbur Gunn moved to Staines, south-west of London, in the 1890s, established the Lagonda company, and sold his first motor cycle in 1900. Although Gunn seems to have had no master plan to break into the motor car market, he was tempted by the rather simple process of incorporating motorcycle technology into a three-wheeler (hence 'tricar') frame. The first Lagonda

tricar was apparently built in 1903 to satisfy an unsolicited order from a motor club secretary; Gunn found this process so straightforward that he decided to make more of them. Officially, therefore, the first 'production' tricar was launched in 1904, was gradually improved, and was not replaced by a more 'car-like' car until 1908.

Tricars are still seen competing in Veteran car events like the London-Brighton run. Although obviously derived from motorcycle engineering, they are sturdy and able to cope with reasonably long journeys (by early 1900s standards). Their layout, of course, was not at all

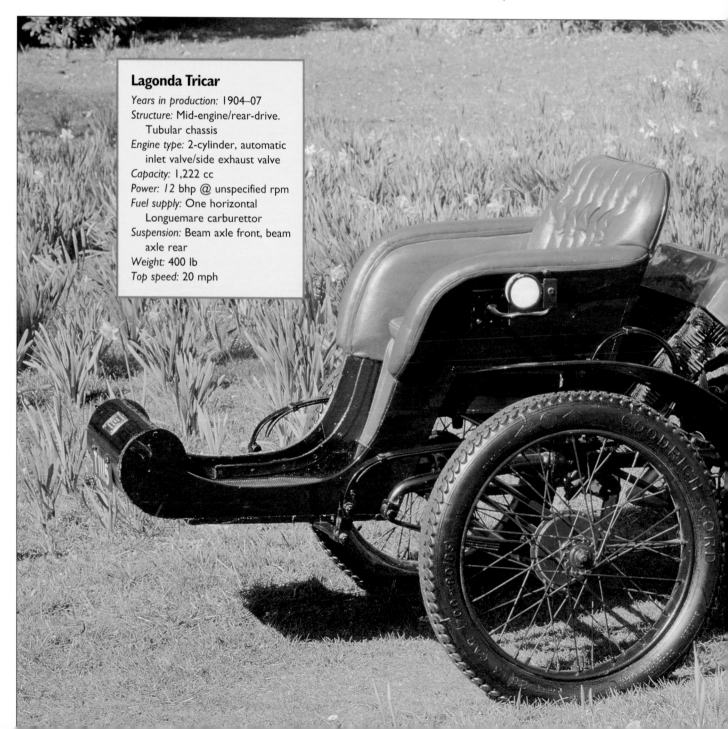

Lagonda Tricar

Years in production: 1904–07
Structure: Mid-engine/rear-drive. Tubular chassis
Engine type: 2-cylinder, automatic inlet valve/side exhaust valve
Capacity: 1,222 cc
Power: 12 bhp @ unspecified rpm
Fuel supply: One horizontal Longuemare carburettor
Suspension: Beam axle front, beam axle rear
Weight: 400 lb
Top speed: 20 mph

like the conventional cars which were soon to appear. There were two wheels up front, attached to a motor cycle-type frame with a single rear wheel; the air-cooled engine was fixed to the chassis tube between the driver/rider's legs, and the rear wheels were chain-driven. Almost all the machinery, including the transmission, was exposed to the elements, and susceptible to mud and road filth of all types.

There was no suspension of any sort on the earliest tricars, (although pneumatic tyres helped to give some resilience) as both front and rear wheels were fixed solidly to the frame, and steering, through a simple linkage, was not from a wheel, but from cycle-type handlebars.

The original tricar specification was not fixed for long, as Gunn reacted to market pressures, providing more powerful engines, and a modicum of creature comforts. Smaller, single-cylinder, or larger air-cooled or water-cooled twin-cylinder engines were available, chassis design was altered significantly, suspension was added, and the Royal Mail even bought a number of these cars, with a delivery 'bin' in place of the passenger's seat.

By 1907, the British tricar fashion had passed, and Lagonda's total output was 69 cars.

Below: Amazingly, the tricar was a two-seater with the passenger accommodated in a seat (often made of wicker) fixed ahead of the driver, ahead of the steering, and between the front wheels. If the tricar ever left the road, or made contact with any other vehicle, pedestrian or horse, it was the unprotected passenger who would act as an involuntary 'bumper' for the rest of the ensemble.

1906 Rolls-Royce 'Silver Ghost'

Henry Royce and Sir Charles Rolls joined forces to produce the very first Rolls-Royce cars in 1904. Royce (later knighted, to become Sir Henry) carried on as the company's titular head until the early 1930s, designing every part of the cars that bore his name.

The magnificent 40/50 hp model, soon nicknamed the 'Silver Ghost', appeared in 1906. In British terms, 40/50 denotes the engine type and its power rating: amazingly, in spite of its huge 7-litre engine, this was probably only 60 bhp, the huge car's top speed being a mere 50 mph.

Compared with any other contemporary car, the Silver Ghost was smooth, silent, ultra-reliable, and amazingly elegant. Around 8,000 were produced between 1906 and 1926, 1,700 coming from a subsidiary in Springfield, Massachusetts, USA. Not even a fast car by mid-1900s standards, it always behaved in a more refined and dignified, manner than any rival. With this model, Rolls-Royce established the 'Best Car in the World' tag that it would flaunt for so many years.

The car was available with a variety of splendidly-

built bodies, though Rolls-Royce never built their shells. There were two wheelbase lengths – 135.5 in or 143.5 in – all cars carrying the same long bonnet and patrician radiator, which had been modelled on the very best in Greek architecture. A really well-equipped limousine with up to seven seats would be driven by a chauffeur, and could weigh up to 5,000 lb. Progress was stately, rather than spirited.

The engine, conventionally laid out, had rocking levers placed between the side-mounted camshaft and the valve stems themselves. With a sturdy crankshaft, which defied the very thought of torsional vibrations, it ran silently at all times. It was quite possible to stand

Rolls-Royce Silver Ghost

Years in production: 1906–1926
Structure: Front engine/rear-drive.
    Separate chassis
Engine type: Six cyl, side-valve
Bore and stroke: 114.3 x 114.3 mm
Capacity: 7,036 cc
Power: Not quoted
Fuel supply: Rolls-Royce/Krebs
    carburettor
Suspension: Beam axle front,
    beam axle rear
Weight: Up to 5,000 lb

alongside an idling Silver Ghost and not realise that the engine was running.

The engine itself was enlarged, to 7,428 cc, in 1909. The original gearbox, an 'overdrive' four-speed design, was replaced by a three-speeder from 1909 to 1913, after which a direct-top four-speed box was adopted.

The original platform-type of leaf-spring rear suspension gave way to conventional leaf springs at an early stage, then to a cantilever layout from 1912.

Other changes included the fitment of a spiral-bevel instead of a straight-bevel rear axle (1923), an engine torsional damper (1911), a dynamo (1919 – instead of a magneto), four-wheel brakes with a Hispano-Suiza type of servo (1924), Hartford suspension dampers (1924) and wire spoke wheels (standard from 1913).

Although the Silver Ghost was never a technological advance, Rolls-Royce ensured that it was always the world's best built and equipped machine. Approved coachbuilders gradually modernised, along graceful lines. A Silver Ghost was instantly recognisable, dignified and suitable for every occasion.

Every owner, Rolls-Royce thought, needed to employ a full-time chauffeur, trained by Rolls-Royce, someone who usually lived in the grounds of his master's house, perhaps over the garage, where there would be a fully-equipped workshop.

When the time came to retire the Silver Ghost, it needed to be replaced by a superb new model, which is why the new Phantom I did not appear until 1926.

Above and left: The huge 7-litre engine had rocking levers and a sturdy crankshaft which ran silently at all times. This was a smooth, ultra-reliable and elegant car whose progress was stately, rather than spirited.

1907 Napier 60 hp 'Six'

With a little more luck, and perhaps a little less hype, Napier might have beaten Rolls-Royce in the British prestige car stakes. Although the two marques fought, head-to-head, until the end of the 1900s, Napier then fell away.

It all began when the cycling and motorcycling pioneer Selwyn F. Edge joined the company in 1900, and became Napier's sole distributor, racing personality and arch-publicist. The first true Napier began as an engine conversion in Montague Napier's own Panhard, producing the car in which Edge competed so successfully in the Thousand Miles trial of 1900.

Early production Napiers were twin-cylinder-engined machines, a four-cylinder type followed almost at once, and the first monstrous racing types followed in 1901. By the time Edge himself had won the Gordon Bennett Cup in 1902, and a new factory had been built in Acton, west London, Napier was on the world map. Edge persuaded Montague Napier that it should build a straight-six-cylinder model, and the Type L49 of 1904 was the world's first successful example of that type. Convinced, Napier developed a whole series of magnificent 'sixes',

1907 Napier 60 hp 'Six'

Years in production: 1905–10
Structure: Front engine/rear-drive. Separate chassis
Engine type: Six-cyl., side-valve
Bore and stroke: 127 x 101.6 mm
Capacity: 7,676 cc
Power: Not stated
Fuel supply: Single Napier carburettor
Suspension: Beam-axle front, beam-axle rear
Weight: Up to 4,500 lb (dependent on body fitted)
Top speed: 60 mph

Above: The Napier 'Six' cars were fitted with a new 'water-tower' radiator cap extension. They had pressed-steel chassis frames and were among the fastest and most prestigious cars on the market.

culminating in the rare circuit racing types with engines of up to 12 litres.

The 60 hp model of 1905–10 was typical, and had a 7.7-litre side-valve engine. (Each cylinder displaced 1,279 cc, which was larger than the entire engine of the first Bullnose Morris, which would shortly arrive.) This was the third variety of Napier's 'sixes', and there would be several more in the following decade.

By later standards, of course, we would not call such a car smooth and silent, though by comparison with its contemporaries, it seemed to be so. Fitted with a distinctive new 'water-tower' radiator cap extension, a pressed-steel chassis frame, and a choice of magnificent formal coachwork, they were among the fastest, most costly, and most prestigious British cars on the market.

By 1908, Napier were offering a plethora of 'sixes' – the 4.9-litre '30' and '40', the 6.1-litre '45', the 7.7-litre '60', and the 9.7-litre '65'. They all used variants of the same Edge-inspired side-valve engine, most of them with shaft drive, and only with rear brakes; there was also a vast 15-litre '90' for which a colossal £2,500 was asked for the chassis alone. After balancing power against grace, style against practicality, the '60' was usually seen as the most desirable of all.

By the early 1910s Napier was offering far too many models from a factory which never built more than 800 cars in a year, and was overtaken in the prestige stakes by the Rolls-Royce 40/50 hp Silver Ghost. S.F. Edge moved on in 1912, and Napier's reputation was never as high again.

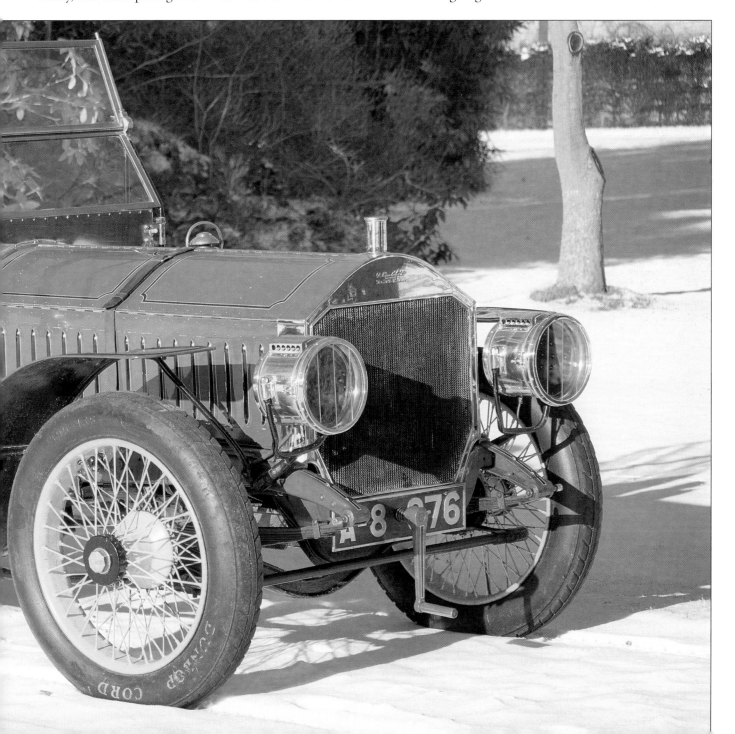

1908 Ford Model T

Although the world famous Ford Model T was not designed in the UK, it was assembled in this country from 1911 to 1927, and was a best-seller for many years. Here, as in the USA and the rest of the world, the Model T re-wrote the motoring script: more than 15 million were produced in the USA, and well over 250,000 were produced at a British factory at Trafford Park, on the outskirts of Manchester.

Henry Ford's first car, the Quadricycle prototype, was finished in 1896, and other Ford production cars followed it, before the all-new Model T appeared in 1908. Designed from the outset to be built in huge numbers, its price fell as production rose.

Although thoughtfully equipped with a large-capacity (2.9-litre) side-valve engine, which produced lots of torque, if not much power, this was a positive disadvantage in the UK, where cars were taxed according to a formula which penalised those with considerable piston area. In spite of its complexities (an epicyclic transmission), and its crudities (an archaic chassis design, with transverse leaf front and rear springing), the Model T was so well serviced by a vast dealer chain, and so easy to fix when it did go wrong, that it immediately found a market.

Although only 10,000 cars were produced in the USA in 1909, no fewer than two million were produced at peak, in 1923. Yet, in spite of this, the Model T changed little mechanically in 20 years, only the multi-farious body styles were updated, from time to time, to represent progress.

The chassis itself was definitely more flexible than some of its competitors, though this, along with the transverse leaf suspension and big wheels, made it possible to pick one's way over the sometimes poor road surfaces of the 1910s and 1920s. The engine was low-revving, but almost totally reliable, while the transmission had only two forward gears, changes being effected by a clutch pedal which was really a 'gear change' pedal. There was no foot accelerator pedal, for engine speed changes were produced

by moving hand levers under the steering wheel which covered throttle opening and ignition advance.

The Model T's low price (less than £250, even at peak, in the 1920s), low running costs, and reliability ensured its sales (7,000 alone in 1915), but the high annual tax (and stiff competition from the Bullnose Morris) eventually killed it off. Ford replaced it with the more conventional Model A in 1928, and were not to be as adventurous again.

Below and left: Idiosyncratic and very popular, it soon acquired nicknames, of which 'Tin Lizzie' was the most memorable. Popular songs like 'Get out and Get Under' followed, and cemented the car's reputation forever.

Ford Model T

Years in production: 1908–27
Structure: Front engine/rear-drive
    Separate chassis
Engine type: 4-cylinder, side-valve
Bore and stroke: 95.2 x 101.6 mm
Capacity: 2,896 cc
Power: 20 bhp @ 1,600 rpm
Fuel supply: One Holley or
    Kingston carburettor
Suspension: Beam-axle front,
    beam-axle rear
Weight: 1,450 lb
Top speed: 45 mph

1911 Lanchester 38 hp

Although Frederick Lanchester designed one of the first (and, for its day, highly advanced) British cars in 1895, his Birmingham-based company was rather slow to get its products into production. Once established in the early 20th century, Lanchester gained a reputation second only to Rolls-Royce, moving smoothly from making twin-cylinder (1901) to four-cylinder cars (1904), and to the first stately six-cylinder machines in 1906, these last having overhead-valve engines of a unique layout.

The main feature of all Frederick Lanchester's production cars was the position of the engine, which was much further back in the chassis than on later conventional machines. Although it was not fair to call a Lanchester 'mid-engined', there was certainly no long snout up front, and front seat passengers usually sat on either side of the engine, which was made as narrow as possible for that reason.

The layout of the 1911 38 hp 'six' (which was revealed at the same time as a smaller, 25 hp 'four' with a similar engine), was typical, although it would be the last of the line. Several varieties were available, and the general style of the cars exhibited a large and spacious passenger compartment, (which was always Lanchester's intention) with a surprisingly short bonnet. Even then the radiator was behind the centre line of the front wheels. This was, however, the first Lanchester to be designed by George, rather than 'Dr Fred', and it signalled a partial change towards a more conventional layout: that change would not be completed until the arrival of the later, 'Sporting Forty' of 1914.

Like earlier Lanchesters, the 38 hp had an engine with horizontal (instead of vertical) overhead-valve, ante-chamber combustion space, and the famous Lanchester wick-type carburettor. Although transmission was still by Lanchester-patented three-speed epicyclic control, it had a conventional clutch pedal and gate-type lever control.

Although this was a fine car, it was the last of that particular line. Production of both six-cylinder and four-cylinder types carried on to 1914, when work for the war effort took precedence, but they were dropped in favour of new machinery thereafter.

Lanchester retained its independence until 1931, when it was taken over by the BSA/Daimler Group. Later Lanchesters, therefore, were really re-developed Daimlers.

Lanchester 38 hp
Years in production: 1911–14
Structure: Front engine/rear-drive. Separate chassis
Engine type: 6-cylinder, overhead-valve
Bore and stroke: 101 x 101 mm
Capacity: 4,856 cc
Power: 63 bhp at 2,200 rpm
Fuel supply: Lanchester wick-type
Suspension: Beam-axle front, beam-axle rear
Weight: Approx. 3,920 lb
Top speed: 65 mph

Below: Because of the forward position of the front seats, the rear seat could also be moved forward, just ahead of the line of the rear axle, ensuring a good ride for the rear occupants, not something that could be guaranteed by Lanchester's similarly-priced rivals.

1913 Argyll 25 hp

Argyll 25 hp

Years in production: 1912–14
Structure: Front engine/rear-drive.
  Separate chassis
Engine type: 4-cylinder, sleeve-valve
Bore and stroke: 100 x 130 mm
Capacity: 4,082 cc
Power: 50 bhp (claimed)
Fuel supply: Single carburettor
Suspension: Beam-axle front,
  beam-axle rear
Weight: Up to 4,500 lb
  (dependent on body fitted)
Top speed: 50 mph

Like Arrol-Johnston, Argyll was a respected Scottish motoring pioneer and built its first Renault-based cars in Glasgow in 1899. Unhappily, its management was deluded enough to build a vast new factory in Alexandria (near Loch Lomond), which it never filled with work, and which never came remotely close to profitability. Burdened with debt (and problems with its sleeve-valve engines), Argyll closed down for the first time in 1914, and the factory turned to other products.

Daimler had been the first British concern to adopt sleeve-valve engines (which oscillated up and down between the pistons and the cylinder block walls, opening and closing inlet and exhaust ports as they did so) and by sheer application made them work well. Argyll, with fewer resources, did not.

The original sleeve-valve Argyll was the big 25 hp (25/50) model first shown in 1911, and on sale in the following year. Except for its engine, which was big, sturdy and carefully detailed both in design and finish, with its cylinder cast in pairs, the 25/50 was an otherwise conventional machine, the top of Argyll's range, and intended to sell to the prosperous who might otherwise be in the market for a Daimler, or similar prestigious motor car.

Not only did the 25/50 hp buyer get a wide choice of stylish, up-to-the-minute coachwork (most of which was erected in the factory at Alexandria), but he got a modern chassis, which included four-wheel brakes (a real innovation by 1912 standards), a quiet and flexible engine, a four-speed transmission which included a rigid torque-tube connection between the gearbox and the back axle, along with a soft and comfortable ride, and a very high level of standard equipment. If the new-fangled engine had worked well from the outset, and if there had not been expensive legal problems about the infringement of another company's patent rights, Argyll's future might have been assured. But with prices of complete cars starting at £640 (a considerable sum for 1912), sales were limited.

Argyll soon decided to apply the same technical principle to its cheaper models, some with engines as small as 1.5-litres. Sleeve-valve engines, however, did not work as well in smaller engines, and since it was those cars which were selling increasingly well in the years before the outbreak of the First World War, Argyll was at a disadvantage.

Argyll was revived as a marque after the war in the original Glasgow factory, although the magnificent 25/50 model was not part of the post-war range. Although 1.6-litre and 2.3-litre sleeve-valve engines continued to be made, but there was no further innovation after 1922, and the last Argylls were produced in 1928.

Right: Early Argylls had conventional (by 1900s standards) engines, but from 1909 they took up the development and manufacture of sleeve-valve engines, which were quieter and technically modern, but required precise technology and manufacturing to work properly.

The radiator badge of a Model T showing the distinctive Ford logo which has been a feature of British motoring since 1908. The present-day corporate lettering still shows a remarkable resemblance to the old logo proving that Ford is only too well aware of the significant role it has played in car history.

Vintage and Thoroughbred

—1919–1939—

Morris Cowley 'Bullnose' ✪ AV Monocar ✪ Vauxhall 30/98

Bentley 3-litre ✪ Sunbeam 12 ✪ Trojan ✪ Austin Seven

Bean 12 ✪ Frazer Nash 'Chain-gang' ✪ Rolls-Royce Phantom I

MG 14/28 ✪ Riley Brooklands ✪ Invicta 4¹/₂-litre

BSA 3-wheeler ✪ Daimler Double Six ✪ Talbot 14/45

Standard Big Nine ✪ Alvis Speed Twenty

Ford 8 hp Model Y ✪ Aston Martin Le Mans

Bentley 3¹/₂-litre ✪ Rolls-Royce Phantom III

Hillman Minx ✪ MG TA ✪ SS-Jaguar SS100

Lagonda V12 ✪ Triumph Dolomite Roadster

Vintage and Thoroughbred

Between 1919 and 1939, Britain's motor industry went through an upheaval. Recovery from the First World War was followed by the glories of what is known as the 'vintage' era, the economic traumas of the Depression of the early 1930s, and the spirited recovery which preceded the outbreak of the Second World War.

The story of this dramatic generation of motor cars must begin with a few statistics. Annual British car production shot up from 25,000 in 1919, to a peak of 341,000 in 1938, and the number of cars on the roads also exploded, from 100,000 in 1919 to just over two million in 1939. That was the good news, but the bad news was that although there were at least 100 different makes of car in production in 1919 (and many more hopeful entrants which never made it beyond the prototype stage), that figure slumped to no more than 35 in the depths of the Depression, and to a mere 32 in 1939–40. Marques which had been popular in the 1920s, such as Bean and Clyno, had disappeared by the 1930s, and marques which had been proudly independent in the 1920s found themselves taken over and transformed within ten years, a fate which befell Bentley, Sunbeam, Talbot, Lanchester and Riley, among others.

While production rose steadily during the 1920s to 170,000 cars a year, the industry, and the type of cars it produced, changed considerably. Until the mid 1920s, even mass-produced cars like the Austin Seven and the Bullnose Morris were built mainly by hand, though in a highly organised way. By the end of the decade mechanisation was sweeping in, bodies were being built from welded pressed steel panels instead of being constructed on a wooden framework, and engines were smaller.

It was only in the mid 1930s, when some die-hards (who had tired of the much cheaper, smaller and flimsier new models which had appeared) started talking of the 1920s as a 'vintage' era. Easy to define but difficult to describe, this usually meant that the cars were sturdily built, simple to maintain and often surprisingly good fun to drive.

By the 1920s a large component supply industry had been established, and engines, gearboxes and axles could be built to order, so it was possible for undercapitalised businesses to announce a new car, to rely on poorly-paid craftsmen to put them together, and to develop a reputation. Even so, of the hundreds of hopefuls who faced the 1920s in this way, few actually became established.

Below: Technological advances during the war meant that the number of cars on the roads was rapidly increasing. This 1920 photograph shows a Calthorpe with a Brooklands Hillman in the background.

THE CRÈME DE LA CRÈME

The best British cars of the 1920s and 1930s were produced for the comparatively small, yet excessively wealthy end of the market: some were as dignified as the Rolls-Royce Phantom and Daimler Double-Six limousines, some as fast and capable as the Bentley 8-litres and Lagonda V12s. Britain's motor cars were at the height of their fame. Big, beefy sports cars from Bentley, Invicta and Lagonda set one standard, while magnificently crafted limousines from Rolls-Royce, Daimler and (for a time) Lanchester maintained another. Although their chassis were never shatteringly modern (compared with the Germans, for instance, the British were tardy in adopting independent suspension, supercharging and V-layout engines), they were invariably well-built, and their coachwork was matchless.

Apart from the few coachbuilders who serviced the latest models from Cadillac, Packard and Duesenberg in North America, no-one could match Britain's coachbuilders. Don't believe anything you may be told about declining standards at this time – merely take a look at an H.J. Mulliner-bodied Rolls-Royce, a Hooper-bodied Daimler, and any number of sports saloons from companies like Park Ward, Gurney Nutting or Barker. 'Makes you proud to be British', was the obvious retort, which was true, as the combination of first-rate styling, a choice of tasteful trim and equipment, high quality materials, and peerless craftsmanship was unmatched. Anyone who could afford such cars – which were extremely expensive, even at 1920s and 1930s price levels – was fortunate to have so much choice.

Yet this was the high tide for such well-crafted cars. In the decades which followed, (particularly after the Second World War) social changes and soaring taxation would decimate the market. Those with an eye to the future rushed to enjoy luxury motoring while it was still practical; happily, a number of these fine cars have survived to this day.

Between 1923 and 1935, cars became much cheaper and thousands more people began driving than ever before.
Above: 1923 Triumph 10/20 hp; Top: 1935 Standard 10.

MIDDLE CLASS MOTORING

Middle class motoring came into existence during the 1920s, and took centre stage in the 1930s. As with so many of the world's innovations, once ways were found of increasing production, costs were driven down, selling prices were reduced, and the market boomed. Car makers who had annually sold dozens in the 1910s sold hundreds in the 1920s, and thousands of cars in the 1930s.

Although a typical manual worker – a factory hand, a miner, or a shipbuilder – could probably not afford a new car at this time, the white collar workers increasingly could. The professions – doctors, solicitors, architects and dentists – were first to join the ranks, followed by the middle-managers. This was a time when few could afford to pay £1,000 for a car, but thousands could afford £500; when Austin, Ford and Morris started asking less than £150 for their small-engined products, the market place exploded.

Even so, it was 'middle class' manufacturers with middle price models, who did so well in the inter-war period. By the 1930s a number of manufacturers had prospered by catering precisely for this new clientele: Alvis, Armstrong-Siddeley, Crossley, Daimler, Lanchester, Riley, Rover, SS-Jaguar, Sunbeam, Talbot, Triumph and Wolseley all competed in this keenly-fought and prestigious sector, all offering smart, well equipped cars.

The 1930s were the high point for such cars and their owners. Motoring became a middle class leisure activity: second-division coachbuilders were able to offer a great deal of visual variety in their car ranges, and magazines were produced to satisfy the curiosity of new car-owners. Advertising was surrounded by an aura of 'British is best', a complacent attitude which seemed to appeal to the motorists of the day.

SPORTY MOTORING

Among the earliest sports cars were the big, expensive Bentleys and Vauxhall 30/98s; these were followed by smaller, individualistic machines such as the Frazer Nash, and finally the small-engined two-seaters from MG, Morgan, Triumph and Singer. These vehicles, particularly those from MG, laid the foundations for the sports car boom which was to follow in the 1950s and 1960s.

There was great demand for fast small cars, if only it could be satisfied. Bentleys, Vauxhall 30/98s, twin-cam Sunbeams, Lagondas and Invictas were all extremely desirable cars, but they were also expensive, and could

only be expected to sell in hundreds, not tens of thousands. Cars such as GNs and Aston Martins were great fun to drive, but prone to fall apart if abused and, as with the most expensive marques, were not backed by a large chain of dealers.

So-called sporty versions of cars like the Bullnose Morris and even the Model T Ford were simply lighter versions of the original, perhaps with the addition of unique bodywork. The breakthrough came when MG, Austin, Riley and Singer all developed truly small cars with unique frames, and tuned-engines: it was with the arrival of M-type Midgets and 9 hp Singer sports cars that demand suddenly expanded. Marques like Triumph and Lea-Francis attempted the same breakthrough, but not in the same numbers.

In only ten years MG grew from being a minor manufacturer to pre-eminence; there was a huge difference – in both engineering and in behaviour – between the Morris-based 14/28 of 1924, and the special overhead-camshaft PAs and Magnettes of 1934. Although the TA which followed was more closely based on Morris and Wolseley models than before, it was still a fine sports car. Morgan joined in, HRG appeared as a bespoke alternative and, quite suddenly, the layout of the traditional British sports car was founded.

In the meantime, the yawning gap between expensive and bargain-basement was also being filled, not necessarily with lightweight two-seaters, but with fine and stylish open models. Lovers of 1920s cars were too blinkered to

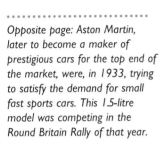

see the merits of many 1930s cars, which ranged from the beefy Jaguar SS100s, to two-seater Riley Sprites; from convertible Triumph Dolomite Roadsters, to the Vanden Plas-styled Alvis Speed Twenty types; from hand-built ACs, to series-production SS-Jaguar, Wolseley and Daimler models. For those in work (and, let's not forget, the effect of the Depression weighed far more heavily on the non-car-owning classes than on the middle class who could afford to buy a new car) there was far more choice of interesting and stylish machinery in the 1930s than there had been just ten years earlier.

MOTORING FOR THE MASSES

Britain's largest car makers were already established before 1914, but it was in the 1920s and 1930s that they truly came to numerical dominance. By the end of the 1920s Morris had market leadership, with Austin close behind, followed by Ford and Standard, with Humber-Hillman (the soon-to-be-named Rootes Group) and Vauxhall ready to join battle. By the end of the 1930s, Austin and Morris were more or less equal, Ford was a definite third, with the other three scrapping for 10 or 12 per cent each of the market place.

In the 1920s, the Austin Seven and the Bullnose Morris were by far the most successful cars of their type, though at the end of the period the tiny Morris Minor and the equally small Singer Junior both came close. In the early 1930s cars rated by the RAC at 8, 9, 10 and 12 hp really took over the market leadership. Every member of the 'big six' had a best-seller in this category, and though they were not technically exciting (and usually unimaginatively titled), they sold in huge numbers. Austin, of course, had the Ten, Morris had the Ten, Standard the Nine, Big Nine and, later, Flying Nine, Rootes had the

ubiquitous Hillman Minx, Vauxhall the Ten-Four and Twelve-Four, while Ford swept into the market with a raft of cars all based on the original 8 hp Model Y, which became the C, evolved into the Anglia, and then spawned the Prefect.

All these cars were available as saloons, convertibles, vans, and were occasionally special-bodied, though the mass-market estate car was a type yet to be invented. Unexciting to drive (in most cases 50 mph was a good cruising speed, no more), and always likely to rot away, they were all very cheap – and motorists loved them. Thus, the scene was set for similar cars to evolve in the 1940s and 1950s.

APOCALYPSE NOW ...

If Adolf Hitler had not decided to conquer the world, the British motor industry might have evolved in a different way. By 1939, the 'big six' were embracing new technology. All-steel bodies and overhead-valve engines were almost universal, unit-construction bodies were already used by Morris, Rootes and Vauxhall, and independent front suspension had arrived at Rootes, Standard and Vauxhall. Exports were going well (nearly 80,000 in 1937), and the market was booming.

Then, at the end of the 1930s, re-armament, tax rises, the opening of aero-engined 'shadow factories' run by car makers and, from the end of 1939, a rapid conversion to military production altered the scene irrevocably. Soon Vauxhall were making tanks, Rootes were producing aircraft, Austin made trucks, while Ford constructed Merlin aero-engines. The transformation was complete: in consequence Britain's industry, and its cars, would never be the same again.

1919 Morris Cowley 'Bullnose'

The original Morris, the much-loved 'Bullnose', was Britain's equivalent – and in competition with – the Ford Model T, though its inventor, William Morris, had different ways of achieving the result. Whereas Ford had concluded that he must make as much of the car as possible in his own factories, Morris used proprietary or 'bought-in' components for some years at first.

Having started out in business by opening a cycle sales and repair shop in Oxford, Morris bought a disused building at Cowley, near Oxford (but one which adjoined open farm land), to produce cars in 1913. First with a car called the 'Oxford', then from 1915 with a smaller-engined version called 'Cowley', he built up a business which was Britain's largest car producer by 1924, when it overtook Ford UK.

The Cowley's design was as simple as that of the Model T. More conventional, it was distinguished by its

rounded, bulbous, radiator style, which soon inspired the unofficial, but lasting nickname. At first almost every component was bought in, ready-manufactured, including engines from Coventry, transmissions from Birmingham, and bodies from a variety of sources. It was only as the 1920s progressed, and as the factory continued to grow, that Morris either bought up his suppliers, or started making components close to the assembly lines.

The RAC rated 'Oxford' types at 13.9 horsepower, and 'Cowley' types at 11.9 hp. They both used versions of Coventry-made engines, and many different body types were available (including super-sports versions which subsequently became the first MGs). By aggressively reducing prices at a time when costs were rising, Morris saw sales rocket.

Having produced only 3,077 cars in 1921, Morris went on to build 54,151 in 1925, by which time the Bullnose was nearly ready for replacement. As with the Model T, this market domination was achieved by cutting prices, which eventually came down to a mere £162 by 1925. No other car or model could match that, for the engines had been specifically designed to take advantage of Britain's tax laws. This, and the way that Bullnose types sold steadily throughout the countries of the Empire, ensured Morris's supremacy.

In the next few years Morris, who eventually became

Lord Nuffield, allowed his business to diversify, so that far too many models were being sold at a time when the market-place was contracting, the result being that Austin rapidly caught up, and that Morris was never again as dominant as it had been in the mid 1920s.

Below: The Bullnose become a British best-seller, and Morris followed up this success by buying other marques and factories (such as Wolseley) to expand even further. His actions helped to kill off many other makes of British car which simply could not compete with Morris's tactics.

Morris Cowley 'Bullnose'

Years in production: 1915–26
Structure: Front-engine/rear-drive. Separate chassis
Engine type: 4-cylinder, side-valve
Bore and stroke: 69.5 x 102 mm
Capacity: 1,548 cc
Power: 26 bhp @ 2,800 rpm
Fuel supply: One Smith carburettor
Suspension: Beam-axle front, beam-axle rear
Weight: 1,750 lb
Top speed: 50 mph

1920 AV Monocar

AV Monocar

Years in production: 1919–24
Structure: Rear-engine/rear-drive.
    Separate chassis
Engine type: Twin-cylinder, air-
    cooled, JAP or Blackburne
Bore and stroke: 70 x 85 mm,
    76 x 85 mm or 85 x 85 mm
Capacity: 654, 770 or 864 cc
Power: Not quoted
Fuel supply: One Capac, or
    Claudel-Hobson, carburettor
Suspension: Beam-axle front,
    beam-axle rear
Weight: 600 lb
Top speed: 40 mph

Viewed from the end of the century, the AV Monocar might look like a joke, but in its day it was a popular and effective little 'cycle car'. This short-lived type of machine was really a cheap half-way house between the motor cycles and more 'grown-up' light cars of the day – and most first owners seem to have graduated to them from motor cycles when they were looking for a little more comfort, and stability. The AV was one of the first of this type, though the later, and more sporting GN became more famous.

AV of Teddington in Middlesex, was founded by Ward and Avey Ltd., who bought a cycle-car design from another struggling designer, John Carden (between 1919 and 1925 there was also a different Carden car), and began producing monocars at Carden's own factory. The first cars were delivered in 1919, and by 1922 prices had fallen to a mere £115. To make such machines profitable at those levels, they had to be more 'cycle' than substantial 'car', and were very cheaply (some say nastily) built.

As its name suggests, the original Monocar was a single-seater, with a wheelbase of only 6 ft 6 in, and it was only 2 ft 6 in wide. It was not, in fairness, a very efficiently packaged car because, within three years, the famous Austin Seven appeared, used a shorter wheelbase, and could carry four people in tolerable comfort.

Although AV's workforce totalled 80 men, this light machine had spidery, minimal, bodywork by Thames Valley Pattern Works, made out of a combination of plywood, papier mâché and mahogany with some aluminium skin panels. Most of the cars seem to have been painted red, with black mudguards (or sometimes merely of polished aluminium). Steering was by wires which passed around strategically located bobbins (which could be very perilous, especially when the unlubricated bobbins began to wear, or fray). From the V-twin air-cooled JAP or Blackburne motorcycle engine, transmission was by chain, through a Sturmey Archer three-speed motorcycle gearbox.

Not even the very low price or weight (the first cars weighed only 600 lb, or twice that of a large motorcycle), could make the Monocar universally popular. Although this was a crude little machine, it was at least simple, and therefore easy to repair when things went wrong (as they often did). Later attempts to broaden its appeal by making it longer, with two tandem seats, or even as a wider Runabout with two parallel seats were not a success.

All cars of this type were eventually defeated by competition from the cheap Austin-Seven, and even from the bulkier Morris 'Bullnose' Cowley, and the last of several hundred AVs were built in 1924. AV reverted to selling other makes of car (notably Jowetts) and survived into the 1950s.

· ·

Right: In the Monocar, the driving position was low, the occupant's legs being angled sharply forwards into the pointed nose, and to make this possible the engine was mounted in the tail, driving the rear wheels.

1920 Vauxhall 30/98

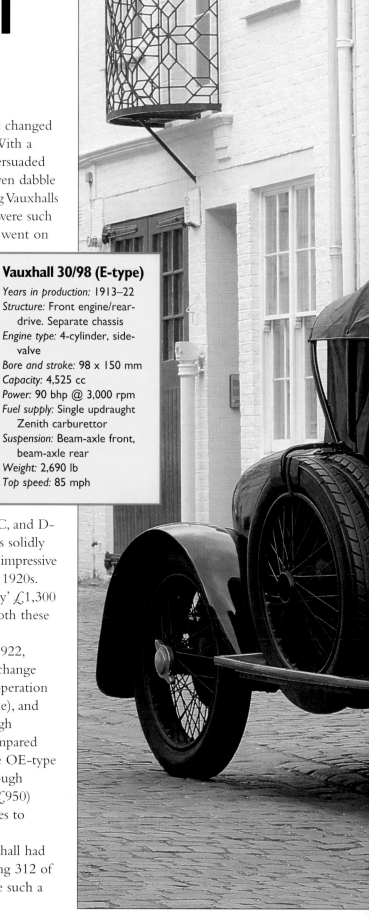

Vauxhall's early cars offered no great distinction, but that changed when L.H. Pomeroy was appointed as chief engineer. With a great love of high-performance engines and cars, he soon persuaded his new bosses that they should back a new sports car, and even dabble with Grand Prix racing. In 1910 the first hand-built sporting Vauxhalls appeared for use in the German Prince Henry trials. These were such a success that a series of road cars, the 'Prince Henry' models, went on sale at £600 each.

The first new Vauxhall model, the 30/98, was built in 1913, as a better, faster and more practical development of the Prince Henry, but its career, as a production car, really belongs to the years after the end of the First World War. With a larger engine than the Prince Henry, it was the fastest sports car of its day, guaranteed to reach 100 mph in stripped-out racing form. This, in effect, meant that it was the Jaguar E-type or McLaren F1 of its day, as it was so much quicker than any rival. The chassis price of £900, however, guaranteed that it would always be rare.

Production of this car, with a simple but effective side-valve engine, got under way properly in 1919, when it was known by the factory (and by the customers) as the 30/98 E-type model – this title following the use of B, C, and D-type Vauxhalls of the pre-war period. The original 30/98 was solidly built, which made it heavy, but it was also fast, and combined impressive performance with good roadholding by the standards of the 1920s. The snag was that its price – £1,670 at first, reduced to 'only' £1,300 in 1921 – made it a direct rival to the Bentley 3-litre, and both these cars were fighting for a very limited market.

About 270 cars were built before a redesign followed in 1922, which produced the equally-legendary OE-type. The main change was to the engine, which was converted to overhead-valve operation on advice from Ricardo (this explains the 'O' of the new title), and produced a rousing 115 bhp. It was an outstanding car, though increasingly this was measured by pre-war standards, and compared with the Bentley it was still a light motor car. Amazingly, the OE-type did not have four-wheel brakes (the Bentley always did), though towards the end of its run, from 1926, (at a chassis price of £950) a 120 bhp version was made available, with four-wheel brakes to control it all.

The last OE was produced in 1927 – two years after Vauxhall had been taken over by General Motors of the USA – there being 312 of that variant. Sadly, GM never again allowed Vauxhall to make such a distinguished machine.

Vauxhall 30/98 (E-type)

Years in production: 1913–22
Structure: Front engine/rear-drive. Separate chassis
Engine type: 4-cylinder, side-valve
Bore and stroke: 98 x 150 mm
Capacity: 4,525 cc
Power: 90 bhp @ 3,000 rpm
Fuel supply: Single updraught Zenith carburettor
Suspension: Beam-axle front, beam-axle rear
Weight: 2,690 lb
Top speed: 85 mph

Below: Solidly built with good roadholding for the 1920's, this car's price, £1,670, made it a direct rival to the Bentley 3-litre – both cars fought for a very limited market.

1921 Bentley 3-litre

W.O. Bentley made his name as an importer of French DFP sports cars before 1914, and for his BR air-cooled rotary aero-engined designs during it. In 1919 he decided to make a car of his own design.

The 3-litre, first seen at the 1919 Olympia Motor Show, was put into production at a factory near Staples Corner, on London's North Circular road, and was first sold in 1921: it was the first of a legendary pedigree of locomotive-like British sports cars. Indeed, it is true to say that the 4.5, 6.5 and 8-litre cars are all recognisably descended from the original 3-litre.

Chassis engineering was conventional in every way, but the engine aroused a great deal of interest. Massively built, tall and elegant, the four-cylinder unit was almost unique in having four valves per cylinder, and an overhead camshaft in a non-detachable cylinder head, a layout which gave the

Bentley 3-litre

Years in production: 1921–28
Structure: Front engine/rear-drive. Separate chassis
Engine type: 4-cylinder, single overhead camshaft
Bore and stroke: 80 x 149 mm
Capacity: 2,996 cc
Power: 80 bhp @ unspecified rpm
Fuel supply: One Smith/two horizontal SU carburettors
Suspension: Beam-axle front, beam-axle rear
Weight: 2,800 lb
Top speed: 80 mph

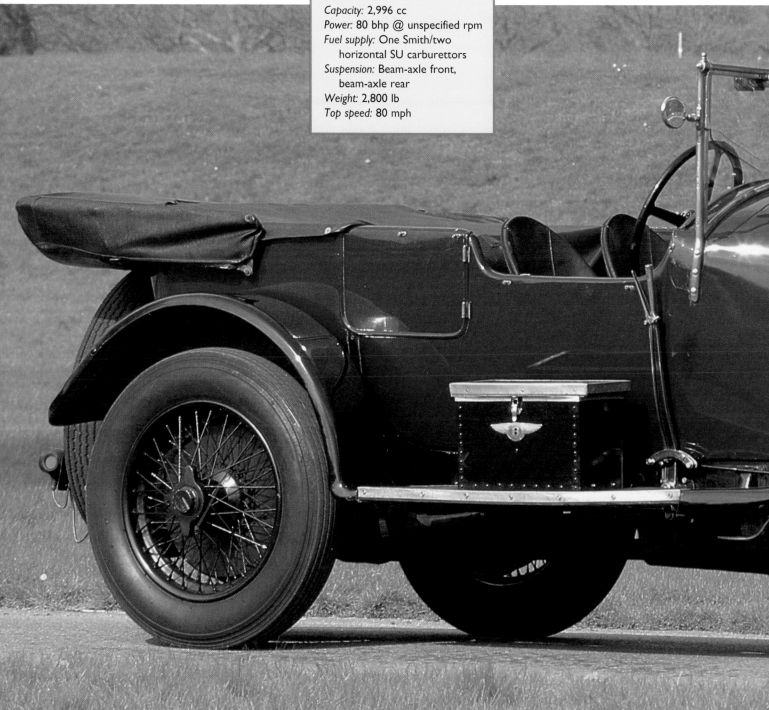

Bentley 3-litre a sparkling performance.

Even though Bentley always seemed to be under-capitalised (it came close to bankruptcy at least three times in the 1920s, before the final collapse in 1931) W.O. Bentley himself always found the time and the money to enter his cars in an ambitious programme of races and high-speed record attempts, telling everyone that this would not only improve development, but would also bring valuable publicity. It was the Le Mans 24 Hours race which meant most to Bentley, where lightweight and tuned-up 3-litres won the race in 1923 and 1927. His cars also raced with distinction in the British Tourist Trophy race (second in 1922), and even in the Indianapolis 500, where W.D. Hawkes's car averaged 81 mph.

The Speed Model, with a tuned-up engine, arrived in 1924, and following the development of the 4.5-litre model (this engine being a technical amalgam of the 3-litre and 6.5-litre 'six' units) a number of common parts were specified. There were three distinct sets of gearbox ratios. The original chassis price was £1,100, which was usually raised to about £1,400, depending on the type of bodywork chosen. By any standards this made the Bentley an extremely expensive proposition, so to stimulate sales the 'Standard' chassis price dropped to £895 in 1924.

Below: Bentley was so confident of his engineering skills that a five-year warranty was offered for the chassis assembly. Three-litre types were in production for seven years, in several basic forms and in three wheelbase lengths.

1923 Sunbeam 12

Sunbeam 12

Years in production: 1923–26
Structure: Front engine/rear-drive.
   Separate chassis
Engine type: 4-cylinder, overhead-
   valve
Bore and stroke: 68 x 110 mm
Capacity: 1,598 cc
Power: 12 bhp
Fuel supply: Single Claudel-Hobson
   carburettor
Suspension: Beam-axle front,
   beam-axle rear

To many vintage car enthusiasts, there has only ever been one real Sunbeam company – that which built cars in Wolverhampton before 1936. Sunbeam, thereafter, became an unwilling part of the Rootes Group, and it was not long before new Sunbeam models had lost their pedigree, and were really no more than Hillmans or Humbers in party dress.

The original Sunbeams of 1901 were weird little creations with wheels in a diamond, rather than conventional formation (and with imported De Dion engines), but Sunbeam's great independent years began in 1909 after the celebrated designer Louis Coatalen joined the company. A range of newly-engineered four-cylinder and six-cylinder types emerged, the 12/16 being such an outstanding car that series production was taken over by Rover during the First World War, to maintain supply for the armed forces.

Sunbeam amalgamated with Talbot and Darracq in 1920 to form the STD combine, and though Coatalen always preferred to design sports, even racing, cars, most touring Sunbeams of the period were cars of great refinement but not outstanding performance. The new generation 12-30 of 1923 was altogether more representative of the genre. Here was a car so typical of the middle class British touring car of the period that the vintage 'rules of engagement' might have been written around it. Both this, and the much larger 16-50 were an evolution of the popular 14 chassis (whose roots lay in a Darracq design), which had been in production for some time, though with new engines, and updated body styles.

The chassis was simple but robust, with channel-section side members, and pressed cross-bracing members, front and rear suspension was by leaf springs (the rear axle being suspended on full cantilever springs), and the 10-spoke wheels were of what was still known as the 'artillery' type. Low-slung by 1920s standards, the frame actually sat well up above the line of the two axles, with the driver sitting atop the frame, not inside the side members. It was still acceptable to fit brakes solely to the rear wheels of this 1.5-litre car, although front brakes became more common as the 1920s progressed.

The engine was a simple, low-revving, rugged overhead-valve four-cylinder unit. It was 1,598 cc instead of the 2,121 cc of the 14 hp model, and was backed by a three-speed transmission, and a gear lever positioned to the outside of the driver's seat.

As with other vintage cars of the period, two immediate problems faced the 12-30, one being that it was obviously based on a larger type, the other being that it was expensive at £570. Although it was better built, with more individual components than the Bullnose Morris, it was no faster, nor did it have better roadholding. Only about 95 cars were ever built.

Right: Typical of the British touring car of the period, the Sunbeam 12 was an expensive car but its roadholding and speed were no better than those of the 'Bullnose' Morris.

1923 Trojan

The best way to describe the Trojan is as eccentric, for its design flew in the face of almost every trend and accepted practice of the period. Leslie Hounsfield laid out this mid-engined machine so well and so successfully, however, that Leyland (the truck specialists), adopted the design and put it into production at Ham, near Kingston-upon-Thames in 1922.

No performance car, and certainly not a looker, it nevertheless appealed to so many that more than 16,000 cars were built in the 1920s alone. Although a Trojan Utility looked conventional enough apart from the radiator and the fuel tank, there was almost nothing under the bonnet, for the hilariously simple (and in theory, quite impractical) two-stroke engine was situated under the rear floor, driving the rear wheels through a two-speed and reverse epicyclic gearbox. The 'self-starter' was a ratchetted lever on the floor, to the right of the driver.

The chassis was a rigid punt-type platform, and although there was plenty of ground clearance and soft cantilever leaf springs at front and rear, the ride was not helped by the presence of very thin, solid tyres. All this, the slow and utterly metronomic quality of the long-stroke engine, and the ability to change gear without a clutch pedal (although one was provided to make timid drivers feel at home), made the Trojan an acquired taste.

The fact that it was an extremely simple vintage car, costing little to run, and almost nothing to maintain (many reached 100,000 miles needing little more than a periodic de-coking of the engine), meant that it soon established its own market, though motoring pundits were never impressed. One of the Trojan's greatest fans, historian Anthony Bird, pointed out that it was almost comic in everything it did, that many professional testers 'praised it with faint damns', and that the motor trade itself was openly hostile to a machine which rarely gave them any work.

No-one bought a Trojan if they were in a hurry, for at any speed above 25 mph, the hammering transmitted through the solid tyres from the poor roads of the period could be extremely uncomfortable. On the other hand, because of its good low-speed engine torque, and its solid rear axle (no differential was fitted), it was a car for climbing every hill, even in the most appalling weather.

One very important, high-profile, fleet contract was obtained: from Brooke Bond, the tea manufacturers, who bought more than 5,000 Trojans over the years for delivery van use, and kept them almost indefinitely, so in cities, at least, the Trojan was always prominent.

Assembly by Leyland ended in 1926, but was revived by Hounsfield himself a year later, in Croydon. Updated only as necessary (which was very little), the 'Utility' became the 'Ten', and maintained a following until the mid-1930s, when car production finally ended.

Trojan

Years in production: 1922–29
Structure: Mid-engine/rear-drive. Separate chassis
Engine type: 4-cylinder, two-stroke
Bore and stroke: 63.5 x 117.5 mm
Capacity: 1,488 cc
Power: 11 bhp @ 1,200 rpm
Fuel supply: One Trojan or Amal carburettor
Suspension: Beam-axle front, beam-axle rear
Weight: 1,315 lb
Top speed: 32 mph

Above: Although this car had a large bonnet behind the
radiator, the engine was positioned under the rear floor.
The solid tyres made any journey very uncomfortable
on the poor road surfaces of the time.

1923 Austin Seven

For years, in the 1920s and 1930s, the tiny Austin Seven was a best-selling little car, which set every standard of small packaging; it seemed cheeky, simple, and promised low-cost motoring. In many ways, it was similar to the Mini which followed decades later.

Everything about the car – everything, including the engine transmission, suspension and choice of bodies – was brand new, for here was a car designed to weigh no more than 800 lb/363 kg, and to be the first (and lowest-priced) car which any new motorist would consider. Initially on sale at £165, (in the UK, only the mass-produced Ford Model T was cheaper), it provided unbeatable value, for although a Seven was slow (anyone who drove faster than about 35 mph was a masochist), and had precarious handling and brakes, it had enormous appeal. The fact that it was worth only pennies by the time it was five years old didn't seem to matter, for even old and rusty Sevens would keep motoring.

The A-profiled (in plan) chassis frame was flimsy and flexible, with a transverse leaf spring at the front, and with cantilever leaf spring at the rear, the brakes rather a bad joke, and the 'in-and-out' clutch fierce in the extreme. It was almost impossible to provide comfortable four-seater bodywork inside the 75 in/1900 mm wheelbase, but Austin tried hard, and sold tens of thousands of these angular machines every year. At first the tiny 747 cc engine produced a mere 10.5 bhp, but this increased gradually over the years, culminating at 17 bhp in the mid-1930s; by this time an Austin Seven could reach more than 50 mph.

Although it was already looking obsolete by the early 1930s, regular re-touching, not only to the style but also to the engineering, meant that it was invariably Austin's best-selling model, and before the last car was produced in 1939, more than 290,000 of all types had been sold. At its peak, which lasted for more than a decade, well over 20,000 cars were being sold, every year. In later life the engine found further use in Reliant three wheelers, and a passion for racing, encouraged by the 750 MC, saw power outputs pushed up to extraordinary levels.

Right: Most factory-built Sevens were two-door saloons or tourers, with a very square style (one could almost say non-style), but there were many special coachwork styles, and even the occasional two-seater.

Austin Seven

Years in production: 1923–39
Structure: Front engine/rear-drive. Separate chassis
Engine type: 4-cylinder, side-valve
Bore and stroke: 56 x 76.2 mm
Capacity: 747 cc
Power: 10.5 bhp @ 2,400 rpm
Fuel supply: One updraught Zenith carburettor
Suspension: Beam-axle front, beam-axle rear
Weight: 800 lb
Top speed: 40 mph

1924 Bean 12

Although glamorous cars like the massive Bentleys, and sports cars such as the Frazer Nash made most of the headlines at the time, the 'vintage era' – roughly speaking the 1920s – saw many more worthy, rather individual, and charming (though slow) family cars go on sale. The Bean, from Dudley, in the West Midlands, was a very popular example of that type.

Bean shot to fame and back to obscurity in only ten years during the 1920s. The business was established immediately after the First World War (the original Bean was actually a remodelling of the 'Perry' light car) and produced more than 4,000 cars a year in the middle of the period. It rapidly faded as the 'Hatfield Bean' and failed to survive the marketing onslaught from cheaper cars like the Morris Cowley and Oxford.

The first Bean of 1919 was a stolidly-engineered and styled 12 hp model (or '11.9'). The factory at Tipton, Dudley was well-capitalised, but the company's ambitions stretched their finances, and survival was always a struggle.

The Bean 12 was updated in 1924, and the larger, heavier and longer 14 was produced in the same year. Rugged but unexciting, both types had a four-cylinder side-valve engine (the 14 having a 2,386 cc type); the 12 had a separate three-speed, while the 14's engine was in a unit with a four-speed gearbox. In both cases the performance was no more than adequate by the standards of the day. Many customers, however, did not mind this, especially as the national speed limit was a mere 20 mph.

Beans were relatively modern and well specified for 1925. Prices ranged from £335 to £395 for the 12 hp, and from £375 for a three-seater Tourer 14, to £585 for a well equipped saloon.

The mid-1920s, however, were the high point for Bean, which had once talked of selling 10,000 cars every year, but never came close to achieving that mark. Although cheaper (and better) than many of their rivals, they were coming under increasing competition from Austin and Morris, with the cheapest Morris Cowley retailing for no more than £175.

By developing a Meadows six-cylinder engined car (the 18/50), Bean found itself saddled with more capital expenditure than it could handle in the long term; other expensive models did not sell as well as planned, and the last cars (but not commercial vehicles) were made in 1929. No fewer than 10,000 11.9s and 4,000 14s were built, figures which dwarfed those achieved by the later models.

Right: From end to end, this was a typical vintage family car, with a high, sturdy chassis, a low revving side-valve engine, and artillery-pattern road wheels with four-wheel brakes and shock absorbers all round.

Bean 12

Years in production: 1919–27
Structure: Front engine/rear-drive.
   Separate chassis
Engine type: 4-cylinder, side-valve
Bore and stroke: 69 x 120 mm
Capacity: 1,795 cc
Power: Not stated
Fuel supply: Single Zenith
   carburettor
Suspension: Beam-axle front,
   beam-axle rear
Weight: 1,550 lb
Top speed: 45 mph

1925 Frazer Nash 'Chain-gang'

No car as special and as uniquely-conceived, as the 'Chain-gang' Frazer Nash comes into existence without precedent. In this case, designer, Archie Frazer Nash, had already been involved in the GN business, where he had proved the worth of the extremely simple, but effective, chain drive transmission.

Setting up on his own in Kingston-on-Thames (though assembly soon moved to Isleworth, in Middlesex), Frazer Nash decided to make a sports car so simply engineered that it could be dismantled like a gigantic Meccano set (some owners got very used to

doing this!), which would use proprietary water-cooled four-cylinder or six-cylinder engines, and a four-speed-and-reverse transmission with dog engagement of various sprockets linked by chain to the rear axle. The first were delivered in 1924, the last in 1939, by which time their popularity had ended.

Chassis were very simple, with stiff cantilever leaf springs at front and rear (Archie Frazer Nash was said to have been mortally offended if any one of

Frazer Nash 'Chain-gang'

Years in production: 1924–39
Structure: Front engine/rear-drive. Separate chassis
TYPICAL, WITH MEADOWS ENGINE:
Engine type: 4-cylinder, overhead-valve
Bore and stroke: 69 x 100 mm
Capacity: 1,496 cc
Power: 62 bhp @ 4,500 rpm
Fuel supply: Two horizontal SU carburettors
Suspension: Beam-axle front, beam-axle rear
Weight: 1,800 lb
Top speed: 85 mph

these was seen to deflect) and high-geared steering. Highly responsive handling was therefore assured.

The chain drive layout was so simple that critics often questioned its efficiency: the drawbacks were that chains could, and often did, snap, and the links had to be cleaned and oiled at least every 500 miles. There was no torque-splitting differential, so the Nash needed a narrow rear track to ensure that tyres were not prematurely worn out: traction, on the other hand, was excellent.

Because the 'Chain gang' (the reason for the nick-name is quite obvious) was light and handled so well, its competitive potential was obvious, even though the styling (and the poor aerodynamic shape) never allowed high speeds to be attained. Over the years, more suitable engines were chosen. Original cars had Power Plus units; British Anzani followed, and Meadows overhead-valve types powered the first batch of 'TT Replica' examples. There was even the choice of twin-cam Blackburne six-cylinder units, and a single-cam 'Gough four'. Many variants were named after sporting successes: 'Shelsley' after the British hillclimb, 'Boulogne' after a French racing circuit, and of course 'TT Replica' after the Tourist Trophy race in the Isle of Man where the cars performed so well.

Below: Low, narrow, open to the elements, and utterly single-purpose, these were singular cars for the individualist. Only about 350 were built in 15 years.

1925 Rolls-Royce Phantom I

'How do you improve on perfection?' was one remark made by Rolls-Royce devotees when the New Phantom eventually succeeded the long-running 40/50 hp Silver Ghost in 1925. But this was to ignore the obvious, which was that the older car had gradually fallen behind the times, mechanically at least, and was overdue for replacement.

To replace one icon with another, Rolls-Royce decided to tackle the job in two stages, first by providing a new overhead-valve six-cylinder engine, and other chassis innovation such as four-wheel brakes; second, an entirely new chassis was developed, which would appear later, and form the basis of the Phantom II. As the new car would have the same bulk as before, and as all Rolls-Royce styling was provided by outside coachbuilders, many potential customers might not even notice the transition.

For the new car, Rolls-Royce produced its second overhead-valve engine (the first had appeared in the new 'small' Rolls-Royce, the 20 hp, in 1922. This was smoother, more modern, and more powerful than before, but otherwise set out to do the same unobtrusive job. Then, as ever, Rolls-Royce motoring was not about performance, but about dignity, silence, almost infallible reliability, and the ability to insulate its owners almost entirely from their surroundings.

The new chassis, therefore, slipped quietly into production, while principal comment seemed to be about styles (the famous radiator grille was not modified), and the details of equipment and furnishing. Rolls-Royce took the big step of producing New Phantoms at a factory in the USA, at Springfield, Massachusetts, where bodies were provided by North American coachbuilders, and were often more flamboyant than their European equivalents.

Purchasers of New Phantoms rarely worried about roadholding, performance and fuel consumption, but if their cars were less than dependable or silent, complaints would surely follow. For some large cars, in any case, this was still the era of the chauffeur, so for the owner (or the occupant, for were bought by companies) it was more important that a New Phantom should have a magnificently trimmed rear compartment with plenty of fittings with which to impress one's colleagues.

And so it did, for no fewer than 2,212 new Phantoms were built at Derby in just four years, with another 1,241 being produced in the USA until American production ended in 1931.

Below: The successor to the Silver Ghost, the Phantom had a new overhead six-cylinder engine, a new chassis and four-wheel brakes. The new engine was smoother and more powerful than before.

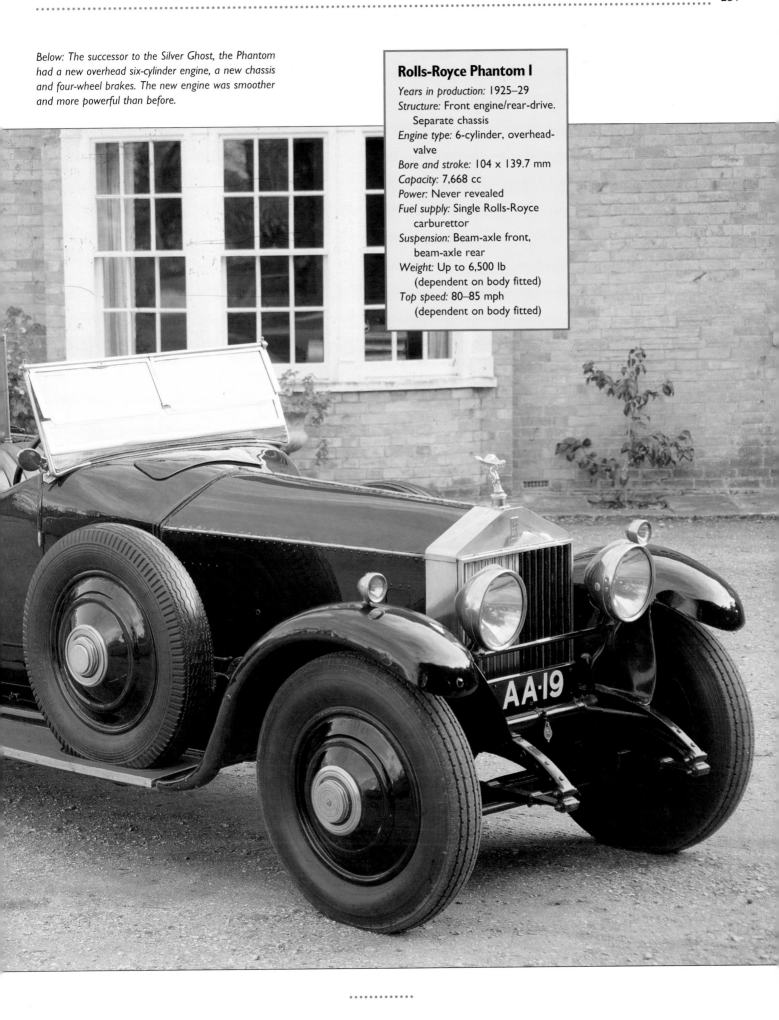

Rolls-Royce Phantom I

Years in production: 1925–29
Structure: Front engine/rear-drive. Separate chassis
Engine type: 6-cylinder, overhead-valve
Bore and stroke: 104 x 139.7 mm
Capacity: 7,668 cc
Power: Never revealed
Fuel supply: Single Rolls-Royce carburettor
Suspension: Beam-axle front, beam-axle rear
Weight: Up to 6,500 lb (dependent on body fitted)
Top speed: 80–85 mph (dependent on body fitted)

1926 MG 14/28

Cecil Kimber, General Manager of Morris Garages, in Oxford started by building special-bodied Morris Bullnose cars in 1923, and made them even more distinguished by adopting the MG (or Morris Garages) badge. The original MG-badged cars were not as sporting as those which followed, but they established a famous sports car marque.

Like the first Morris 'specials' which had preceded them in 1923, the MG 14/28 types were based on the simple chassis and running gear of the mass-produced Morris Bullnose, but now they had larger and more powerful engines, and even more distinctive body styling. During the life of the car, engines became more distinctive, for all were stripped, rebuilt and modified by the Morris Garages' mechanics. At first the cars were assembled in a corner of the Morris workshops at Alfred's Lane, Oxford, the chassis being delivered direct from Morris's Cowley factory on the outskirts of the city. Kimber's craftsmen then made a multitude of improvements, including flattening the springs, re-raking the steering, changing the suspension dampers and altering the overall gearing.

Early MGs used the well known Bullnose radiator, but with the MG octagon badge fixed to it, though from late 1926 these were replaced by a more MG-like flat-nose style. Coachbuilding skills were prolific the time, and it was easy for Kimber to find bodies in two-seat, four-seat and a variety of saloon styles and shapes; Carbodies of Coventry provided most of them.

To call this pioneering MG a 'super sports' was really advertiser's hype (at which Kimber was adept), but there was no lack of demand for the model. The first two-seaters cost £350, though one could pay up to £460 for a four-seater saloon. The first factory move (to Bainton Road) followed in 1925, and further expansion would follow in 1927.

These sporty and extrovert machines were further improved in 1927 with the introduction of the revised Morris 'flat-nose' chassis, which was shorter, stiffer and heavier. Before long, production had risen above ten cars a week, but this was only the first of many expansions. The restless Kimber was not content to leave the 14/28 unmodified for long, so it was joined by a very similar car called the 14/40 in 1927, though the changes were mainly cosmetic. By 1928, however, MG had more exciting models under development – including the first of the tiny Midgets – so this pioneering MG model was soon phased out. Although about 1,300 14/28s and 14/40s of all types were built, very few now survive.

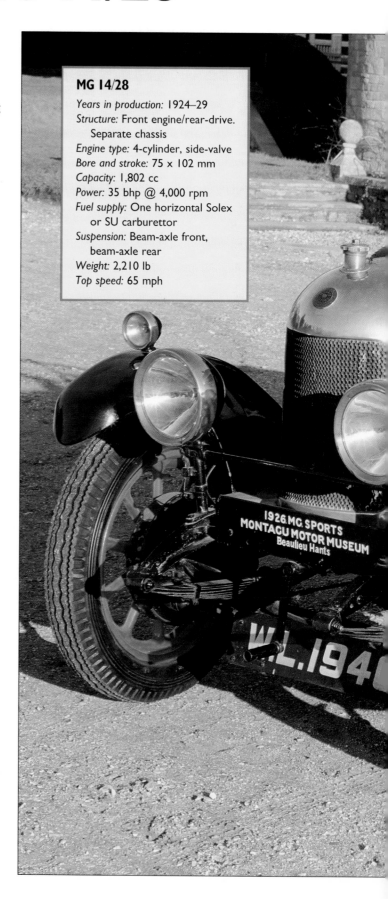

MG 14/28

Years in production: 1924–29
Structure: Front engine/rear-drive. Separate chassis
Engine type: 4-cylinder, side-valve
Bore and stroke: 75 x 102 mm
Capacity: 1,802 cc
Power: 35 bhp @ 4,000 rpm
Fuel supply: One horizontal Solex or SU carburettor
Suspension: Beam-axle front, beam-axle rear
Weight: 2,210 lb
Top speed: 65 mph

Below: Although the engines were modified from mundane side-valve Morris 'Oxford' types, they pushed out a creditable 30–35 bhp, which was enough to give the cars a 60–65 mph top speed.

1927 Riley Brooklands

Once Riley had announced its brand-new, and technically advanced twin-high camshaft 1,087 cc engine, complete with part-spherical combustion chambers, it became a prime target for sporting use. Even though Riley had not, so far, made a small sports car, the temptation to break into this new market was immense. The result, first seen in 1927, was the wickedly low and purposeful 'Brooklands' two-seater.

The engine had already been used in the Riley Nine family car of 1926, which was selling well, and clearly had a great deal of potential. Race driver and entrepreneur J.G. Parry Thomas had already started work on a 'Brooklands Special' before he was killed in a Land Speed Record attempt, and his work was continued by Reid Railton.

The first, and so far only, car was shown in mid 1927, with a unique low short-wheelbase chassis frame, and skimpy two-seater bodywork. A production version, the 'Speed Model', was put on sale months later,

Riley Brooklands
Years in production: 1927–32
Structure: Front engine/rear-drive. Separate chassis
Engine type: 4-cylinder, over head-valve
Bore and stroke: 60.3 x 95.2 mm
Capacity: 1,087 cc
Power: 50 bhp @ 5,000 rpm
Fuel supply: Two horizontal SU (or Solex) carburettors
Suspension: Beam-axle front, beam-axle rear
Weight: Never specified
Top speed: 80 mph

though this car had another totally different type of frame, a two-piece full-width screen and some rather skimpy all-weather equipment to make it more practical for road use. Priced at £395, and with a 50 bhp version of the engine (which was a very high specific output by late 1920s standards), it was obviously a fast little machine.

The whole car was tiny, light, nervous in its handling, and had a top speed of more than 80 mph (which made cars like the original MG M-type Midget look very slow indeed), though there was obviously much more to come as Reid Railton's race car lapped Brooklands at 98.62 mph on its very first outing. Almost immediately in 1929 it became known as the 'Brooklands' Riley, a glamorous nickname for any machine, particularly one priced at £420. With the aid of sponsored runs in long-distance trials like the Land's End (where Sammy Davis's car won a Gold Medal), it was soon seen to be versatile, strong, and very likeable.

No-one ever bought a Brooklands as a runabout, no-one attempted to carry more than two friendly occupants, and there was never any question of transporting luggage or even many parts. It was, after all, a hard-sprung, super-sporting, utterly convincing sports car (or perhaps a competition sports car?), which made no compromises, and it was well loved because of that. The market for this car was very limited, however, and although Riley are known to have produced at least 30,000 Nines of all types, only 200 of them were Brooklands models.

Below and right: In its day, the Brooklands was an immensely appealing little car, with low lines, purposeful detailing, and not a line, or superfluous bit of kit, out of place.

1928 Invicta 4½-litre

The Invicta was a short-lived and essentially 'vintage' phenomenon, but its reputation lives on. Conceived by Noel Macklin, and financed by the Lyle family (the sugar millionaires) in the 1920s, a range of fine hand-built machines emerged from Surrey and were only on the market from 1925 to 1933. Smaller Invictas followed, but Macklin had already turned his enthusiasm to making American-based Railtons instead, and post-war Invictas died through lack of custom.

Each and every 'vintage' Invicta was a sporting car; most were open, and all had that indefinable 'built like a battleship' quality which Bentley had already made so familiar to British motorists. The company was small, and under-equipped, so Invicta only changed their design slowly, and used a large number of 'bought-in' or proprietary components, particularly their engines. Original Invictas used a Coventry-Climax engine, but from 1925 the team turned to Henry Meadows of Wolverhampton, who supplied its rugged six-cylinder power unit in a variety of sizes, most notably the famous 4½-litre size, which was also supplied to Lagonda and other concerns.

Apart from the impressive front-end styling, which featured riveted bonnet panels, and in imitation of the contemporary Rolls-Royce, the cars' styling was unexceptional.

By 1930 the 4½-litre Invicta was available in two forms: as the high-chassis 'A' type, and the entirely different and much-lowered 'S' type, both at prices which approached those of the current Bentley and Rolls-Royce vehicles. The S-type (sometimes nicknamed the 'flat iron') Invicta was usually supplied with a lightweight open sports car body, and could be an extremely successful competition car.

Although one car (driven by *The Autocar*'s sports editor, Sammy Davis) was involved in a lurid crash at Brooklands, another in the hands of Donald Healey won the 1931 Monte Carlo Rally. Built like a battleship, and with the sort of stump-pulling torque for which such vintage engines were famous, this was a car which appealed strongly to those who could afford one. Yet by the early 1930s, rich sportsmen were few and increasingly cautious with their money, so Invicta found itself running out of clients. According to Noel Macklin, there were two solutions: one was to produce a much smaller-engined car (which was a complete failure); the other was to turn to an altogether cheaper type of car, which appeared as the Railton.

All in all, no more than 500 4½-litre Invictas were ever made, only 77 being the charismatic S-type sports cars.

Invicta 4½ litre

Years in production: 1928–33
Structure: Front engine/rear-drive. Separate chassis
Engine type: 6-cylinder, overhead-valve
Bore and stroke: 88.5 x 120.6 mm
Capacity: 4,467 cc
Power: 115 bhp @ unspecified rpm
Fuel supply: Two horizontal SU carburettors
Suspension: Beam-axle front, beam-axle rear
Weight: 2,800 lb
Top speed: 90–95 mph

Below: Every one of the original Invictas was developed around the same general chassis layout, which featured rock-hard half-elliptical front and rear suspension, and rod-operated drum brakes which were often inadequate for the car's performance.

1929 BSA 3-wheeler

BSA of Birmingham was famous for many years as a manufacturer of guns and other armaments, before it started to make cars. The fact that it was already producing motor cycles, and had acquired Daimler in 1910, must have influenced its plan to produce small, cheap, cars, as a half-way house between the two types.

Although the original BSA car of 1921–25 was a four-wheeler with an air-cooled power unit, the second model which followed in 1929, was a quirky and individualistic three-wheeler. With two front wheels and a single rear, but with front-wheel-drive (itself a real novelty) this was a distinctive and surprisingly successful car for the next few years. In seven years, until further rationalisation of the business ensued, BSA built at least 5,200 machines at its motorcycle factory at Small Heath, Birmingham.

Only a company as well founded as BSA could have produced a car like this, particularly as it reached maturity in the depths of Britain's depression. Although Morgan had already linked air-cooled two-cylinder engines to three-wheeler motoring, this was the first British application of front-wheel-drive; on the BSA, the rear wheel's only use was to hold the rear end of the 'duck-tail' bodywork off the ground.

The air-cooled 90-degree V-twin engine had overhead valves, and was a Hotchkiss design, a modified version of that used in the earlier BSA Ten of the early 1920s. Unlike any other engine of its day, it drove forward to a three-speed gearbox, which powered the front wheels, independent front suspension being by clusters of cantilever quarter-elliptic leaf springs.

Although this was no sports car (the engine, whose power was not stated, was not nearly as powerful as that of the Morgan three-wheeler) it was a brisk and surprisingly willing runabout, usually sold as a rather flimsily built two-seater (or three-abreast, if everyone was friendly) soft-top. Cruising speeds were no higher than 40 mph, but with complete car prices starting at no more than £130, it was an intriguing alternative to contemporary four-wheelers like the Austin Seven and the Morris Minor.

BSA persevered with this car for several years, making a few four-wheeler models (FW32 types) in 1932, while a four-cylinder water-cooled engine type followed in 1933.

Below: The chassis frame was simplicity itself, with members surrounding the engine/transmission unit, and with a single backbone member leading back to a neat cantilever spring/trailing link type of rear wheel suspension.

BSA 3-wheeler

Years in production: 1929–36
Structure: Front engine/front-wheel-drive. Separate chassis
Engine type: V2-cylinder, side-valve
Bore and stroke: 85 x 90 mm
Capacity: 1,021 cc
Power: Not revealed
Fuel supply: Single updraught Solex carburettor
Suspension: Independent front, independent rear
Weight: Never specified
Top speed: 50 mph

1929 Daimler Double Six

Between 1908 and the mid 1930s, Daimler of Coventry built a string of famous sleeve-valve-engined cars, with smooth and unobtrusive power units, which produced a slight but characteristic blue haze of engine oil smoke. The most famous of all, and a genuinely successful rival to Rolls-Royce, was the Double Six family, first launched in 1926.

Daimler's chief engineer, Laurence Pomeroy (Senior) persuaded his directors to authorise a series of magnificent and complicated V12 engines, which used many existing parts from current Daimler six-cylinder power units. It was called 'Double Six' because in many ways, such as the duplication of carburation, water pump and ignition systems, it was a double six-cylinder unit. The original, massive and imperial 'Fifty' was effectively two sets of 25/85 six-cylinder blocks set at an angle of 60 degrees.

With a capacity of 7.1 litres, and a declared output of 150 bhp (Rolls-Royce never dared to reveal their own peak figures, which were not impressive), this provided a huge, silent, power unit with more torque, which was ideal for the powering of massive limousines and (occasional) fast sporting models. Lever-type hydraulic dampers were standardised, and a vacuum servo was definitely needed to help power up the four-wheel drum brakes. Naturally, there was no power-assistance for the steering (such systems had not yet been invented), so the chauffeur had a hard job. Later models, at least, were available with Daimler's new pre-selector/fluid-flywheel transmission, which made them even smoother than before.

The typical Double Six '50' had a lofty limousine body, which could seat up to seven people, might weigh 6,200 lb/2,812 kg, and would cost around £2,500 – definitely Rolls-Royce levels. Not surprisingly, this model was popular with the British royal family, who purchased several, over the years. Fuel consumption could be worse than 10 mpg, but no-one seemed to worry about that.

To expand the range in 1928, the '50' was joined by the Double Six '30', which had an altogether different and smaller 3.8-litre V12; this model itself was replaced by the 5.3-litre '30/40' in 1930.

Even without the effects of the Depression, Double Six sales would always have been low, but economic problems hurt their prospects further, so the programme was gradually run down during the early 1930s, and the cars were eventually replaced with conventional straight-eight cylinder/poppet-valve cars. Less than 500 Double Six cars were built in the 1920s, even fewer after that.

Below: Chassis, though conventional in design, were always colossal, typically with a wheel-base of 155.5 in/3950 mm or even 163 in/4140 mm.

Daimler Double Six

Years in production: 1927–30 (1931–35 as developed 40/50 model)

Structure: Front engine/rear-drive Separate chassis

Engine type: V12-cylinder, double sleeve-valve

Bore and stroke: 81.5 x 114 mm

Capacity: 7,136 cc

Power: 150 bhp @ 2,480 rpm

Fuel supply: Two updraught Daimler carburettors (one per bank)

Suspension: Beam-axle front, beam-axle rear

Weight: Up to 6,200 lb (dependent on body fitted)

Top speed: 80 mph (dependent on body fitted)

1929 Talbot 14/45

Although the British Talbot concern was part of the larger Anglo-French Sunbeam-Talbot-Darracq (STD) combine, it was struggling to stay in business when Swiss-born engineer Georges Roesch returned to the company in London in 1925. Starting with a new six-cylinder engine, in the 14/45 of 1926, he transformed the prospects of the business, and was only ousted when Talbot fell into the hands of the Rootes Group in 1935.

Faced with almost non-existent sales of the older models, which had ageing technical features, Roesch was encouraged to start again – and did, from the ground up. The first of the new-generation cars was the 14/45. Its chassis, like that of the other 'Roesch Talbots' which would follow, was conventional enough, but the engine was quite superb.

Even in original form, when it measured a mere 1,666 cc, and had only four crankshaft main bearings, it seemed to be years ahead of contemporary British opposition: in later years, developed, enlarged and even more magnificent, it

Talbot 14/45

Years in production: 1926–35
Structure: Front engine/rear-drive. Separate chassis
Engine type: 4-cylinder, overhead-valve
Bore and stroke: 61 x 95 mm
Capacity: 1,666 cc
Power: 46 bhp @ 4,500 rpm
Fuel supply: One Zenith carburettor
Suspension: Beam-axle front, beam-axle rear
Weight: 2,630 lb
Top speed: 65 mph

would reach 3,377 cc and 123 bhp. At first it had only a single carburettor, but its potential was obvious.

The 14/45 model started life as a full five-seater saloon on a 120 in/3048 mm wheelbase. Other bodies – open, closed, 'family' and sporting – soon followed, and renamed the '65', the car sold until 1935. Clearly under-powered (or too heavy, depending on one's viewpoint), it was a car at the very beginning of its development life, but the quality of its engineering shone out from every corner. The asking price of £485 in 1926 ensured that it was a hit, and order books were immediately full, to the very limit of the North Kensington factory's capacity. Soon at least 50 14/45s were being built every week.

The chassis itself was neatly detailed, with deep side members and sturdy cross-bracing, and came complete with quarter-elliptic leaf spring rear suspension, a right-hand gear change, and torque tube transmission to the spiral bevel rear axle. Bodies were neat and impressive, rather than beautiful, but it was the obvious potential of the design, particularly of the engine, which attracted so much custom.

Motor traders, they say, did not like the new-fangled 14/45s because they required skilled, specialist attention, but the customers loved them. The handling was good, the quality of the engineering was high, and future prospects were enormous. By 1930 Roesch had developed the Talbot 90, with its 2.3-litre engine, the 3.0-litre-engined Talbot 105 followed in 1931, and an impressive string of race and rally results ensued. It was no wonder that the 14/45 was so popular, and before it finally died out (as the 65) no fewer than 11,851 cars had been produced.

Left: With good handling and high quality of engineering on these cars, customers flocked to buy this impressive five-seater saloon.

1931 Standard Big Nine

Until the end of the 1920s, Standard was a relatively small Coventry car maker, but the advent of Captain John Black, first as general manager, and later as managing director, galvanised it into further expansion. Black wanted Standard to be one of the 'big six' manufacturers, an ambition he achieved partly thanks to popular mass-market cars like the 'Big Nine'.

Like the Ford Model T (which had already disappeared) and the Ford 8 Model Y which soon followed, the Big Nine was intended to serve the mass market at a price they could afford, so it was engineered and equipped accordingly. Supported by Standard's ever-growing dealer chain, it was the sort of car the emerging middle class motorist could buy, use for business or enjoy at weekends: commuting, as a habit, was still rare in those days.

The first of the Big Nines was launched in 1928, and was one of the first Standards to use a new type of four-cylinder side-valve engine which (in four-cylinder and six-cylinder form) would find a home in many Standards and SS models in the next decade. The definitive Big Nine of 1930, though, was the first to combine coil ignition, a spiral bevel axle, and a new radiator style – but, unlike its predecessors, no union flag badge or mascot.

In many ways the first of Standard's mass-production cars, it influenced the Standards of the early 1930s in many ways, with its angular six-light saloon body style, its simple engine and transmissions (a choice of three-speed or four-speed), and its amazingly low prices, which started at only £195. In spite of what the traditionalists would insist, many aspiring motorists had not been able to afford a hand-built 'vintage' car, and it was this type of mass-produced machinery which was eventually going to put them on the road.

This was not a quick car, for its comfortable, and natural, cruising speed was no more than 40-45 mph, but at least it could record up to 40 mpg in daily use, and was simple, robust, and easy to service and maintain. In its road test, *The Autocar* called it 'a remarkably attractive car, especially in view of its moderate price.' Tens of thousands of Big Nines were eventually made, and their characteristics passed to the later, more stylish, Flying Nines; Standard's future was assured.

Standard Big Nine
Years in production: 1930–33
Structure: Front engine/rear-drive. Separate chassis
Engine type: 4-cylinder, side-valve
Bore and stroke: 63.5 × 102 mm
Capacity: 1,287 cc
Power: 25 bhp @ 3,200 rpm
Fuel supply: One Zenith carburettor
Suspension: Beam-axle front, beam-axle rear
Weight: 1,960 lb
Top speed: 54 mph

Below: The Standard Big Nine was a car intended to serve the mass market at a price they could afford and was easy to service and maintain.

1932 Alvis Speed Twenty

Although the first Alvis cars were not sold until 1920, they rapidly built up a fine reputation in the vintage era, not only because they were solidly-constructed machines, but because they had a great deal of sporting character too. While T.G. John was managing director, and Capt. G.T. Smith-Clarke was chief design engineer, the marque's future was safe.

During the 1920s a series of cars had all used the same type of four-cylinder engine, but the first six-cylinder Alvis, the 1,870 cc 14.75 SA, appeared in 1927. It was this engine and its enlarged descendants which powered almost every subsequent Alvis made until the outbreak of war in 1939. The original engine was later bored out, given a longer stroke, and generally modernised as the years passed, for it was an ideal 'building block' for Alvis's

future. From 1,870 cc, it became 2,148 cc, then 2,511 cc, 2,762 cc – and there was still more to come.

The Speed Twenty (the title indicated its official British RAC rating) was launched in 1931 as one of Alvis's first true post-vintage thoroughbred models, and came complete with the ex-Silver Eagle power unit of 2,511 cc. For the time, its peak power rating – 87 bhp – was quite outstanding, as was its top speed of nearly 90 mph.

In spite of its small size, (it rarely built even 1,000 cars in a year) Alvis, was always technically ambitious, so the Speed Twenty was improved significantly in four years. By 1933 not only was there a new chassis with independent front suspension, but also a modern synchromesh gearbox, both these features being years ahead of other British mass-market concerns.

All this, of course, came at a price, for the original Speed Twenty cost £695, while later saloons cost up to £850. Even so, by producing 1,165 examples, Alvis made the Speed Twenty its highest-selling pre-war car, during which time there were four sub-types, all of them with triple SU carburettor engines. By the mid 1930s, with the Speed Twenty reaching maturity, Alvis cars had become progressively larger, so the next generation of six-cylinder engines had 3.5-litre engines, and aimed for an even more rarified market than before.

Alvis Speed Twenty

Years in production: 1932–35
Structure: Front engine/rear-drive. Separate chassis
Engine type: 6-cylinder, overhead-valve
Bore and stroke: 73 x 100 mm
Capacity: 2,511 cc
Power: 87 bhp @ 4,000 rpm
Fuel supply: Three horizontal SU carburettors
Suspension: Beam-axle front, beam-axle rear
Weight: 2,912 lb
Top speed: 89 mph

Below: This was always a low-slung car with impeccable road manners, and (depending on the body style chosen) a variety of attractive styling. The whole car was led by that characteristic red triangular radiator badge.

1932 Ford 8 hp Model Y

If the Model T Ford was vital to Ford-USA's future, the Ford 8 hp Model Y was the single model which set Ford-UK on the way to market leadership. It was Ford's first truly small car, their cheapest-ever car, and it opened up Ford motoring to the masses.

Until the 1930s, Ford-UK's fortune was tied up in the assembly of American models such as the Model T and the Model A. The building of a new factory at Dagenham, in Essex, and the onset of the Depression in Europe made Ford desperate for something smaller, cheaper – and domestic. Although the Model Y was British-made, it was engineered and styled entirely in the USA. Those were the days when Ford ruled its world-wide empire from Dearborn, near Detroit, with a rod of iron. Every part of the car – the chassis, the tiny side-valve engine, and its style, came from the other side of the Atlantic.

The result was a car whose blood lines were still in evidence at Ford until the end of the 1950s, when the last of the Popular models was built. In 27 years, all the cars in this family were based on the same simple chassis frame, with transverse-leaf spring suspension on front and rear beam-axles, and with a version of the side-valve engine. Early Model Ys boasted 933 cc and 23 bhp, while the last, definitive units had 1,172 cc and 36 bhp.

Sold from mid-1932 as a cheap and cheerful two-door (Tudor) saloon for little more than £120, the Model Y immediately carved out a 40 per cent share of the 8 hp market, which had hitherto been dominated by the Morris Minor and the Austin Seven. The Model Y was so outstanding that when the Minor was renewed, it was replaced by a clone of the small Ford.

Model Ys provided marginal motoring at a very low cost, with tiny maintenance costs from an expanding line of Ford dealerships; nothing was allowed to push up the price. Four-door saloons soon joined the range, and there were specials from outside coachbuilders. The high point (the low point, really, in pricing terms) was when the stripped-out Popular of 1935 was launched, at a retail price of only £100 – the first time this had ever been achieved for a British series-production saloon.

The Model Y was slow, it only had a three-speed gearbox, and it had a tendency to wander from side to side on the road as its suspension flexed, but (like the Model T which preceded it), it provided unbeatable value and ample space for a complete family. Nearly 158,000 were produced in five years, before the re-styled and somewhat larger Model C 8 hp and 10 hp Fords took over in 1937. In that short time a principle had been established, which continues to this day in the current Ford range.

Right: This was Ford's first truly small car, their cheapest-ever which opened up Ford motoring to the masses with the bloodline of its design still in evidence until the end of the 1950s with the Ford Anglia and Ford Prefect.

Ford 8 hp Model Y

Years in production: 1932–37
Structure: Front engine/rear-drive
   Separate chassis
Engine type: 4-cylinder, side-valve
Bore and stroke: 56.6 x 92.5 mm
Capacity: 933 cc
Power: 23 bhp @ 4,000 rpm
Fuel supply: One downdraught
   Zenith carburettor
Suspension: Beam-axle front,
   beam-axle rear
Weight: 1,484 lb
Top speed: 59 mph

1933 Aston Martin Le Mans

The first Aston Martin cars were built in 1922, but the marque had a chequered financial record for many years. Prices were high and sales were low, because of the cars' specialised nature, and because the business was small.

There were several important changes of management in the first decade of production, and stability was finally established when Sir Arthur Sutherland took control in 1932. The well-liked four single overhead camshaft engine appeared in 1927, and would be used in one form or another for the next ten years. At the same time 'Bert' Bertelli rejuvenated the company, putting the cars into important races with considerable success.

The Sports and International models were established from 1927, but were costly to build. With the company fast fading away, Sir Arthur introduced revised cars, using bought-in proprietary components to reduce costs, and with a new chassis frame. The result was the launch of the new International and Le Mans models which sold steadily and consistently for the next two years.

The latest cars combined a new chassis frame, developed versions of the overhead-camshaft engine, and a proprietary Moss transmission, with a choice of wheelbase lengths and body styles. The Le Mans (so named after the team's motorsport appearances) was closely related to the new International, but had a lowered radiator, slab fuel tank, and chassis modifications.

Compared with the multitude of mundane engines offered by other makers, the Aston Martin's single-cam was not only efficient – 70 bhp from 1.5 litres was outstanding by early 1930s standards – but well specified, and was prepared to run for ever. Until 1932 an International Le Mans had sold (very slowly!) for £650, while the latest (1933) model retailed at £595.

Aston Martin was so encouraged by the car's reception

that they made haste to offer alternative wheelbase lengths – of 102 in/2591 mm or 120 in/3048 cc – in future seasons, with a choice of open two-seater of four-seater bodywork. Long, low, and immediately recognisable by their unique radiator style, these cars had great character, riding hard, but making all the appropriate mechanical noises. They were exclusive too, for in 1932 and 1933, only 130 Aston Martins of all types were produced. Although the marque name survived, later, post-war, Aston Martins were completely different.

Aston Martin Le Mans

Years in production: 1932–33
Structure: Front engine/rear-drive
    Separate chassis
Engine type: 4-cylinder, single
    overhead camshaft
Bore and stroke: 69.3 x 99 mm
Capacity: 1,495 cc
Power: 70 bhp @ 4,750 rpm
Fuel supply: Two horizontal SU
    carburettors
Suspension: Beam-axle front,
    beam-axle rear
Weight: 2,128 lb
Top speed: 85 mph

· · · · · · · · · · · · · ·

Below and above: By the standards of the early 1930s, these were not only speedy cars (the Le Mans' top speed was about 85 mph which compared well with the pace of the cheaper MG and Singer sports cars of the day), but were also significantly cheaper than before, retailing at £595.

1933 Bentley 3½-litre

Although the legendary 'W.O.' Bentley cars built a fine reputation in a mere ten years, they were not a commercial success, so after the company had run through at least three tranches of capital, it went broke for the last time in 1931. After a rather sordid courtroom battle, Bentley was bought up by Rolls-Royce, and re-developed in its own image. There was a two year hiatus, while the last surviving 'W.O.' cars were bodied and sold off, and a new model was developed.

The cars which appeared in 1933 shared only a radiator badge with their earlier namesakes. Marketed under the banner of the 'Silent Sports Car', the first 'Rolls-Bentley' (or 'Derby Bentley') was the 3½-litre model of 1933, which leaned heavily on the existing Rolls-Royce 20/25 model for its running gear. The two cars, however, had little in common. Although they shared the same basic 3.7-litre six-cylinder engine, that used in the Bentley was much-

modified and more powerful (we were never told how powerful, though). This was used with the Rolls-Royce transmission in a new chassis which, in spite of what the traditionalists might say, was much lighter and more capable than ever before.

The new Bentleys were bodied by independent coachbuilders, a good proportion being clothed by Park Ward, Barker and Gurney Nutting, each producing noticeably more rakish styles than anything normally committed to a Rolls-Royce base. Although prices crept up in the years which followed, an early 3½-litre would cost about £1,500 to put on the road – a price which one should compare with the £100 Ford 8 hp saloon of the period.

To call it a 'sports car', would stretch the point, but this new Bentley was certainly a fast and capable 'grand tourer'. A 90 mph top speed, which was

> **Bentley 3½ litre**
>
> *Years in production:* 1933–36
> *Structure:* Front engine/rear-drive
>   Separate chassis
> *Engine type:* 6-cylinder,
>   overhead-valve
> *Bore and stroke:* 88.9 x 114.3 mm
> *Capacity:* 3,669 cc
> *Power:* Never revealed
> *Fuel supply:* Two horizontal SU
>   carburettors
> *Suspension:* Beam-axle front,
>   beam-axle rear
> *Weight:* 3,920 lb
> *Top speed:* 95 mph

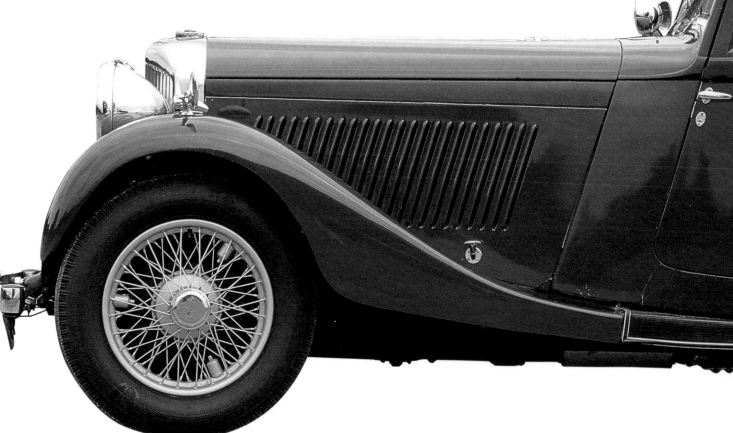

Below and left: The new Bentleys were fast, capable of a top speed of 90 mph. These were light and appealing cars, sharing the same radiator badge as the 'W.O.' Bentleys.

normal for these original cars, was very fast by the standards of the day. The Bentley's character, too, was very light and appealing, something proved by the hundreds of cars which still survive.

As competition increased, and as the weight of the cars inexorably crept up, more performance was needed, so from 1936, the 4¼-litre model took over (with a 4,257 cc engine), while a four-speed 'overdrive' gearbox was

standardised from 1938, though none ever achieved 100 mph in standard coachwork form. By the summer of 1939 the range was at the height of its fame, and its replacement by a brand new generation Rolls–Bentley was only prevented by the outbreak of the Second World War with Hitler's Germany.

In six years nearly 2,500 Bentleys were produced, 1,191 of them the original 3½-litre types.

1935 Hillman Minx

A motor car does not have to be beautiful or incredibly fast, to become a classic. It must, above all, stand out as a great example of what was right for its day. Just as there were important sports cars between the wars, so were there also commercially successful family cars. The Hillman Minx of 1935–39 was one of them.

Until 1928, Hillman had been independent, but following its purchase by Rootes Ltd (motor traders and distributors whose guiding light was 'Billy' Rootes, of Maidstone), it was rapidly turned into a mass production concern. Along with Humber, it became a major constituent part of the Rootes Group, which immediately became one of the British 'big six' car makers.

The original, and all-new Minx was previewed in 1931, and went on sale in 1932, but it was the second-generation Minx (the 'Minx Magnificent', as its bonnet badge advertised) which finally established the type. From then until the 1970s, there would always be a Hillman Minx in the Rootes Group line-up.

Mechanically it was conventional, with a separate chassis, beam-axle front and rear suspensions, and a side-valve engine, but there was interest in the detail, and it may be significant that both Bill Heynes (later legendary at Jaguar) and Alec Issigonis (of Mini fame) were both employed at Rootes at this time.

The most popular version was a rounded four-door saloon (Pressed Steel supplied the bodies), but a few limited-edition styles were also produced. It was neither fast (the top speed was about 60 mph), nor temperamental, but it was reliable, refined by

Hillman Minx

Years in production: (Second generation car) 1935–39
Structure: Front engine/rear-drive. Separate chassis
Engine type: 4-cylinder, side-valve
Bore and stroke: 63 x 95 mm
Capacity: 1,185 cc
Power: 30 bhp @ 4,100 rpm
Fuel supply: One downdraught Solex carburettor
Suspension: Beam-axle front and rear
Weight: 2,130 lb
Top speed: 60 mph

the standards of the 1930s, and roomy enough to carry four or even five adults.

More than all this, a Minx was remarkably cheap, for in 1935 British prices started at a mere £159. No wonder the first 10,000 were built in a matter of months, or that a total of 92,095 cars were built in only four full years and the side-valve engine itself would be used in Rootes Group cars until 1957.

Above: Built in large quantities in Coventry, it was the highest-selling Rootes Group car of the day, and eventually donated its running gear to more up-market machines such as the Talbot Tens of the period.

1936 Rolls-Royce Phantom III

Looking back over the decades, one has to ask what inspired Rolls-Royce to build a car as complex as the Phantom III, for this was the very first British car which had ever been designed around a V12 engine. Logically, however, one can see that Rolls-Royce had to compete with Hispano-Suiza, who also had a V12, and particularly with Cadillac, who were selling limited numbers of V16-engined machines. In the most discreet way, too, there must also have been a good marketing reason to supplement the efforts of the aircraft engine division, which had just started building the famous V12 Merlin engine, which would power the Spitfires, Hurricanes, Lancasters and Mosquitoes of the RAF in the Second World War.

As the successor of the existing company flagship, the Phantom II, the new Rolls-Royce was entitled Phantom III. Although no larger than before, it had a new chassis frame, complete with independent front suspension (which had been copied very carefully from the latest General Motors layouts), but all other mechanical attention was centred on the V12 engine. Not only was this a real leviathan, at 7.34 litres, but it also featured hydraulic tappets ('valve lifters', as Americans always called them), and was more powerful than any previous Rolls-Royce engine. It needed to be, for the coachbuilt machines could be extremely heavy, and they carried such craggy bodywork with a vast frontal area that top speeds were rarely more than 90 mph.

Most owners, it has to be said, were far more interested in buying a car in which they could not even hear the engine running, and in which they could luxuriate in total comfort.

To their shame (though the news rarely got out at the time), Rolls-Royce found that these engines were troublesome (particularly if the new tappets got sludge in their mechanisms), so there were no long-term plans to improve the power unit in the 1940s. The advent of war, and the post-war chance to start again, must have been a relief, although another consequence was that very few V12-engined Phantom IIIs survive into the classic car era. Only 710 were ever built.

Right: The Rolls-Royce Phantom III – if one had to ask the price, one could probably not afford it, for these were the most exclusive and expensive of all late-1930s British motor cars.

Rolls-Royce Phantom III

Years in production: 1936–39
Structure: Front engine/rear-drive Separate chassis
Engine type: V12-cylinder, overhead-valve
Bore and stroke: 82.5 x 114.3 mm
Capacity: 7,338 cc
Power: Never officially revealed
Fuel supply: Single downdraught carburettor
Suspension: Independent front, beam-axle rear
Weight: 5,400 lb
Top speed: 90 mph

1936 MG TA

The watershed of MG's early years came in 1935, when the company's guardian, Lord Nuffield, transferred its ownership to his vast new Nuffield Organisation. At the same time, his managing director, Len Lord, decreed that future MG sports cars should use many more off-the-shelf components than before.

One early result was the launch of the TA, the first of a long and successful line of T-series cars, which launched MG even faster down the road to world-wide fame. Longer, wider, heavier, but simpler than the PB model which it replaced, the TA was a classic MG sports car.

Although it was built around a simple ladder-style chassis frame, and had a body shell assembled around a wooden frame – both of which were traditional MG in every way – the TA's real innovation as far as the customers were concerned was in its engine and transmission. For the first time in eight years, this was an MG without an overhead-camshaft engine, and it was also the first to have a synchromesh (as opposed to a 'crash') gearbox.

The TA, in fact, had been laid out in the Nuffield design offices, where the engineers had chosen to use modified versions of the latest Morris/Wolseley engines and running gear. According to the traditionalists (who were wrong) this ruined the MG's character, but Nuffield's planners produced a car that was simpler, faster, and more reliable than before. Before long, the TA was selling faster than any previous MG, and only one look at its style spelt out the reason. Here was a two-seater car with all the established MG virtues of sweeping front wings, proud free-standing headlamps, and an unmistakable radiator grille. Not only that, but it was probably the first Midget to have a cockpit large enough for two adults.

Although the 1,292 cc engine was neither as specialised, nor as high-revving, as its predecessors, it delivered the goods, for this was the fastest Midget yet. In some ways it was almost an embarrassment for MG, as it was also little slower than the six-cylinder Magnettes, which were still available.

With the virtues came all the expected failings – a rock-hard ride, sensitive steering, sketchy all-weather equipment, and a tendency to leak water in heavy rain-storms – but no-one seemed to care. Like earlier Midgets, this was a car with a heart and soul, which seemed to relate to every owner's yearnings.

The TA set MG on a new sports car path, for the re-engined TB took over successfully in 1939, and the TC (a lightly-modified TB) would be a huge success in the late 1940s. It was a very important Midget: before the arrival of the TA, MG's commercial future had been in doubt, but afterwards the subject was never mentioned again.

MG TA

Years in production: 1936–39
Structure: Front engine/rear-drive. Separate chassis
Engine type: 4-cylinder, overhead-valve
Bore and stroke: 63.5 x 102 mm
Capacity: 1,292 cc
Power: 50 bhp @ 4,500 rpm
Fuel supply: Two horizontal SU carburettors
Suspension: Beam-axle front, beam-axle rear
Weight: 1,765 lb
Top speed: 78 mph

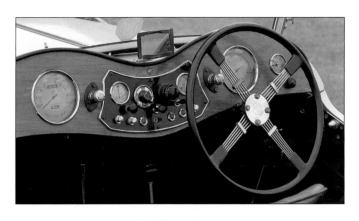

Below and above: The TA sold faster than any earlier MG. It was a simple, fast and reliable two-seater with the famous MG badge displayed prominently above its distinctive radiator grill.

1936 SS-Jaguar SS100

SS and SS-Jaguar came from nowhere to lead the middle class car market, during the 1930s, which was a credit to William Lyons and his single-minded enterprise. Whereas the original 1932 SS1 had used humble side-valve Standard engines, late 1930s SS-Jaguars had powerful, purpose-designed overhead-valve 'sixes'. That, and a line-up of elegant styles, made them extremely desirable.

New for 1936, the SS-Jaguars had four-cylinder and six-cylinder engines, saloon and drop-head coupé body styles, along with one very special derivative – the rakish two-seater SS100 sports car. Using a short wheelbase version of the touring cars' chassis, but with the same engines, transmissions and other running gear, the SS100 was a wickedly attractive two-seater which came as close to sex-on-wheels as its descendant the E-type a quarter of a century later.

Running on a 102 in/2591 mm wheelbase chassis, with hard beam-axle suspension and rather heavy and imprecise steering, the SS100 did not even attempt to give its occupants a peaceful ride, but inspired excitement at every turn. Its sweeping front wings were dominated by huge headlamps; the bonnet was long, low, and covered in louvres; the engine bay was full of impressive power, while the rear wings were abbreviated and rather coquettishly curved. Cutaway doors, a slab fuel tank, and a fold-down windscreen all added to this car's irresistible visual appeal.

Original SS100s had 2.7-litre engines, a 95 mph top speed, and cost £395, but from 1938 there was the option of a 125 bhp/3,485 cc power unit, from which 101 mph was available, all for a mere £445. There was much petty jealousy from SS-Jaguar's rivals, but none of them could counter the colossal (by 1930s standards) performance, the eye-catching looks, or the amazing value-for-money pricing.

The fact that sales were so limited – only 198 2.5-litre and 116 3.5-litre types were produced in four years – reflected the heavy annual taxation of the period, rather than the car's limitations. It was, admittedly, one of those machines one only ever bought as a 'toy' (there was virtually nowhere to stow baggage, and rather sketchy all-weather accommodation), but its excitement-per-pound rating must have been one of the most impressive of all time.

SS-Jaguar considered making a closed two-seater coupé version of the same car, but this never progressed beyond a single prototype. In the more sober motoring period which followed the Second World War, there was no place for an SS100 in the line-up, but the vast majority of these machines seem to have survived.

SS-Jaguar SS100

Years in production: 1936–39
Structure: Front engine/rear-drive. Separate chassis
Engine type: 6-cylinder, overhead-valve
Bore and stroke: 73 x 106 mm/82 x 110 mm
Capacity: 2,663 cc/3,485 cc
Power: 102 bhp @ 4,600 rpm/125 bhp @ 4,250 rpm
Fuel supply: Two horizontal SU carburettors
Suspension: Beam-axle front, beam-axle rear
Weight: 2,576 lb
Top speed: 94/101 mph

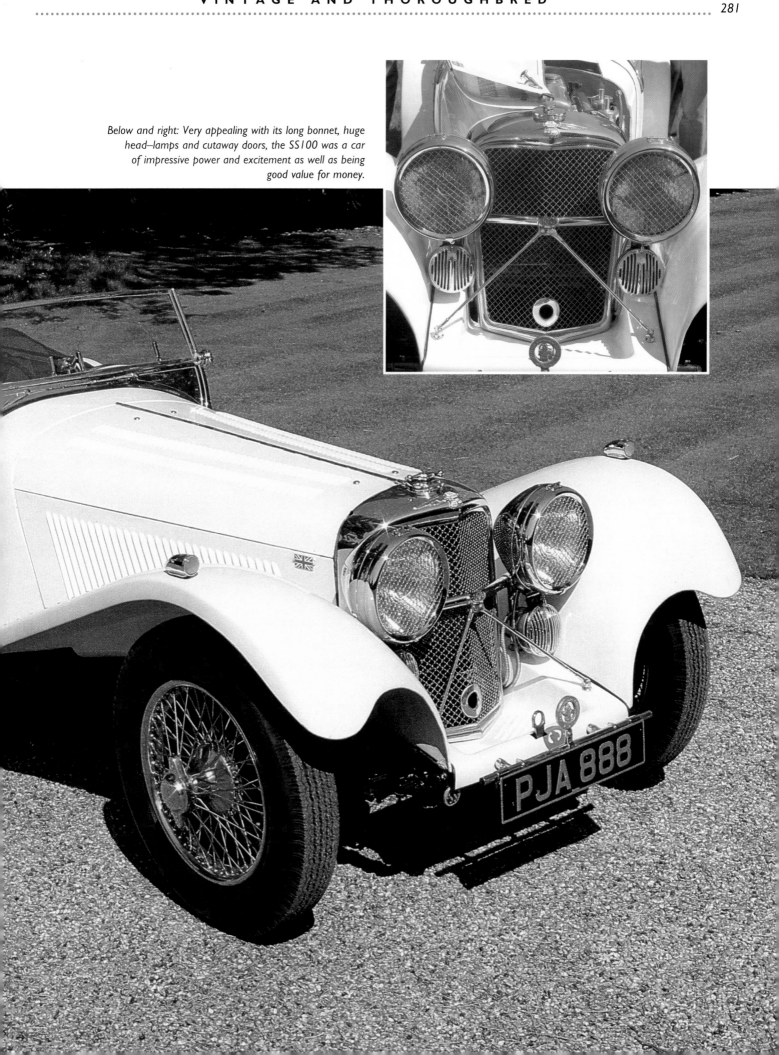

Below and right: Very appealing with its long bonnet, huge head–lamps and cutaway doors, the SS100 was a car of impressive power and excitement as well as being good value for money.

1937 Lagonda V12

Those who didn't know that the extremely desirable Lagonda V12 was inspired by W.O. Bentley could surely have guessed, for here was a massive, locomotive-like machine, with an engine producing immense torque, and all the characteristics of the legendary 'vintage' Bentleys. Those cars, at least, had carried the famous badge, but the Lagonda V12 was a latter-day 'W.O.' by another name.

Bentley himself, the confident and renowned engineer, had been tied to Rolls-Royce since the take-over of 1931, but was eventually released in 1935, after which he immediately joined the small Lagonda company, which made its cars at Staines, in Middlesex. Current Lagondas

of the early 1930s were worthy but rather rough sports and saloon cars, which used massive Meadows six-cylinder engines. Bentley's new team quickly refined what they found, developed a new chassis, and finally set about the design of a new engine, an ambitiously-detailed 4.5-litre V12. Although the prototype was shown at the Olympia Motor Show of 1936, it was still not complete, and production units were not delivered until 1938.

Lagonda V12

Years in production: 1937–39
Structure: Front engine/rear-drive. Separate chassis
Engine type: V12-cylinder, single overhead-camshaft
Bore and stroke: 75 x 84.5 mm
Capacity: 4,480 cc
Power: 180 bhp @ 5,500 rpm
Fuel supply: Two downdraught Solex carburettors
Suspension: Independent front, beam-axle rear
Weight: 4,440 lb
Top speed: 101 mph

The V12's chassis was solid, well detailed, and modern. It shared many of the various body styles with the LG6 type (Meadows six-cylinder-engined) which ran alongside it, so all attention was concentrated on the engine. This was only the second British V12 to go on sale (Rolls-Royce, with the Phantom III having the first), though Hispano-Suiza also had such a power unit. It had an overhead-camshaft valve gear and 'two of everything' – SU carburettors, electrical coils and fuel pumps – so this was a smooth and effective power unit, which not only produced 180 bhp, but was the most powerful of all pre-war British engines.

Available in saloon, drop-head coupé, limousine, tourer and other derivatives, each and every V12 had to be hand-built – and in fact only 189 were built before war broke out.

The engine went on to have a fine career in light naval craft, but was not revived after the war.

Below: Undeniably expensive cars, (from £1,550 in 1938, at a time when the Bentley 4.25-litre cost only £1,430), they were bound to sell slowly, but because every type had a top speed of more than 100 mph, they were very popular.

1937 Triumph Dolomite Roadster

Donald Healey might not have been a trained engineer, or a trained stylist, but he always managed to inspire his teams to produce exceptional cars. The distinctively shaped Triumph Dolomite Roadster was a fine example.

Already famous for winning the Monte Carlo Rally in 1931, Donald Healey joined Triumph in 1933, soon rising to become the company's technical director. Having been allowed one expensive indulgence, which was the supercharged Dolomite Straight Eight, he then up-graded Triumph's production

car range of Glorias and Vitesses. The arrival of a new Dolomite range (no relation) denoted the launch of a new family of four- and six-cylinder engines.

One feature of the new Dolomites in 1936 was their 'waterfall' style of radiator grille, which stylist Walter Belgrove had produced as an obvious inspiration from the latest Hudson Terraplanes. This was distinctive enough, but when added to the style of body which appeared in 1938, it produced a real effect. Well trimmed and furnished, the Dolomite Roadster, which was produced in very limited numbers,

Triumph Dolomite Roadster

Years in production: 1937–39
Structure: Front engine/rear-drive. Separate chassis
SPEC. FOR 2-LITRE
Engine type: 6-cylinder, over head-valve
Bore and stroke: 65 x 100 mm
Capacity: 1,991 cc
Power: 75 bhp @ 4,500 rpm
Fuel supply: Three horizontal SU carburettors
Suspension: Beam-axle front, beam-axle rear
Weight: 3,304 lb
Top speed: 80 mph

was more 'drop-head' than 'roadster', and it was available in two forms: a four-cylinder 1,767 cc type, or a six-cylinder 1,991 cc model with a longer (and even more elegant) wheelbase. On this body the waterfall grille was matched to a two-seater front compartment, and a long sweeping tail concealed a lift-up panel which hid two further 'dickey' seats. Although this was already an obsolete feature, and the whole thing was a trifle over-the-top, it was striking, and attractive.

When the six-cylinder engine was fitted, the top speed was around 80 mph, enough to make it a useful rally car. For the well-to-do middle class sportsman, who could choose between Triumph, SS-Jaguar, Riley, MG and other substantial cars, this was an intriguing contender and, at £450 for the 116 in/2,946 mm wheelbase version, it was good value.

Seat trim was in pigskin-grained leather, winding windows were provided in the doors, there was a disappearing front arm rest between the seats, and discreet steps were fitted to allow access to the dickey seats, for which there were no doors. In the rather genteel British motoring competitions of the day it was a sure-fire contender for Concours awards.

Elegant by the standards of the day, it died at the outbreak of war, for post-war Triumphs were really modified Standards, and a new-generation Roadster was not nearly as smart as the original.

Below and right: Distinguished by the 'waterfall' style of its radiator grille, the Dolomite Roadster had a sweeping tail which concealed a lift-up panel with two middle 'dickey' seats.

The superb radiator grill and huge headlamps contributed to the eye catching looks of the 1936 SS100 Jaguar.

The Classic Years

——— 1945–1970 ———

Morgan 4/4 ✪ Riley RM Series ✪ Allard Sports Car
Jowett Javelin ✪ Jaguar XK120 ✪ Land-Rover ✪ Morris Minor
Bond Minicar 3-wheeler ✪ Healey Silverstone ✪ Dellow Sports Car
Rover P4 ✪ Ford Consul/Zephyr Six ✪ MG TD
Standard Vanguard ✪ Bentley Continental R-Type ✪ Triumph TR2
MG MGA ✪ Armstrong-Siddeley Star Sapphire ✪ Austin-Healey Sprite
Lotus Elite ✪ Triumph Herald ✪ Austin-Healey 3000
Austin-Morris Mini ✪ Jaguar 3.8 Mk II
Jaguar E-Type ✪ AC Cobra ✪ Aston Martin DB5 ✪ Hillman Imp
Sunbeam Tiger ✪ Jensen FF & Interceptor ✪ Range Rover

The Classic Years

For Britain's motor industry, the Second World War changed everything. When Britain's car makers returned to their peacetime businesses in 1945, they faced a different reality. The market-place, clientele, social climate and economy had all been transformed.

It was not only the factories which built the cars, but also the nations and the individual customers who bought them which had been badly battered by the fighting; furthermore, prices had more than doubled in six years. In order to raise revenue, the British government (almost bankrupt by the sheer cost of the war) had introduced a purchase tax on what they defined as luxury items – which naturally included cars. Even so, if economic conditions had not then been turned on their heads, British car makers might still have been able to carry on where they left off in 1939.

A Labour government took over for the first time since 1931, a government which indulged in an orgy of nationalisation, raised taxes to pay for this, followed a long-term policy of austerity, and kept rationing of everything from bread to petrol going for years longer than was really justified. There was a shortage of all

materials (and national reconstruction had the utmost priority), and it was obviously going to take years to bring truly new post-war cars to the market. To fill the gap, therefore, the motor industry mostly re-started by building mildly up-dated versions of their 1939 models.

HUGE DEMAND

After six years in which private car production had ceased, and in which many older cars had been worn out, abandoned or destroyed, there was a huge demand for new cars all over the world. Almost any car, however old-fashioned, or crudely developed, found sales in the first post-war years.

Until the 1950s, therefore, Britain's motor industry thrived in this climate. Although a government recommendation for car makers to follow a 'one-model policy' never really took off, a new type of flat-rate taxation influenced the architecture of future engines, and an 'export or die' philosophy obliged companies to export most of their output (strictly monitored steel supply quotas saw to that). This meant that British customers had to join huge waiting lists, and originally had to sign

Below: After crossing the Atlantic from New York in the liner Queen Elizabeth, a Rolls-Royce Silver Cloud is re-fuelled by a three-wheel Scammell Esso transporter at Southampton dockside in 1960.

Above: In 1966 an E-Type Jaguar Coupé was regarded as the height of fashion, driven by pop and film stars; its enduring beauty means it can still turn heads today.

'covenants' to stop them re-selling recently delivered new cars for profit on to a black market. Cars were only available to priority customers at first (doctors and other 'essential workers' among them). For the private individual, new cars ordered in 1946 would often not arrive until the early 1950s, sometimes to an entirely different and later specification.

For the motor industry, this was a financial golden age, and several car makers became complacent about their future. Only one large merger (of Austin with the Nuffield Organisation in 1952, to form BMC) took place, and this was never pursued to its logical conclusion. Aston Martin also merged with Lagonda, but this was at the expensive end of the market, and was less significant.

To satisfy the demand on their own terms, and with new export opportunities, the 'big five' car makers churned out more and more conventional machinery. Insatiable demand and great enthusiasm from private owners, however, encouraged the production of new styles and ranges. Thoughtful companies like Rover went into a new market sector with the Land Rover, old-fashioned types such as Jowett (with the Javelin and the Jupiter) sought to change their image, while thrusting businesses like Jaguar set up entirely new ranges (such as the XK120 sports cars and the Mk VII saloons). They were joined by brash new makes such as Allard, Bristol, Healey and Lotus, who used different materials where there was no steel, ingenuity instead of conventional engineering where there was an opportunity, and crossed fingers

where there was a lack of finance.

Among the mass-producers, some designers were allowed to look into the future, and it wasn't long before modern cars (which have subsequently become known as 'classics' began to appear. The bulbous Morris Minor of 1948 set new small-car standards, if not of performance, then certainly in chassis behaviour; the Consul/Zephyr series from Ford introduced a whole list of technical novelties, while the Rootes Group (Hillman, Humber and Sunbeam) developed the art of product planning (or squeezing many models out of restricted resources).

NEW ENTERPRISE

The big advances in styling, engineering and sheer motoring excitement came from the independent makers. If they could not buy sheet steel, they made do with aluminium, with steel tubes and with fibreglass. Smaller companies were early innovators; they were the first to exploit aerospace construction such as multi-tube space frames and disc brakes, and were always ready to pioneer strange aerodynamic shapes or materials to make their point. An AC, an Allard, a Bristol, or even a Bond three-wheeler might not appeal to everyone – but they were available and they all had their merits.

Then, in the 1950s, came the boom in British sports cars. MG and Jaguar, both well-established, blossomed with new types, while Austin-Healey, Triumph and Sunbeam all joined in. Though staid car makers like Alvis, Jowett and Daimler all tried to surf this tidal wave, they failed, and one of the few new companies to become permanently established was Colin Chapman's Lotus. North America, in particular, loved Britain's TR2s, MGAs, Alpines and Austin-Healey 100s, but that love-affair became even more intense in the 1960s with the arrival of small sports cars like the Triumph Spitfire, the Austin-Healey Sprite, MG Midget and the sensational Jaguar E-type.

This, if only the pundits had known it, was really the start of the now-recognised 'classic' era, where individual motor cars of all types became available at amazingly attractive prices. The appeal of sports cars was obvious, but Britain also produced fascinating new models such as the famous front-wheel-drive BMC Mini, and technically interesting cars such as the Triumph Herald and the Hillman Imp.

Yet this was not before time, as Europe's car makers had made a strong recovery from the devastation of war, and had always produced more interesting cars than the British. Say what you like about the looks of the VW Beetle, or of the crudities of the Fiat 600 and Renault Dauphine types, they sold in vast quantities, and quite overshadowed many British machines.

Below: The new Ford Anglia de Luxe 1959/60 with an aerodynamic body tested in wind tunnels. The car featured a unique reverse angle rear screen. It is fondly remembered by many as the car chosen for summer holiday hire in the early 1960s.

RATIONALISATION

Much of the romance of making motor cars was squeezed out of Britain's industry in the 1960s as a wave of mergers and many transatlantic methods swept through the workshops. Ford and Vauxhall both prospered under American ownership, and were joined by the Rootes Group, who fell to Chrysler.

Standard-Triumph was taken over by Leyland (the truck maker with big ideas) in 1961, who eventually swallowed up Rover and Alvis too. BMC, complacent as ever, thought they were above all this, though they bought up Jaguar just to be sure. Then, in 1968, government pressure saw Leyland merge with BMC-Jaguar, producing the ill-fated British Leyland combine.

Jaguar, Lotus and Aston-Martin-Lagonda were almost the only survivors of the famous old marques. Many fell by the wayside and the roll-call of the vanished makes was heartbreaking: Allard, Alvis, Armstrong-Siddeley, Healey, Invicta, Jowett, Lea-Francis and many others all closed their doors, and worse was to follow. Although the industry closed ranks, concentrating on fewer and fewer groups, British car production continued to rise – from 522,515 units in 1950 to 1,352,728 in 1960, and onwards to 1,640,966 in 1970, but this wasn't all unblemished good news. In the same period, imports of foreign cars rocketed from 1,375 in 1950 to 157,956 in 1970, and this was only the beginning.

Rationalisation, expansion and sheer caution meant that cars like the Ford Cortina, the Morris 1100, the

*Above: The Aston Martin Lagonda DB6 Mk2. This new-look
Aston Martin had fuel injection and DBS safety features.
It first went on sale on August 21, 1969.*

Hillman Minx and the Vauxhall Viva sold in large numbers, and truly interesting and inspiring cars (particularly sports cars) languished in the shadows. Yet it was still Britain's most individual cars from Lotus, Jensen, Range Rover and Austin-Healey which made all the headlines.

It was at this point that motoring history began to repeat itself. In the 1930s observers had tired of the cars currently on offer, had looked back longingly to the cars of the 1920s and started calling them 'vintage'. In the early 1970s many enthusiasts harked back to the 1950s and 1960s, sad that such individualism seemed to have gone for ever. In the 1930s, traditionalists had yearned for a 'vintage' car, but now, having settled on a new definition, they wanted a 'classic'. They didn't really need to know that a dictionary defined classic as being, 'of acknowledged excellence; outstandingly important; remarkably typical...' – for they knew that already, and this was the sort of motor car they wanted to remember from the period.

DOOM AND GLOOM

It was almost by accident that the 'classic car' movement was founded at the same time as the first energy crisis erupted, and it was almost coincidental that the most

enterprising of British (and overseas, for that matter) car makers began to pull in their horns at the same time. Britain's original *Classic Cars* magazine was first published in 1973 as inflation soared out of control, as the miners struck, putting the lights out, and as British Leyland became a national joke.

Faced with the threat of petrol rationing, of open-road speed limits almost everywhere (West German autobahns being a notable exception), and of more and more performance- and character-sapping legislation, many motorists feared that all the world's best cars might already have been built. Companies as big as Ford started cancelling sporty models and withdrawing temporarily from motorsport, and all except the brave started developing bigger and better safety bumpers, ever-more varieties of economical engines, and continued to worry about safety regulations.

Only the most optimistic drivers thought that the most exciting cars were still to come. So, what if our sports cars were rapidly losing their markets in the USA, and so what if we were faced with paying a lot more money for our cars in the 1980s? We could still look back on this Golden Age ....

1946 Morgan 4/4

Although the original four-wheeler Morgan was shown in the mid-1930s, it was overshadowed by the company's older three-wheeler models until the end of the Second World War. From that point, while altering the original style only slightly as the years passed by, Morgan concentrated on their four-wheeler sports cars.

Morgans were first made by a family-owned business in 1910 (a situation which has never changed), and even

the first cars employed a type of sliding-pillar independent front suspension which is still used to this day.
Assembly was always by hand, always at a leisurely pace,

Morgan 4/4

Years in production: 1945–50
Structure: Front engine/rear-drive.
    Separate chassis
Engine type: 4-cylinder, overhead-
    valve
Bore and stroke: 63.5 x 100 mm
Capacity: 1,267 cc
Power: 40 bhp @ 4,300 rpm
Fuel supply: One downdraught
    Solex carburettor
Suspension: Independent front,
    beam-axle rear
Weight: 1,590 lb
Top speed: 77 mph

and even in the post-war years it was a good week
which saw more than ten complete cars leave the gates
in Malvern Link.

The post-war 4/4 retained the simple ladder-style
chassis and the rock-hard suspension for
which the marque is noted, and still
looked like its 1939 predecessor. It used
to be said that the ride was so hard that
if one drove over a penny in the road, a
skilled driver would know whether
'heads' or 'tails' was uppermost. Although
pre-war cars had been powered by
Coventry-Climax, the post-war chassis
was exclusively fitted with a specially-
manufactured overhead-valve Standard
1,267 cc engine (which never appeared
in Standard or Triumph models).
Although this engine only produced 40
bhp, the Morgan was such a light car that
it could reach 75 mph, while handling in a way that
made all MG Midget owners jealous.

The style was what we must now call 'traditional
Morgan' – it was a low-slung two-seater with sweeping
front wings, and free-standing headlamps, along with
cutaway doors and the sort of weather protection which
made one drive quickly for home in a shower, rather
than stop to wrestle with its sticks and removable panels.
Up front, there was a near-vertical radiator, flanked by
free-standing headlamps, while the coil spring/vertical-
pillar front suspension was easily visible from the nose.
Most 4/4s were open-top two-seaters, though a more
completely trimmed and equipped two-seater drop-
head coupé (with wind-up windows in the doors) was
also available. Bodies were framed from unprotected
wood members, with steel or aluminium skin panels
tacked into place, and were all manufactured in the
Morgan factory.

Here was an old-style, no-compromise sports car made
in modern times – a philosophy which Morgan has never
abandoned. Requests for a more modern specification
were politely shrugged off, waiting lists grew, and Morgan
has been financially healthy ever since. Before the 4/4
was replaced by the altogether larger 2.1-litre Plus 4 of
1950, a grand total of 1,720 4/4s were sold.

*Left: Hand assembled, these low-slung two-seater sports
cars had cutaway doors and a near vertical radiator which
was flanked by free-standing headlamps. Most were open
topped and had rock-hard suspension.*

1946 Riley RM Series

Although Riley of Coventry, whose proud advertising slogan was, 'As Old as the Industry', had hit financial problems in 1938, it was rescued by Lord Nuffield, added to the Nuffield Organisation's quiver of marques, and encouraged to grow again after the Second World War. The new RM (Riley Motors) Series models of the post-war era were a remarkable tribute to that rebirth.

Riley retained the justly famous twin high-camshaft 1.5-litre and 2.5-litre four-cylinder engines as part of the new range, but used them to power a truly sleek, low and stylish family of four-seater saloons, which shared the same cabin, but different wheelbases. With torsion bar independent front suspension and rack-and-pinion steering, the chassis was advanced and effective, and although the body style had only semi-recessed headlamps reminiscent of the 1930s, it was never-the-less elegant and nicely proportioned, with a series of rakish lines.

Riley RM Series

Years in production: 1946–55
Structure: Front engine/rear-drive. Separate chassis
Engine type: 4-cylinder, overhead-valve
SPEC. FOR 2½-LITRE
Bore and stroke: 80.5 x 120 mm
Capacity: 2,443 cc
Power: 100 bhp @ 4,500 rpm
Fuel supply: Two horizontal SU carburettors
Suspension: Independent front, beam-axle rear
Weight: 3,136 lb
Top speed: 95 mph

The 1½-litre model, which had a top speed of 78 mph, was available first, but it was the 2½-litre model, which not only had a longer wheelbase, but 100 bhp instead of 55 bhp, which caused such a stir. Although the 1½-litre was an appealing sports saloon, it was quite expensive (£710 at first) and not outstandingly fast; the 2½-litre version, on the other hand, was a much more serious proposition. Here was a car which not only had remarkably good handling, and steering so accurate that it made most other British cars of the day look sluggish, but it had a top speed of 95 mph, and was equipped in that typically British combination of wood, leather and carpet which made every owner feel special.

Although traditional Riley enthusiasts did not like to admit it, here was a car which was superior to any Riley

Left and above: Hand-built, these sports cars had aluminium-panelled bodies.

model ever built by the original family concern. The car looked good, behaved impeccably, and it was an easy match for its competition. Later in the 1940s, final assembly was moved from Coventry to the MG factory at Abingdon, and a four-seater convertible version of the original style also appeared, along with a very limited number of three-seater Roadsters, but it was always the saloons which dominated the sales charts.

Finally, in 1953 the 2½-litre car was discontinued (it was replaced by the Nuffield-designed Pathfinder, which was not a good car), though a facelifted Riley 1½-litre continued until 1955. No fewer than 13,950 1½s, and 8,959 2½s, had been made.

1946 Allard Sports Car

The Allard was one of those hand-built, individually-designed sporting cars which flourished briefly after the Second World War, and died away as soon as shortages and waiting lists disappeared. Inspired by London motor trader Sydney Allard, the first 'Allard Specials' were trials cars built in the 1930s, but production of a big, and unmistakably styled road car followed in 1946.

The original Allard was based almost entirely on Ford V8 running gear – chassis, engine, transmission and suspension items – which were modified to suit Syd's own ideas, although the aluminium-panelled bodies (complete with their long, swooping noses) were all his own invention. An Allard, therefore, combined the simplicity and easy availability of Ford parts, with a certain exclusivity, which had a great

charm at a time when new cars were scarce. Even by late-1940s standards, the ride, handling and steering were no more than adequate, but the performance was encouraging. Standard Ford side-valve engines produced only 85 bhp, but enlarged (Mercury), more highly-tuned examples were also available to make them into truly fierce machines.

The first Allard of 1946 was the J1 competition two-seater, which was closely followed by a longer and heavier K-type, while the L-type was a full four-seater tourer. All shared the same type of divided-axle/transverse-leaf spring front suspension, and the same frontal styling.

An early Allard's appeal was not entirely in its performance, nor even in its styling, but in its extrovert character, and its

Allard Sports Car

Years in production: 1946–53
Structure: Front engine/rear-drive. Separate chassis
Engine type: V8-cylinder, side-valve
Bore and stroke: 77.8 x 95 mm
Capacity: 3,622 cc
Power: 85 bhp @ 3,800 rpm
Fuel supply: One downdraught Zenith carburettor
Suspension: Independent front, beam-axle rear
Weight: 2,240 lb
Top speed: 85 mph

relatively easy availability. Although an Allard cost as much as a Jaguar XK120, it was simpler to maintain and repair, and the fact that private owners also started winning rallies in it helped enormously.

By the early 1950s massively powerful Cadillac V8-powered J2s and J2Xs (pictured) were on the market, an all-new tubular chassis frame was being designed, and touring Allards like the P1 saloon and the M2X convertible had fleshed out the range. Sydney Allard's famous P1 victory in the 1953 Monte Carlo Rally made many headlines, but Allard's short career was almost over. The last of these V8-engined cars was made in 1955. All in all, about 1,800 of this family were produced.

Above: These were hand-built cars, individually designed but using freely available Ford engine parts. The bodywork was made of aluminium panels and the cars were as expensive as the Jaguar XK120, but easier to maintain and repair.

1947 Jowett Javelin

Few cars are designed by one man, but the Jowett Javelin certainly qualifies for that honour. Although its engine was a flat-four, the entire design was laid out by Gerald Palmer, who had already learned much of his craft at MG and in the Nuffield Organisation.

For far too long, Jowett cars, which were made in Bradford, had been simple, rugged, but technically backward, so for its post-war project the company hired Palmer, to give them valuable new ideas. Designed while the Second World War was still blazing, the Javelin made its debut in the austerity years which followed, and immediately drew praise because of its style and performance.

By Jowett standards, there was innovation everywhere, not only in the style and the engine, but in the body construction and the use of independent front suspension. Based around a unit-construction four-door saloon body shell, which was supplied by Briggs Motor Bodies in Doncaster, the new Javelin had a high nose but a long sweeping tail, which by the standards of the day was remarkably wind-cheating. Creditable in any other make of car, by Jowett's previous standards it was breathtakingly novel.

The flat-four engine was completely new, and once a series of teething problems had been sorted out, it also proved to be remarkably tuneable. This ensured that Palmer could endow it with sparkling performance – it was at least 10 mph faster than other comparable British 1.5-litre cars of the day – and very capable roadholding. The Javelin soon began to get a name for itself, especially in long-distance rallies, and the arrival of a specialised sports car (the Jupiter) based on the same running gear all helped transform Jowett's reputation. Successful Javelin outings in the French Alpine and Monte Carlo rallies, and by the Jupiter in the Le Mans 24 Hour race, all confirmed the pedigree.

Unfortunately Jowett did not have a vast dealer network with which to tackle their bigger rivals (Ford, Austin and Morris) head on, nor could they sell the Javelin cheaply enough to seriously threaten them, so it was never financially possible to facelift the original style, nor to invest in a new one. Well known transmission reliability problems didn't help; a high selling price also took its toll, and by the early 1950s the Javelin was well past its peak. Even though a new generation Jupiter sports car was being designed, the last cars were built in 1953.

In seven years a total of 22,799 Javelins, and 899 Jupiters, were produced.

Below: The style of the car drew praise with its high nose and long sweeping tail. It had good roadholding and its performance was at least 10 mph faster than other comparable cars of the day.

Jowett Javelin

Years in production: 1947–53
Structure: Front engine/rear-drive. Monocoque body/chassis
Engine type: Flat-four, overhead-valve
Bore and stroke: 72.5 x 90 mm
Capacity: 1,486 cc
Power: 50 bhp @ 4,100 rpm
Fuel supply: Two downdraught Zenith carburettors
Suspension: Independent front, beam-axle rear
Weight: 2,156 lb
Top speed: 78 mph

1948 Jaguar XK120

The XK120 caused a sensation when launched in 1948, and it still turns heads today. Not only was it beautiful, but it was also very fast, had a new type of twin overhead camshaft engine, and was always sold at unbelievably low prices. Yet it had all been developed in a tearing hurry, and was never meant to sell in large numbers.

Jaguar (once known as SS-Jaguar) had started planning for its post-war existence while the bombs were still falling on Coventry. The centre of its strategy was to be the production of new twin-cam engines, which would power a big new saloon car. The problem for Jaguar's founder, William Lyons, was that the engine was ready long before the new car could be finalised. In frustration, therefore, Lyons decided on a short-term solution. After instructing his design team to produce a short-wheelbase version of the new torsion-bar chassis (with a 102 in/2,591 mm wheelbase instead of the original 120 in/3,048 mm), to use the intended engine, transmission and suspension, he personally set about styling a sleek open two-seater sports car body style.

Even though it was revealed in October 1948, the XK120 was not ready for sale until mid 1949. Early cars had wooden body framing clad in aluminium panels, but by 1950–51 this had all changed, and a series production steel body shell of the same shape had taken over. By 1954, when the XK120 gave way to the similar XK140, the open car had been joined by a bubble-top coupé, and by a more fully-equipped drop-head coupé.

The 3.4-litre twin-cam engine was one of the most powerful in the world, ensuring that every XK120 could top 120 mph. Not only that, but it was one of the silkiest and most refined engines Jaguar had produced, the car being equally happy to potter along at 30 mph in towns, or at a stress-free 100 mph on open roads. The engine was so outstanding that it later powered the C-types and D-types which won at Le Mans in the 1950s.

These days we would criticise the XK120's lacklustre drum brakes and the heavy steering, but no-one ever whinged about the acceleration, the style, or the sheer animal character which was built in to every car. Not only was the XK120 wildly successful all over the world, but it was also a great rally car, and in some events a useful race car too. In six years, 12,055 cars were produced.

To replace it, Jaguar would need an excellent car. Fortunately the XK140, based on the same design but with more power, and most of the draw-backs eliminated, was just that. The XK pedigree continued until 1961 when the first of the equally amazing E-types appeared, while the last of the XK engines was not built until the 1990s.

> **Jaguar XK120**
> *Years in production:* 1949–54
> *Structure:* Front engine/rear-drive. Separate chassis
> *Engine type:* 6-cylinder, twin-over head-camshaft
> *Bore and stroke:* 83 x 106 mm
> *Capacity:* 3,442 cc
> *Power:* 160 bhp @ 5,000 rpm
> *Fuel supply:* Two horizontal SU carburettors
> *Suspension:* Independent front, beam-axle rear
> *Weight:* 2,856 lb
> *Top speed:* 125 mph

*Left and below: This car caused a
sensation when it was launched.
It was very successful worldwide
and a great rally car.*

1948 Land Rover

Here is a classic case of the stop-gap project which soon outgrew its parent. Before the Land Rover appeared, Rover had been building a relatively small number of fine middle class cars. By the 1950s they were building many more Land Rover 4x4s, and the cars were very much a minor part of the business.

Immediately after the war, Rover found itself running a massive former 'shadow factory' complex at Solihull, and needed to fill it. (A 'shadow factory' was an aero-engine factory established during the rearmament of the 1930s.) Faced with material shortages, it could not build many private cars, and elected to fill the gaps with a newly-developed 4x4, which it would base unashamedly on the design of the already legendary Jeep from the USA.

Early Land Rovers shared the same 80 in/2,032 mm wheelbase as the Jeep, and the same basic four-wheel-drive layout. The Land Rover, however, was much more versatile than the Jeep, in that it was built in myriad different guises, shapes and derivatives, and it used aluminium body panels, which ensured that it was virtually rust-free. Apart from the fact that it was not very fast or powerful, (though time and further development would solve those problems) the Land Rover could tackle almost any job, climb almost any slope, and ford almost every stream, which made it invaluable for farmers, contractors, surveyors, explorers, armies, public service companies – in fact almost anyone with a need for four-wheel-drive traction, and the rugged construction which went with it.

It wasn't long before the original pick-up was joined by vans, estate cars, short and long wheelbases to choice, petrol and diesel engines. A long list of extras became available: winches, extra-large wheels and tyres, and liaison with specialist companies ensured that it could be turned it into an impromptu railway shunting vehicle, a portable cinema truck, an equipment hoist, and a whole lot more. Its short-travel leaf spring suspension gave it a shatteringly hard ride and the Land Rover engineers stated that this, at least, limited cross-country speeds to keep the chassis in one piece.

Later models grew larger, longer, and more powerful, but it would not be until the 1960s that the first six-cylinder type appeared, not until 1979 that the first V8 Land Rover was sold, and not until the early 1980s that coil spring suspension finally took over. Sales, however, just went on and on, with the millionth being produced in the mid 1970s. By the late 1990s, when the 'Freelander' model appeared, 1.5 million Land Rovers had been manufactured, although by then it had been renamed 'Defender' and was sold exclusively with diesel engines.

Right: Based on the American Jeep car, this British 4x4 used aluminium panels to produce a virtually rust-free vehicle in a variety of shapes and styles.

Land Rover

Years in production: (Series I)
1948–57
Structure: Front engine/four-wheel-
drive. Separate chassis
Engine type: 4-cylinder, overhead-
inlet-valve/side exhaust
Bore and stroke: 69.5 x 105 mm
Capacity: 1,595 cc
Power: 50 bhp @ 4,000 rpm
Fuel supply: One downdraught
Solex carburettor
Suspension: Beam-axle front,
beam-axle rear
Weight: 2,594 lb
Top speed: 55 mph

1948 Morris Minor

The Morris Minor, like the Mini, is one of those cars that everyone recalls, affectionately, with a nostalgic smile. 'Ah, yes,' we all say, 'I used to have one of those when I was young....' Morris Minors are now seen as fully paid-up classic cars, not for their performance, nor for their style, but for their unmistakable character. Then, as now, no-one drives a Morris Minor if they are in a hurry, for although the roadholding was peerless by late 1940s standards, the acceleration was distinctly leisurely.

It all started in 1942-43, when Morris Motors' Alec Issigonis first sketched out his ideas for a new post-war small car. Egged on by the vice-chairman, Miles Thomas, his small team designed the 'Mosquito' around a squat unit-construction body shell, which was to be powered by a new type of flat-four cylinder engine. Post-war shortages and a lack of capital caused delays, the new engine was swept away in favour of an ancient side-valve unit, and the entire shell was widened at the last minute, but the Morris Minor which went on sale in 1948 was still an intriguing proposition. At a time when most British cars looked narrow and old-fashioned, the new-shape Minor was arresting, had torsion bar front suspension to provide great handling, and rack-and-pinion steering to provide precise direction.

The fact that the top speed was little more than 60 mph, and that the styling was not to everyone's taste (Lord Nuffield himself is supposed to have likened it to 'a bloody poached egg') made no difference. For the next two decades Nuffield (and later BMC) sold Minors just as fast as they could be made.

Here was a range that grew and grew. Over the years saloons, open-top tourers, estate cars, vans and pick-ups were all eventually made in large numbers; the floor pan and suspension was adapted for use under the Wolseley 1500/Riley 1.5-litre models, while the cars were assembled locally in several parts of the Commonwealth.

From 1952 Series II Minors got a new overhead-valve engine, but no more performance, and from 1956 they became Morris Minor 1000s, with a more powerful 948 cc engine. The last Minors of all had 1.1-litre engines, but by that time they had become institutions, and no-one really measured the performance.

Minor styling changed little over the years, although the headlamp position was raised in the early 1950s, and bow windows front and rear) were part of the Minor 1000 package of 1956. The splendid

> **Morris Minor**
>
> *Years in production:* 1948–71
> *Structure:* Front engine/rear-drive. Monocoque body/chassis
> ORIGINAL TYPE:
> *Engine type:* 4-cylinder, side-valve.
> *Bore and stroke:* 57 x 90 mm
> *Capacity:* 917 cc
> *Power:* 27 bhp @ 4,000 rpm
> *Fuel supply:* One horizontal SU carburettor
> *Suspension:* Independent front, beam-axle rear
> *Weight:* 1,735 lb
> *Top speed:* 62 mph

roadholding, the rather boomy exhaust note, and the way it acquired and kept its 'district nurse's car' image all remained constant.

The sales figures tell their own story, for in 21 years, 1948–71, no fewer than 1.3 million Minors (and another quarter-million vans and pick-ups) were sold. In later years some were also made in Sri Lanka, and it is still possible to recreate a Morris Minor today. To some people, there has never been a more practical car.

Above and right: These are cars which evoke nostalgia as their character is what made them so popular. Produced in a wide range of styles, the cars were to become an institution and they never lost their 'district nurse's car' image.

1948 Bond Minicar 3-wheeler

Cars like the Bond could only have prospered in a motoring climate which was starved of both cars and fuel – which explains why these ingeniously-detailed three-wheelers were so successful in the 1940s and 1950s. Over the years, several generations were produced around the same basic structure, where the engine was mounted close to the single front wheel, driving and steering with it; reverse gear was not offered.

Lawrie Bond, sometimes described as an eccentric genius, designed the original car before selling the manufacturing rights to Sharps Commercials of Preston, Lancashire, who were soon building 15 cars every week. The Minicar's secret was its tiny, two-seater size, its light but amazingly effective aluminium structure (there was no separate chassis), and for the way the air-cooled single-cylinder motor cycle-type engine was arranged to drive the single front wheel by chain, and to pivot with that wheel when it was turned to steer the car.

Crude in almost every other way, it was nevertheless an amazingly compact little car: the original models had no rear suspension, (the rear wheels' only function was to keep the rear end of the car off the ground), 30 mph was really the limit of the cruising speed, and creature comforts were in line with the low price. Lacking a reverse gear, it could be driven by anyone possessing a motor cycle licence, though because the front wheel could be steered to a full 90 degrees in each direction on later cars, the lack of that reverse was no big loss; the Minicar, quite literally, could turn in its own length.

Yet, for all this, the original Minicar cost only £199 (half the price of a Morris Minor), there was a serviceable hood and removable side screens, the cars often returned an amazing 100 mpg on two-stroke fuel, and they would not, of course, rust. To drive and enjoy a Bond, however, needed a certain attitude of mind, for all journeys tended to be slow, long and tedious, the driver always felt vulnerable when surrounded by other traffic, and if social status mattered to him, he was advised to choose another mode of transport.

Many ex-motorcyclists, and marginal motorists, shrugged off all this, and a whole series of Minicars, which became progressively larger, more streamlined, and more expensive, followed, until the last was produced in 1966. By then Sharps had turned to producing the Bond Equipe sports coupé, a much more upmarket machine – yet 26,500 Minicar sales, in 18 years, told its own success story. In spite of their rust-resistant construction, very few seem to have survived.

Bond Minicar 3-wheeler

Years in production: 1948–51
Structure: Front engine/front-wheel-drive. Aluminium monocoque body/chassis
Engine type: 1-cylinder, two-stroke
Capacity: 122 cc
Power: 5 bhp @ 4,400 rpm
Fuel supply: One horizontal Amal carburettor
Suspension: Independent front, Solid/no suspension rear
Weight: 308 lb
Top speed: 35 mph

Left and below: These three-wheelers were very successful due to their tiny size and their rust-free aluminium structure. They had no reverse gear and could be driven by anyone with a motorcycle licence.

1949 Healey Silverstone

Although everyone now remembers Donald Healey for the famous Austin-Healey sports cars which bear his name, his reputation was secure well before then. Triumph's technical chief in the 1930s, he established his own sports car business immediately after the Second World War, and a whole family of sports saloons, drop-head coupés and two-seaters evolved around the same chassis. The Silverstone, of which only 105 cars were ever made, was the most sporty of all.

The chassis was a simple, but rigid, box-section design, with a 102 in (2591 mm) wheelbase, which featured trailing-arm/coil spring independent front suspension. Although originally intended to use Triumph running gear, (Healey tried to sell the rights to his one-time employer), it was finally powered by the impressive twin high-camshaft Riley 2.5-litre engine, whose 104 bhp output was among the highest of all early post-war British cars. Backed by a Riley gearbox and rear axle, this was a formidable base on which to build various body styles.

Original cars, pre-viewed in 1946, were two-door four-seater machines called Westland (an open roadster) and Elliot (a saloon), but although both could reach 100 mph, they were really too heavy to be competitive in motorsport. The two-seater Silverstone, which was announced in 1949, changed all that.

Using the same chassis, the Silverstone was fitted with a stark and very basically equipped open-top aluminium body shell in a traditional two-seater style. With separate front wings closely cowling the front wheels, the head-lamps were hidden away behind a narrow radiator grille – where they can have done little to improve the air flow through the radiator. The Silverstone was 450 to 500 lb (204 to 227 kg) lighter than the four-seater types, and the trade-off for minimal accommodation was much faster acceleration, and better roadholding. One of the entertaining quirks of this car, by the way, was that the spare wheel was mounted horizontally, and semi-externally

in the tail, where it acted as a bumper. There was no front bumper.

Functionally, this was a purposeful machine, the only marketing problem being that it was handbuilt and, by definition, expensive. Unhappily, some potential customers wanted a fast car as an alternative to, say, the Jaguar XK120, but were frightened off the Silverstone because it was such an individual machine. It might have been effective, but as there was virtually nowhere to stow any luggage, here was a single-purpose car, made with motorsport in mind.

Only 105 Silverstones were made, and all today's survivors are regarded as rare, and desirable machines.

Healey Silverstone

Years in production: 1949–50
Structure: Front engine/rear-drive. Separate chassis
Engine type: 4-cylinder, overhead-valve
Bore and stroke: 80.5 x 120 mm
Capacity: 2,443 cc
Power: 104 bhp @ 4,500 rpm
Fuel supply: Two horizontal SU carburettors
Suspension: Independent front, beam-axle rear
Weight: 2,072 lb
Top speed: 105 mph

Below and right: Made of aluminium, these cars had their headlamps hidden away behind the radiator grille. The spare wheel was mounted horizontally, and semi-externally in the tail, where it acted as a bumper. Handbuilt, these were expensive cars and survivors are very rare.

1949 Dellow Sports Car

With great shortage of new cars after the Second World War, almost any product calling itself a sports car found a market. The Dellow, which was produced by a small garage business near Birmingham, was one such. Its instigators, K.C. Delingpole and Ron Lowe, were production car trials enthusiasts, so they produced a car which could be used as both a two-seater sports car on the road and as a trials car.

Built around a simple tubular chassis frame, it used mainly Ford Ten/Prefect components, including the rugged 1,172 cc side-valve engine and a three-speed gearbox, with the old-fashioned transverse leaf suspension. The original cars were bodied in stark two-seater open-top style, using aluminium skin panels on a tubular frame work. Naturally, there were no doors, a skimpy soft-top was only provided as an apology for keeping out the worst of the bad weather, while two trials-orientated features were the big (15 gallon) fuel tank, and the twin spare wheels, both of which hung out over the rear of the car, thus increasing the weight over the driven rear wheels.

The result was a perky, quirky, but above all light, cheap and appealing little two-seater, which soon built up its own small coterie of fans. Eventually outclassed in trials, where more specialised machinery eventually took over, the Dellow was also a good car for use in driving tests and some rallies.

Compared with almost any other British car of the day – and certainly any family car – the original Dellow was outrageously stark and purposeful. Even though the side-valve-engined Fords were nothing special, and the three-speed gearbox was a positive drawback, this car was so light that it was brisk and appealing. Even in standard form they could reach 70 mph, but when super-tuned, speeds of 80 mph (which felt and sounded most impressive) were seen.

Later Dellows had coil spring suspension on their beam-axles, but by the mid-1950s their time had passed. No more than 500 cars of all types were ever made.

Dellow Sports Car

Years in production: 1949–57
Structure: Front engine/ rear-drive. Separate chassis
Engine type: 4-cylinder, side-valve
Bore and stroke: 63.5 x 92.5 mm
Capacity: 1,172 cc
Power: 30 bhp @ 4,000 rpm
Fuel supply: One down-draught Zenith carburettor
Suspension: Beam-axle front, beam-axle rear
Weight: 1,344 lb
Top speed: 69 mph

Above: This open-topped two-seater, was a car with no opening doors and aluminium skin panels. The cars were light, cheap and appealing with two spare tyres mounted on the rear of the car.

1949 Rover P4

If ever there was a model which deserved the famous nickname of 'Auntie Rover', this was it. The legendary P4 saloon, first seen in 1949, but gradually developed, was the epitome of everything Rover's guiding light, Spencer Wilks, was trying to do. High performance meant nothing to him, but refinement, high quality and dignity was of utmost importance. At this time Rover's measured, gradual but totally focused approach to building, equipping and marketing its cars had been maturing for well over a decade, for it was the arrival of Wilks as Rover's managing director in the 1930s which had made it all possible.

The P4 (which indicated that this was the first phase in a long-term plan of model development) was much like its predecessors, though it looked more modern and incorporated a number of mechanical innovations. Based around a four-door saloon style on a rock-solid separate chassis, the car's original engine was a 2.2-litre 75 bhp straight-six, and the '75' set about providing motoring for the 'mobile drawing room' class.

This was not a car in which one set out to drive fast; instead one motored in great comfort, safety and with pleasure. It was quiet, it felt quite insulated from the world outside, and it never seemed to be in a hurry. The P4 had all the old-fashioned virtues of grace, understated good taste, long experience, and a certain standing in society, so it was no wonder that, quite without Rover's intention, it soon became known as 'Auntie Rover'. In the same way that many people's favourite aunt might be well dressed and immaculately turned out, so a P4 was impressively equipped, the inside having wood, leather and pile carpets in abundance.

Rover had invested heavily in the P4; it intended to sell it for a long time, gradually making logical changes and improvements. The only startling feature of the original shape was the central 'Cyclops' lamp in the grille, but this disappeared in the first facelift, while later alterations squared up the rear of the body a little, and increased the size of the rear window.

Over the years, therefore, the main changes were to the engines and the transmission. Using the model name to indicate peak power output, the six-cylinder unit was eventually enlarged and pushed out through '90', '95', '100' and finally '110' (the fastest of these cars could reach 100 mph), while at one time there were also four-cylinder '60' and '80' varieties. All these, and the choice of freewheel, overdrive or automatic transmissions meant that there was plenty for the customers to choose from.

A typical P4 customer, by the way, might be a doctor, a solicitor, a bank manager or an accountant, but one rarely found sporting types such as racing drivers or young tycoons signing an order form. According to Rover, this was exactly as it should be, and before the P4 was finally displaced by the very different P6 2000 in 1964, more than 130,000 cars had been built.

Rover P4

Years in production: 1949–64, all models
Structure: Front engine/rear-drive.
   Separate chassis
ORIGINAL 75 MODEL
Engine type: 6-cylinder, overhead
   inlet/side-exhaust-valve
Bore and stroke: 65.2 x 105 mm
Capacity: 2,103 cc
Power: 75 bhp @ 4,200 rpm
Fuel supply: Two horizontal SU
   carburettors
Suspension: Independent front, beam-
   axle rear
Weight: 3,265 lb
Top speed: 82 mph

Above: This high quality, four-door saloon was well-equipped with wood, leather and pile carpets. Built for comfort, safety and pleasure, this was not a fast car.

1950 Ford Consul/Zephyr Six

Until the 1950s, British Fords were always affectionately known as 'Dagenham Dustbins' (cars were built at Dagenham, in Essex), with their engineering derided, and their low selling prices highly respected. All that changed forever when the first post-war Fords were introduced. The closely related Consul and Zephyr models completely changed the face of the company.

After 1945 it took several years to convert the British motor industry to a forward-looking peacetime economy. Even at Ford, a ruthlessly efficient operation, early post-war cars were simply warmed-over 1930s types until the introduction of the Consul/Zephyr models, classics of their type, and classic to this day. Inside Ford, and out, these cars represented a design revolution. They were the first Fords to use unit construction (chassis-less), the first to use independent front suspension, and the first to use overhead valve engines. Later, as the model range developed, they would be the first to offer a steel-bodied estate car derivative, the first to offer automatic transmission as an option, and the first Fords to go on sale with front-wheel-disc brakes.

Even if they had looked dreadful, they would have been classics of their period, but this excuse was never needed. Styled by Ford-USA in Detroit, they were modern, streamlined, distinctive shapes by the standards of the late 1940s.

Inside their cabins, of course, they were pure Detroit, complete with bench-type front seats, and with steering-column gear change controls.

Under the skin, Consuls had four-cylinder and Zephyrs had six-cylinder versions of the same design, while the front suspension was a new and mechanically simple layout known as 'MacPherson strut' (after its American inventor) which was carefully patented to eliminate direct copies. The mechanical elegance of this system was such, however, that rivals all round the world made haste to make their own versions (and to employ the best patent lawyers to advise them).

Consuls had a soft ride, but were quite slow, while

Ford Consul / Zephyr Six

Years in production:
  1950–1956
Structure: Front engine/
  rear-drive. Monocoque
  body/chassis
Engine type: 4-cylinder/
  6-cylinder, overhead-valve
Bore and stroke: 79.37 x 76.2 mm
Capacity: 1,508 cc/2,262 cc
Power: 47 bhp @ 4,400 rpm/68 bhp @ 4,000 rpm
Fuel supply: One downdraught Zenith carburettor
Suspension: Independent front, beam-axle rear
Weight: 2,296 lb/2,604 lb
Top speed: 74 mph/80 mph

Zephyrs (which had a longer wheelbase) were faster, but with rather skittish roadholding. Their value, however, was not in doubt, and after a 'works' Zephyr had won the Monte Carlo Rally in 1953, their reputation was sealed.

Shortly, a better-trimmed and equipped version of the Zephyr, called 'Zodiac', arrived, after which developments of these cars dominated their market sector for more than 20 years, until the first Granadas replaced them. As model followed model, rivals would snipe about their styling, their equipment, and their rather obvious transatlantic pedigree, but Ford, who knew what sort of value they were offering, never flinched.

Between 1950 and 1956, no fewer than 231,481 Consul/Zephyrs were sold.

Above: This was an innovative car from Ford. Their style was distinctive, modern and streamlined. They were styled by Ford-USA and had bench front seats and steering-column gear change controls.

1950 MG TD

If ever there was a car which introduced American drivers to the British sports car, it was the MG TD. Earlier T-Series cars had reached the USA in limited numbers, but it was the TD – the first MG sports car to have a left-hand-drive option, and the first to have independent front suspension – that converted them. Of a total production of nearly 30,000, more than 23,000 were originally sold in North America.

Building on the reputation of its earlier Midgets, MG had launched the first T-Series car in 1936, but until 1950 they had a 1930s layout, complete with a flexible chassis, a narrow-hipped body and a bone-shattering ride. The TD, which was developed in a tearing hurry, set out to change all that.

Although the TD followed the same visual philosophy as previous Midgets – a wooden-framed body tub, flowing front wings, separate free-standing headlamps, and an upright, instantly recognisable radiator grille – it was different in almost every detail. Not only had the chassis, hidden underneath, been changed, but the proportions of the body shell had altered too.

The first prototype used a much-changed version of the MG YA chassis, but for production there was a new frame, much stiffer than ever before, with wider wheel tracks, rack-and-pinion steering and coil spring independent front suspension. Although the engine and transmission similar to the TC Midget which it replaced, the TD turned out to be a much more capable car, if only because its roadholding was so much better than before.

This was, in other words, a new type of sports car which, quite perversely, continued to look old. Except that it was wider and somewhat more squat than before, it could easily have been engineered in the 1930s, and was built on the same sort of rudimentary jigging and tooling. For a time, at least, absolutely no-one complained, especially when they discovered the famous XPAG-type engine which could withstand super-tuning, and realised that the car could develop spirited acceleration. Nothing, however, could give the TD a high top speed, as its body had all the aerodynamic qualities of a mature barn door.

Until two new and much more modern looking sports cars appeared – the Triumph TR2 and the Austin-Healey 100 – the TD was Britain's most successful sports car, and deservedly so. It was probably a mistake for MG's bosses to insist that it was than facelifted (to the TF) instead of commissioning a completely new style, but these cars won, and have always retained, a huge following, especially now that the cult of the classic car has mushroomed so strongly.

Right: The TD differed from previous Midgets in its chassis and body shell. These cars had much better roadholding than earlier models and went on to become Britain's most successful sports car.

MG TD

Years in production: 1949–53
Structure: Front engine/rear-drive. Separate chassis
Engine type: 4-cylinder, overhead-valve
Bore and stroke: 66.5 x 90 mm
Capacity: 1,250 cc
Power: 54 bhp @ 5,200 rpm
Fuel supply: Two horizontal SU
Suspension: Independent front, beam-axle rear
Weight: 1,930 lb
Top speed: 77 mph

1951 Standard Vanguard

Standard Vanguard
Years in production: 1948–53
Structure: Front engine/rear-drive.
   Separate chassis
Engine type: 4-cylinder, overhead-
   valve
Bore and stroke: 85 x 92 mm
Capacity: 2,088 cc
Power: 68 bhp @ 4,200 rpm
Fuel supply: One downdraught
   Solex carburettor
Suspension: Independent front,
   beam-axle rear
Weight: 2,620 lb
Top speed: 78 mph

Standard's original post-war Vanguard may not be classic in terms of its performance or roadholding, but it was in terms of what it set out to do. Immediately after the Second World War, Britain's car makers were exhorted to adopt one-model policies, and for a time this was Standard's response.

The government's 'one-size-fits-all' policy was never going to produce thoroughbreds, but with exports to the Empire in mind, and by designing a new engine which was ideal for use in the Ferguson tractor, Standard produced an ordinary but remarkably rugged machine. In a clever and patriotic move they chose to name it 'Vanguard', after Britain's only surviving modern battleship.

Although the rather short-wheelbase chassis layout was very ordinary, and the original body style rather too obviously derived from transatlantic trends, its origins were fascinating. Concluding that early 1940s Plymouths were among the most attractive of American shapes, Standard's managing director had sent his chief stylist down to London, to sit outside the American embassy, and to sketch any Plymouth he found parked outside.

The engine was a heavy four-cylinder affair, with slip-fit 'wet' cylinder liners. Inspired by the current front-wheel-drive Citroen power unit, it would survive for more than 20 years, to power Vanguards and Ferguson tractors, as well as a long line of fast, reliable and successful Triumph TR sports cars.

Purists did not like the style, the use of bench front seats, the three-speed gearboxes or the steering column gear change, but export customers clearly did, especially as they soon found that the Vanguard could put up with rough treatment, misuse and neglect on a grand scale. Vanguards were soon found not only in London, but in Cape Town, Sydney and North America. The armed forces bought them in large numbers, and to keep up with the demand Standard also made them available in saloon, estate, van or pick-up form ('ute', to use the Australian phrase, where these versions were built).

Although bodies tended to go rusty (but what post-war British car did not, because of poor quality steel being supplied?), the rest of the running seemed to last forever, so many of these cars still survive. The original car was re-styled, into the notchback Vanguard Phase II, in 1953, then an entirely different type of car, the monocoque chassised Mk III, followed in 1955. The theme changed completely in the mid 1960s, when a much better car, the Triumph 2000 took over.

Right: Heavily based on the American Plymouths, these cars were soon very popular all over the world. They were produced in saloon, estate, van or pick-up form and many cars still survive.

1952 Bentley Continental R-Type

After Rolls-Royce took over Bentley in 1931, it was more than 20 years before the new owners produced another truly sporty new model. But the wait was worthwhile. The R-type Continental of 1952–55 was a great car by any standards, which not only looked sensational, but was also extremely fast.

Even before 1939, Rolls-Royce had dabbled with super-streamlined prototypes (one of them being called a 'Bentley Corniche'), but production cars had to wait until after the war. Using only slightly modified versions of the existing Bentley Mk VI saloon car's chassis, but with a superbly detailed two-door four-seater coupé designed by the coachbuilder, H.J. Mulliner, the company produced an extremely fast (115 mph), exclusive, and very expensive car, whose title told its own story.

The Continental certainly did not gain its high performance by being light, but by a combination of high (unstated) horsepower, and by the remarkable aerodynamic performance of the bulky, yet sleek shell. There was, of course, no way of taming the drag of the proud Bentley radiator grille, but the lines of the rest of the car were as wind-cheating as possible, the long tapering tail being a delight to the eyes. Like all the best 1930s Bentleys, it had two passenger doors, and a full four-seater package. Leather, carpet and wood abounded – for no concessions were made to ensure a high performance.

Bentley Continental R-type
Years in production: 1952–1955
Structure: Front engine/rear-drive. Separate chassis
Engine type: 6-cylinder, overhead-valve inlet/side exhaust
Bore and stroke: 92.1 x 114.3 mm/ 95.25 x 114.3 mm
Capacity: 4,566/4,887 cc
Power: Not revealed
Fuel supply: Two horizontal SU carburettors
Suspension: Independent front, beam-axle rear
Weight: 3,700 lb
Top speed: 115/118 mph

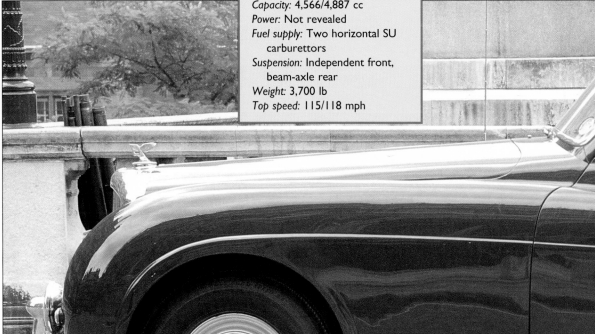

Here was an expensive grand tourer for the connoisseur and, by definition, it was likely to sell in small numbers. Put on sale in 1952 at £7,608 (at a time when Morris Minor prices, for instance, started at £582), it was ideal for the 'sportsman' who liked to drive far and fast, wherever conditions allowed. It was produced in the traditional Bentley/Rolls-Royce style, for the engine was low-revving, the steering and most other controls quite heavy, and the fuel consumption ferocious – but the fit, finish and quality of every component (especially the interior trim) were of the very highest quality.

As ever, Rolls-Royce/Bentley never thought it necessary to reveal the power output of the big six-cylinder engine, whose overhead inlet/side exhaust valve layout was only shared with one other British make of car – the Rover of the period. Needing only to point out the easily provable performance of their cars, they let acceleration figures speak for themselves.

In a career of only three years, the R-type Continental needed little improvement, for the engine was a very powerful 4.5-litre unit. Only 208 were ever built.

Above and below: A great sporty new model which looked sensational and performed very well. They had a long tapering tail and leather, wood and carpet built into the interior design which was of the highest quality.

1953 Triumph TR2

Although Triumph was originally an independent car-maker, it was taken over by Standard in 1944. Several early post-war attempts to sell 'Standard-Triumphs' all failed, but after Standard also failed to take over Morgan, Sir John Black told his engineers to develop a rival sports car.

Work on the 20TS project began in 1952, the prototype being shown at Earls Court in October of that year. A very tight budget obliged the engineers to base the original design around a modified 1930s-style Standard Flying Nine frame, which was clearly not stiff enough. That first car was neither fast enough, nor attractive enough, and lacked proper road behaviour.

A rapid and complete re-design produced the definitive TR2 of 1953, which had a new and more rigid chassis frame, coil spring independent front suspension, a 90 bhp development of the Standard Vanguard engine, modified and more chunky rear-end styling, and a top speed of more than 100 mph. The first production cars were delivered in the autumn of 1953 at the bargain price of £787, and were immediately seen as serious competition for MG, whose old-fashioned TF's top speed was 20 mph slower.

Although the TR2 was fast and remarkably cheap, its handling was still somewhat suspect, and it was fortunate that an outright win in the 1954 RAC Rally of March 1954 brought an instant competition record to the notice of motoring enthusiasts. Sales rose gradually (especially in North America) as the car improved, and as the available extras (including a removable hard-top, wire-spoke wheels, and overdrive) proliferated. The remarkable fact which also began to emerge from countless magazine road tests was that a TR2 could not only be a race and a rally winner, it could also be extremely economical: 32-35 mpg was normal for the early cars.

In the autumn of 1955, only two years after the first TR2 had been delivered, it was replaced by the TR3, which had minor styling changes, and 95 bhp. In the next year the engine power crept up again – to 100 bhp – and from late 1956 the TR3 became the world's first quantity-production sports car to have front-wheel disc brakes as standard.

More improvements followed. From the autumn of 1957 (for launch in January 1958) the car was built

with revised front-end styling and other equipment improvements. Soon affectionately known as the TR3A, this was a title never officially adopted by the Triumph concern. It was the TR3A which really found great popularity in North America, where most sales were made, and which established the marque's fine reputation in that continent in advance of the introduction of Spitfires and newer TRs in the 1960s.

A 2,138 cc engine became optional in 1959, after it had been used successfully in the 1958 Alpine Rally by the factory team, though few cars with this engine appear to have been sold. TR3A production continued until 1961, when the model was replaced by the TR4, which had a completely new body shell. A final series of cars was built in 1962 to satisfy Triumph's North American dealers. Unofficially known as TR3Bs, and only for sale in the USA, most had 2,138 cc engines, and all used the TR4-type synchromesh gearbox.

There were 8,628 TR2s, 13,377 TR3s and 58,236 TR3As, along with 3,331 TR3Bs. The vast majority of these cars were exported, most of them to the USA.

Triumph TR2

Years in production: (TR2–TR3B) 1953–1962
Structure: Front engine/rear-drive. Separate chassis
Engine type: Four-cylinder, overhead-valve
Bore and stroke: 83 x 92 mm
Capacity: 1,991 cc
Power: 90 bhp @ 4,800 rpm
Fuel supply: Two horizontal SU carburettors
Suspension: Independent front, beam-axle rear
Weight: 1,848 lb
Top speed: 103 mph

Above and below: This was a car which was seen as serious competition for the MG. It could be both an economical road car and a race and rally winner.

1955 MG MGA

In the 1930s and 1940s, MG established a world-wide reputation for producing small, neat, two-seater sports cars with lots of character. By the 1950s, however, the traditional styles on which they had concentrated were beginning to look dated, so MG enthusiasts were delighted when the all-new MGA was announced in 1955.

Compared with the long-running T-series cars, which it replaced at Abingdon, the MGA was different in every respect. Not only did it have a new, broad-based chassis frame, and a modern and very stylish body, but it was the first MG sports car to use BMC (Austin-based), instead of Nuffield-based running gear. All previous MGs had used engines derived from Morris and Wolseley family cars, while the MGA used engines which had been designed for use in new BMC family cars.

Inspiration for the MGA originally came from a special body which MG built for a T-series model to race at Le Mans in 1951. It was refined and made more 'pro-duction' over the next four years. Smooth where previous MGs had been craggy, wide where they had been narrow, and roomy where they had been cramped, it was an elegant leap into the future.

Sitting on a new, squat and very sturdy chassis frame, the new MGA body was the first all-new MG styling since the arrival of the Midgets in the 1930s. Built entirely from steel pressings (though wooden floor boards were retained), it married a sloping version of the familiar MG grille with a flowing, sexy, shape.

The engine was a tuned-up BMC B-series, previously used in the MG Magnette sports saloon, and although traditionalists complained about this at first, it proved to be just as tuneable as any previous MG power unit. Even when rated at 72 bhp, it gave the MGA a top speed approaching 100 mph, while up to 100 bhp was available in racing form.

The MGA not only looked beautiful, but also had a

MG MGA

Years in production: (All types)
1955–62

Structure: Front engine/rear-drive.
Separate chassis

Engine type: 4-cylinder, overhead-valve

ORIGINAL 1500:

Bore and stroke: 73.02 x 88.9 mm

Capacity: 1,489 cc

Power: 72 bhp @ 5,500 rpm

Fuel supply: Two horizontal SU
carburettors

Suspension: Independent front,
beam-axle rear

Weight: 1,988 lb

Top speed: 98 mph

soft ride, very good roadholding, and seemed to be stuffed full of 'Abingdon magic'. It immediately began to outsell any previous MG car, and when a neat bubble-top coupé, with wind-up windows, was added, the range was complete.

Over the years the MGA was progressively improved: the 1600 of 1959 had a larger engine and front disc brakes, and finally the Mk II of 1961, which had 86 bhp and a 101 mph top speed. For a time, too, there was even an expensive, difficult-to-maintain MGA twin-cam, with a unique engine. A great car was needed to improve on the MGA, and the MGB was just that. In seven years, no fewer than 101,470 MGAs were built, then an Abingdon record.

Above: A beautiful car with good roadholding and a soft ride. They were the first MGs to use BMC engines as opposed to the Morris and Wolseley in previous models.

1958 Armstrong-Siddeley Star Sapphire

It is ironic that the best and most handsome of all Armstrong-Siddeley saloons was also the last car it ever made. In the UK, the market for large, middle class machines was increasingly dominated by Jaguar, and though the Sapphire and Star Sapphire types had fine engines and attractive styles, they could not compete on price.

its 125 bhp/3.4-litre six-cylinder engine, could reach more than 90 mph, and went on sale for £1,728, intending to capture sales in the Jaguar Mk VII market sector. Complete with its noble radiator shell and emblem, and elegant four-door styling, it was a fine machine. With the 150 bhp engine which was also available, it could just reach the magic 100 mph mark.

Above: The noble radiator shell and emblem.
Right: The elegant cars of Armstrong Siddeley faced strong competition from Jaguar, Alvis and Daimler.

From the 1920s to the 1950s, Armstrong-Siddeley had built a series of well engineered, dignified, but essentially mainstream middle class cars. Then, buoyed up by the profits from their successful aero-engine business, they invested in a new and more advanced range of cars, the Sapphire.

This car had a separate chassis frame and would retain the pre-selector type of transmission for which the marque was noted, but there were two other major innovations. One was that Armstrong-Siddeley elected to assemble their own smart new four-door body shells, and the other was that they designed a new six-cylinder engine, with part-spherical combustion chambers and complex valve gear. The Sapphire of 1953, originally with

Right from the start, however, the Sapphire had to face formidable competition, not only from Jaguar, but from Alvis and Daimler. Easier availability, lower prices and a bit more performance would all have helped, but Armstrong-Siddeley's Coventry factory was not capable of mass production, and the Sapphire became rather an exclusive car.

A massive limousine version was soon made available, but it was the much-improved Star Sapphire, built from 1958 to 1960, which was the star of this range. Looking like, but not identical to, the original car, the 'Star' had a 165 bhp/ 4-litre version of the engine, Borg Warner automatic transmission, power-assisted steering and front wheel disc brakes, in what was a very appealing package.

The price of this most comprehensively equipped car, unhappily, had shot up to £2,646, which was too costly to sustain high sales, and although it was a nicely-built, well equipped and very capable saloon, demand slowly ebbed away. Rootes, in the meantime, had copied the engine for a new Humber Super Snipe, in return for letting Armstrong-Siddeley build Sunbeam Alpine sports cars.

In 1960 Armstrong-Siddeley decided to concentrate on making aircraft engines, and pulled out of the car business completely. Between 1953 and 1960, 8,568 cars in this family were produced.

Armstrong-Siddeley Star Sapphire

Years in production: 1958–60
Structure: Front engine/rear-drive. Separate chassis
Engine type: 6-cylinder, overhead-valve
Bore and stroke: 97 x 90 mm
Capacity: 3,990 cc
Power: 165 bhp @ 4,250 rpm
Fuel supply: Two downdraught Stromberg carburettors
Suspension: Independent front, beam-axle rear
Weight: 3,920 lb
Top speed: 100 mph

1958 Austin-Healey Sprite

Everyone wanted small sports cars in the 1950s, but none were available. Until, that is, BMC asked Donald Healey to design a small two-seater for the Austin-Healey stable. The result was the Sprite, a car which started a new trend. An ever-improving family of Sprites emerged from the MG Abingdon factory until 1971, and the MG Midget which derived from them would be made until 1979.

Spiritually, the new Sprite was related to several earlier BMC cars (MG T-series Midgets because of their size, MGAs and Austin-Healey 100 Sixes) because of the way they also used so many existing parts, such as engines, transmissions and suspension units. Although the car's monocoque structure was new and unique, with a neat way of locating the rear axle by

cantilever leaf springs, almost all its running gear was lifted from the BMC 'parts bin', which meant that it would be easy to maintain, and support, at dealerships all over the world.

By using Austin A35 and Morris Minor 1000 pieces (including a tuned-up version of the famous 948 cc engine), Donald and Geoffrey Healey produced a simple and rugged little two-seater, into which they built a great deal of sports car behaviour, and appealing character. Simple to the point of being rather starkly-equipped at first, the Sprite cut costs to the bone by specifying plastic side curtains, and by making the soft-top a simple item with a build-it-yourself frame.

No sooner was the new car launched, of course, than its unique styling, with

Austin-Healey Sprite

Years in production: 1958–61
Structure: Front engine/rear-drive. Monocoque body/chassis
Engine type: 4-cylinder, overhead-valve
Bore and stroke: 62.94 x 76.2 mm
Capacity: 948 cc
Power: 43 bhp @ 5,200 rpm
Fuel supply: Two horizontal SU carburettors
Suspension: Independent front, beam-axle rear
Weight: 1,328 lb
Top speed: 87 mph

headlamps grafted on to the top of the bonnet panel, inspired the affectionate nickname of 'Frog Eye' (or, in the USA, 'Bug Eye'). This, however, was a feature forced upon the company at a late stage. Prototypes had fold-back headlamps designed to preserve a smooth line, but cost considerations forced a change to the fixed position on production cars. The entire bonnet/front wings assembly was hinged at the passenger bulkhead, and could be lifted up for access to the engine bay and front suspension assemblies. The result was a car which lacked aerodynamic purity, but had unmistakable looks. Perhaps by chance, it also made this car look 'cute': when added to its undeniable performance and spirited handling, this was a great marketing advantage.

The new Sprite was instantly a great success, especially in North America, where British sports cars were in great demand; over the next few years it also gained a reputation in sports car racing. Engine tune-up kits, suspension modifications and even special bodywork all helped to make it a successful race car.

In three years, no fewer than 48,987 'Frog Eye' Sprites were built, but this was only the beginning of a long success story. A restyled Mk II, with more conventional looks, then took over, and a near-identical MG Midget was also introduced; these cars then continued to sell at a phenomenal rate until the end of the 1970s. All in all, nearly 356,000 cars in this family were built, and every survivor is now revered as an affordable classic.

Above and below: This was a popular two-seater sports car designed by BMC which used many exisiting parts and which was easy to maintain.

1958 Lotus Elite

Right from the start, when he built his original special-bodied Austin Seven trials car, Colin Chapman showed signs of engineering genius. Setting up Lotus, he sold his first car kits in the early 1950s, and soon progressed to building advanced racing sports cars. The first true Lotus road car, however, was the very advanced Lotus Elite.

First shown in 1957, but not available until a year later, the new two-seater Elite coupé was irresistibly attractive. Even though Lotus was still a small company, Chapman had laid out a car which pushed technology to the limit. In particular, he decided to make the Elite without a separate chassis, using a fully-stressed fibreglass monocoque body which would only include steel sections for a few local reinforcements.

Not only was this amazing machine to be powered by

a race-proved overhead-camshaft engine from Coventry-Climax, and had four-wheel independent suspension, but it was achingly beautiful, and was quite amazingly light in weight. No-one, it seems, was ever likely to confuse the Elite with any other car, for its tiny, smooth and always curving lines had no rivals. Looking back into history, its only real drawback was that the door windows could not be wound down, but had to be removed to provide better ventilation.

In engineering terms, though, 'adding lightness' often adds cost too, and there was no doubt that the Elite was always going to be a costly car to make and sell. The fibreglass monocoque body shells proved to be difficult to make in numbers, major bought-in items like the Coventry-Climax engine were very expensive, and owners soon found that a great deal of maintenance and loving

care was needed to keep the new sports car running. Refinement was not then a word which Lotus understood and the Elite was a rather crudely equipped and finished machine at first; the interior environment was very noisy, for there was little attempt to insulate the drive line and suspension fixings from the monocoque, which acted like a fully matured sound box.

As the years passed, the Elite's specification changed, with the power of the engine gradually being pushed up to 100 bhp (which brought the top speed to more than 120 mph, quite amazing for a 1.2-litre car), a ZF gear-box adapted and (for Series II cars) a different type of rear suspension geometry specified.

> **Lotus Elite**
>
> *Years in production:* 1958–62
> *Structure:* Front engine/rear-drive. Fibreglass monocoque body/chassis
> *Engine type:* 4-cylinder, single-overhead-camshaft
> *Bore and stroke:* 76.2 x 66.6 mm
> *Capacity:* 1,216 cc
> *Power:* 83 bhp @ 6,250 rpm
> *Fuel supply:* Two horizontal SU carburettors
> *Suspension:* Independent front, independent rear
> *Weight:* 1,455 lb
> *Top speed:* 118 mph

Special Elites, particularly when prepared at the factory, were outstandingly successful class cars in GT racing, even appearing with honour in major events such as the Le Mans 24 Hour and Nurburgring Six Hour events. Years later Colin Chapman admitted that the Elite had never made profits for Lotus, which may explain why he was happy to phase it out in 1962, ahead of the arrival of the backbone chassised Elan. Nothing can ever detract from the gracious style and inventive engineering which went into the car. A total of 988 Elites were made.

Below: Committed owners usually forgave the Elite for the car's failings, as here was a car which drove and handled like no other rival. Light by the standards of the day, it was not only fast, but remarkably economical too.

1959 Triumph Herald

Compared with the dumpy Standard Eights and Tens which it replaced, the Triumph Herald was a totally different type of car. Stylish where the old Standards had been dull, and technically exciting where old Standards had been boring, the Herald was the first of a big family of saloons and sports cars which sold hugely for more than ten years.

In 1957 the Herald's design (which was masterminded by Harry Webster) came together quickly, and by happenstance. Standard-Triumph wanted to build a conventional replacement for the Standard Eight/Ten using the same running gear, but could find no supply of unit-construction body shells. Electing to revert to separate-frame construction, they then hired the prodigious young Italian, Giovanni Michelotti, to style the car, which he did, with great flair. From there, it was a short step to adopting all-independent suspension, an unbeatable tight turning circle (which could match the best of London taxis), to decide to construct the body from bolt-up major sections, and to engineer a whole series of derivatives – saloon, coupé, estate car and van – on the same basis.

In their class, the original Heralds had competitive performance, but it was their styling which gave them a marketing advantage over their rivals, where cars like the Ford Anglia and (soon) the Vauxhall Viva looked ordinary by comparison; the major rival, of course, was the Mini, which no other car in the world could match.

Eventually, there would be more variety: somehow a six-cylinder engine was shoe-horned into place, producing the Vitesse, while a shortened chassis, with impeccable Michelotti styling, became the Spitfire (4-cylinder) and GT6 (fastback 6-cylinder) sports cars. This was an entirely new venture for Standard-Triumph, and early problems were inevitable. Original 948 cc Heralds were perhaps overweight, and too expensive, their handling often seeming suspect, but steady improvement produced the larger-engined Herald 1200 in 1961, the car became increasingly popular in the mid 1960s.

Although the Herald saloons and convertibles were always the best sellers in this range, it was the Spitfire (for glamour) and the Vitesse (for smooth six-cylinder character) which added the gloss to an already successful image. Since this was also a time when the TR sports car was at the height of its fame, Triumph had an extremely good image in the 1960s, which the Herald did much to support.

Lasting fame was assured even before the final Heralds were made in 1971, for by this time they were 13/60s with 1.3-litre engines, and were the last separate-chassis cars on UK sale. In later years, particularly in sporting form, they became much-loved classics.

Triumph Herald

Years in production: (All types)
1959–71
Structure: Front engine/rear-drive.
Separate chassis
Engine type: 4-cylinder, overhead-valve
ORIGINAL 948 CC TYPE:
Bore and stroke: 63 x 76 mm
Capacity: 948 cc
Power: 34.5/45 bhp @ 4,500/5,800 rpm
Fuel supply: Single Solex/two horizontal
SU carburettors
Suspension: Independent front,
independent rear
Weight: 1,764 lb
Top speed: 71 mph/79 mph

Left and below: A totally different type of car, the Herald was designed by the Italian Michelotti with great flair, and sold in huge numbers for more than ten years. Their individual style gave them a significant marketing advantage over their rivals.

LKX 326H

1959 Austin-Healey 3000

Mention the famous phrase 'Big Healey', and some-one will automatically add 'hairy–chested' to the description. Originally announced in 1952 as a beautiful two-seater sports car using a four-cylinder Austin A90 engine, this was a car which would grow larger, heavier, faster and more characterful in a full 15-year career. The last of the famous line was the Austin-Healey 3000, which went on sale in 1959.

The original 'Healey 100' began as a private venture from Donald Healey's small company, and was supposed to use Austin/BMC running gear. However, as soon as that company's chairman, Len Lord, saw the car, he tied up a deal with Healey – that the car would be manufac-tured by BMC at Longbridge, that its name would be changed, and that the Healey company would be retained as sports car design consultants thereafter. First deliveries of Austin-Healey 100s followed in 1953.

From 1952 to 1956 these four-cylinder cars sold well, especially in the USA. They were then re-engineered with BMC's new six-cylinder engine, becoming the '100 Six'. Three years later, with an enlarged engine, the same cars were rebadged as the '3000', which it remained for the next eight years. In 1957 final assembly was moved to the MG factory at Abingdon, two-seater or 2+2-seat options were made available, along with optional hard-tops, optional overdrive, single or duo-tone colour schemes, and a mass of accessories.

Earlier cars were raced at Le Mans and Sebring, and were used in a number of high-profile long distance record attempts. Healey produced more and more, perfor-mance-raising options. By the 1960s in much-modified and 'works' prepared form, the 3000 was a formidable rally car, and a good sports car racer, its most famous achievement when Pat Moss (Stirling's sister) won the gruelling Liège-Rome-Liège Rally of 1960.

If standard production types had a problem, it was that they were a little too low slung, and that they passed far too much engine heat into the cockpit, but in view of their style, their performance and their character, enthusiasts forgave them everything. From 1962, in any case, the body was re-engineered with wind-up windows and a curved screen, while from 1964 the interior was also rejigged and the ground clearance raised.

The last of all, the Mk IIIs, were the best. In total, there were more than 58,000 six-cylinder engined cars, and more than 73,000 of all types.

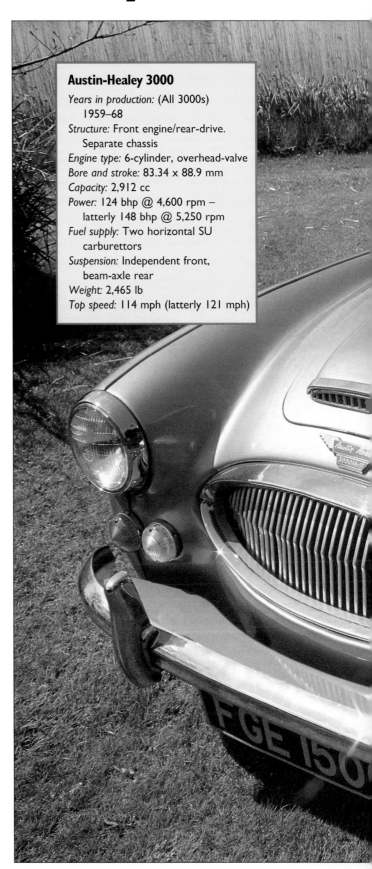

Austin-Healey 3000

Years in production: (All 3000s) 1959–68
Structure: Front engine/rear-drive. Separate chassis
Engine type: 6-cylinder, overhead-valve
Bore and stroke: 83.34 x 88.9 mm
Capacity: 2,912 cc
Power: 124 bhp @ 4,600 rpm – latterly 148 bhp @ 5,250 rpm
Fuel supply: Two horizontal SU carburettors
Suspension: Independent front, beam-axle rear
Weight: 2,465 lb
Top speed: 114 mph (latterly 121 mph)

Below: Every six-cylinder car had the same butch character, made all the right noises when pressed hard, and had the same sort of rugged dependability which sports car enthusiasts enjoyed.

1959 Austin-Morris Mini

Announced in 1959, and still manufactured 40 years later at the end of the century, Alec Issigonis's cheeky little Mini-Minor changed the face of motoring. The world's first car to combine front-wheel-drive and a transversely-mounted engine in a tiny ten-foot long package, was the most efficient and effective use of road space that had ever been seen. In so many ways, this must

qualify as the 'car of the century'.

In scheming up the car Issigonis and his team, which had already designed the Morris Minor, was given a difficult brief by the British Motor Corporation. In the aftermath of the Suez Crisis, and threatened world-wide petrol rationing, Issigonis was asked to provide a minimum-size, minimum-price four-seater package – all built around an

Austin-Morris Mini

Years in production: Introduced 1959

Structure: Front engine/front-drive. Monocoque body/chassis

Engine type: 4-cylinder, overhead-valve

Bore and stroke: 62.94 x 68.26 mm

Capacity: 848 cc

Power: 34 bhp @ 5,500 rpm

Fuel supply: One horizontal SU carburettor

Suspension: Independent front, independent rear

Weight: 1,380 lb

Top speed: 72 mph

existing BMC engine. Choosing front-wheel-drive and the A-series engine, he then minimised the size of the car by turning the engine sideways, and mounted the transmission under the engine. Tiny (10 in /254 mm) diameter road wheels, independent suspension by rubber cone springs, and a careful packaging of the cabin, all helped to provide one of the most amazing little cars of all time. So what if the driving position was cramped, and the steering wheel too vertical? This was a Mini, after all.

Although Issigonis insisted that he was only providing a super-small, super-economy saloon, almost by chance his Mini had superb handling, precise race-car-like steering and unmatched agility. Even before more powerful versions were available, the Mini had started winning rallies, and showing well in saloon car racing: later, in Mini-Cooper S form, size-for-size it was unbeatable. Originally sold only as two-door saloons in near-identical 'Austin' and 'Morris' forms, Minis soon spawned derivatives. Not only would there be vans, estate cars and pick-ups, but plusher Riley and Wolseley types followed, as did the stark 'top-less' Mini-Moke machines.

Engines were eventually enlarged, tiny front-wheel disc brakes were added, the Mini-Cooper and Mini-Cooper S followed, and by the mid-1960s this was a car which had won the Monte Carlo Rally on several occasions. For years there was nothing a Mini could not do, for it appealed to everyone, and every social class, from royalty to the dustman, bought one. At peak, production in two factories (Longbridge and Cowley) exceeded 300,000 every year, BMC's only problem being that it was priced so keenly that profit margins were wafer thin.

Even the arrival of the larger Mini Metro in 1980 could not kill off the Mini, whose charm was unique. By the 1980s, with larger wheels, re-equipped interiors and wind-up windows, the Mini was a better car than ever, and, looking much the same, it was still selling steadily at the end of the 1990s: more than five million had already been made.

In the 2000s, we are told, there will be a New Mini, but this will be larger and heavier than before.

Far left: The steering wheel was nearly vertical in the little Mini.

Left and below: The Suez Crisis led to the need for a small, economical saloon. The Mini had superb handling, precision steering and great agility, and in so many ways could qualify as the car of the century.

1959 Jaguar 3.8 Mk II

To see a Mk II in action these days, merely switch on the TV and watch any recycled British 'cops and robbers' programme of the 1960s and 1970s. If the police are not using one as a pursuit car, the 'baddies' will be driving one as a getaway car. One car, at least, is usually crashed in every episode – so it is a miracle that many have survived!

For the first ten post-war years, Jaguar produced only sports cars or big saloons with separate chassis frames: the 2.4 of 1955 was the first Jaguar to have a unit-construction body shell. This was the first of a large family of 'compact' four-door saloons which would follow in the next 13 years.

Although the original 2.4/3.4 types were rather dumpily styled, with thick windscreens and window surrounds, the Mk II versions which followed in 1959, were altogether more graceful. Styled by Jaguar's founder, Sir William Lyons, the Mk II built on the theme of the Mk I,

Jaguar 3.8 Mk II

Years in production: 1959–67
Structure: Front engine/rear-drive. Monocoque body/chassis
Engine type: 6-cylinder, twin-over head-camshaft
Bore and stroke: 87 x 106 mm
Capacity: 3,781 cc
Power: 220 bhp @ 5,500 rpm
Fuel supply: Two horizontal SU carburettors
Suspension: Independent front, beam-axle rear
Weight: 3,304 lb
Top speed: 125 mph

but had a larger window area, a wraparound rear window, lighter detailing, and an improved chassis, with a wider choice of equipment. The original front engine/rear-drive layout was retained, along with a beam rear axle retained by cantilever leaf springs. The latest cars had a much wider wheel track and handled much better than earlier models. Four-wheel disc brakes had been standardised, so they also felt much safer too.

Most importantly, Mk IIs were available with a choice of XK six-cylinder engines – 2.4-litre, 3.4-litre and 3.8-litre types – along with manual, overdrive, or automatic transmission, disc or wire spoke wheels, and a raft of desirable extras. With Jaguar sales rising past 500 cars every week, the choice seemed endless.

As the years passed, Daimler V8-engined versions also appeared, as did the long-tail S-type (which had independent rear suspension), the 420 of 1966 being the final version. Predictably, the most glamorous Mk IIs were the 3.8-litre types, which were amazingly powerful and flexible, preferably built in a bright colour (fire engine red was popular, for instance), with overdrive transmission and chrome-plated wire-spoke wheels. Not only were they exciting 125 mph cars, virtually peerless in open road use, but they were thoroughly practical and versatile four-seater saloons as well.

Unleashing the booming straight-line performance was one thing, but controlling it was quite another; radial ply tyres were still rare, and tyre grip was, in any case, primitive. To drive a Mk II fast on twisty, slippery roads required supreme skill – for it could bite back swiftly. A well prepared Mk II, however, was a formidable racing saloon car, unbeatable for years except by vast-engined American saloons. From 1959 until 1968, when it finally gave way to the XJ6, it was one of the most enjoyable and affordable sports saloons.

Left and above: A common sight in old movies, these graceful cars were the first in a series of large four-door saloons. The Mk II had a larger window area, a wraparound rear window and a wider choice of equipment than its predecessor.

1961 Jaguar E-type

By almost any reckoning, Jaguar's original E-type was the sexiest motor car ever launched. It looked wonderful, it was extremely fast, and it was always sold at extremely attractive prices. For more than a decade, it was the sports car by which all other supercar manufacturers had to measure themselves.

Originally conceived in 1956 as a successor to the D-type racing sports car, the E-type was not to be used for that purpose. Re-engineered and re-developed, it became an outstanding road-going sports car, taking over from the last of the XK cars – the XK150 – in 1961. Like the D-type, its structure acknowledged all the best contemporary aerospace principles, utilising a multi-tubular front chassis frame which surrounded the

engine and supported the front suspension and steering, and was bolted up to the bulkhead of the pressed steel monocoque centre and rear end.

Power came from the very latest version of the famous XK six-cylinder twin-cam engine, with three SU carburettors and no less than 265 bhp (according to American SAE ratings). It was matched by all-independent suspension, four-wheel disc brakes, and a unique, wind-cheating body style. As with the C- and D-type racing cars, the E-type's shape had been designed by ex-aircraft industry specialist Malcolm Sayer, who combined great artistic flair for a line with the ability to calculate how the wind would flow over a car's contours. For practical purposes, the E-type's nose might have been too long,

Right: Considered to be the sexiest car ever launched, the E-type was a fast and outstanding sports car. Designed by an ex-aircraft specialist, it had a remarkable aerodynamic performance.

its cabin cramped, and its tail too high to hide all of the chassis components, but all this was forgiven by its remarkable aerodynamic performance – and its enormous visual appeal.

Open and fastback two-seaters were available from the start, and although a 150 mph top speed was difficult for an ordinary private owner to achieve, this was a supercar in all respects, being faster than any other British road car of the period (and, for that matter, for many years to come). Much-modified types eventually won a series of motor races at just below world level, for they were really too heavy for this purpose. Only three years after launch, a 4.2-litre engine, allied to a new synchromesh gearbox, was adopted, and a longer wheelbase 2+2 coupé followed in 1966.

The E-type sold well all around the world, especially in the USA although new

safety laws caused the car to lose its power edge, and its headlamp covers before the end of the 1960s. The Series II's performance did not match that of the original, and by 1971, the E-type was a somewhat emasculated car. A final Series III type was powered by Jaguar's new 5.3-litre V12 engine, and a top speed of 150 mph was once again within reach.

Drivers did not seem to mind the small cabin and less than perfect ventilation, but in the end it was more safety regulations and changes in fashion that caused this wonderful motoring icon to fade away. The last of 72,520 E-types was built in 1975, when it was replaced by an entirely different type of sporting Jaguar, the larger, heavier and not so beautiful XJ-S.

Jaguar E-type

Years in production: (all types) 1961–75
Structure: Front engine/rear-drive. Monocoque body/chassis, tubular front chassis
ORIGINAL CARS:
Engine type: 6-cylinder, twin-overhead-camshaft
Bore and stroke: 87 x 106 mm
Capacity: 3,781 cc
Power: 265 bhp @ 5,500 rpm
Fuel supply: 3 horizontal SU carburettors
Suspension: Independent front, independent rear
Weight: 2,688 lb
Top speed: 149 mph

1962 AC Cobra

Here was the most extrovert sports car of all, British-built but with American V8 power. No-one ever bought a Cobra and expected to remain anonymous, for almost everything it did was noisy, flamboyant and spectacular.

In 1961 the former American racing driver, Carroll Shelby, approached AC, suggesting that they should supply Ace body/chassis assemblies to him in California, where he would insert Ford-USA V8 engines and transmissions for sale in the USA. AC, whose Ace was in any case approaching the end of its career, was delighted to do this business. In future years there would be arguments about the car's design provenance, its source, and even its true name. Everyone now knows it as a Cobra, but the Americans always wanted to call it a Shelby American Cobra, while the British insisted on their right to retain the famous AC badge.

In many ways the first Cobra was a thoroughly re-engineered Ace, which retained the same twin-tube chassis frame, all-independent suspension (by transverse leaf springs), and sleek aluminium-panelled 'Barchetta' style body. Compared with the Ace though, the tubular chassis was much stronger, there was a massive new rear axle, four-wheel disc brakes, and flares over the wheel arches to cover wider wheels and tyres.

Soon after deliveries began, a 4.7-litre V8 engine replaced the original 4.2-litre type, while rack-and-pinion steering was also standardised. Helped along by its extrovert character, and by a flamboyant motor racing programme which eventually saw the Cobras beating Ferrari production sports cars, it became a cult car in 1960s America. Shelby even went so far as to develop the Daytona Cobra race cars, with a dramatically different fastback coupé style, extremely rare cars which won the 1965 World Sports Car Championship.

On the road, a Cobra never did anything by halves, bellowing when the accelerator pedal was pressed, squealing its tyres at any excuse, and generally looking impressive and aggressive. All this was eventually tempered by technical improvements, for from 1965 a new chassis with coil spring suspension took over, wheel tracks were further widened (with body styling modified to suit), and an even more powerful version, the 7-litre powered Cobra 427, joined the range.

Production of the original Cobra (which was also sold in the UK as the AC 289) eventually ran out in 1968 after 1,137 cars had been made. This was by no means the end of a complicated saga however. In the 1970s enterprising specialists all over the world pirated the design, marketing what they called Cobra 'replicas' (though this transgression was speedily seen off by AC's lawyers). AC's successor company started building cars again in small numbers, and in the 1990s Carroll Shelby himself reactivated a series of unallocated original chassis plates to build new-old Cobras once again.

Many more Cobras, or so-called Cobras, now exist than were ever originally constructed in the 1960s, all them having the same sort of extrovert character as the originals. Although the name had changed, the Cobra's pedigree had not died away and, when it does, be sure that it will not go quietly.

Left and below: A British built car with Ford-USA V8 engines, the Cobra was to become a cult car in 1960s America. With the 4.7-litre V8 engine it was able to beat Ferrari production sports cars.

AC Cobra

Years in production: 1962-present
Structure: Front engine/rear-drive.
   Separate chassis
Engine type: V8-cylinder, overhead-valve
ORIGINAL AC 289:
Bore and stroke: 101.6 x 73 mm
Capacity: 4,727 cc
Power: 195 bhp @ 4,400 rpm
Fuel supply: One vertical Ford
   carburettor
Suspension: Independent front,
   independent rear
Weight: 2,315 lb
Top speed: 138 mph

1963 Aston Martin DB5

Fame comes in strange and unexpected ways. Although the Aston DB4 and DB5 models were already respected by the cognoscenti, the DB5 did not become world-famous until used as James Bond's personal transport in the film *Goldfinger*. Although not equipped with Bond's ejector seat, it appealed to millions, and the DB5's reputation was secure for ever. Technically, of course, Aston Martin had always been a marque of distinction.

Following the success of the DB2, DB2/4 and DB Mk III models of the 1950s, Aston Martin commissioned a totally new and larger series for the 1960s, beginning with the DB4 in 1958. Built around a simple steel platform chassis, it was clothed in a sleek light-alloy fastback body style by Superleggera Touring of Italy (but built at Newport Pagnell). The skin panels were fixed to a network of light tubing, a method patented by Superleggera. Power (and what power!) came from a magnificent new 3.7-litre twin-cam six-cylinder engine, which soon proved to be strong and reliable in motor racing. The DB4 came close to matching anything so far achieved by Ferrari. All this, allied to a close-coupled four-seater cabin, and high (traditionally British) standards of trim and equip-

ment, made the expensive DB4 very desirable.

The DB5, which was launched in 1963, was a direct development of the DB4; it had a full 4-litre engine, a more rounded nose with recessed-headlamps, and many equipment improvements. Two varieties of engine – the most powerful with a claimed 314 bhp – were on offer, as were non-sporting options such as automatic transmission, which came a full decade before Ferrari stooped to such action.

It was such a complicated, mainly hand-built, machine that it had to sell at high prices. The saloon cost an eye-watering £4,175 in 1963 (there was also a convertible version, at £4,490) and because assembly was a lengthy and careful business, sales were limited to only ten cars a week. It was not for years, incidentally, that it became

clear that even these prices did not cover costs, for Aston Martin was merely the industrial plaything of its owner, tractor magnate David Brown.

DB5s could safely reach 140 mph, with roadholding, steering and brakes to match, all the time producing the characteristic booming exhaust notes for which they became famous. Although they looked sinuous and dashing, they were heavy machines and there was no power-assisted steering on this model.

Clearly, this was a bespoke GT machine which would run and run, as the longer and more spacious DB6 which took over in 1965 would prove. In only two years, a total of 1,063 cars (123 convertibles, and 12 of them very special estate car types) were produced. Almost all have survived.

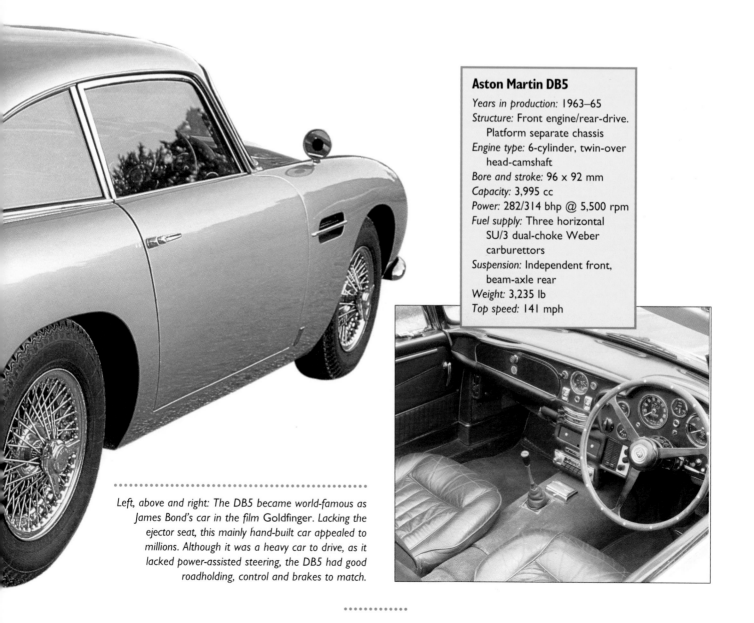

Aston Martin DB5

Years in production: 1963–65
Structure: Front engine/rear-drive. Platform separate chassis
Engine type: 6-cylinder, twin-over head-camshaft
Bore and stroke: 96 x 92 mm
Capacity: 3,995 cc
Power: 282/314 bhp @ 5,500 rpm
Fuel supply: Three horizontal SU/3 dual-choke Weber carburettors
Suspension: Independent front, beam-axle rear
Weight: 3,235 lb
Top speed: 141 mph

Left, above and right: The DB5 became world-famous as James Bond's car in the film Goldfinger. Lacking the ejector seat, this mainly hand-built car appealed to millions. Although it was a heavy car to drive, as it lacked power-assisted steering, the DB5 had good roadholding, control and brakes to match.

1963 Hillman Imp

Hillman's rear-engined Imp, launched in 1963 and built until the mid-1970s, was the right car at the wrong time. If it had not had to compete with BMC's well established Mini, and if it had not been made by a financially ailing Rootes group, it could have been a great success. The design, in other words, was much more successful than its sales.

For the Rootes Group, already famous for building a series of conventional Hillmans, Humbers and Sunbeams, the decision to develop a new small car was extremely brave. Having looked closely at cars like the Mini, the Ford Anglia and the Triumph Herald, Rootes cast convention to the winds and opted for a rear-engined car – the 'Apex' project.

The engine was located in the tail, and the transmission ahead of it. This meant developing a new alloy engine (which was based on a Coventry-Climax racing design), transmission and all-independent suspension layout. Swing axle front suspension, and semi-trailing arms at the rear were remarkably effective, much of the luggage was stowed up front, but there was also space behind the rear seats, ahead of the engine.

Functionally, the new 'Apex' (which would

Hillman Imp

Years in production: 1963–76
Structure: Rear engine/rear-drive. Monocoque body/chassis
Engine type: 4-cylinder, single overhead camshaft
Bore and stroke: 68 x 60.4 mm
Capacity: 875 cc
Power: 37 bhp @ 4,800 rpm
Fuel supply: One downdraught Solex
Suspension: Independent front, independent rear
Weight: 1,530 lb
Top speed: 78 mph

eventually carry Hillman, Singer, Sunbeam and Commer badges) was advanced and successful. The style of the saloons was craggy in the extreme (the rear-engined Chevrolet Corvair was thought to be an inspiration), but it was much more roomy than the Mini, and had a useful lift-up rear window feature. Though the Imp's weight was heavily biased towards the rear, the handling was remarkably good, the steering inch-perfect, and the traction superb. If only the first cars' reliability had been better, and the prices a little lower, the Imp might have successfully established itself.

The problem, however, was that for political and employment purposes, Rootes had been obliged to build Imps at a factory near Glasgow, in Scotland, with an inexperienced workforce, while engines and transmissions were assembled in the Midlands, and much shuffling of components ensued. To make a great car from this framework was almost impossible.

Early reliability problems were eliminated within two or three years, but in spite of a facelift, and the introduction of sporty versions, the Imp project always struggled to make its mark. Yet this was unwarranted. Singer types were much better furnished, Sunbeams had more powerful engines and 90 mph performance, while the fastback coupé versions (notably the Sunbeam Stiletto) were chic and well specified. A successful race and 'works' rally programme (which included success in the British Saloon Championship) helped underpin the image. More than 440,000 of all varieties were made before 1976. Now that these cars are retired, they have an enthusiastic following.

Above: The rear-engine design of Hillman Imp was a great success. However, due to the political pressure, Rootes built the car with an inexperienced Scottish workforce, which contributed to early reliability problems and undermined sales.

1964 Sunbeam Tiger

If the AC Cobra of 1962 was the first attempt to mate American V8 power with a British sports car chassis, the Sunbeam Tiger of 1964 was the first to tackle the same feat in quantity production. It was the same entrepreneur, Texan Carroll Shelby, whose engineers built the first of both versions, but in the case of the Tiger, final development was a joint effort between the British Rootes Group, and its sub-contractors, Jensen.

Introduced in 1959, the Sunbeam Alpine was a stylish British sports car, which combined a short-wheelbase version of the Rapier's platform and running gear, with a very smart new two-seater sports car style. Compared with its rivals – the MGA and the Triumph TR3A – it was under-powered, so a proposal to fit a 4.2-litre Ford-USA V8 (and give the car a new title) looked like a great opportunity.

Rootes arranged for Pressed Steel to supply complete body shells to Jensen, who modified them as appropriate, and then assembled the whole cars. Announced early in 1964, the newly-named Tiger had the body style of the Alpine IV (in which the rear fins had been cut down, and the interior improved), and was available in soft-top or detachable hard-top form. In the first year, 1964–65, all supplies went to the USA, but the Tiger was put on sale in the UK from 1965.

With 164 bhp instead of the contemporary 1.6-litre Alpine's 82 bhp, the Tiger was a much fiercer proposition, which gave, as the Americans said, 'more bangs per buck', and soon began to build a following. It was the sort of car which seemed eager to spin its rear wheels – and many owners did just that. Unhappily, compared with the Alpine, there were only minor styling changes, and no opportunity was available to beef up the chassis, so Tiger customers soon found that the original type was not yet a completely balanced package.

Even so, a short-lived motor racing programme (two Tigers competed at Le Mans in 1964), and an altogether more successful 'works' rally programme began to promote the message that here was a car with performance and durability. All would have been well if Rootes, in the meantime, had not sold out to the Chrysler Corporation, who took an instant dislike to a car which was powered by the engine of one of its deadliest rivals.

Second thoughts are often better than the first, but although Rootes introduced the Tiger II in 1967, complete with a 200 bhp/4.7-litre engine and four-wheel disc brakes, Chrysler soon insisted that it be killed off and these rare, but fully-formed machines, became both the best, and least-known Tigers of all.

Sunbeam Tiger

Years in production: (All types) 1964–67
Structure: Front engine/rear-drive. Monocoque body/chassis
Engine type: V8-cylinder, over head-valve
Bore and stroke: 96.5 x 73 mm
Capacity: 4,261 cc
Power: 164 bhp @ 4,400 rpm
Fuel supply: One downdraught Ford carburettor
Suspension: Independent front, beam-axle rear
Weight: 2,525 lb
Top speed: 117 mph

Right and below: A stylish sports car, the Tiger's production halted when Chrysler bought Rootes, as the engine was powered by a rival company.

1966 Jensen FF and Interceptor

Established by the Jensen brothers in West Bromwich in the 1930s, Jensen's first cars were stylish, but otherwise technically mundane machines. Even by the 1950s and early 1960s their successors' appeal was more in what they looked like, than how they were equipped. Then, buoyed up by the profits from a great deal of contract work (Jensen built complete bodies for the Austin-Healey 3000, and tackled complete assembly of the Sunbeam Tiger sports car), the decision was taken to modernise. The result was the launch of two stunningly handsome four-seater coupés, known as the Interceptor and the FF.

Jensen Interceptor and FF

Years in production: (All types)
   1966–76
Structure: Front engine/rear-drive
   (FF = four-wheel-drive).
   Separate chassis
Engine type: V8-cylinder, over
   head-valve
ORIGINAL TYPE:
Bore and stroke: 108 x 86 mm
Capacity: 6,276 cc
Power: 325 bhp @ 4,600 rpm
Fuel supply: One downdraught
   Carter carburettor
Suspension: Independent front,
   beam-axle rear
Weight: 3,500 (FF = 4,030)lb
Top speed: 133 mph

Right and below: With Italian styling, the Jensen was a well-equipped coupé, easy to handle with a large expanse of glass. The introduction of anti-lock brakes and four-wheel drive was a massive technical breakthrough.

By combining the existing Jensen tubular chassis frame with a vast Chrysler V8 engine and automatic transmission, and swathing the whole in a body styled by Touring of Italy, the result was a modern-looking coupé, with graceful lines, a great deal of glass, and a well equipped cabin. This new Jensen, however, broke new ground, not just for Britain, but for the entire world of motoring. By

co-operating with Harry Ferguson Research, Jensen offered one version of the car, the FF, with four-wheel-drive. This, and the use of Dunlop Maxaret anti-lock braking, was a massive technical breakthrough.

To do all this, the drive was split behind the main gearbox, a second propeller shaft was threaded forward alongside the engine, and the car's wheelbase had to be stretched by four inches to accommodate a front axle ahead of the engine. By modern standards the installation looked crude, but it was a world 'first', and remarkably effective.

The FF was much more expensive than its rear-drive cousin: in 1966 the UK prices were £5,340 and £3,743, at a time when a new Rolls-Royce cost £6,670, and sales were always limited. It was the Interceptor which sold in quantity and helped give Jensen an entirely new image.

Not only were these very fast cars (an Interceptor could reach 133 mph, and an FF about 130 mph), but they were also easy to handle, enjoyable grand tourers in spite of their bulk. By the time the specification had settled down, they had power-assisted steering, were effortless to drive, and the equipment had received two upgrades. Demand was strong.

Although only 320 FFs were made before production closed down in 1971, the older the Interceptor became, the faster it sold. By the mid-1970s one version, powered by a 385 bhp Chrysler engine, could reach 145 mph, while convertible and hard-top versions added to the variety.

Unhappily, the after effects of the 1973 Energy Crisis, and Jensen's other problems connected with the Jensen-Healey dragged down the Interceptor, which died in 1976 after 6,639 cars had been produced. Later attempts to revive the Interceptor, first in the 1980s, and then in the 1990s, both failed.

1970 Range Rover

Rover never hid the fact that their original Land Rover 4x4, which went on sale in 1948, was inspired by the famous US military Jeep. The Range Rover of 1970, however, was unique. Bigger, heavier, better equipped than any previous Land Rover, it opened up an entirely new type of market. Although it was conceived simply as a 'bigger Land Rover', even before it went on sale it had become more of a gentleman's 4x4, and less of an all-can-do workhorse, and that process carried on inexorably over the next 25 years. By the time

the last Range Rover 'Classic' was produced in 1995, no fewer than 317,615 had been built.

The first Range Rovers had a 100 in (2540 mm) wheelbase, were powered by a de-tuned version of Rover's ex-GM V8 engine, had a newly-engineered four-wheel-drive layout, and their beam front and rear axles ran on long-travel coil springs. Not only did the light-alloy-clad estate car body shell look smart, but this was also a vehicle with quite unrivalled on- or off-road abilities.

Although Rover originally looked on the Range

Rover as a hard-working and versatile tool which could be used in the most awful conditions (which, indeed, it was, and could), they soon found that more and more customers were using it as a large, high-capacity, estate car which rarely left surfaced roads. Quips that Range Rovers rarely attempted anything more than wet gravel in a supermarket car park were met by Rover with broad smiles and the response: 'Look at the sales figures'.

Although the styling altered only slightly over the years, the specification advanced considerably. Automatic transmission, five forward speeds instead of four, and eventually a fuel-injected version of the engine were

> ### Range Rover
>
> *Years in production:*
>   (First generation) 1970–95
> *Structure:* Front engine/four-wheel-drive. Separate chassis
> *Engine type:* V8-cylinder, overhead-valve
> ORIGINAL TYPE
> *Bore and stroke:* 88.9 x 71.1 mm
> *Capacity:* 3,528 cc
> *Power:* 135 bhp @ 4,750 rpm
> *Fuel supply:* 2 SU carburettors
> *Suspension:* Beam-axle front, beam-axle rear
> *Weight:* 3,880 lb
> *Top speed:* 99 mph

all added in the 1980s. A five-door body option within the same overall package was an instant best seller, limited-edition packs called 'Vogue' soon became regular options, while the specification, equipment, fittings and features all gradually increased.

By the late 1980s the Range Rover was also available with a diesel engine option (which was much more popular in certain export markets and with businesses than ever it was with private British buyers), and before long the most expensive, highest-specified versions had 200 bhp 4.2-litre engines, longer wheelbase bodies and self-levelling suspensions. Early cars which had a top speed of 92 mph were quite outclassed by these machines, which could top 110 mph, though the fuel consumption was very heavy (worse than 15 mpg).

During the 1990s, the Land Rover Discovery appeared, using the original 'short' Range Rover chassis, and from 1994 there was a completely new-generation Range Rover, even faster, more expensive and glossier than ever before. In 20 years, the Range Rover had established an entirely new market sector which left its rivals struggling to catch up.

Left and above: Bigger and heavier than the Land Rover of 1948, the Range Rover was the first high capacity estate car, which preceded the explosion in 4x4 vehicles of the 1990s.

It is easy to recognise the 1958 Lotus Elite; its stream-lined design and smooth bodywork were unrivalled.

Modern-Day Classics

—1970–1995—

Rover 3500 SD1 ✪ Rolls-Royce Corniche
Bentley Mulsanne Turbo ✪ Morgan Plus 8
Lotus Esprit X180 ✪ Jaguar XJ-S Convertible
Jaguar XJ220 ✪ TVR Griffith
Ford Escort RS Cosworth ✪ McLaren F1
MG MGF

356 ·

CLASSIC BRITISH CARS

Modern-Day Classics

For British motorists in the late 1970s, the miracle was that the climate for motoring changed so fast. Even though there had been two vicious energy crises and a long period of horrifyingly high inflation, fine cars were still being made, space was still available to drive them, and new styles were still being developed. It was amazing. Only ten years after the first energy crisis had made most people fear for their future mobility, all the fun in motoring had returned. Maybe there were not as many sports cars as before, but high-performance saloons and hatchbacks seemed to be everywhere.

By the late 1980s, and following a long world-wide economic boom, Britain produced a series of magnificent supercars. Some, like the first Ford Sierra RS Cosworth, seemed easily affordable, while others, like the Jaguar XJ220, were merely there to be admired by many, but owned by very few. That didn't matter. By the 1980s and 1990s what truly mattered was that the definition of a 'classic' car altered. It was clear that there would be 'classics', 'modern classics' and 'sleepers'. Even better, cars came on to

the market and were immediately hailed as 'instant classics' – the Bentley Mulsanne Turbo and the Ford Escort RS Cosworth being typical.

CONSOLIDATION

Car makers struggled to survive during the 1970s, and no important new marques were established. Some, like Lotus and TVR, made bigger, glossier and more costly models, but others, like AC, Jensen and even Triumph barely remained in business.

By the end of the decade British Leyland (which included Jaguar, MG and Rover) had gone bankrupt and then been nationalised, but otherwise the 'big four' looked stable, though more change was yet to come. Ford had established market leadership in the 1970s, BL (which soon became Austin-Rover) tucked in behind them, with Vauxhall and Peugeot-Talbot (who acquired the ex-Rootes, ex-Chrysler business in 1978) bringing up the rear. Without exception, they forged stronger links with overseas combines – Ford's move into Ford-of-

· ·

Below: The Rolls-Royce continued to be the best built car in the world using the highest quality materials and offering all important exclusivity.

*Above: The TVR Griffith is symbolic of the continued survival
and prosperity of the privately owned Blackpool car maker.*

Europe being first, and BL's tie-up with Honda last –
which meant that individual British characteristics were
bound to fade away with time.

Individual companies, which survived in remarkable
numbers, sometimes absolutely on their own, tried to
retain their integrity. Aston Martin went through a series
of rich, paternalistic, owners before finally selling out to
Ford in 1987, while Jaguar broke loose of British Leyland
in 1984 (the government privatised that side of the
business) but were then absorbed by Ford in 1989. Lotus
survived until 1982, when the founder Colin Chapman
died, and when Toyota took a stake, though it wasn't until
1986 that General Motors took control. For a short time,
too, Lotus had technical links with DeLorean, of
Northern Ireland, though that enterprise collapsed in
1982, its proprietor accused of financial skullduggery. In
and around all this, TVR survived and prospered by
operating with only two benevolent owners in the
technical backwater of seaside Blackpool.

Most car makers exercised caution. The sleek Jaguar E-
type had given way to the craggy XJ-S. MG Midgets and
MGBs were built for years after their appeal had faded,
for British Leyland never planned any successors, and the
rival TR7s were not good enough to supplant them. Ford
Escort RS models gradually faded away. Other classics –
Range Rover and Morgan among them – continued,
apparently *ad infinitum*, their sponsors lacking the drive or

the inclination to produce anything new. Then, in the
1980s, inflation was slashed and industrial optimism
returned. Except for Jaguar, Britain's motor industry
found that it could survive without the North American
market, and that it could continue to design and build
great cars that the rest of the world wanted to buy.

Jaguar's case history tells us so much about the period.
By the mid-1970s their business was in disarray, the
E-type dead, and their products criticised for poor build
quality. The big cats roared back in the 1980s: the XJ-S
matured with honour, special Jaguars won the Le Mans
24 Hour race (and later, the World Sports Car
Championship), and from 1989 they received the
benevolent and long-term backing of Ford. The XJ6
saloon was rejuvenated as the V8-engined XK8, and a
new smaller car (the S-type) was added in 1999. In almost
every case, 1980s and 1990s Jaguars were 'instant classics',
as we will surely discover in the 2000s and beyond.

Lotus, too, had a hard time, but survived, albeit under
their third (or was it their fourth?) owner since Colin
Chapman's death. Poorly-built Esprits of the 1970s
became re-styled and more powerful Esprit V8s for the
1990s. A bravely-engineered front-wheel-drive Elan
project only failed because it was too costly, and in more
recent times a super-light, super-sporting Elise two-seater
sold in higher numbers than almost any previous Lotus.
Pedigree and soul, it seems, will usually prevail.

In the case of Triumph and the 'classic' MG, it did not, but in the case of the revived MG, and Aston Martin, it did. In the 1970s Triumph continued to outsell MG, but both were eventually killed off when BL stopped making sports cars. Then came an astonishing re-birth. Two owners down the line (for BMW took control in 1994), the MG sports car was back, first as the disgracefully paunchy RV8, which was pastiche in every way, but later as the mid-engined MGF.

Here was a classic British car reborn, created by a team who clearly understood what the magic initials 'MG' and 'sports car' should mean. Like the MGAs and the MGBs of old, the car was built around existing saloon car parts (in this case, Rover 100/200/400 types), but with a unique style, sporty handling, and a great deal of character.

This was the sort of car on which British automobile engineers became increasing expert in the 1970s, 1980s and 1990s. They knew how to build character into a new model without letting costs run out of control, they knew that good handling cost no more than bad, and that beautiful lines were just as easy to manufacture as ugly ones. The problem, however, was that they were rarely allowed to prove it.

In some cases, as with the gently-changing family of Rolls-Royce and Bentley, cost was not such a cramping factor: build-quality and exclusivity were all-important. By that time, it was said, a Rolls-Royce was no longer the 'Best Car in the World' (which had once been their proud advertising claim), especially when performance

and roadholding was taken into consideration, but it seemed that it was always the best built. No matter how hard their rivals (at home and overseas) tried, it seemed that these cars had the very best quality materials, were the most carefully built, were the most rigorously tested, and offered a unique package of virtues. 'What would happen if a sub-standard Rolls-Royce left the building ?' a spokesman was once asked. 'The security guard would never let it out of the gate', he replied without hesitation.

Cars produced by small bespoke companies such as Aston Martin could not quite approach Rolls-Royce standards (though their performance was usually much higher). Even in the 1970s and 1980s, when their commercial existence sometimes hung by a thread, Aston Martins were always fast, well presented, impressively and uniquely styled, with very high performance. Things actually improved at Aston Martin after Ford took over, for new models and new methods could be considered for the first time in many years. The new DB7 of 1994 (which had many Jaguar components hidden away) was immediately seen as more 'classic', more desirable and of even better value than before. It was this approach to making desirable cars which gave the British motor industry a lead over its rivals.

By the 1990s, however, 'instant classic' British cars were being produced for two different reasons – one because they had a single-purpose job to do, the other being that they had to offer the very pinnacle in automotive engineering. Some 'single-purpose' cars which, by defini-

Opposite page: The Ford Escort RS Cosworth of 1992 became a highly desirable, instant classic with four-wheel-drive and a turbo-charged engine derived directly from motor sport.

Above: The mid-engined MG MGF was the result of an astonishing rebirth of this classic car in 1994 and points the way forward for British car makers into the new millenium.

tion were 'outstandingly important', and therefore potentially of classic status, came along to satisfy motorsport regulations. This explains the series of fine limited-production Fords starting with the 200-off RS200 of 1985, and culminating in the four-wheel-drive Escort RS Cosworth of 1992. If a car needed four-wheel-drive, a turbocharged engine, and positive downforce to make it competitive, then it should have it, Ford concluded. If, along the way, it became highly desirable, this was a bonus.

Britain's two fastest-ever cars, the Jaguar XJ220 and the McLaren F1, were built for an entirely different reason. Each, in its own way, was meant to be the ultimate car. The XJ220 was built to meet a small and prestige-conscious market of millionaires, pop stars and playboys who wanted the biggest toys and were ready to pay for them. The McLaren F1 which followed was looking for the same clientele, but wanted to offer even more. Technically, both cars were a huge and instant-classic success, but commercially both were failures. They were aimed at a fragile market which could (and did) disappear, but both proved, without question, that British engineers could

still provide superlative cars ahead of their competitors.

For the 21st century the prospects are good, and there could well be more cars like these. In spite of everything, it seems classic British motor cars will continue to appear, to be loved by motoring enthusiasts and to be revered as they grow old. Compared with earlier generations, however, almost all of them will be specialist models, built for a specific purpose. In all honesty, because of the stifling legislative climate, I cannot foresee a new generation of British family car ever attracting as much praise as the sheer breathtaking charm of a BMC Mini.

There will, on the other hand, certainly be great new Millennium cars to take over from the MGF, the McLaren F1 and from sumptuously hand-built cars like the Bentley Mulsanne Turbo. Each will probably fulfil a small, specific, but definite need, and will be distinct and desirable because of that. As one famous motoring personality said in the depths of a 1970s energy crisis: 'It doesn't matter what fuel we have to use, if the cars are still fun. I don't care if I have to feed a car Mars Bars to make it run, just as long as it makes me smile....'

1976 Rover 3500 SD1

In the post-war years, Rover's image changed considerably. First they built staid and dignified saloons, then Land Rover 4x4s were added to the range, they dabbled with gas-turbine powered cars, and finally turned to the technically advanced Rover 2000 range.

Taken over by Leyland in 1967, Rover carried the process a stage further and the launch of the 3500 confirmed an attempt to satisfy the mass market. Designed under the guidance of Spen King, the new 'SD1' (the acronym stood for 'Specialist Division, Project 1') was a big five-door hatchback which effectively took the place

of two older cars – the Rover 2200/3500 range, and the Triumph 2000/2500.

Although the cabin was laid out as a five-seater, with a bench rear seat, in traditional Rover fashion it was really more comfortable as a four-seater.

Simpler than originally expected, the original car mated the well known light-alloy V8, in a front engine/rear-drive layout, with a well located beam rear axle. Faster and easier to handle than previous Rovers, the new 3500 made many friends as a sports saloon, but it also began to make enemies

Rover 3500 SD1

Years in production: (All types) 1976–86
Structure: Front engine/rear-drive. Monocoque body/chassis
Engine type: Various 4-cylinder/ 6-cylinder/V8-cylinder, petrol and diesel
ORIGINAL TYPE:
Bore and stroke: 88.9 x 71.1 mm
Capacity: 3,528 cc
Power: 155 bhp @ 5,250 rpm
Fuel supply: Two horizontal SU carburettors
Suspension: Independent front, beam-axle rear
Weight: 2,989 lb
Top speed: 123 mph

because of the quality problems which afflicted many British Leyland models of the period.

As with many modern cars, this Rover was not just one model, but a complete range, and by 1982 the original V8 had been joined by a 2-litre four, 2.3-litre and 2.6-litre six, and a 2.4-litre diesel power unit. By this time, too, final assembly had been moved from the original Rover plant in the Midlands to the British Leyland factory at Cowley, and the car had been treated to a subtle but definite styling facelift. British Leyland also dabbled with an estate car version, but although prototypes were seen in public, they never went on sale.

The Vitesse, the fastest SD1, was introduced at the end of 1982, with a 190 bhp fuel-injected version of the V8 engine. Complete with a vast rear spoiler, the Vitesse had a top speed of 132 mph, and outstanding roadholding to match. Before long, highly-tuned Vitesses were winning Touring Car races all over Europe, and it was not until special turbocharged Fords were introduced that they were regularly defeated.

Over the years, the SD1 built up a real following, especially among the racing fraternity, and V8 examples, particularly Vitesses, are still prized. 300,000 cars of all types were produced before the last were built in 1986.

Below: The style, which was influenced by existing Italian supercars, (the Ferrari Daytona in particular), was smoother and more elongated than any previous Rover, and with no obvious visual links to its predecessors.

1979 Rolls-Royce Corniche

When Rolls-Royce announced its ground-breaking Silver Shadow range in 1965, which had an all-in-one chassis-less four-door body shell, pessimists forecast the imminent end to special-bodied models. Coachbuilders who had found it easy to build coachwork for fitment to separate-chassis models found it almost impossible to work the same magic on cars with monocoque, or unit-construction structures, where pressings and welding had to take over from hand-crafting and simple construction.

Rolls-Royce, therefore, decided to invest heavily at their Mulliner Park Ward subsidiary, and performed this miracle them-

selves. Starting in 1966, and using the saloon's platform, they announced a sleek two-door saloon, following it in 1967 with a convertible version of the same car. Rolls-Royce and Bentley versions were both sold. Those cars, updated and more powerful, were rebadged as 'Corniche' models: although the saloon was dropped in 1980, the convertible sold steadily until the mid-1990s.

Mechanically, every Corniche was closely related to the Rolls-Royce four-door saloon of the day – Silver Shadows until 1980, Silver Spirits thereafter – which is to say that they

Rolls-Royce Corniche

Years in production: (All types)
 1971–94
Structure: Front engine/rear-drive.
 Monocoque body/chassis
Engine type: V8-cylinder, over
 head-valve
Bore and stroke: 104.1 x 99.1 mm
Capacity: 6,750 cc
Power: Not revealed
Fuel supply: Two horizontal SU
 carburettors/Bosch fuel
 injection
Suspension: Independent front,
 independent rear
Weight: 4,816 lb
Top speed: 120 mph

used 6.75-litre V8 engines, automatic transmission, self-levelling suspension and full power braking. Power, never officially revealed, was always described as 'adequate', and was enough to give the cars a top speed of around 120mph. The two-door coachwork was smooth and dignified, fitted out and finished to every expected Rolls-Royce standard, with leather seating, a wooden fascia panel, deep pile carpets, and a full array of instruments and controls. Automatic air-conditioning was standard – even in convertibles which might be expected to be used hood-down, on many occasions.

Although this was a thoroughly and carefully developed motor car, the Corniche was not a machine to be used day in and day out, but was really a rich man's indulgence. It could take him far and fast in great luxury, in every climate. Somehow, it seemed, it was most at home on a Riviera boulevard, or on Rodeo Drive in Los Angeles.

The convertible version was topped off by a sumptuously detailed and furnished power-operated soft-top

which covered the spacious four-seater interior. Such was the company's attention to detail that it regularly took up to two weeks to manufacture, fit and adjust before new cars could be delivered.

Chassis improvements paralleled those of the saloons, but from 1979 the platform, and particularly the rear suspension, was upgraded to the new Silver Spirit level, making the cars even more silent and dignified than before. From 1984 the Bentley version was re-badged as a Continental, though without mechanical changes. Then, as later, Rolls-Royce put ride comfort ahead of roadholding – it was always more comfortable to drive a Corniche in a measured manner than to try to hurry along.

In a good year, more than 200 Corniches would be made, and almost 6,000 convertibles were produced in 23 years.

Below: The convertible version of the Corniche two-door saloon had a power-operated soft-top, as well as automatic air-conditioning and leather seating.

1982 Bentley Mulsanne Turbo

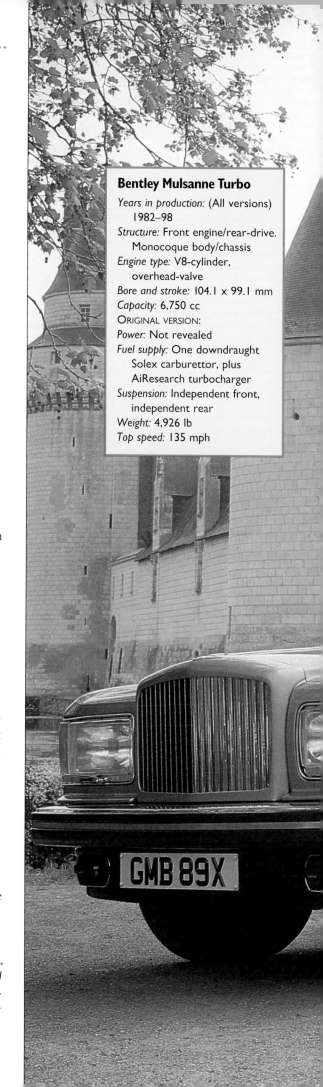

By the 1980s, Bentley's original sporting pedigree was long forgotten. The big 'vintage' sports cars designed by W.O. Bentley in the 1920s had long gone, for Rolls-Royce had bought up the bankrupt company in 1931. Thereafter, new Bentleys ('Rolls-Bentleys' as they were often christened) became sporty versions of Rolls-Royce cars, though even this new pedigree was diluted as the years past. By the end of the 1970s, every Bentley characteristic, it seemed, had been extinguished, and sales were falling fast. Rolls-Royce's chief executive, David Plastow, then had a brainwave. After hiring Broadspeed to develop a turbocharged version of Rolls-Royce's vast V8 engine, he installed it in a Bentley Mulsanne saloon (which was really no more than a rebadged Rolls-Royce Silver Spirit), and the whole car was re-aligned as the ultimate millionaire's sports saloon.

When the new car, the Bentley Mulsanne Turbo, was launched in 1982, it caused a real stir. Faster than any existing Bentley or Rolls-Royce, the power output figure was not originally revealed although it is now known to have been 300 bhp. With a top speed of 135 mph and acceleration to match, this was a magnificent Bentley. The high-tech chassis, with self-levelling all-independent suspension and full-power brakes, and sumptuous trim, carpeting and equipment contributed to an irresistible, if expensive car.

Even though the first cars cost £58,613 (then, as later, they were among the most expensive new cars in the world) they immediately began to sell well. The fact that they held the road no better than other Rolls-Royces and Bentleys (for although the ride comfort was remarkable, the suspension and damping was still very soft) was no deterrent, for they provided an unrivalled level of high-speed comfort.

The Bentley Mulsanne Turbo, however, was only the first of a long line of turbocharged Bentleys, the last of which were still being made in the year 2000. The Bentley Turbo R of 1985 had much better roadholding, a fuel-injected engine was added a year later, suspension-adaptive damping was added for 1990 and a four-speed automatic transmission followed in 1991.

A whole series of sporty two-door versions also evolved from this chassis – notably the Continental R, the Azure convertible and the short-wheelbase Continental T. By that time, the venerable turbocharged 6.75-litre V8 engine produced up to 420 bhp, and some cars could reach 160 mph. By the end of the 1990s, well over 8,000 turbocharged Bentleys in this family had been sold.

Bentley Mulsanne Turbo

Years in production: (All versions) 1982–98
Structure: Front engine/rear-drive. Monocoque body/chassis
Engine type: V8-cylinder, overhead-valve
Bore and stroke: 104.1 x 99.1 mm
Capacity: 6,750 cc
ORIGINAL VERSION:
Power: Not revealed
Fuel supply: One downdraught Solex carburettor, plus AiResearch turbocharger
Suspension: Independent front, independent rear
Weight: 4,926 lb
Top speed: 135 mph

Right: An irresistible millionaire's car, the Mulsanne Turbo sold well from its launch, despite its vast price. Superbly equipped, the car provided an unrivalled level of high speed comfort.

1984 Morgan Plus 8
(with fuel injection)

Morgan styling rarely changes, and then only slightly. Unless one is a true Morgan fanatic, it would be difficult to look at almost any Plus 8 and know what decade, let along what year it was built in. Thirty years after the launch of the original Plus 8 in 1968, it still looked almost the same. Not only that, but all Plus 8s looked much like the Plus 4s of the 1950s and 1960s that they had replaced.

Yet Morgan have always had a firm grip on their market, and seem to know exactly what their customers want. Televised advice from management guru, John Harvey-Jones, that they should boost production and raise prices was ignored, and no-one complained. Production may have crawled up from 10 cars a week to about 11 cars a week, but there is still no rush at the factory at Malvern Link, a stuffed owl keeps birds out of the paint shop, and waiting lists are still measured in years.

Like the earlier Plus 4s and 4/4s, the Plus 8 was an evolutionary step on what Morgan had been doing so well for some time. Although the style, almost pre-war in concept and detail, was little changed, this time it covered a wider and longer chassis frame, and was the first

Morgan to be powered by Rover's light-alloy V8 engine.

Open two-seaters with detachable side screens, all Plus 8s used the same type of rather flexible frame, with sliding pillar independent front suspension, and rock-hard rear leaf springs. The first cars, crude in many ways because of their old-style Moss gearboxes, had 155 bhp and a 120 mph top speed, but as the years passed they were widened, became available with optional light-alloy bodies, became more refined and better equipped, and (by Morgan standards) were more sophisticated.

Later cars got five-speed Rover transmissions and wider-rim alloy wheels, the cockpit was somehow

Below and top right: Styled much as previous models, the more powerful Plus 8 had a basic cramped interior with detachable side screens.

Morgan Plus 8

Years in production: (all types) introduced 1968
Structure: Front engine/rear-drive. Separate chassis
Engine type: V8-cylinder, over head-valve
FIRST FUEL-INJECTED VERSION:
Bore and stroke: 88.9 x 71.1 mm
Capacity: 3,528 cc
Power: 190 bhp @ 5,250 rpm
Fuel supply: Bosch-Lucas fuel injection
Suspension: Independent front, beam-axle rear
Weight: 1,900 lb
Top speed: 120 mph

softened and equipped better, but the real advance came in 1984 when a fuel-injected 190 bhp version of the Rover engine was fitted for the first time. This, and the standardisation of rack-and-pinion steering, made the Plus 8 an even more appealing car, though the barn-door aerodynamics of the old-fashioned shape meant that no Morgan was ever likely to go faster than 130 mph.

Little, however, could be done (and there is no sign that Morgan wanted to do it, anyway) about the limited wheel movement, the hard spring and damper settings, and the creaky bodywork which tended to leak in heavy rain, though more modern Morgans had been given wooden-framed bodies steeped in preservative. The customers knew all about the problems, but they knew all about the cars' animal appeal too – and demand stayed solid. Perhaps it always will.

1987 Lotus Esprit X180

By the end of the 20th century, the Lotus Esprit family had been on sale for nearly 25 years, which is a measure of the car's technical worth and of the original style which had been produced for Lotus by the Italian genius, Giorgetto Giugiaro. Although Lotus smoothed out the style in 1987 (to what is often known as the 'X180' shape), the car's character was not lost.

stylists to produce the more rounded 'X180' shape which would continue only lightly modified, to the end of the century.

In turbocharged SE form, the revised Esprit was good for around 160 mph, but there still seemed to be a demand for more performance, so in 1996 the long-rumoured Lotus 3.5-litre V8 engine, with 349 bhp, was finally introduced, making it a 175 mph car. Along the

The mid-engined Esprit was designed as a replacement, but altogether larger, faster and more specialised, for the Europa, which had been Lotus's first mid-engined road car. Like the Europa, the Esprit was a two-seater with a tiny cabin mounted on a folded steel backbone chassis frame, with Lotus's own newly designed 16-valve twin-cam 2-litre engine positioned behind the cabin. The rolling chassis was wrapped in a fibreglass body full of sharp edges and planes, unmistakably from the hand of Giugiaro himself. None but a company already steeped in motor racing could ever have produced a car whose chassis promised so much, and delivered it all with such aplomb.

The first Esprits were delivered in 1976 and were cars which took time to mature, first gaining reliability and longevity, then larger engines, and finally a turbocharged version of the power unit. In 1987, with the established design well past its tenth birthday, Lotus used its in-house way, a whole variety of Esprit Turbos were built, some in very limited quantities, the most powerful of all being the 302 bhp variety, which traded refinement for sheer performance.

Each and every Esprit was a sports coupé with the accent on sports, majoring on function rather than convenience, for the cabin was always a snug fit for only two people, luggage space was small, and noise levels

were always above average. Except that it needed a brave and expert driver to get the very best out of the chassis, no-one ever complained about the Esprit's handling, just as no-one ever seemed to find fault with the car's style and character. By the end of the 1990s, the Esprit was selling only slowly, but there were still those drivers who would not swap its agility, small size, and sheer appeal for any other.

Below: With the established Esprit design well-past its tenth birthday, Lotus produced the more rounded X180 shape which continued to the end of the century.

Lotus Esprit (X180 style)

Years in production: (All types) Introduced 1987
Structure: Mid-engine/rear-drive. Separate chassis
Engine type: 4-cylinder, twin-overhead-camshaft
Bore and stroke: 95.28 x 76.2 mm
Capacity: 2,174 cc
Power: 172 bhp @ 6,500 rpm/ 215 bhp @ 6,500 rpm
Fuel supply: Two horizontal twin-choke Dellorto carburettors/turbocharging
Suspension: Independent front, independent rear
Weight: 2,590 lb/2,800 lb
Top speed: 135 mph/150 mph

1988 Jaguar XJ-S Convertible

The original Jaguar XJ-S, which was unveiled in 1975, was the last car whose styling had been influenced by Jaguar founder Sir William Lyons before his retirement. Before it was launched, however, that style was modified to comply with US legislation. The result was that this bulky four-seater was a car which did not appeal to the same clientele as the XK, and E-type owners.

The XJ-S took its inspiration from the peerless XJ6/XJ12 saloon, for it was built around a shortened version of that car's pressed steel platform. Apart from saving a fortune in time, cost, and tooling investment, one obvious benefit was that the XJ-S also shared the same independent suspension, and the same outstanding qualities of ride and handling. No other car in the world had felt – and been – as refined as the XJ6, and the XJ-S could match it in all respects.

Like the XJ12 saloons, original XJ-Ss were all fixed-head coupés fitted with 5.3-litre V12 engines, and all but a handful had automatic transmission. Wide and squat, they were fitted with controversial 'flying buttresses' which linked the roof panel to the rear corners of the shell. Although four seats were fitted, customers rarely used them as more than spacious two-seaters with mountains of stowage space.

Very high performance and excellent ride and handling qualities had to be measured against the styling, and often ferocious thirst for fuel, but this was still a package which appealed, especially to North American buyers. Once the early quality problems had been eradicated, sales rose steadily, and the addition of 3.6-litre straight-six engines, and a clever cabriolet body style, made this a more versatile prospect.

Originally, though, there was no full convertible type. A private enterprise conversion from the USA finally persuaded Jaguar to engineer its own type which finally appeared in 1988 in V12 form. After a rear-end restyle in 1991 made the buttresses less blatant, it became even more popular in the USA, becoming the best-selling XJ-S variant. Once a more efficient 4.0-litre six-cylinder version went on sale in the early 1990s, it became another Jaguar success.

By 1996, when the XK8 finally took over from the long-running XJ-S, a total of 115,413 cars of all types had been made, of which more than 30,000 of these were XJ-S convertibles. Solid, well-engineered and reliable, they were classics from the start, and should remain so well into the 21st century.

Jaguar XJ-S Convertible
Years in production: (Convertible) 1988–96
Structure: Front engine/rear-drive. Monocoque body/chassis
Engine type: V12-cylinder, single-overhead-camshaft
Bore and stroke: 90 x 70 mm
Capacity: 5,343 cc
ORIGINAL TYPE:
Power: 291 bhp @ 5,500 rpm
Fuel supply: Bosch-Lucas fuel injection
Suspension: Independent front, independent rear
Weight: 4,055 lb
Top speed: 151 mph
Note: A 4-litre 6-cylinder version was also available from 1991.

Below: Most models were four seater, fixed-head coupés with very high performance and excellent handling qualities.

E814 LAC

1989 Jaguar XJ220

As the prosperous 1980s unfolded, a growing number of rich car enthusiasts demanded more and more motoring excitement, so a select number of supercars were designed to satisfy them. With the exception of the McLaren F1, the mid/rear-engined Jaguar XJ220 was the fastest and most practical of all.

By any standards this was a car of huge excesses: very powerful, very fast, very beautiful, and very expensive. It was high geared and somehow bulky, so even a millionaire would not choose it for everyday use, especially as it was strictly a two-seater and, frankly, hard work to drive.

But with such exceptional good looks, no-one seemed to care. The original prototype of 1988 was only meant to be a one-off, and was even bigger than the production car which followed, using Jaguar's famous V12 engine, and four-wheel-drive. Although it had not even turned a wheel when exhibited, it carried the XJ220 title as an indication of its proposed top speed.

Reaction was so positive that Jaguar handed over the project to Tom Walkinshaw's Jaguar Sport organisation (with whom it was in partnership), to turn it into a reality. The 'Walkinshaw' XJ220 was shown a year later, this time significantly smaller than before, with a twin-turbo V6 engine of the type being used in current Jaguar racing sports cars, and only with rear drive.

Not that this deterred the customers, for although Jaguar said they would only build 350 cars at a newly-developed factory near Banbury, more than 1,200 customers wanted to buy one, and priority of orders had to be applied.

> **Jaguar XJ220**
>
> *Years in production:* 1992–94
> *Structure:* Mid-engine/rear-drive. Monocoque body/chassis
> *Engine type:* V6-cylinder, twin-overhead-camshaft
> *Bore and stroke:* 94 x 84 mm
> *Capacity:* 3,498 cc
> *Power:* 542 bhp @ 7,200 rpm
> *Fuel supply:* Zytec fuel injection, plus twin Garrett turbochargers
> *Suspension:* Independent front, independent rear
> *Weight:* 3,210 lb
> *Top speed:* 213 mph

Built around a relatively conventional light-alloy hull, the XJ220 was really a civilised version of a race car, though with equipment which included air-conditioning and a fully-trimmed cockpit. Surprisingly, ABS anti-lock braking could not be developed in time for sales to begin in 1992.

Even though the XJ220 was tested at 213 mph, and everyone seemed to love its styling and general behaviour, Jaguar could do nothing about the general collapse in economic confidence in the early 1990s. In 1989 every customer had been obliged to sign a legal agreement when ordering the car, and to make hefty payments towards the £403,000 price, but many of them tried to wriggle out of the contract while the cars were being built.

The result was that only 271 cars were produced in three years, many of which languished un-delivered at Jaguar until the late 1990s. Amazingly, this supremely fast and beautiful Jaguar supercar now goes down in history as a commercial failure, tainted by the economic conditions of the day, rather than its own short-comings. The question is who can possibly afford to run such a car in the future?

Below: Of all the supercars developed at the time, the XJ220 was the fastest and most practical of all. Air-conditioning was standard in the fully trimmed cockpit. The cars were extremely expensive at £403,000.

1991 TVR Griffith

Throughout its life, the TVR sports car has always lined up behind the same marketing formula – all models were two-seater sports cars, all had sturdy multi-tube chassis frames, all had fibreglass bodywork, and all had outrageously extrovert characters. Each and every car has been made in dilapidated premises in Blackpool.

The second-generation Griffith (which was no relation to an earlier TVR built in the 1960s) was faithful to every facet of the original TVR character, with one additional feature: it was out-standingly beautiful. Previous TVRs had been handsome, rugged in some cases,

but none had ever achieved such sinuous styling.

This was a car which had been shaped lovingly by hand in a small workshop in Blackpool (no over-hyped consultant was ever involved, for this was the work of chairman Peter Wheeler, and his chief designer John Ravenscroft), where mundane things like bumpers were omitted from the equation, and where every straight line had been banished. Cockpit equipment was lavish, though in typical (and tradi-tional) TVR style, the standard of fixtures and fittings were sometimes rather casually achieved.

As ever with TVR, the Griffith

TVR Griffith

Years in production: (all types)
Introduced 1991
Structure: Front engine/rear-drive. Separate chassis
Engine type: V8-cylinder, over head-valve
ORIGINAL VERSION:
Bore and stroke: 94 x 77 mm
Capacity: 4,280 cc
Power: 280 bhp @ 5,500 rpm
Fuel supply: Bosch-Lucas fuel injection
Suspension: Independent front, independent rear
Weight: 2,304 lb
Top speed: 161 mph

which went on sale in 1992 was very different from the prototype of 1990, for it used a modified version of the racing Tuscan's frame. Power came from a much-modified light-alloy Rover V8, backed by the same company's sturdy five-speed transmission – and the car's specification could be boosted by larger and more powerful versions. Like all other TVRs, the Griffith had independent suspension, there was unassisted rack-and-pinion steering, four-wheel disc brakes, and large dollops of that indefinable piece of specification – character.

Early Griffiths had 280 bhp and 4.3-litres, but it wasn't long before TVR also offered a slightly milder version (with 240 bhp/4.0-litres), then from 1993 a brawny

325 bhp/5.0-litre derivative was added. Even the 4.0-litre car could top 150 mph, and the top speed of a full 5.0-litre type was best investigated on wide open spaces!

Performance was tyre-stripping, for these were cars which could rush up to 100 mph in little more than 11 seconds, the performance being accompanied by squeals from the overworked rear tyres, and aggressive bellows from the exhaust system. It was no wonder that more than 600 cars were made in the car's first full year (which made this one of the fastest-selling TVRs so far), and it was only the advent of new and even more extrovert TVRs which thrust the Griffiths back into the mainstream.

Below: The TVR Griffith had no bumpers front or back and the interior trimmings were lavish. Shaped lovingly by hand, the car bodywork was made from glassfibre and was full of character.

1992 Ford Escort RS Cosworth

When Ford-UK needed a new rally car for World Championship use in the 1990s, it combined the best of Sierra engineering, the best of Cosworth's engine-tuning expertise, and a brave approach to aerodynamics, to produce the Escort RS Cosworth. Although this car looked something like the mainstream front-drive Escort of day, it had a four-wheel-drive chassis, and hid much Sierra RS Cosworth heritage under its bewinged skin.

Starting on the basis of a shortened Sierra Cosworth 4x4 platform, and adapting a three-door Escort body superstructure to that, Ford spent time in its wind tunnels, eventually endowing the new car with a large and entirely functional rear spoiler. This, along with other add-ons, louvres and detail changes, produced a car which not only looked aggressively purposeful, but which developed positive downforce at high speeds. As speeds rose, the car was actually pressed further down onto its suspension, loading up the tyres and increasing potential grip.

With 227 bhp available from its 2-litre turbocharged engine in standard form, the Escort RS Cosworth was already a comfortable, reliable, exhilarating and extremely capable road car, but with 300 bhp or more, and a whole host of extra equipment in place, it became a phenomenal rally car. Road cars, equipped with fat and soft-compound Pirelli P Zero tyres, handled like no previous Ford had ever done, and because they were so small and agile, they soon attracted a cult following. The looks, perhaps, were an acquired taste, but no-one ever argued about the abilities of the package.

Ford Escort RS Cosworth

Years in production: 1992–96
Structure: Front engine/four-wheel-drive. Monocoque body/chassis
Engine type: 4-cylinder, twin-over head-camshaft
Bore and stroke: 90.82 x 76.95 mm
Capacity: 1,993 cc
Power: 227 bhp @ 6,250 rpm
Fuel supply: Weber-Marelli fuel injection, with Garrett turbocharger
Suspension: Independent front, independent rear
Weight: 2,882 lb
Top speed: 137 mph

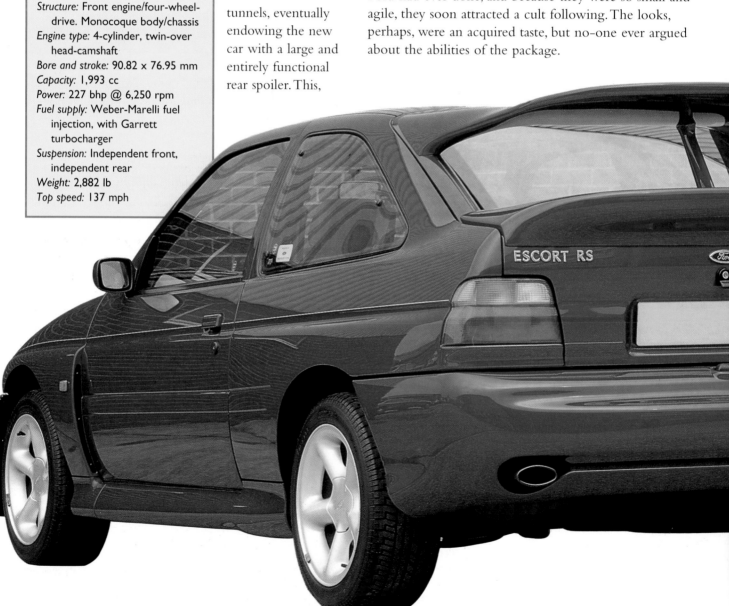

Right: Although it resembled the mainstream Escorts of the day, the Escort RS Cosworth had four-wheel-drive and an aerodynamic shape.

Road cars went on sale in 1992, cars started winning World Championship rallies in 1993, and by 1995 this had become one of the most successful Ford competition cars of all time. Victory in the Monte Carlo Rally (in 1994 and 1996) established the car's reputation for good, and in a final evolution, as the Escort WRC rally car, it was good enough for Carlos Sainz to win several world-class events.

The problem, as so often with these cars, is that the Escort RS Cosworth was too costly (£23,500 at first) to appeal to the mass market, too complex for Ford's dealer chain to understand, and far too special for the companies who had to insure it, so Ford never sold more than about 3,000 cars in a year. The final version, shorn of its big spoiler and with a small turbocharger, was a better road car, but not ideal for use in motorsport.

Commercial success, however, was never the most important factor in this charismatic car's career. By the time the last one was built in 1996, Ford enthusiasts had already christened it a classic, had found ways of extracting up to 400 bhp from its engine, and were defying Ford to produce even better cars in the future.

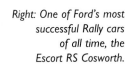

Right: One of Ford's most successful Rally cars of all time, the Escort RS Cosworth.

1993 McLaren F1

At the end of the 1980s, the fashion for making and marketing supercars with colossal performance was short-lived. At a time when rich men had money to splash around, supercars were very popular, but as recession followed, the market for expensive fast cars collapsed. All the cars in this class, such as the Bugatti EB110 and the Jaguar XJ220, could easily beat 200 mph, but few owners ever found a place to exercise that top speed. The McLaren F1 was probably the best of this exclusive breed – not only did it have a top speed of 230 mph and more, but it was stylish rather than brutally sexy, beautifully engineered and built with a unique layout.

McLaren, already famous for its Grand Prix cars, invited ex-Brabham F1 designer Gordon Murray to join them at Woking, where he concentrated on the new road-car product, which they decided, confusingly, to call 'F1'. Predictably enough, he laid out a mid-engined coupé, but there were important differences. Not only did McLaren persuade BMW to develop a unique alloy 627 bhp/6.1-litre V12 engine to power the car, but Murray laid out the interior as a three-seater, where the driver sat in the middle, ahead of his two passengers.

To keep the weight down, every possible high-tech. aerospace standard material was used: this was the world's first carbon-fibre chassised road car, and similar materials cropped up in detail all round the car – and the performance was stupendous. No British source, not even McLaren, could test the 230 mph-plus top speed in the UK, so a trip to the enormous circular test track at Nardo in southern Italy was made to prove the point. As expected, though, the acceleration figures were outstanding (and, as the climate for motoring has changed, may never be surpassed). The F1 could sprint from rest to 100 mph in 6.3 seconds, and to 200 mph in a mere 28 seconds. All this was accompanied by average fuel consumption of better than 15 mpg, the driver achieving it all in air-conditioned comfort.

Although the F1 was not meant to be a car for everyday use (significantly, it lacked features such as ABS braking, and power-assisted steering), it was small enough (only 71.6 in/1,820 mm wide) and light enough at 2,510 lb/1,138 kg, to be used in heavy traffic, or in normal conditions, but this was to waste the potential of a magnificent machine.

Even McLaren would now admit that it arrived on the market too late, for at the huge price of £540,000, it was never likely to sell in significant numbers. Although thousands of enthusiasts were impressed by it, very few (all multi-millionaires) bought an F1. After less than four years, in which only 100 cars (including a large proportion of special racing versions) were built, McLaren brought this loss-making project to a close. For sheer performance, such a car, it is thought, will never be beaten.

Right: The world's first carbon-fibre chassis road car. A three-seater, the driver sat in the middle ahead of his two passengers. Capable of 100 mph in 6.3 seconds from rest.

McLaren F1

Years in production: 1993–98
Structure: Mid-engine/rear-drive.
  Monocoque body/chassis
Engine type: V12-cylinder, twin-
  overhead-camshaft
Bore and stroke: 86 x 87 mm
Capacity: 6,064 cc
Power: 627 bhp @ 7,400 rpm
Fuel supply: Bosch fuel injection
Suspension: Independent front,
  independent rear
Weight: 2,509 lb
Top speed: 230 mph +

1995 MG MGF

By the 1970s, British Leyland was in such a financial mess that several factories had to be closed down, one of them being the MG plant at Abingdon. This meant the death of the long-running MGB – and the end of MG sports car production for more than a decade. After several changes of control in the 1980s, British Leyland became Rover, who were determined to revive MG sports cars. The retro-engineered MG RV8 of 1992 was the first new model, but it was the all-new mid-engined MGF of 1995 which caused such a stir.

By any previous MG standards, the layout of the new MGF was sensational enough, but the commercial deal which made the project viable was equally bold. Rover planned to make only 15,000 cars a year and needed an investment partner. They found it in the Mayflower business of Coventry, which not only produced all the body shell tooling and built all the bodies, but financed that operation too.

Sleek, rounded, compact and arranged purely as a two-seater, the MGF had a new unit-construction body shell, with all-independent suspension, but (in the very best historic MG traditions) almost all the engine, transmission and chassis components were lifted, only slightly modified, from mass production family cars in the parent company. The twin-cam four-cylinder engine was a highly-tuned version of the 16-valve K-series units already found in Rover 100, 200 and 400 models, and was linked to a neat, five-speed transmission, the entire assembly being placed closely behind the passenger cabin. There were two engine tunes, the most powerful having technically advanced VVC, or Variable (Timing) Valve Control. Hydragas suspension, interconnected from front to rear, as used in the Rover 100

sensitive electric power assistance which was also available.

By any standards this was a fast and well equipped little car, which kept its high performance (131 mph on the VVC-engined cars) in check with four-wheel discs, and ABS braking on the VVC version. Fuel injection, electric windows, a catalytic converter and part leather trimming in the cockpit made it an appealing little car which sold well – and continued to sell – from the moment it went on sale.

British customers originally had to pay £15,995 for the 'base' car, £17,995 for the VVC-engined machine, but there were waiting lists at first. For the first time, though, this was an MG sports car which was not to be sold in the USA. Five years after its launch, the MGF had gained a detachable hard-top option, but few other changes, and it looked exactly the same as in 1995. The co-financing deal had already paid off handsomely, and for the 2000s its future looks secure.

(the former Metro) was modified to include separate telescopic dampers and anti-roll bars at each end of the car, which ensured sports car handling allied to a soft and supple ride. Rack-and-pinion steering was as expected, though not the speed-

MG MGF

Years in production: Introduced 1995
Structure: Mid-engine/rear-drive. Monocoque body/chassis
Engine type: 4-cylinder, twin-over-head-camshaft
Bore and stroke: 80 x 89.3 mm
Capacity: 1,795 cc
Power: 118/143 bhp @ 5,500/ 7,000 rpm
Fuel supply: Lucas fuel injection
Suspension: Independent front, independent rear
Weight: 2,366 lb
Top speed: 123/131 mph

Below: Sleek, rounded and compact, the new lay-out of the MG MGF caused a stir at its launch.

Tracing its ancestry all the way back to the MG 14/28 of 1926, the mid-engined 1994 MG MGF is the living embodiment of the British Classic Car, and points the way forward for British car makers into the next century.